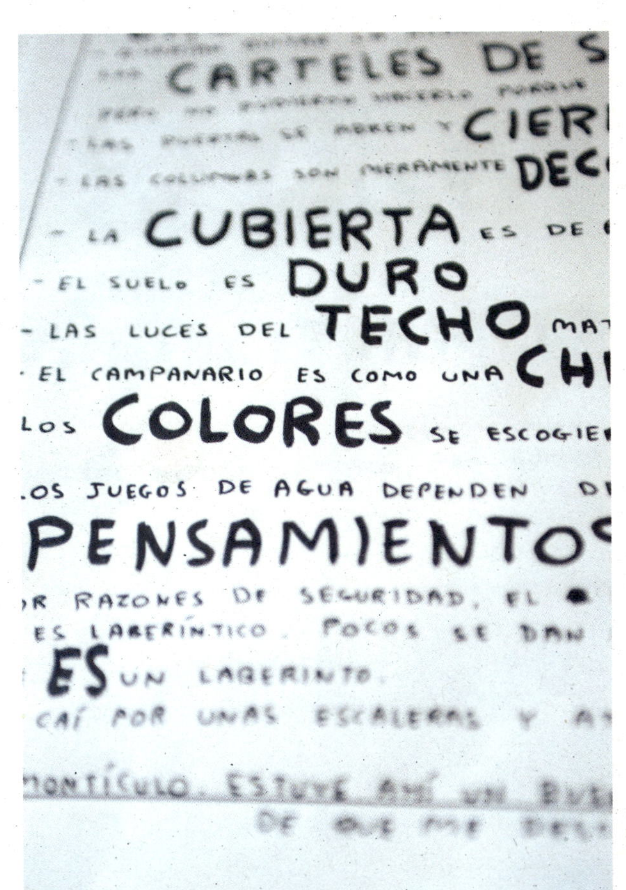

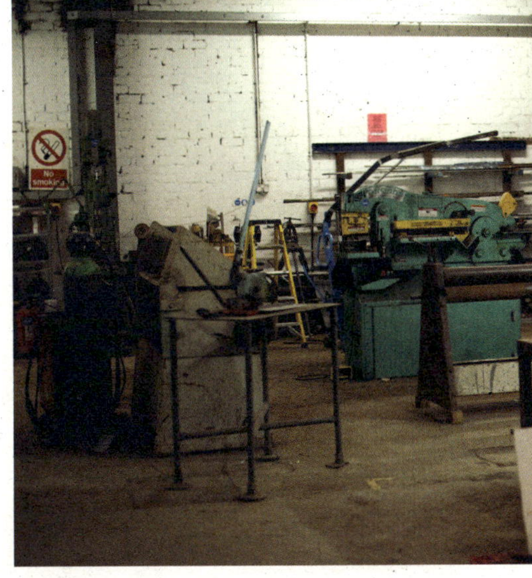

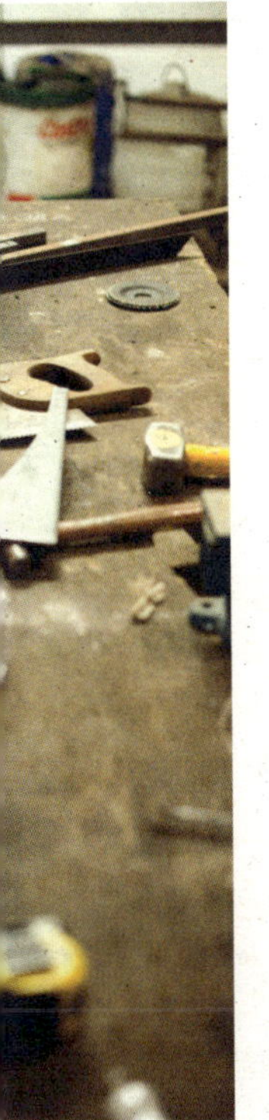

YOGA

THE KEY TO

Better Health

Keener Mind

Happier Disposition

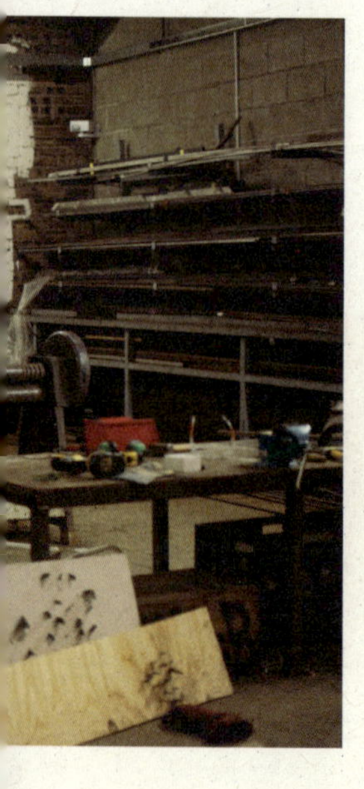

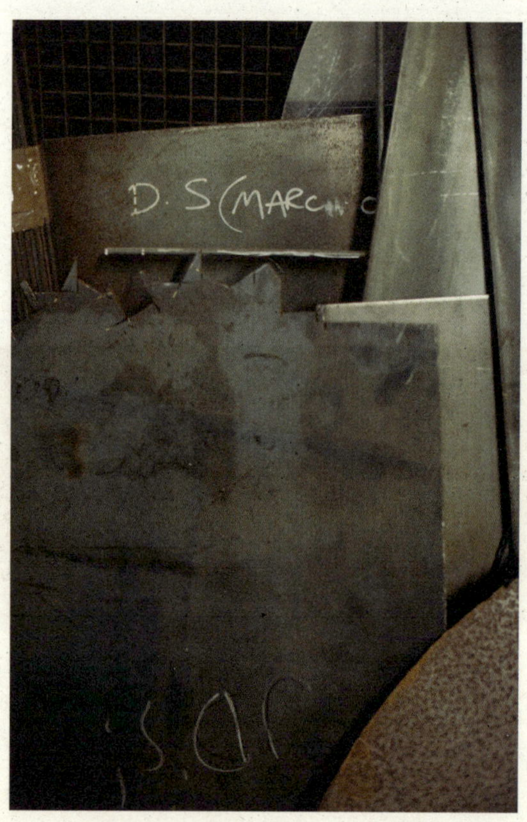
D. S (MARCH

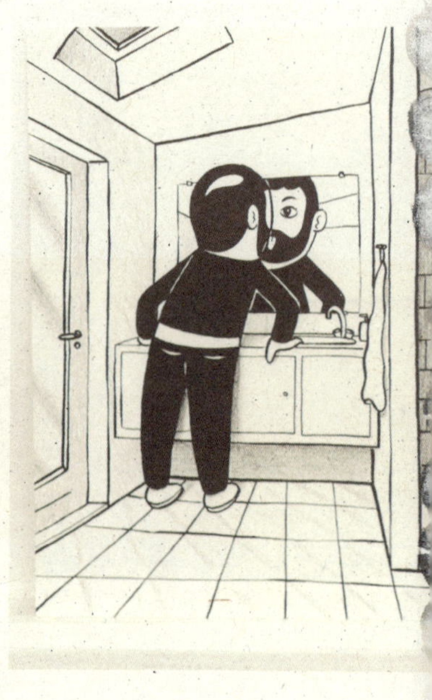

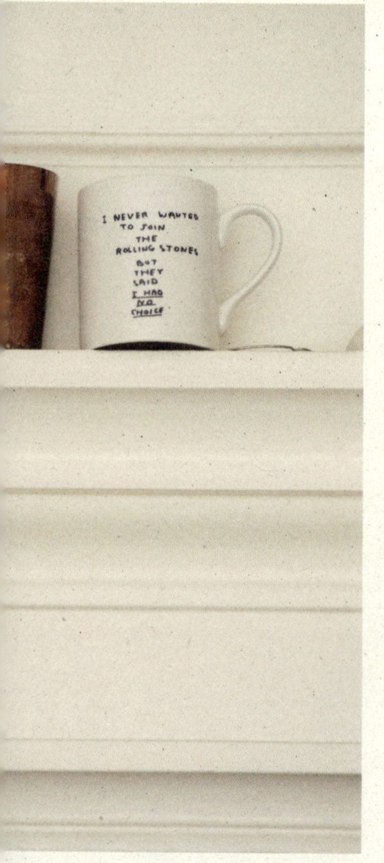
I NEVER WANTED
TO JOIN
THE
ROLLING STONES
BUT
THEY
SAID
I HAD
NO
CHOICE

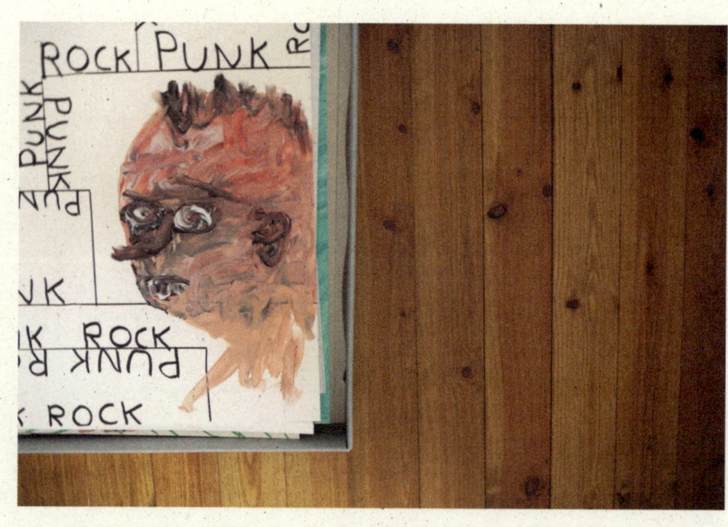
ROCK PUNK R
PUNK
PUNK
PUNK
PUNK
UNK
PUNK ROCK
PUNK R
ROCK

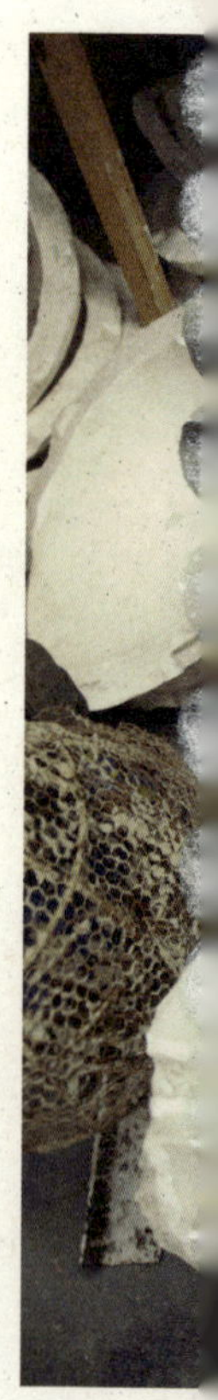

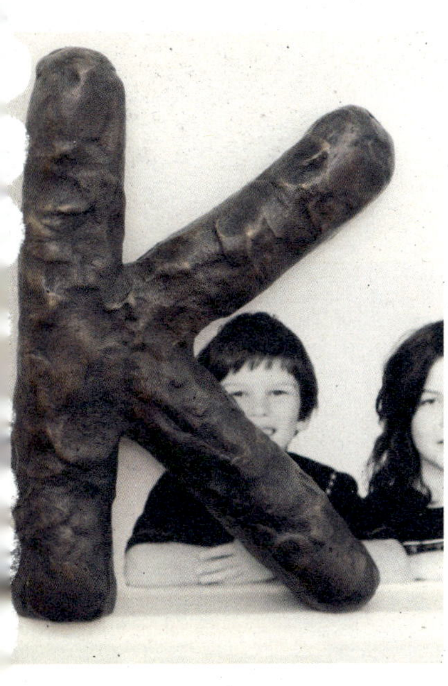
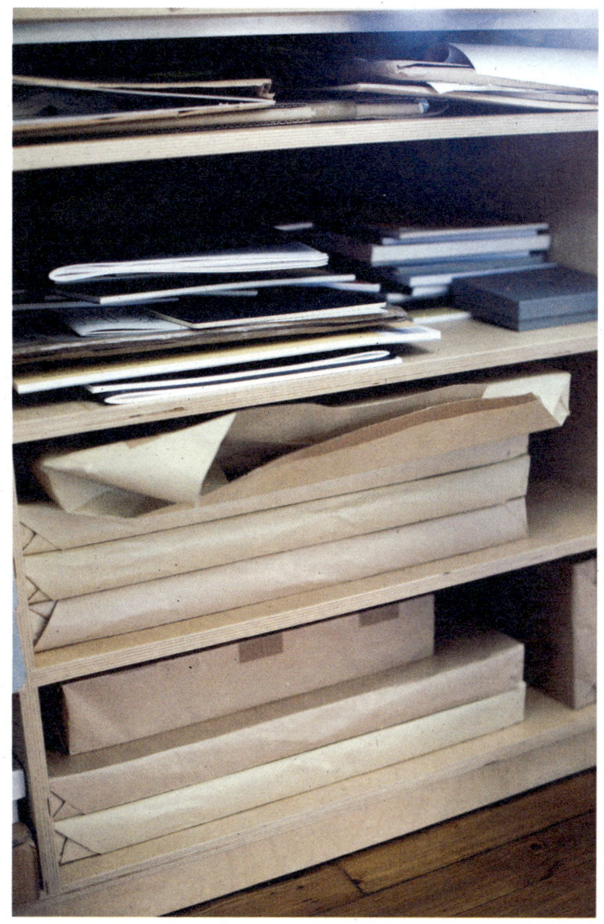
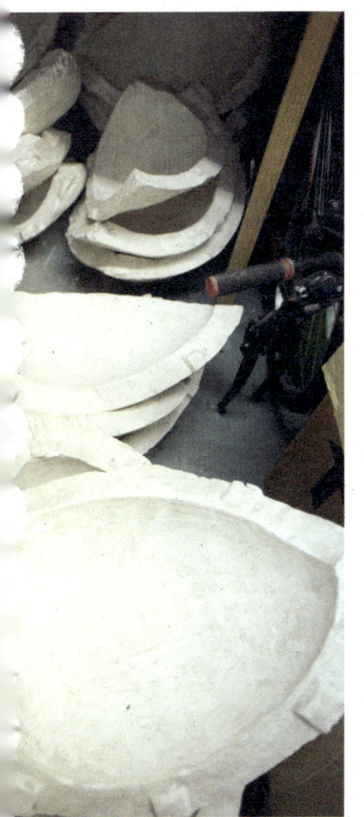
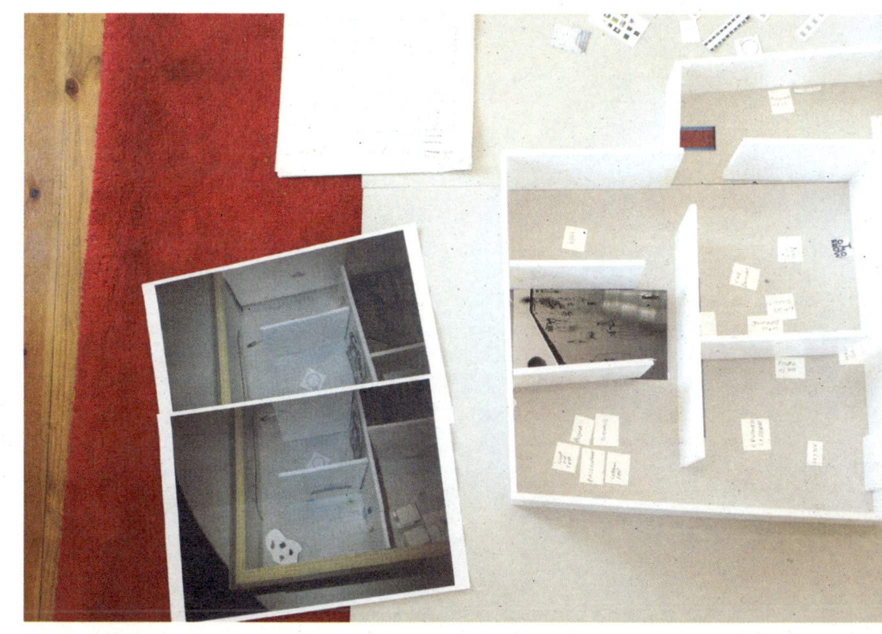

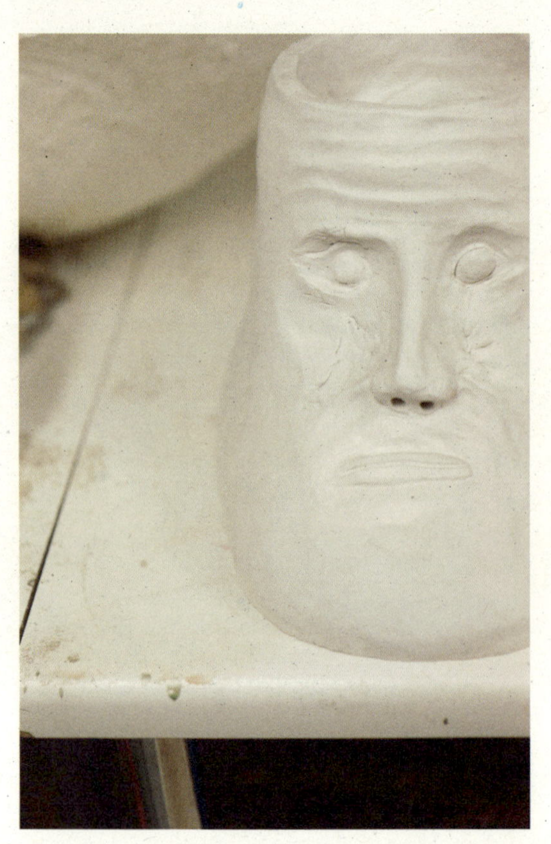

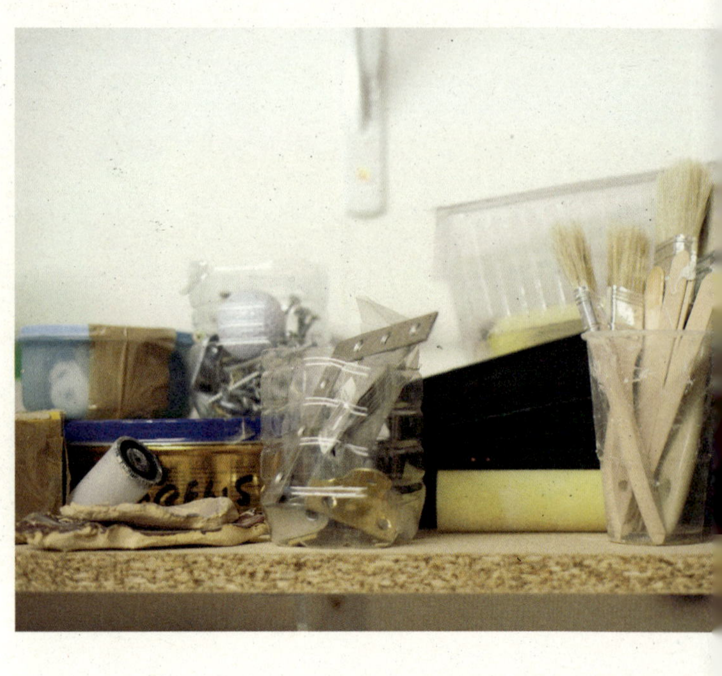TOOLS

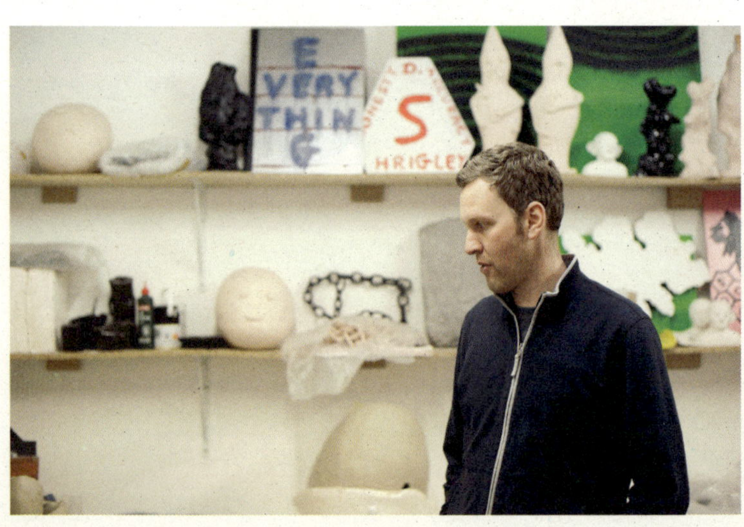EVERY
THIN
G
S
HRIGLEY

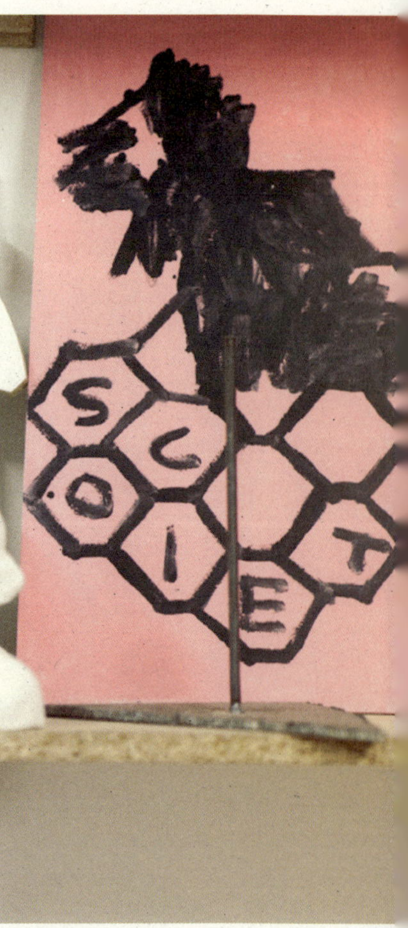S
C
O
I
E
T

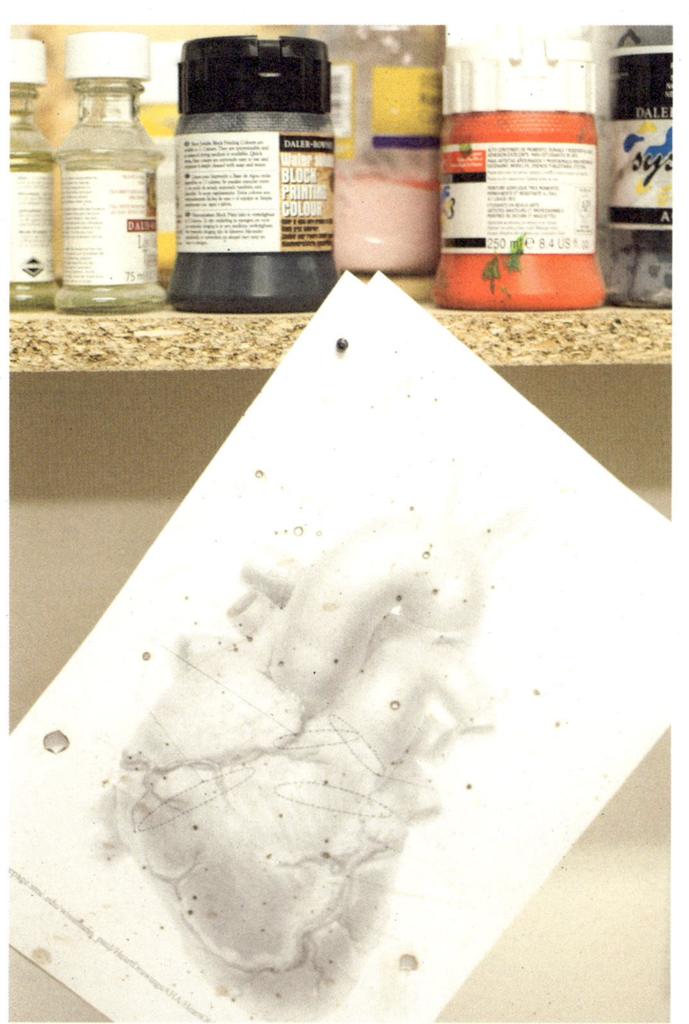

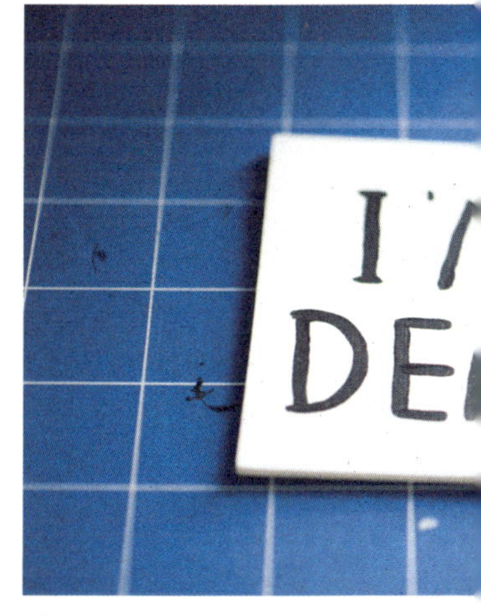
I'
DE

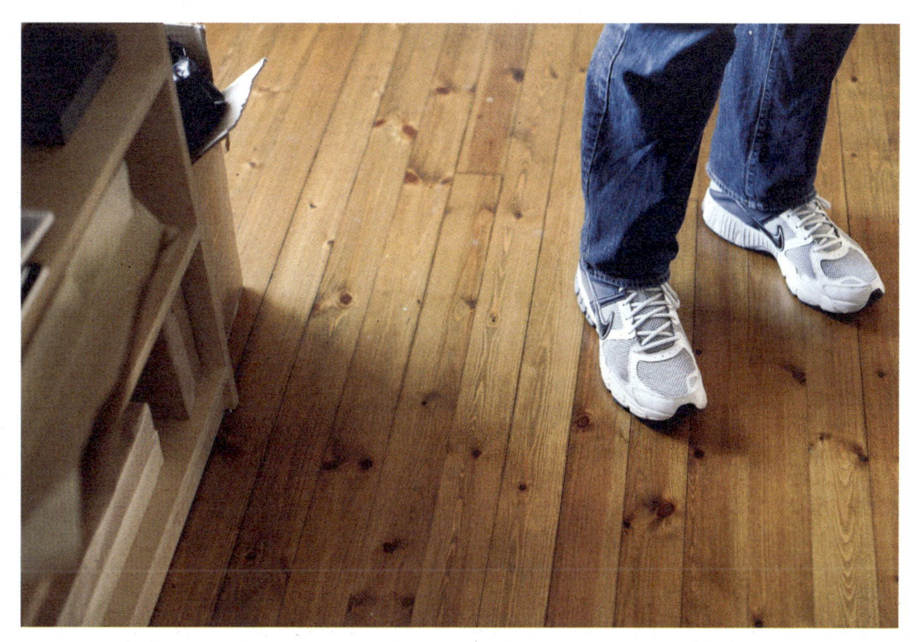

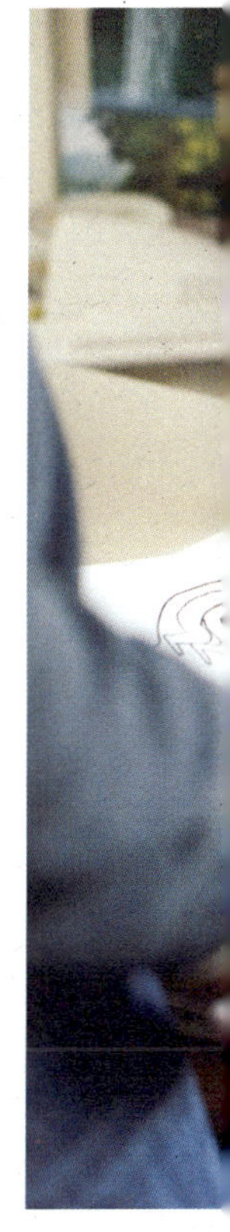

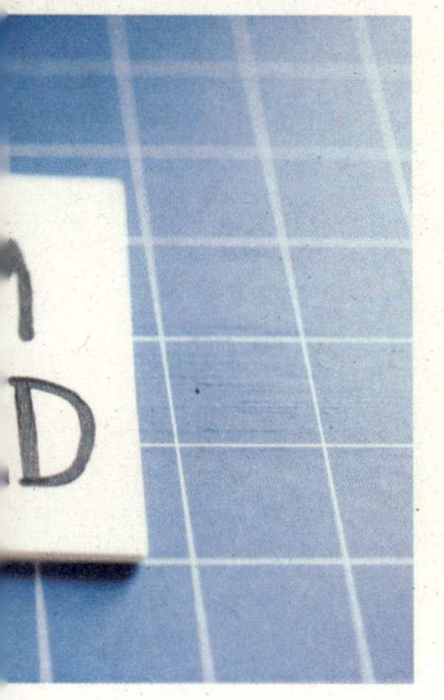

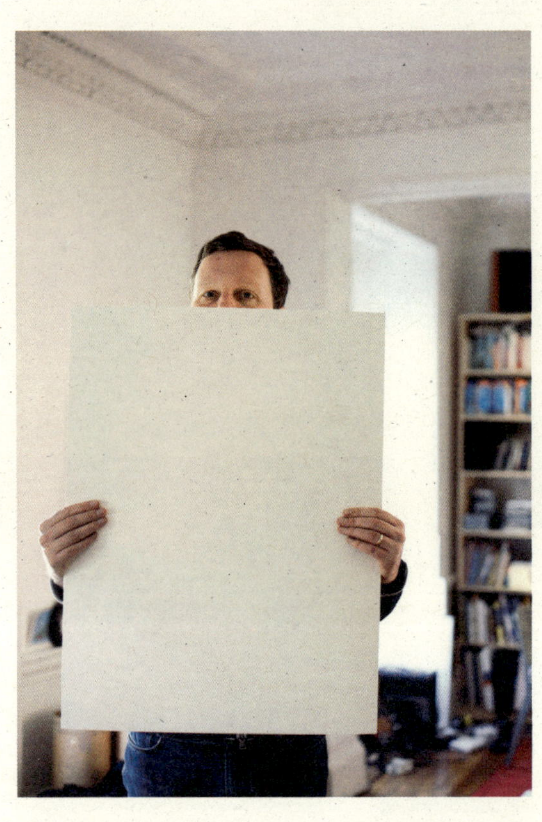

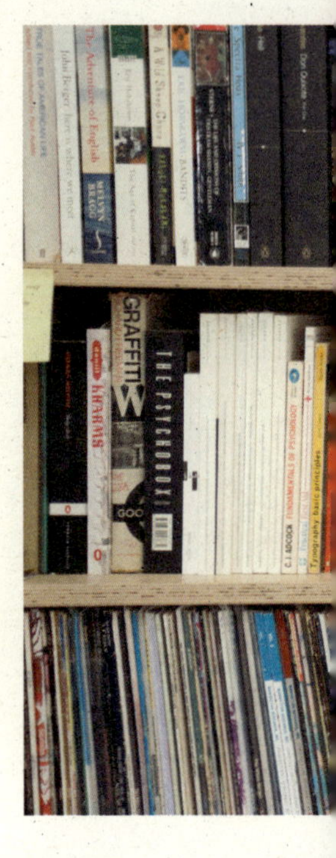

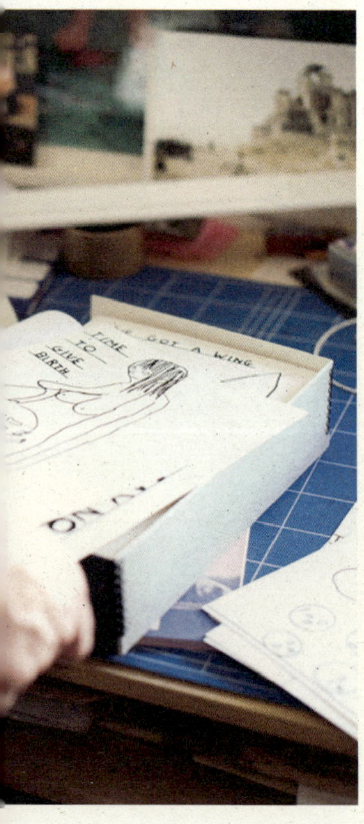
I DIE
TO
GIVE
BIRTH

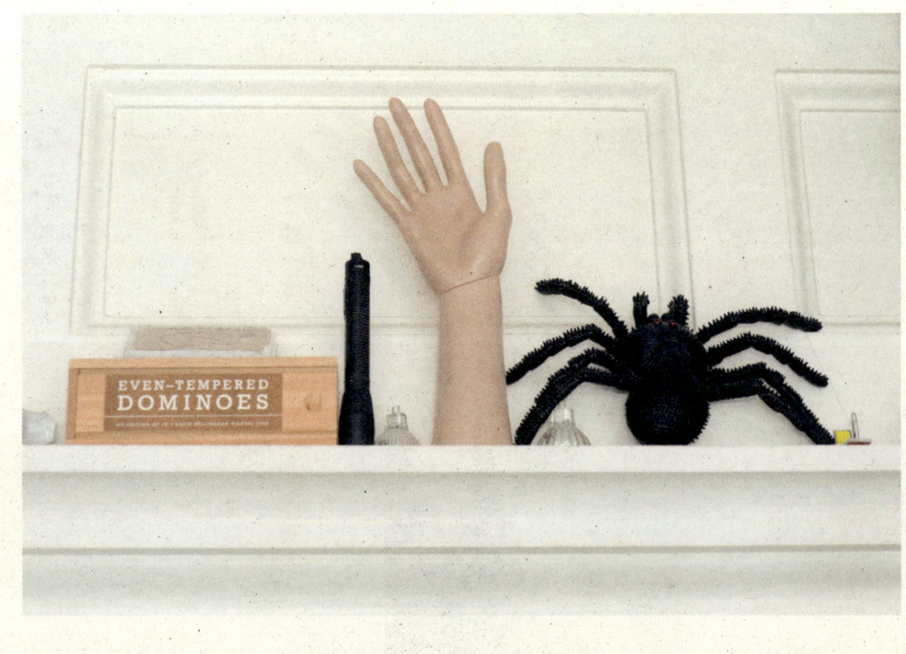
EVEN-TEMPERED
DOMINOES

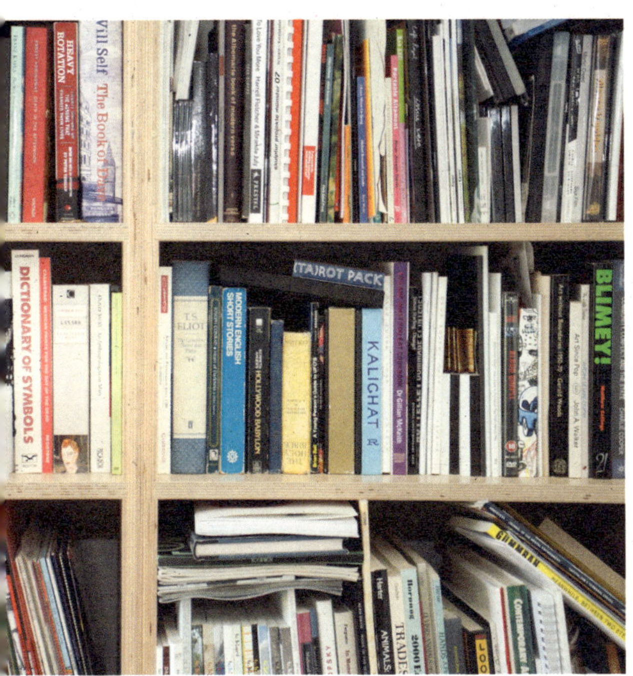
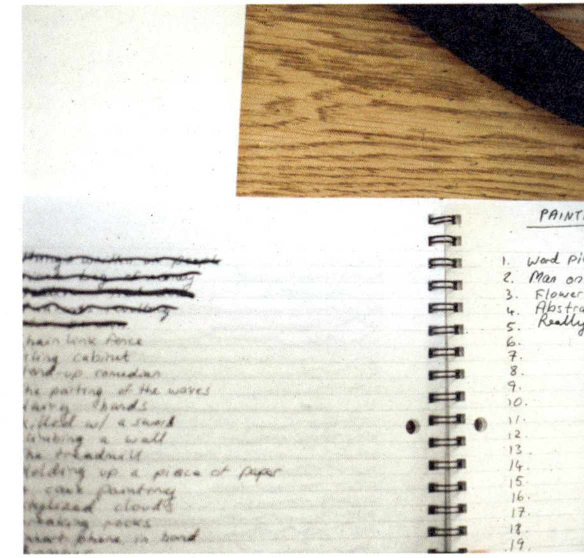

chain link fence
filing cabinet
stand-up comedian
the parting of the waves
fairy hands
field w/ a sword
climbing a wall
the treadmill
holding up a piece of paper
cave painting
airbrushed clouds
breaking rocks
mobile phone in hand
PAINTI
1. Word Pic
2. Man on
3. Flower
4. Abstrac
5. Really
6.
7.
8.
9.
10.
11.
12.
13.
14.
15.
16.
17.
18.
19.

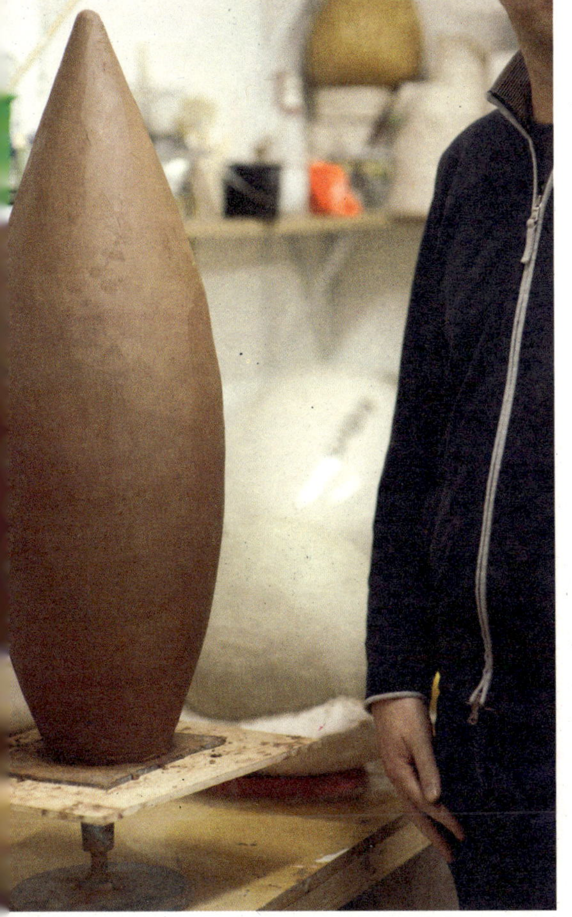
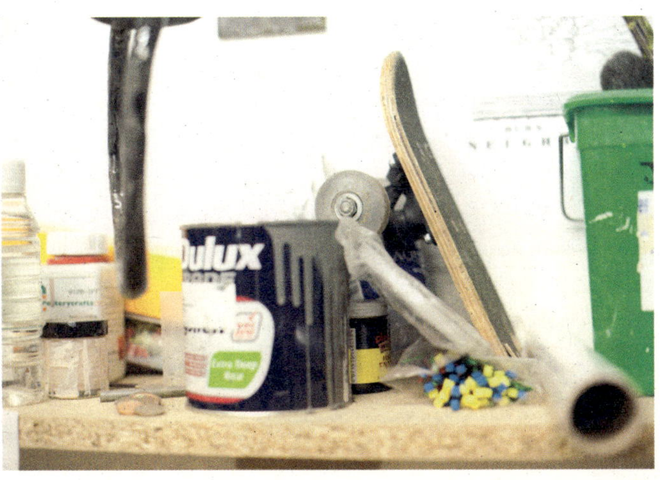

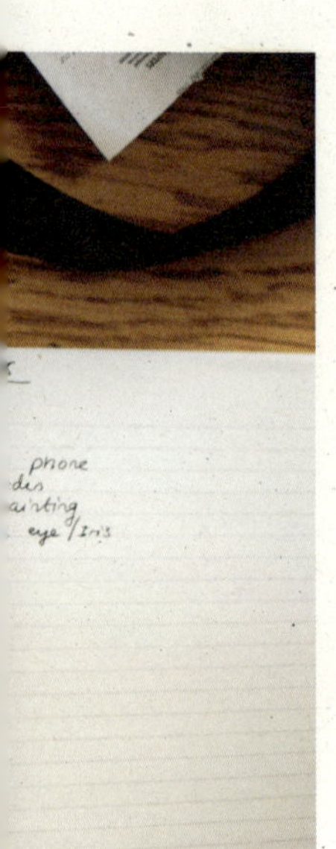
phone
das
eye / ins

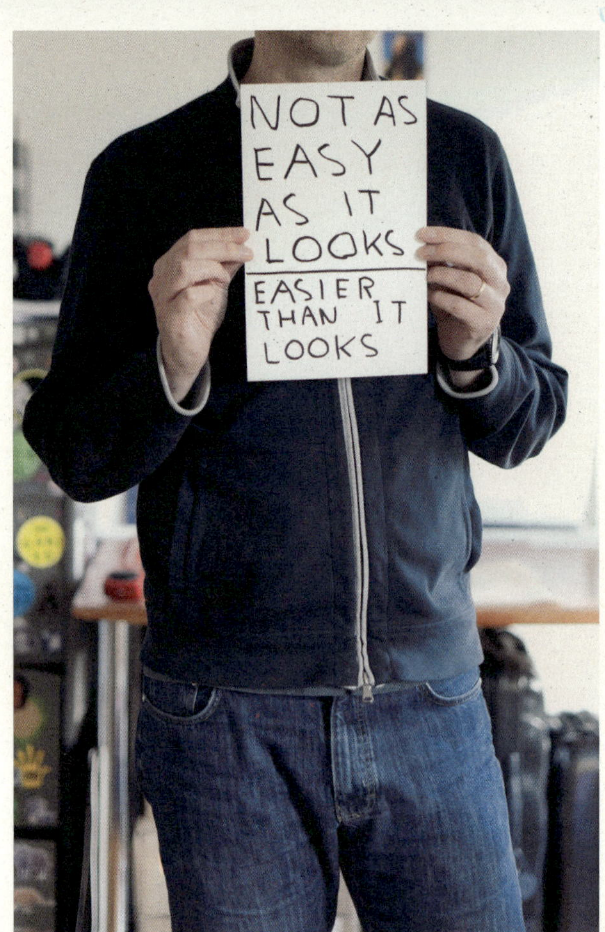
NOT AS
EASY
AS IT
LOOKS
EASIER
THAN IT
LOOKS

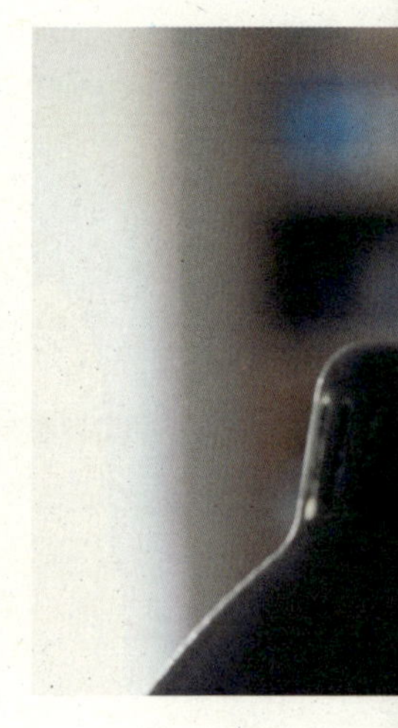

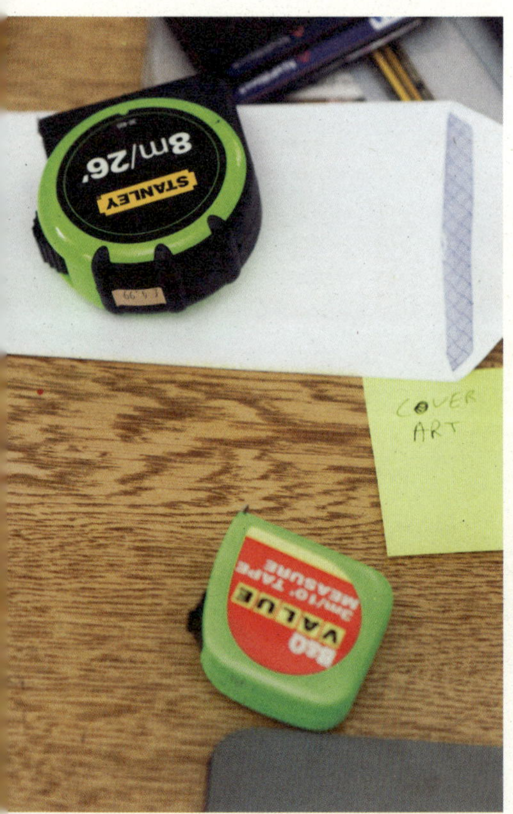
STANLEY
8m/26'
VALUE
3M/10' TAPE
MEASURE
COVER
ART

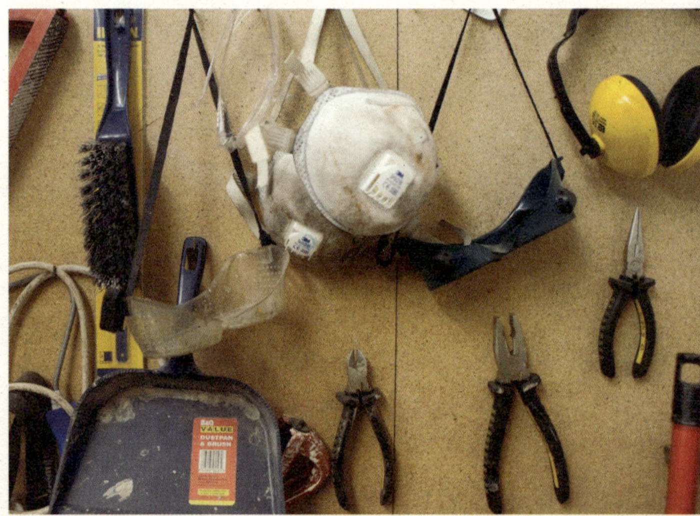
VALUE
DUSTPAN
& BRUSH

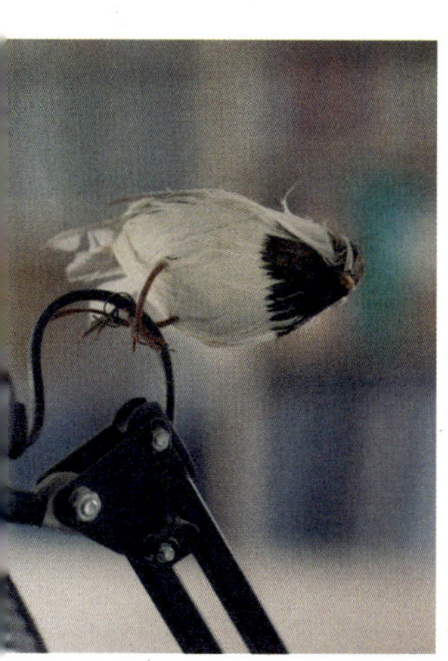

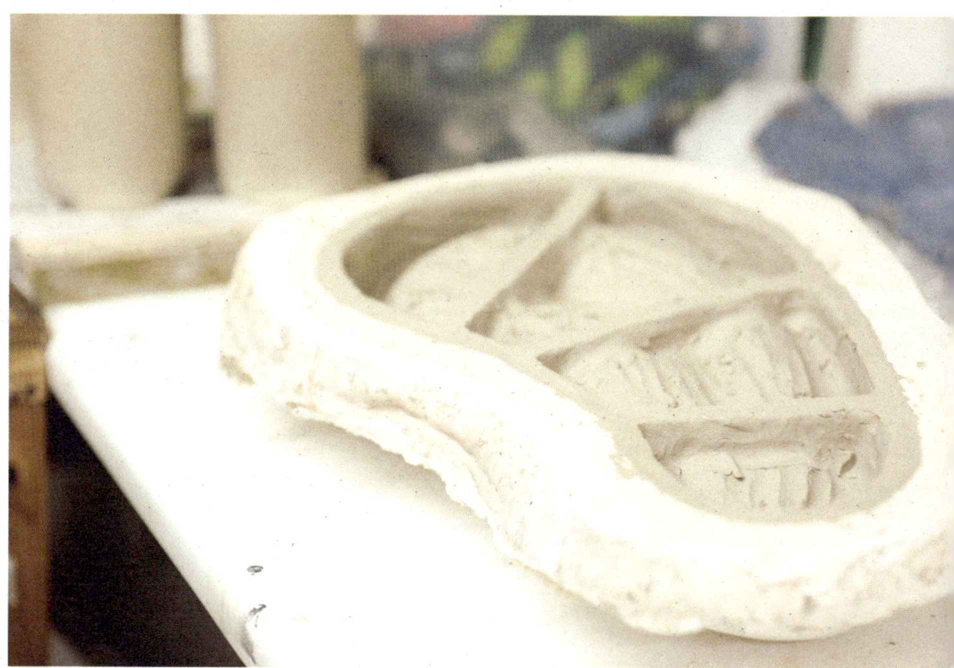

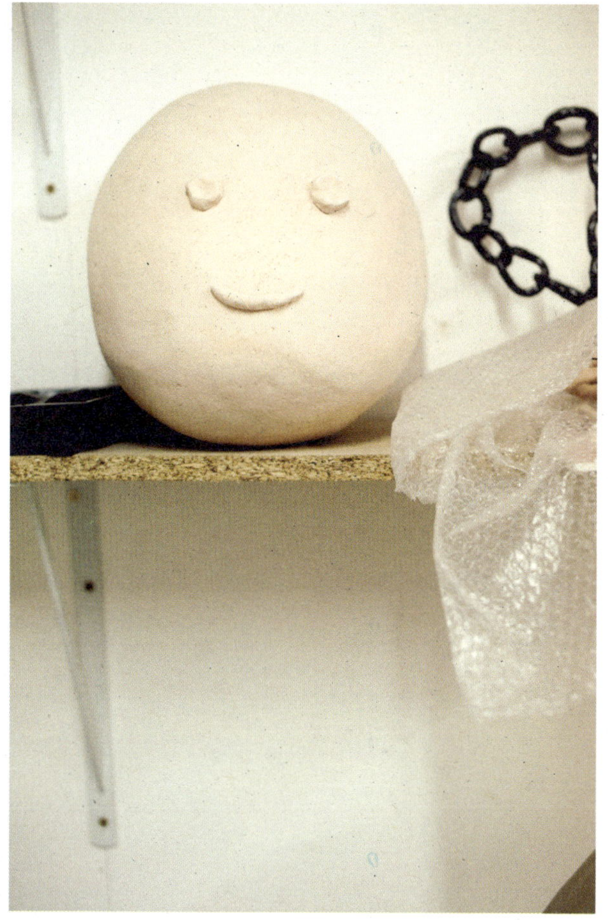

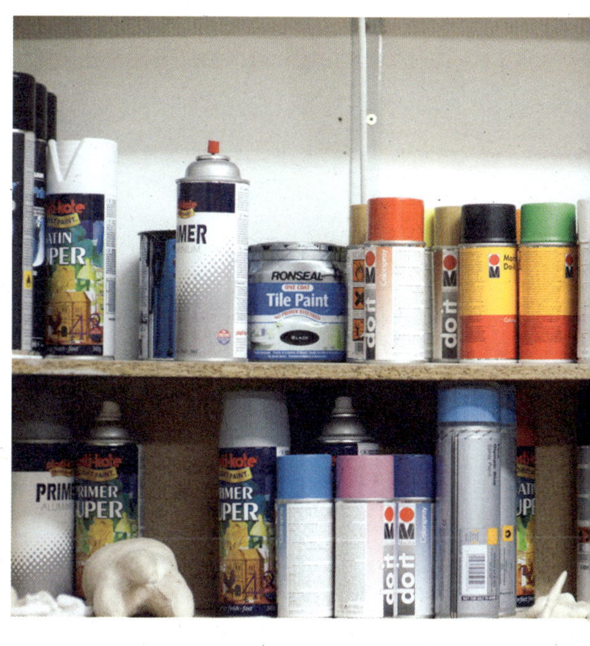

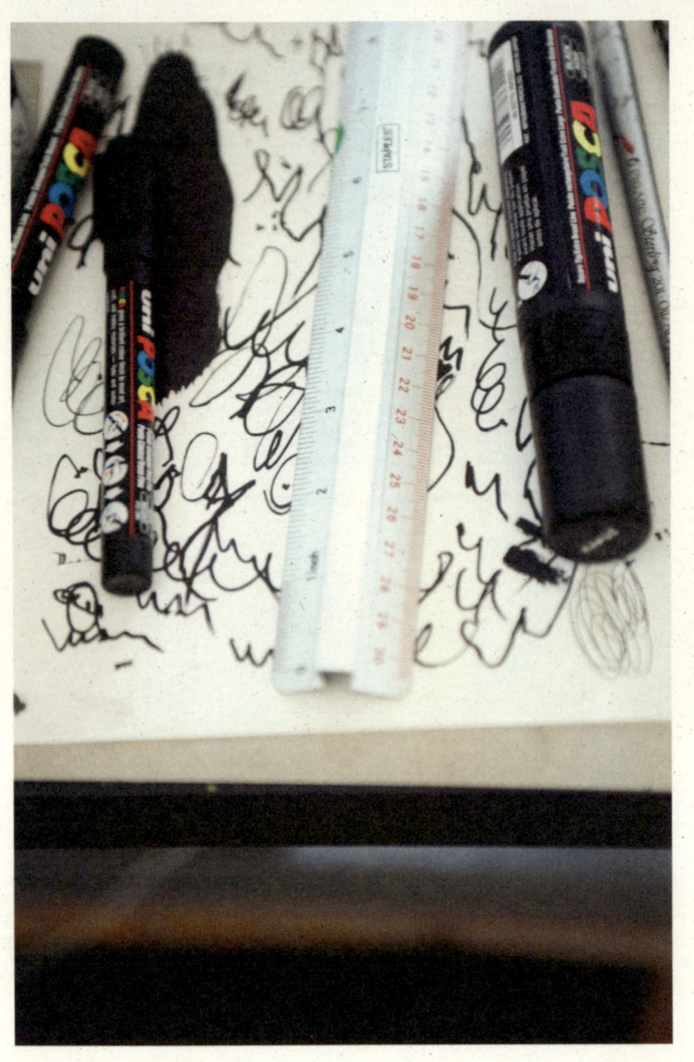
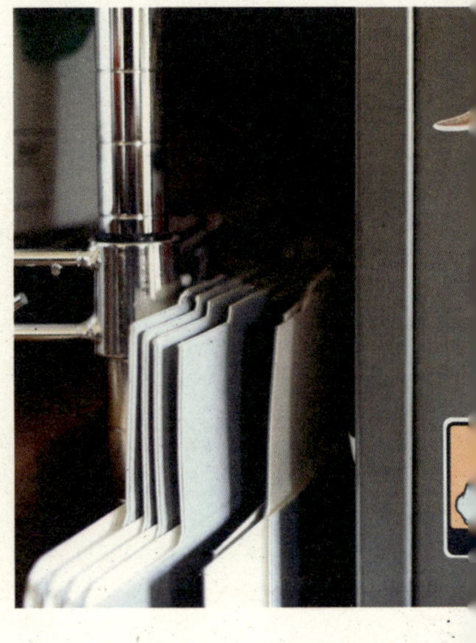
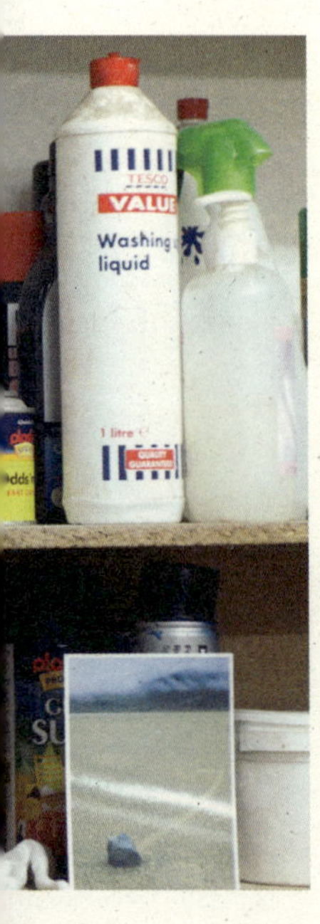
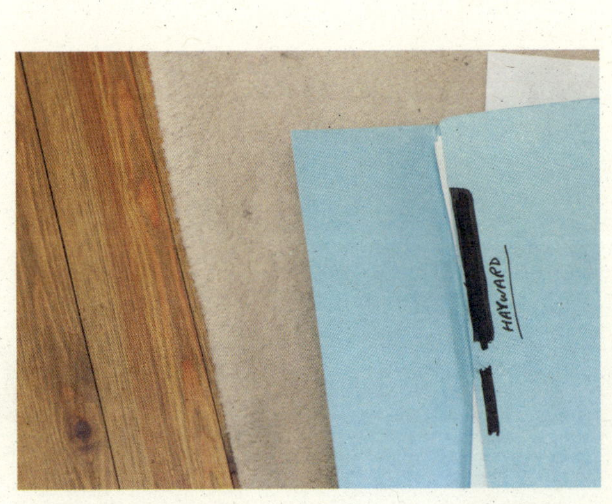
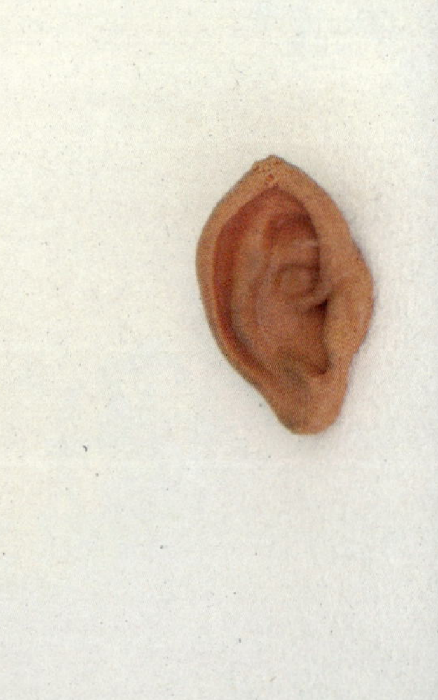

David Shrigley
— Brain Activity

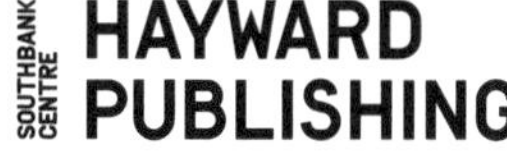

DAVID SHRIGLEY

BRAIN ACTIVITY

Contents

Foreword

For over two decades, David Shrigley has been making some of the most darkly humorous and slyly disquieting art of our times. He first became known for his stripped-down drawings, usually accompanied by words, which displayed an inventively mordant wit, while encapsulating the banalities and failures of everyday life and society. This exhibition – his first survey in the United Kingdom – includes a substantial selection of these drawings, but also focuses on the many other types of work that the artist produces, including sculpture, painting, photography, video and installation. Featuring new commissions as well as salient examples from every phase of his career, *David Shrigley: Brain Activity* reveals the full range of his imaginative and aesthetic reach, and conveys his underlying impulse to use minimal means in order, as he says, to 'communicate as simply and directly as possible'.

We are very grateful for all the time and energy that David has put into realising this exhibition, and for his enthusiasm in developing new ideas for its installation at the Hayward. In addition, this show could not have been realised without the generosity of the different institutions and individuals who have loaned works from their collections. We are also grateful for the assistance and loans provided by David's galleries: Stephen Friedman Gallery, London, Galleri Nicolai Wallner, Copenhagen, Anton Kern Gallery, New York, Galerie Yvon Lambert, Paris, Galerie Francesca Pia, Zurich and BQ Berlin.

Hayward Curator, Cliff Lauson, who spent a great deal of time in discussions with the artist and closely engaging with his work, deserves praise for putting together a deftly considered and energetic survey. Hayward Exhibitions Assistant Jessica Cerasi provided indispensable support in organising the show.

This catalogue features lively and thoughtful texts that explore different aspects of David Shrigley's art, and we are grateful to Dave Eggers, Martin Herbert and Jonathan Monk, as well as Cliff Lauson, for their highly original contributions. Hayward Art Publisher, Nadine Monem, did a superb job managing all aspects of this publication. Thanks also go to David Lane and Robert Boon from Inventory Studio for their excellent and fresh design of this book.

Hayward Operations Manager Ruth Pelopida and Senior Technician David Wood adroitly managed the planning and installation of the exhibition. I also wish to thank Hayward Assistant Registrars Vicky Skelding and Charlotte Booth; Hayward Interpretation Manager Helen Luckett and Hayward General Manager Urszula Kossakowska. Finally, this exhibition has benefited from the support of Southbank Centre CEO Alan Bishop and Artistic Director Jude Kelly as well as Southbank Centre's Board of Trustees, and Arts Council England.

Ralph Rugoff
Director, Hayward Gallery

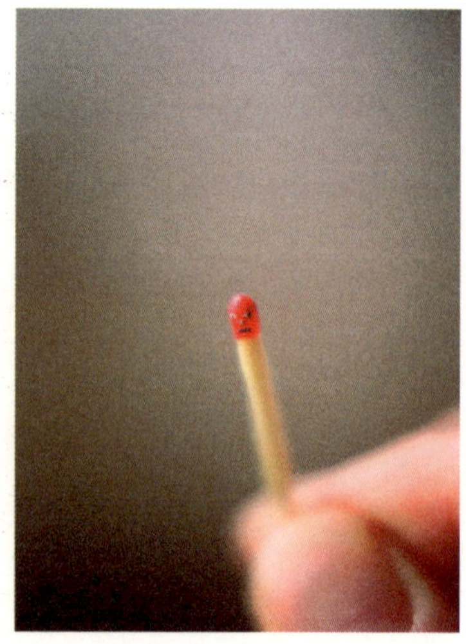

01.

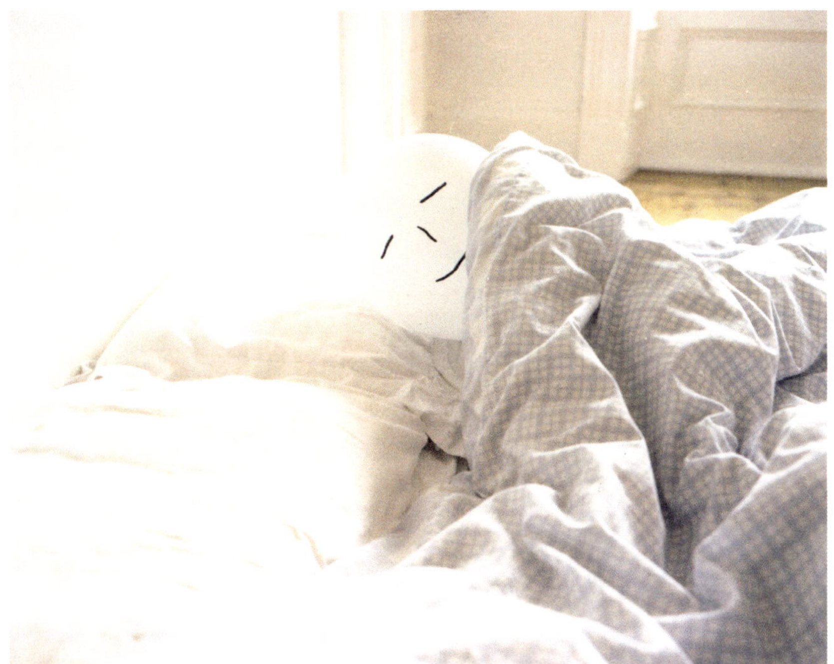

02.

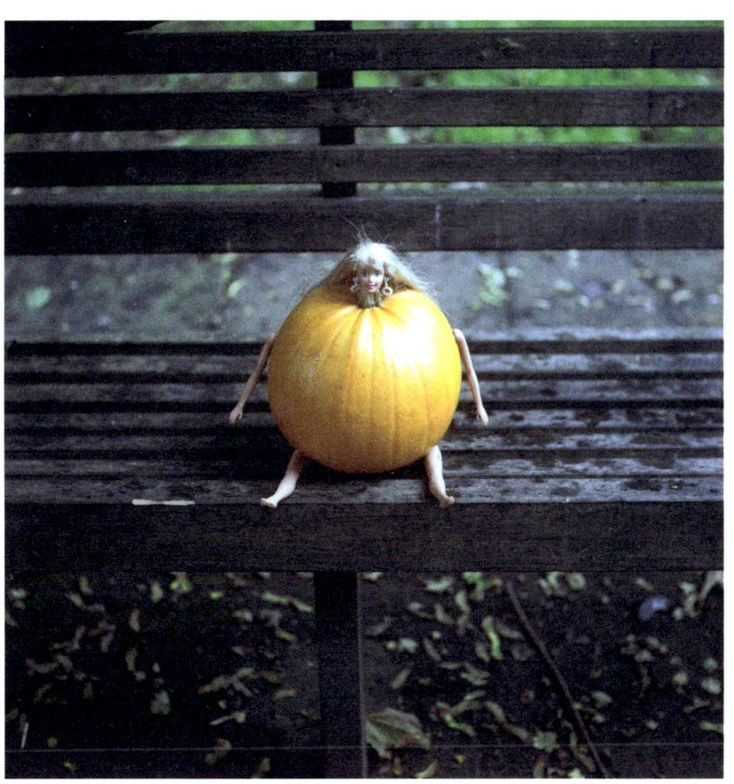

03.

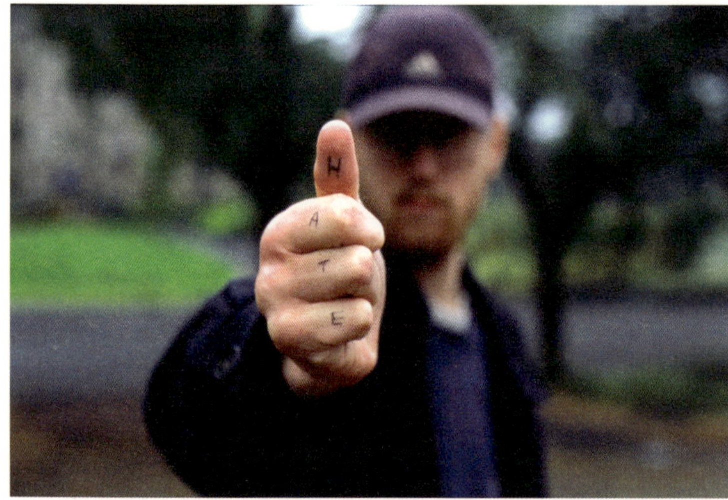

04.

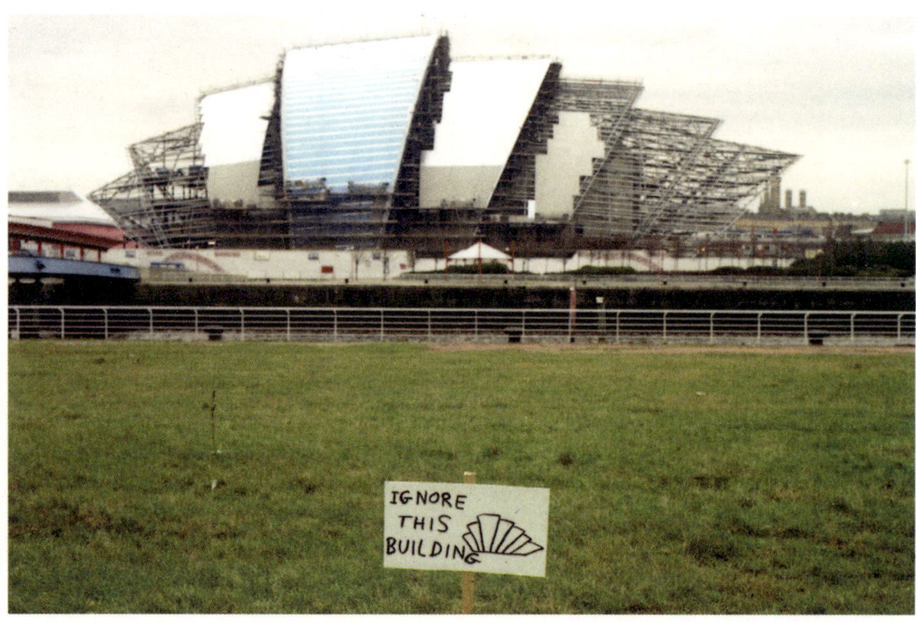

05.

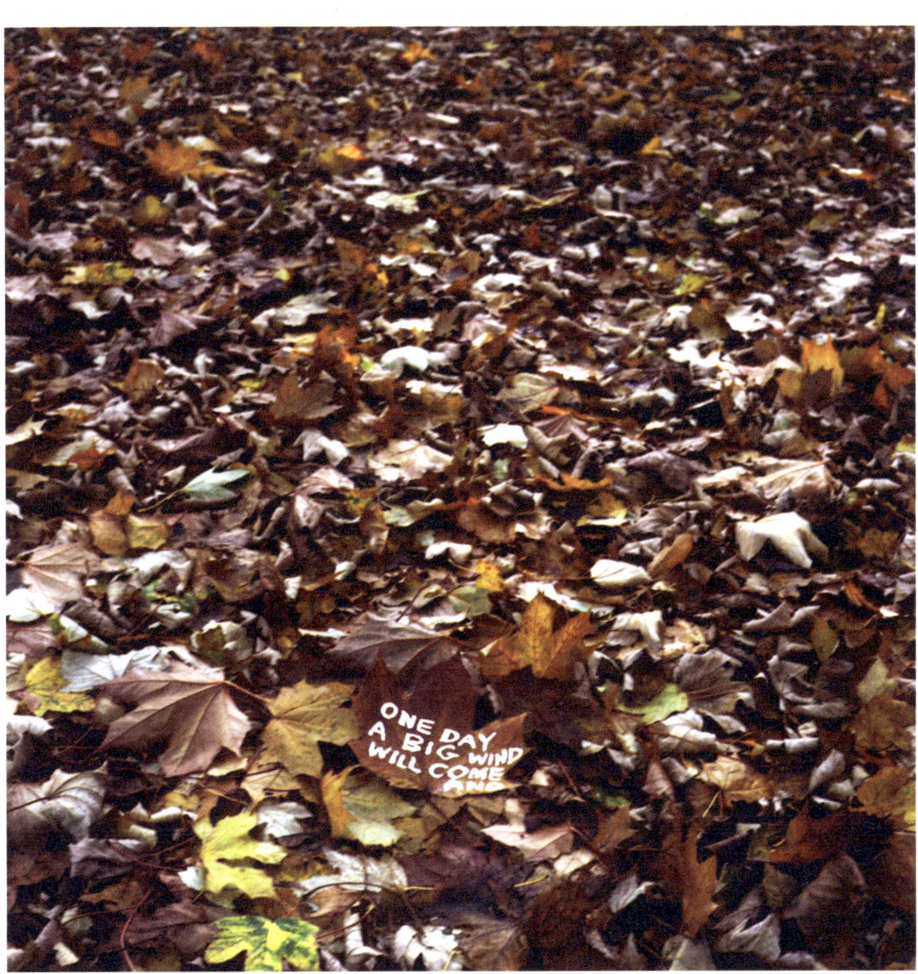

06.

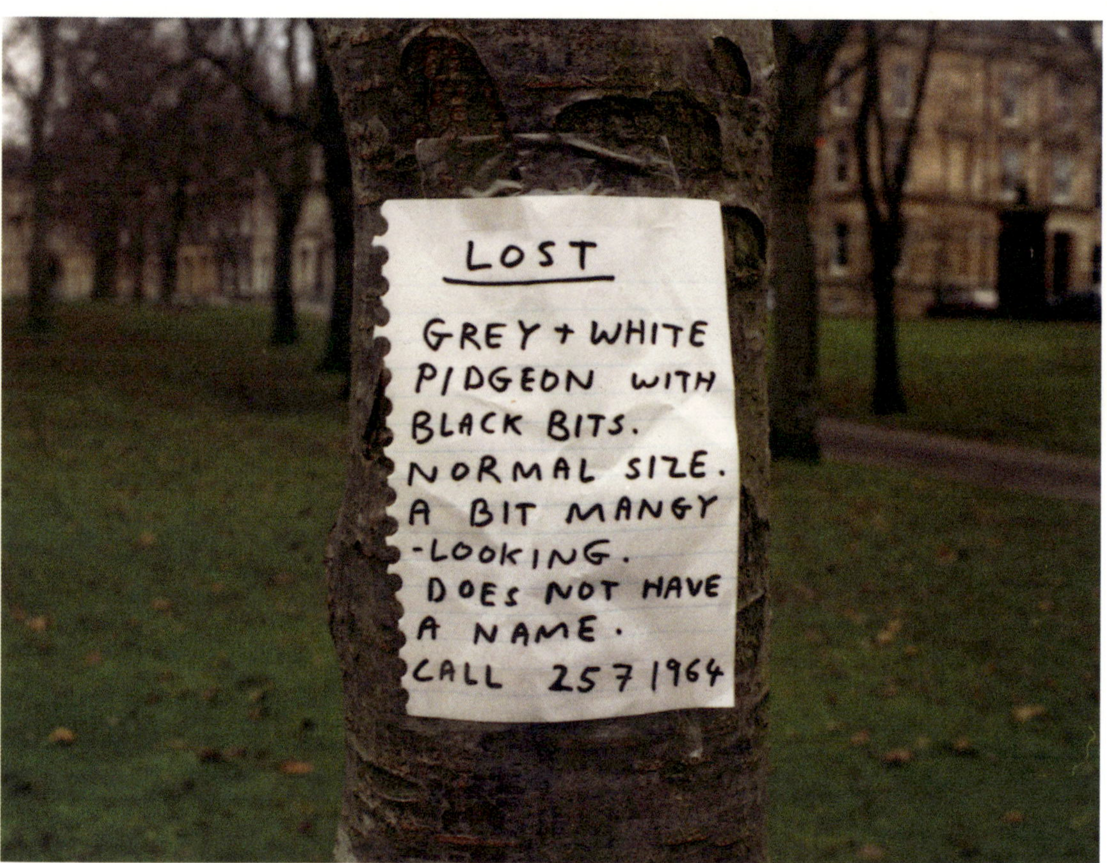
LOST

GREY + WHITE
PIDGEON WITH
BLACK BITS.
NORMAL SIZE.
A BIT MANGY
-LOOKING.
DOES NOT HAVE
A NAME.
CALL 257 1964

07.

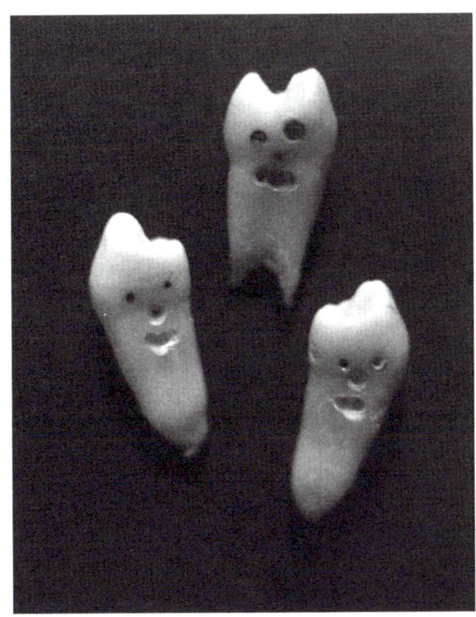

08.

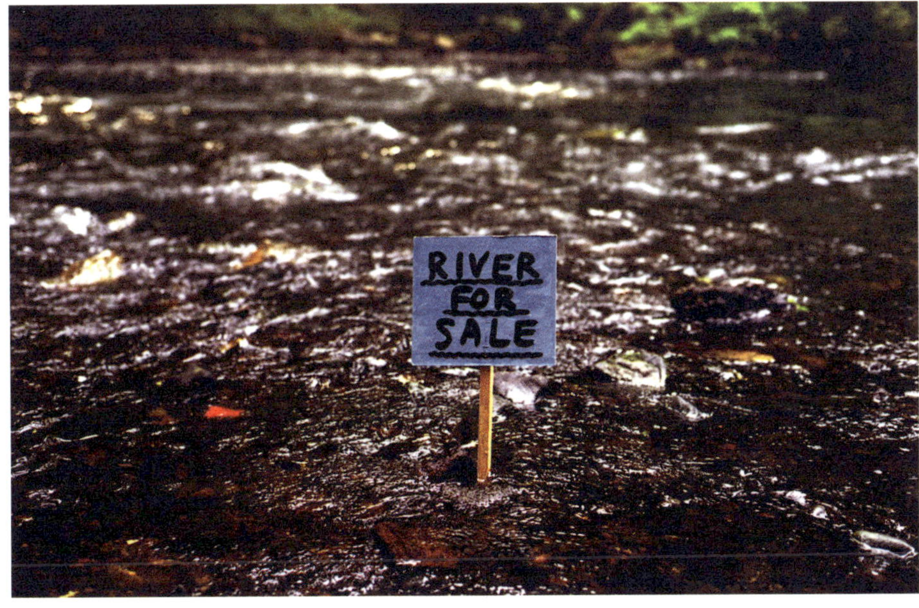

09.

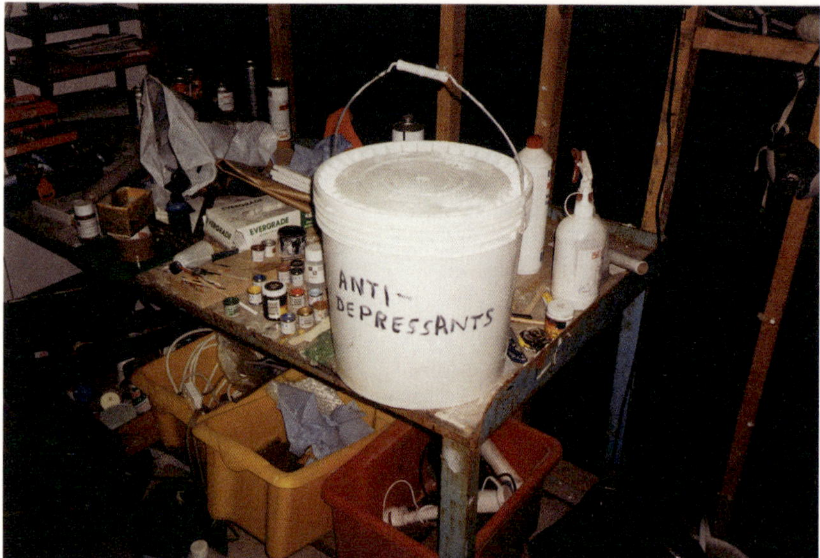

10.

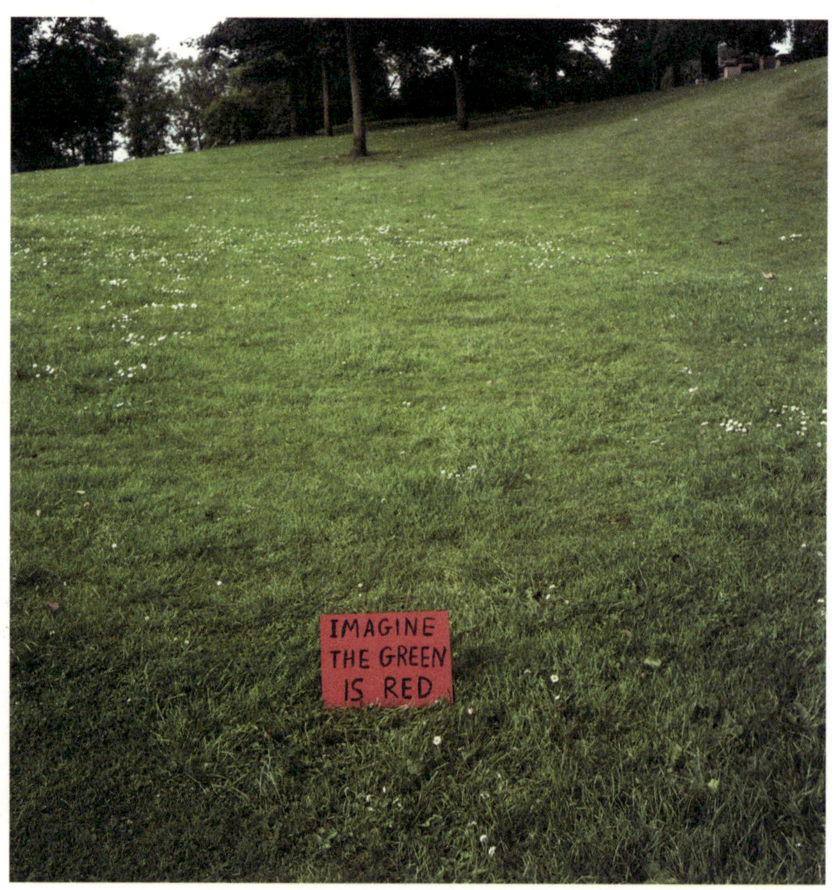

11.

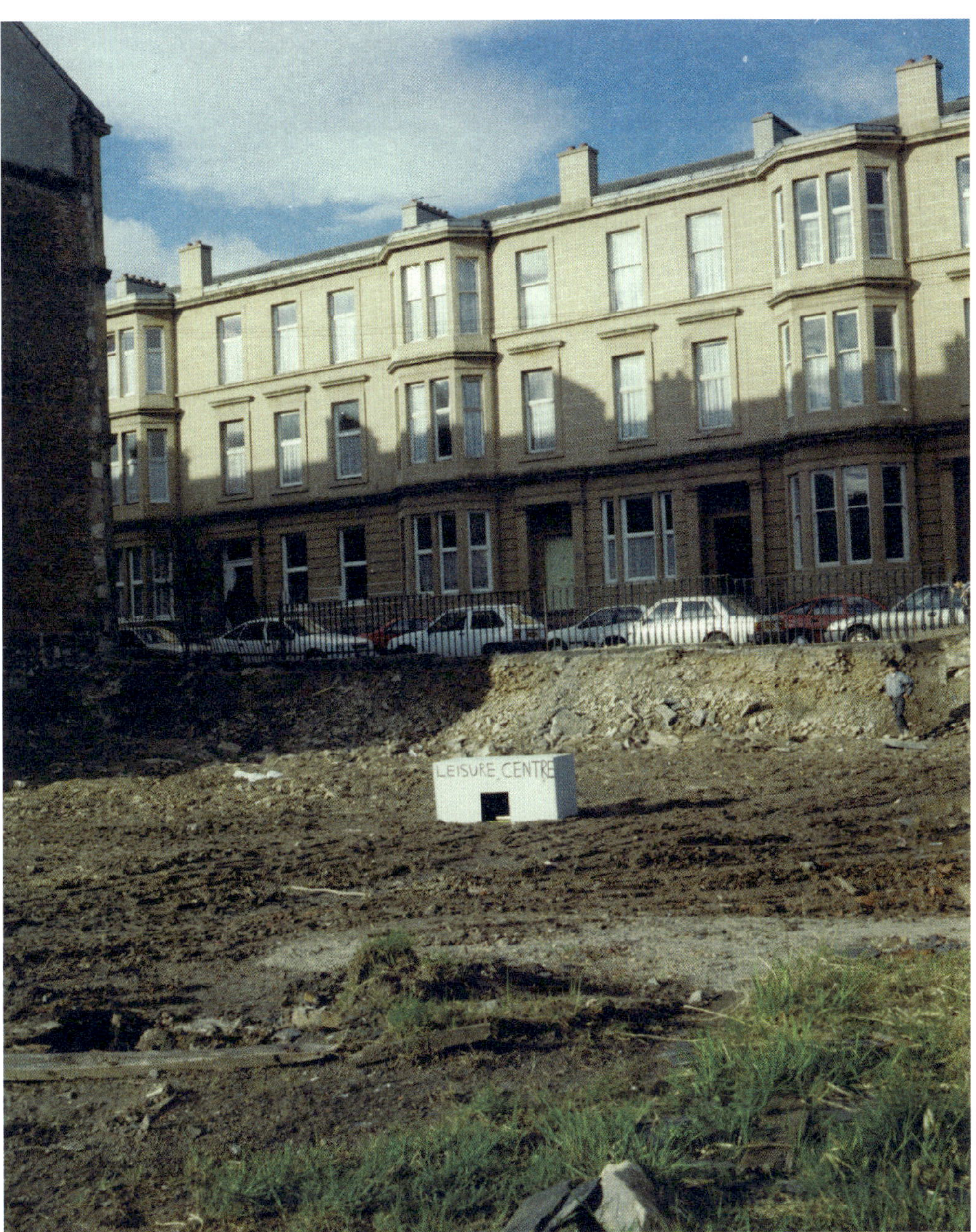

12.

David Shrigley: Larger Than Life (And Sometimes Death)
— Cliff Lauson

Judging by the title of David Shrigley's animation *Who I Am and What I Want* (2005), one might think the film presents a straightforward portrayal of an individual, perhaps even of the artist himself. The seven-minute animation, however, features a character named Muck (but you can call him Pete) who tells the story of his weird and wonderful life, each scene brought to life in Shrigley's crude style of drawing. Pete generally seems to lead a rather humdrum existence, tending to everyday tasks and chores, but also experiences some rather extreme situations, such as growing up in a swamp, living in a zoo aviary enclosure, and dealing with bouts of insanity.[1] As the film progresses, Pete's daydreams and fantasies start to blur with reality and the result is a visually chaotic descent into his psyche – 'If I could meet god what would he say? What if I lived amongst the dinosaurs? What if I was fried in a pan with butter and garlic? What would happen if I executed myself?' The film is a surreal tale of a blissfully naïve character whose mental state oscillates between normalcy and psychosis.

Who I Am and What I Want is typical of Shrigley's overall practice, which makes witty and incisive commentary on the objects and experiences of everyday life, often with an absurd and dark comedic sense. While Shrigley is best known for his amusing drawings, his artwork has proven to be remarkably diverse, crossing a variety of media, including sculpture, painting, photography, printmaking, digital animation and music. At the heart of all of these works is Shrigley's sense of humour, a highly unusual foundation for an art practice. Indeed, while many contemporary artworks are funny, few artists have been able to consistently mine the genre, as Shrigley has done over the past two decades, to achieve international recognition both in fine art and more diverse circles of popular culture. He accomplishes this by using different types of humour, from the one-liner joke to the tragicomic narrative, and also by involving different genres including (but not limited to) situational, black humour and dead-pan. Drawing inspiration from everyday life, Shrigley's work brings to light and pokes fun at all of the dilemmas, moral crises and burdens of responsibility that fill our lives, usually in a very condensed or metaphorical way. A sculpture like *What Decay Looks Like* (2001, see p.47), an oversized tooth riddled with holes standing in front of a mirror, seems to be invested with this kind of emotional weight. Close to becoming overwhelmed by cavities, it must surely be wrestling with the meaning of life, and all of the existential complexities that come with being an oversized premolar.

Shrigley's interest in humour was not exactly something that he was taught at the Glasgow School of Art (GSA), where he studied in the late

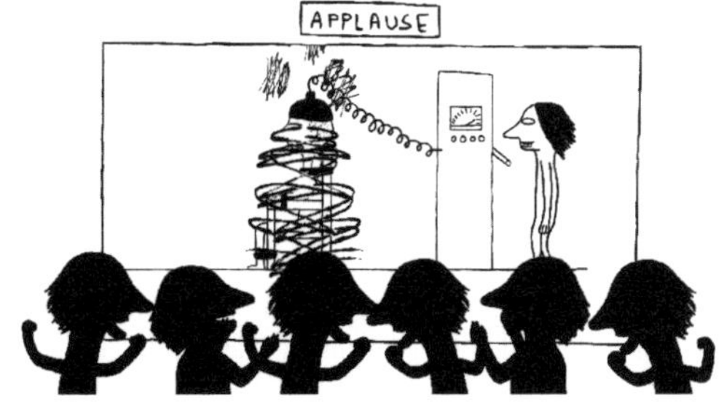

David Shrigley and Chris Shepherd
Still from *Who I Am and What I Want,* 2005

1980s to early 90s, along with conceptual artist and friend Jonathan Monk. He has always possessed a very dry sense of humour, but this did not necessarily find acceptance as art in a learning context dominated by a Neo-Expressionist painterly aesthetic embraced by artists such as Georg Baselitz, Jean-Michel Basquiat and Julian Schnabel. In contrast, Shrigley (and Monk) were more interested in post-conceptual strategies and in the pop cultural references employed by Mike Kelley or Haim Steinbach. Taking a course in Environmental Art (the only refuge for artists at GSA not committed to working in a single medium), Shrigley developed an aptitude for making work that responds incisively to its context. His take on situational humour is evident in a body of photographic work made throughout the 1990s in which he makes small interventions into nondescript situations such as a landscape, room or street. *Leisure Centre* (1992, see p.23) depicts an undeveloped plot in the midst of which Shrigley has placed a small white box, with a cut-out door, that is labelled 'LEISURE CENTRE', an ironic critique of public services. *Lost* (1996, see p.20) mimics the format of a photocopied lost pet poster affixed to a tree, only Shrigley's 'pet' is a mangy and anonymous pigeon. As a whole, this body of photographic work recalls Richard Wentworth's ongoing archive *Making do and getting by* (1970–), which documents objects that have been used in an incongruous way. As in Wentworth's series, it is the dead-pan tone and adoption of the casual snap-shot aesthetic that make Shrigley's work not only whimsical, but also unexpectedly funny. Each one of Shrigley's photographs is almost a study of how a small textual or graphic intervention suddenly overturns or disrupts a 'first glance' reading of an overall image. The effect that this incongruity has on the viewer, like the classic comedic trope, is often a double-take.

   To a degree, the mantra for the GSA Environmental Art course – 'The context is half the work' – explains the situational humour that Shrigley applies throughout his broader practice, which ranges from unexpected occurrences in the gallery to musical collaborations: the drawing *Why We*

Richard Wentworth
London 1999. From the series *Making do and getting by*, 1970–

Got The Sack From The Museum (1998, for all drawings mentioned in this essay, see pp.102–103) sees miscreants taking paintings from the gallery walls and jumping on them; while the album *Worried Noodles* (2007) features famous bands playing songs with awkward lyrics and themes penned by the artist. When presenting work in the gallery, Shrigley attempts to generate surprise at every turn by using unconventional architecture or by creating sculptural interventions that leave the viewer wondering if what they are seeing – a large tooth stuck behind a radiator, for example – is an undisclosed artwork or something that they should report to security. For a 2007 exhibition at Malmö Konsthall in Sweden, Shrigley divided the space into no less than 26 separate stalls in which to show his work. This series of small spaces created the feel of a marketplace at odds with conventional museum installation aesthetics. In these ways, Shrigley's interventions and installations tend to be relatively organic and site-specific, responding to each context and situation in ways that best heighten the artworks' comedic effects.

   Since the mid-1990s, drawing has been the mainstay of Shrigley's practice. During and in the years immediately following art school, his drawings had been largely consigned to his sketchbook as a sideline activity. After graduating, he experimented with becoming a commercial cartoonist, but ultimately found the cartoon style to be too polished and contrived, and chose instead to self-publish (as The Armpit Press) a few books of drawings with a rougher feel to them, like those in his sketchbooks. These books, such as *Merry Eczema* (1992) and *Blanket of Filth* (1994), were cheaply printed and distributed by the artist to a small social circle. It was only after attaining recognition for them, which had started to spread by word of mouth, that he was offered his first gallery exhibition at Glasgow's Transmission Gallery (1995). Since then, Shrigley has deftly managed to excel in two parallel arenas: with the same drawings he is able to achieve recognition with audiences who know little about art but appreciate his humour, and with galleries and collectors who support a limited number of international artists. To date, he has published over 30 books and, ironically, he also eventually returned to cartooning, but firmly on his own, now-established stylistic terms, creating drawings for the *Guardian*, *The Independent* and the *New Statesman*.[2] Fine art, however, remains his central focus. As he has said, 'I seem to have this reputation as an illustrator or a cartoonist-type person, so a lot of people don't realise that I have this other background in fine art… Fine art is the thing I couldn't forsake. I couldn't stop being a fine artist and be someone who just designs record covers.'[3]

That many of Shrigley's drawings were made with publication in mind is important, both in terms of their design and distribution. His drawings have a recognisable style – often heavily outlined, scratchy, crude, with accompanying text – and are sometimes arranged by the artist to sit together on facing or sequential pages. Superficially, these visual aspects seem to align Shrigley's work with the graphic style found in comic books. However, it is important to note that they are neither literary nor structured as sequential narrative 'stills'. Instead, the artist's aesthetic demonstrates a kind of compressed and minimal vocabulary of gestures that find their best expression through drawing: 'I started to draw in the way that I do as an attempt to reduce my ideas to their barest form; to communicate as simply and directly as possible.'[4] Drawing here is used almost as a form of notation or

paraphrase in which the simplest set of marks can refer to objects and subjects of much greater breadth and complexity. Shrigley's drawings have a lightness and ease of access to them that belies the incisiveness of his observations. Rather than appropriating the existing comic genre for use in art, he defines his own aesthetic, which speaks equally to spheres of popular culture and fine art. His work therefore transcends the long-standing 'high and low' debate between comics and fine art, most obviously demonstrated by his pocketable publications that are both novelty purchases as well as artist's books.[5] The book format offers easy accessibility as well as massively increased distribution compared to the otherwise limited opportunity of seeing the drawings presented in a formal gallery context. And as they have become increasingly popular, Shrigley has been able to shape the books into more self-contained and sometimes self-referential projects. For example, *Err* (1996) parodies the published format itself, with deliberate typos, formatting and illustration errors, as if produced by the world's worst publisher, editor and designer.

All of Shrigley's drawings, regardless of their final output, are made intuitively in a fairly disciplined manner, at an easel in his organised studio, even if their rough, scrawling and sometimes child-like appearance contrasts dramatically with this working method. He draws at a sustained stretch, completing tens or even hundreds of drawings within a short space of time. Whatever rigour they appear to lack in individual precision – wayward lines, mistakes and corrections all record the process of making – they gain through editing. Shrigley leaves his drawings in his 'artistic distance box' for a time before deciding on which ones to keep, and he usually destroys about three-quarters of them. This is a careful process of consideration that belies the seeming spontaneity of the humour within each drawing, and means that for the 7,000 or so drawings that he has officially made public since the beginning of his career, he has in fact made at least 25,000. It is a vast amount of work for an artist only in his early 40s, and their sheer quantity amusingly recalls one such drawing in

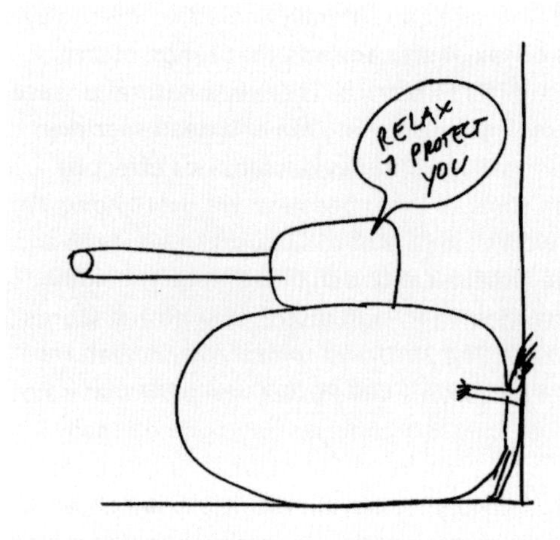

Dan Perjovschi
Relax, I protect you, 2005

which a monster who has had his arm cut off also unfortunately has carpal tunnel syndrome.

Shrigley's drawings can also be seen as part of a more general rise in interest in contemporary art involving drawing as a medium, which also includes 'expanded notions' of drawing, beyond the pencil and paper. But rather than present delicate or intricately rendered scenes such as those made by Raymond Pettibon or Paul Noble, Shrigley's marker-based 'sketches' have more in common with Dan Perjovschi and Nedko Solakov, who are also known for their humorous and pared-down graphic forms. All three artists use text in their work to steer the readings of their drawings, sometimes taking the shape of a speech bubble and other times acting as a title or statement. With Shrigley's work, there is often more of a disjunction between image and text, generating humour out of the frisson between the two. And, while Perjovschi and Solakov make political drawings and often draw directly on walls as a form of graffiti-like intervention, Shrigley's work tends to be less concerned with ideology and more in dialogue with the materiality of the page: in addition to being printed in books, his drawings are presented both as individually framed unique objects and as reproduced posters (see pp.86–87).

As central as drawing is to Shrigley's art, it is only one aspect of an *œuvre* that includes a broad diversity of media and which shares thematic, humorous and historical influences. Dada and Surrealist strategies are important precursors for his work, not only in terms of drawing, but also as the entry points into art for the absurd, unexpected and humorous. Marcel Duchamp is the obvious arbiter in this regard with, for example, his graffitied moustache on a reproduction of Leonardo da Vinci's *Mona Lisa* and his accompanying inscription, which translates as 'she has a hot ass' (1919). As in Shrigley's photographs, this work demonstrates the power of a single gesture to undermine the whole image. There is also something of the comedic anticipation of Duchamp's 'trap', *Trébuchet* (1917), an upturned coat-rack nailed to the gallery floor, in Shrigley's word sculpture *IT* (2010, see pp.52–53). Standing at less than six inches high and cast in bronze from hand-pressed wax, this sculpture is named as such only because, in stumbling, the gallery-goer is likely to exclaim, 'I tripped over it!'. Belgian Surrealist René Magritte is another major influence, particularly his paintings that typify the incongruous image and often rely on the tension between image and text. Shrigley's (barely) *trompe-l'œil* painting *Door* (2007, see p.147) surely owes much to Magritte's famous painting *The Treachery of Images* (1928–29) in its appeal to a common-sense logic that is often undermined through verbal shorthand – obviously it is not a door; it is a painting of a door. Working in the reverse way, *Hanging Sign* (2007, see p.39) a hanging sign on which appear the words 'HANGING SIGN', is so plainly factual that our instinctive response is to laugh at the obvious tautology. Shrigley's work oscillates between the delightfully unexpected and the painfully obvious, and jars best in a work like *Five Years of Toenail Clippings* (2002, see p.113), which is both unexpected *and* obvious.

The artist's consistent return to the theme of death and use of dark humour also finds precedents in Surrealism. The term 'black humour' was first coined by André Breton in his 1940 anthology of texts, which traces the literary history of satirising death to 'peculiarly liberating and elevating effect'.[6]

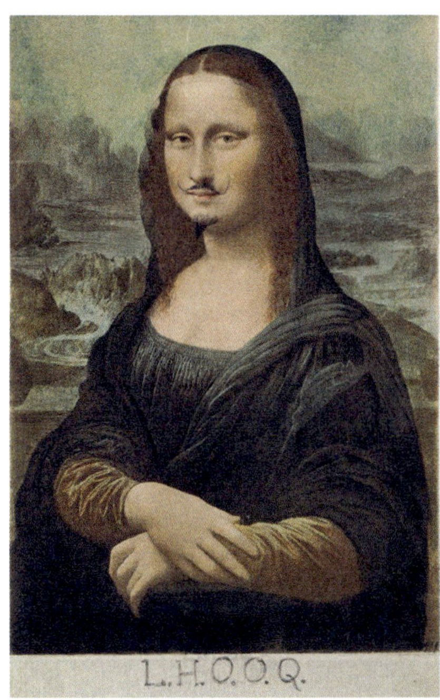

Marcel Duchamp
L.H.O.O.Q, 1919

For the Surrealists, absurdities and desensitisation to death were both a consequence of and a reaction to the atrocities of the First World War. Black humour was a form of political and psychic disruption in fine art, a way of subverting rational thinking. For Shrigley, obsessing over death is a way of making light of the human condition, of finding the limit of humour against what is usually the most serious and emotional of topics. He even treats atrocity on a level with the everyday in, for example, his recent sculpture *The dead and the dying* (2010, see p.58), a group of 40 miniature clay figurines in various states of collapse. While grim in overall content, the figures are artfully arranged in a neat circle as if fine porcelain collectibles, a presentation that ultimately undermines their tragic condition. From the seeming profundity of *Gravestone* (2008, see p.48), a massive headstone inscribed with a mundane shopping list, to the banner-like drawing *Heaven is the New Hell*, Shrigley treats death and misfortune with a well-worn cynicism.

Death is also quite literally embodied in Shrigley's series of taxidermy animals that range in size from squirrel to ostrich. There is a natural unease surrounding the presentation of a dead specimen in an art gallery; Shrigley doubles this effect by making some of them headless. His best-known *I'm Dead* works are part of this unusual menagerie and feature either a cat or dog (heads intact) holding up a hand-written sign inscribed with the words 'I'M DEAD'. The 2010 version of this work features a white and brown Jack Russell (see p.61) that is not only cute but, as a common pet, is emotionally close to us and already somewhat anthropomorphised. Shrigley makes this artificially animated state even more unnatural by posing him on his hind legs, using his tail to form a tripod, to make the Frankenstein-like proclamation. The fact that the sign itself, a white card on a wooden stick, has the look of a quickly-made protest placard seems to imply that even the dog himself objects to being dead or made to look alive, or likely both. This, of course, is a subtle point that comes second to the fact that dogs (and cats) are not capable of writing in the first place. In these death-related works, Shrigley draws upon an uncomfortable, *schadenfreude* humour, tending towards the macabre, for effect. Considering whether or not to laugh at this participates in what the artist calls a 'moral conundrum'.

If the taxidermy animals are disconcerting, other, more subtle, works within Shrigley's sculptural practice are uncanny or awkward, perhaps evoking more of a nervous laughter in the viewer. Exaggerated scale, one way in which the artist makes the familiar seem strange, is evident in the ongoing series of large *Keys* (2007, see pp.50–51) or *Big Nut* (1996, see p.56), which are impossibly unwieldy, or in *Ceramic Ear* (2010, see p.115), an enormous ear within which nestles a little man. These oversized objects recall Claes Oldenburg's sculptures, such as a spoon, clothes-pin or ice-cream cone, that are drawn from the everyday and elevated to monumental status through a process of enlarging (many intended as actual public monuments). Not wanting to make such grandiose gestures, Shrigley is more interested

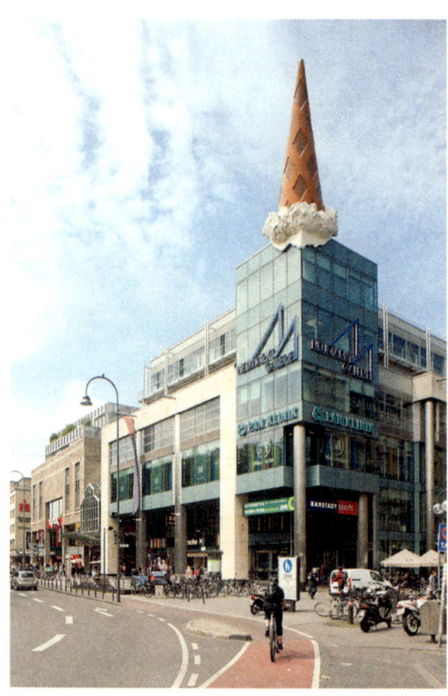

Claes Oldenburg
Dropped Cone, 2001. Installation in Cologne, Germany

in attenuations of scale in relation to the body –
a very long finger for example (*Finger*, 2010, see
pp.44–45) or a head with a protruding bearded chin
(*The Philosopher*, 2008, see p.119). His group of
20 ceramic boots (*Boots*, 2010, see pp.36–37) are
slightly too big to be human-sized and, although
they come in pairs, are neither left- nor right-footed.
Like Eleanor Antin's photographic postcard series
100 Boots (1971–), Shrigley's black boots appear
to have arrived out of place, in the wrong context.
Their orderly line-up suggests a preceding journey,
a marching army with no trace of their owners.[7]
These works are humorous by virtue of their awkward-
ness and weirdness as sculpture – they pun on the
word 'funny', as in 'funny-looking'. Indeed, this seems
a fitting description for the peculiar variety of objects
that are ferried along in the animation *Conveyor
Belt* (2008, see p.110–11), ranging from a head with
tentacles to a less easily identifiable hairy blob.

Other than simply looking slightly bizarre,
Shrigley's works do have a seemingly crafted and
handmade quality to them. Whether drawing at

the easel or welding in the metal workshop, he
is a studio-based artist who pays particular atten-
tion to materials and to the process of making.
His glazed ceramics, cast bronze and welded metal-
work require the craftsmanship of an artisan
and, at scale, works such as *Eggs* (2011, see pp.156
–57) or *Very Large Cup of Tea* (2012) present
technical challenges that require a sophisticated
understanding of the medium to overcome. Yet,
despite their craftsmanship and high degree of polish, Shrigley's sculptures do not look like beautifully
made objects. Rather, like his drawings, they are
often a bit haphazard, slightly misshapen, or like
parodies of ideal forms. They are clearly handmade
and imperfect. The lumpy, pock-marked texture of
the artist's clay maquettes for sculptures are trans-
lated directly, without smoothing or refining, into
ceramic or bronze through the process of casting.
Still other sculptures are made of unexpected materials (also a classic Surrealist strategy) – a wooden
cake (*Black Forest Gateaux*, 2001, see p.112), a
ceramic bomb (*Bomb*, 2010, see p.114) or stainless-
steel peas (*Peas*, 2007). And finally, Shrigley creates
works using a variety of 'lo-fi' materials such as con-
struction timber or expanding foam, improvising
with what is at hand, including found objects (*Cheers*,
2007, see p.43). The overall impression of these
works is thus one of amateurism, of a certain degree

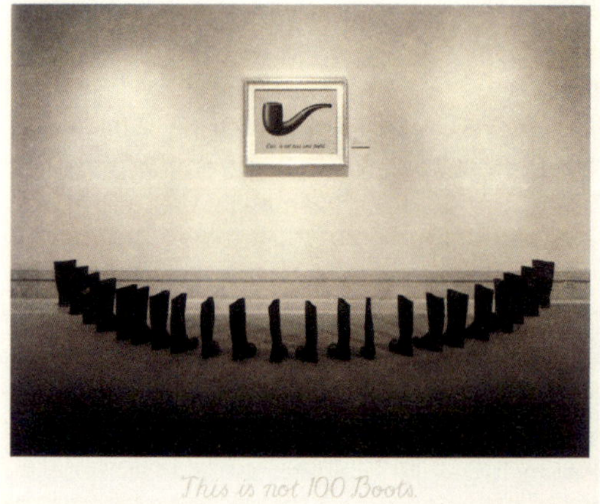

Eleanor Antin
This is not 100 Boots, 2002

John Baldessari

I will not make any more boring art, 1971

of technical competence, but with an accidental or deliberately imperfect aesthetic. For Shrigley, it is a way of animating the inanimate, of breathing life into his objects: 'I like the personality of things being a bit half-finished, of basically *having* a personality.'[8]

If Shrigley's work has a character, it is dry, witty, and a relatively discreet one, almost never exuding emotion or sentimentality. These are characteristics of the dead-pan genre of comedic acting, a form of economy in humour that involves 'physiognomic reduction and impassive restraint' as opposed to the exaggerated gestures of slapstick and vaudeville.[9] In terms of the dead-pan in art, Shrigley's work owes much to 1970s conceptual art practices, particularly to the way in which artists such as John Baldessari, Bas Jan Ader or William Wegman included humour in their work as a way of resisting the increasingly serious tone adopted by the more philosophically-inclined conceptual artists.[10] The most famous case of this polarisation is the opposing artistic stances of Joseph Kosuth and Baldessari, the former actually having attempted to ostracise the latter from the conceptual art movement for not taking art seriously enough. It is indeed very hard to suppress one's laughter at works such as *Baldessari Sings LeWitt* (1972) or *Teaching a Plant the Alphabet* (1972), which seem to undercut the philosophical propositions and systems that position his work as art in the first place. Baldessari's delivery is absolutely dead-pan, completely straight and poker-faced,

not even flinching when singing off-key or when the plant continues to offer no acknowledgement of its education. Shrigley's work gives away nothing more than this, drawing heavily on the tension between the austerity of the white cube gallery space and the absurdity of his works to heighten their effect. If 'the context is half the work' is one mantra that Shrigley had drilled into him at art school, perhaps another is the statement *'I will not make any more boring art'*, written in school-like cursive repetition in Baldessari's 1971 print.

Linked to the adoption of a dead-pan style, Shrigley's work also reflects the legacy of conceptual art in other ways. Over time his drawing method has become more overtly systematic: for a recent show he first made a list of hundreds of ideas and then proceeded to draw multiple versions of each to be later subjected to the usual selection process. This practice underlines the continuing importance of image and text for Shrigley, and reveals the very direct relationship between his ideas and the illustration of them as artworks. The latter linkage is also true of a number of the artist's short animations such as *Ones* (2009, see pp.126–27), in which a hand rolls a die repeatedly, always landing on one. Though the concept of the repeated action is brief and singular, something of a narrative starts to unfold as the anonymous person attempts to restore random chance through a variety of shaking and throwing methods, and predictably fails each time. A similarly anonymous hand in *Light Switch* (2007, see pp.128–29) prods a switch repeatedly, plunging the whole film into darkness every time it goes off. A kind of homage to conceptual artist Martin Creed's *Work No. 227: The lights going on and off* (2000), Shrigley's work puts the spectator at the mercy of either a child or an annoying adult who has a tireless appetite for pressing the switch. As much as these animations seem to be one-liner jokes in terms of content, they actually develop over the films' duration, albeit minutely, to explore narrative potential within the established constraints of the scene or action.

In contrast to his early film, *Who I Am and What I Want*, Shrigley's recent animations, such as those mentioned above, are far more concise and condensed. While no less humorous, they demonstrate what Shrigley calls 'the economy of telling stories', a way of considering the structure of humour, of finding the threshold for communicating an absurdity or crafting a narrative with the least amount of information possible. It is no coincidence that the restrained nature of dead-pan humour is well suited to Shrigley's equally economic graphic style and to the succinct nature of his work in general. From the pared-down nature of his drawings to his awkward sculptures, Shrigley communicates humour efficiently and accessibly. In his work, the expected becomes surprising, the quotidian becomes profound and death becomes a laughing matter. His work proves that art does not have to be sombre and serious nor reliant upon complex theoretical frameworks; it can be funny and fleeting and thoroughly enjoyable. But Shrigley's art also occupies a darker realm of uncanniness, violence and death. His extraordinary ability is to deftly combine both the pleasurable and the distressing – all while keeping a straight face – as in his spoken word track 'Don'ts', which offers little helpful hints to avoid serious bodily injury:

> Don't stick your hand in the blender.
> Don't use the hairdryer while you're in the bath.
> Don't point the crossbow at your friends.
> Don't trim your toenails with a carving knife.
> Don't climb inside old freezers at the junkyard.
> Don't put your nephew in the microwave.
> Don't summon demons with the ouija board.
> Don't try to make new holes in your belt while you are still wearing it.
> Don't try to swim to the island.
> Don't throw darts at people.
> Don't climb on the roof.
> Don't throw stones at me to try to attract my attention.
> Don't shut your eyes while you're driving.
> Don't drink the grey wine… [11]

[1] Based on the 2003 book of drawings of the same name, the film *Who I Am and What I Want* was a collaboration with Chris Shepherd and was commissioned by animate!.

[2] Additionally, Shrigley is known for a number of commissions, including music video animations for Blur and Bonnie Prince Billy, record covers for Deerhoof and Thee Oh Sees, the opening sequence to the film *Hallam Foe* (2007), advertising for Monorail, Pringle and Stussy, and animations for the BBC, Channel 4 and the 2010 UK Save the Arts Campaign.

[3] Neil Cooper, 'Top Drawer', in *MAP*, no. 8, 2006, p.42.

[4] 'Portrait: David Shrigley', in *les inrockuptibles*, no. 583, 2007, p.28.

[5] This debate reached its climax in Pop art, which directly appropriated comic-book characters and printing techniques. See Albert Boime,'The Comic Stripped and Ash Canned: A Review Essay', in *Art Journal*, vol. 32, no. 1, 1972; and Sheena Wagstaff, 'Comic Iconoclasm', in *Comic Iconoclasm*, exhibition catalogue, Institute of Contemporary Arts, London, 1987. It is also important to mention that Shrigley's work is not influenced by punk, graffiti, children's art, naïve or outsider art.

[6] André Breton, 'Lightning Rod' [1939], in *Anthology of Black Humour*, Telegram, London, 2009, p.25.

[7] '[The Boots] meet cows in a meadow, lounge on the porch, enjoy a shady grove, bask in the sun by a pond, even, it would appear, fall in love with a ballerina, who quickly sends them packing. Down and out, they look for work, first in the oil fields, and then, out of a job once again, at the carnival. Finally, unable to avoid the draft, they go to war, asserting their status as an *avant-garde* in both military and art world sense of the term.' Henry Sayre, 'A Return Address', in *100 Boots by Eleanor Antin*, Running Press, London, 1999, n.p.

[8] Caroline Muntendorf, 'Crooked Penmanship', *in mono. kultur*, no. 9, 2006–7, p.4.

[9] John C. Welchman, '"Don't Play It for Laughs": John Baldessari and Conceptual Comedy', in John C. Welchman (ed.), *Black Sphinx: On the Comedic in Modern Art*, JRP/Ringier, Zurich, 2010, p.255.

[10] Specific examples include Bas Jan Ader's *I'm too sad to tell you* (1971), which features the crying artist too upset to actually say anything, and William Wegman's *Spelling Lesson* (1973–74) in which the artist teaches his dog, May Ray, the difference between the words 'beech' and 'beach'.

[11] Excerpt from 'Don'ts', from the album *Forced To Speak With Others* (2006).

Ostrich, 2009

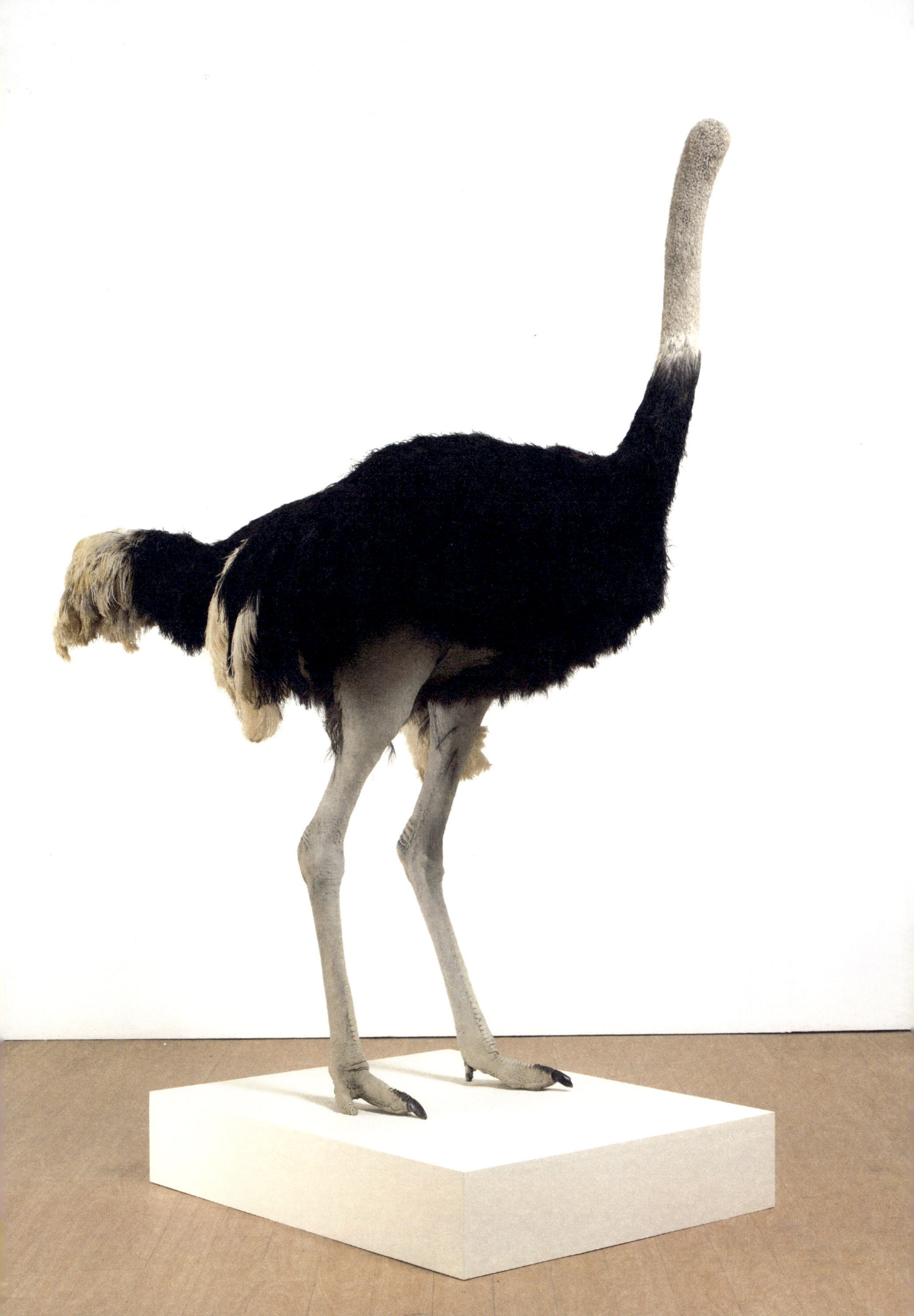

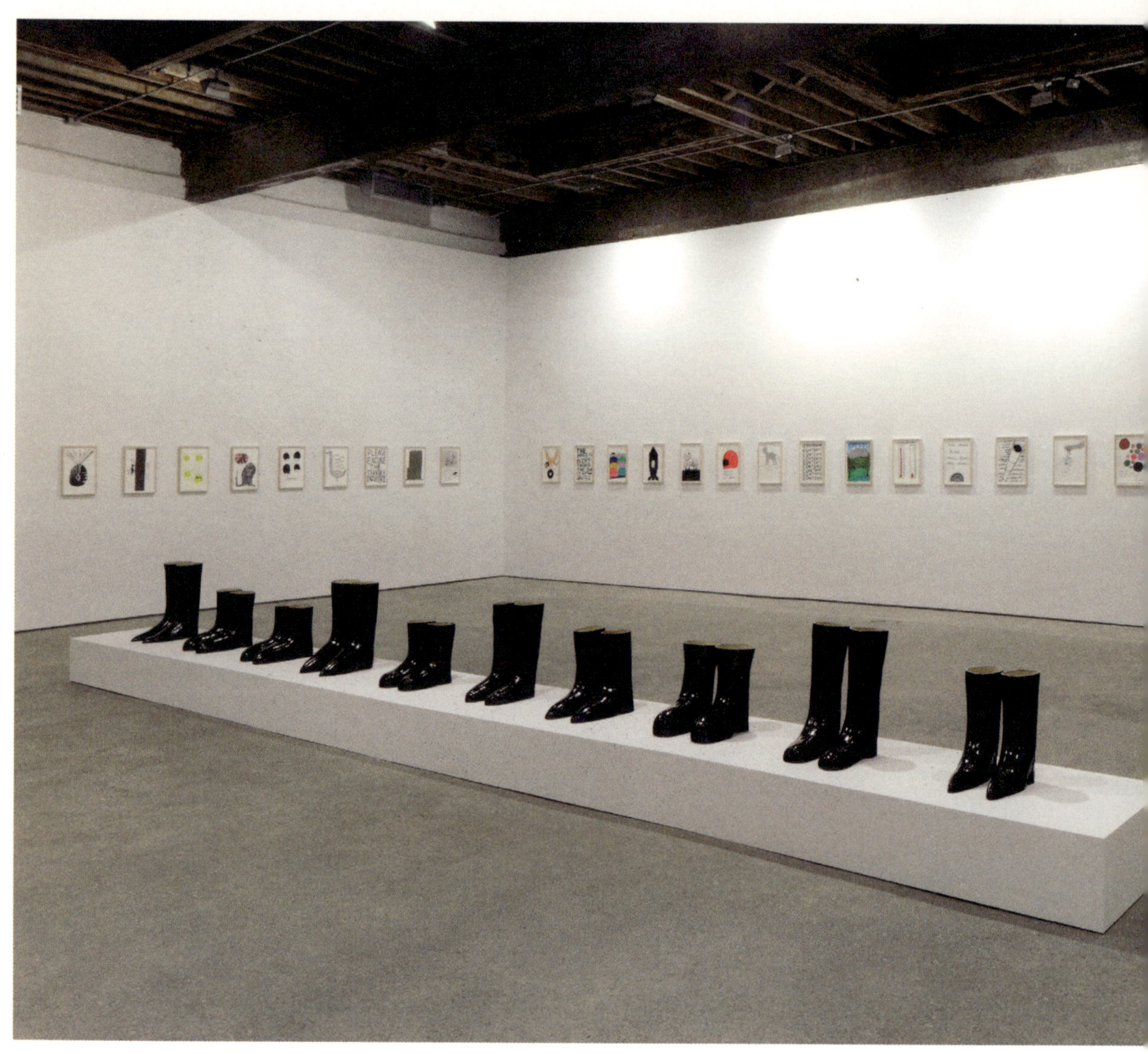

Boots, 2010. Installation at Anton Kern Gallery, New York

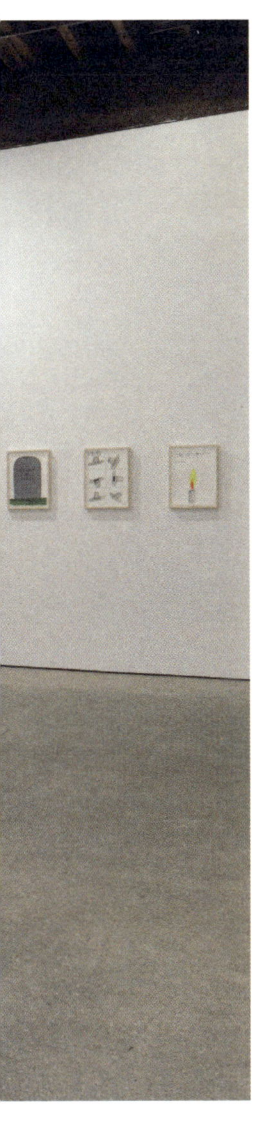

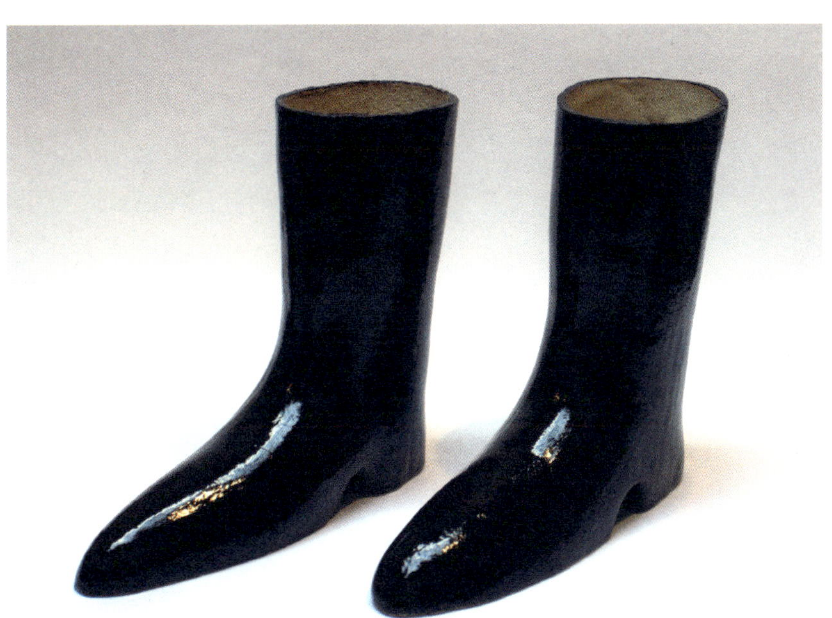

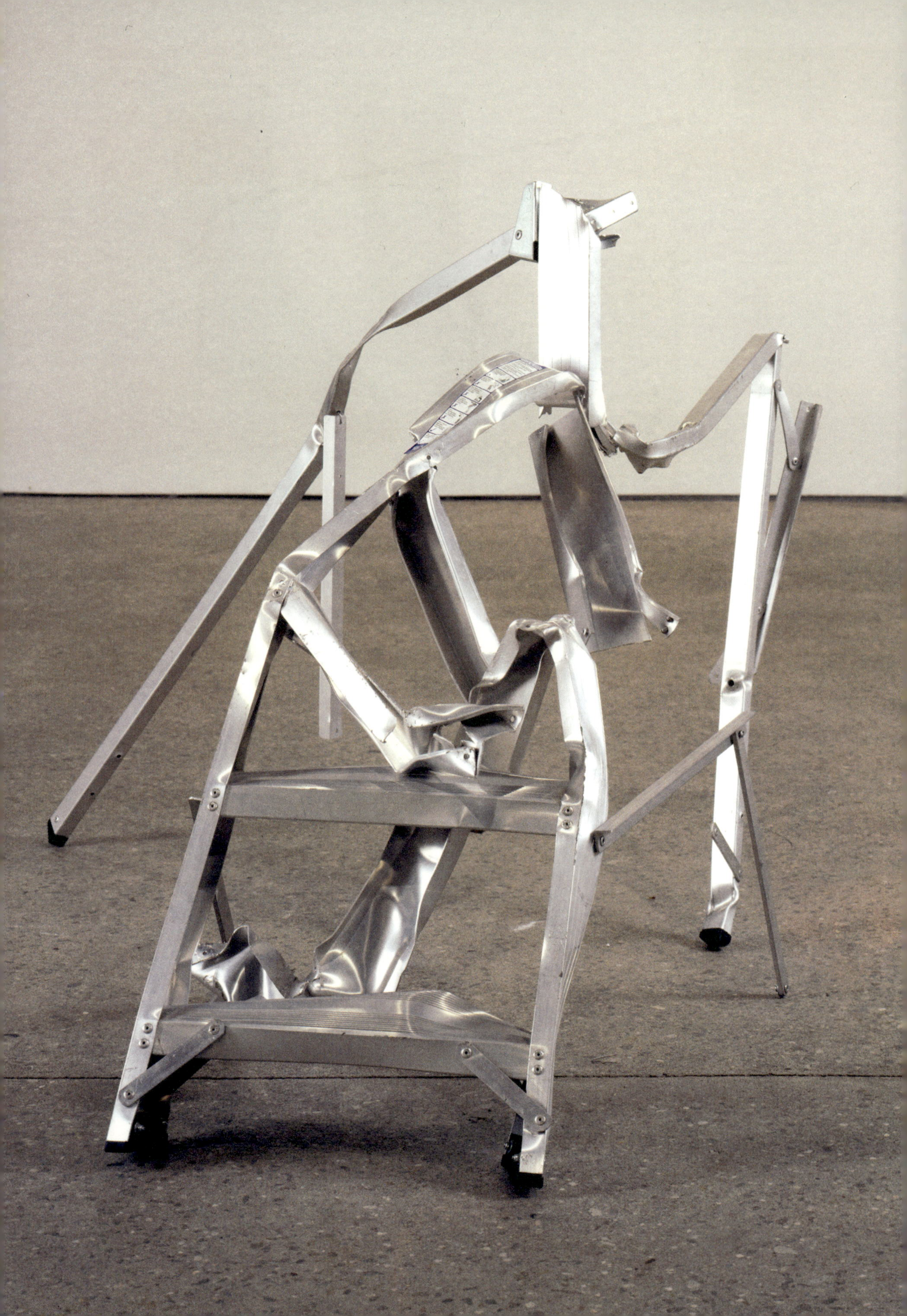

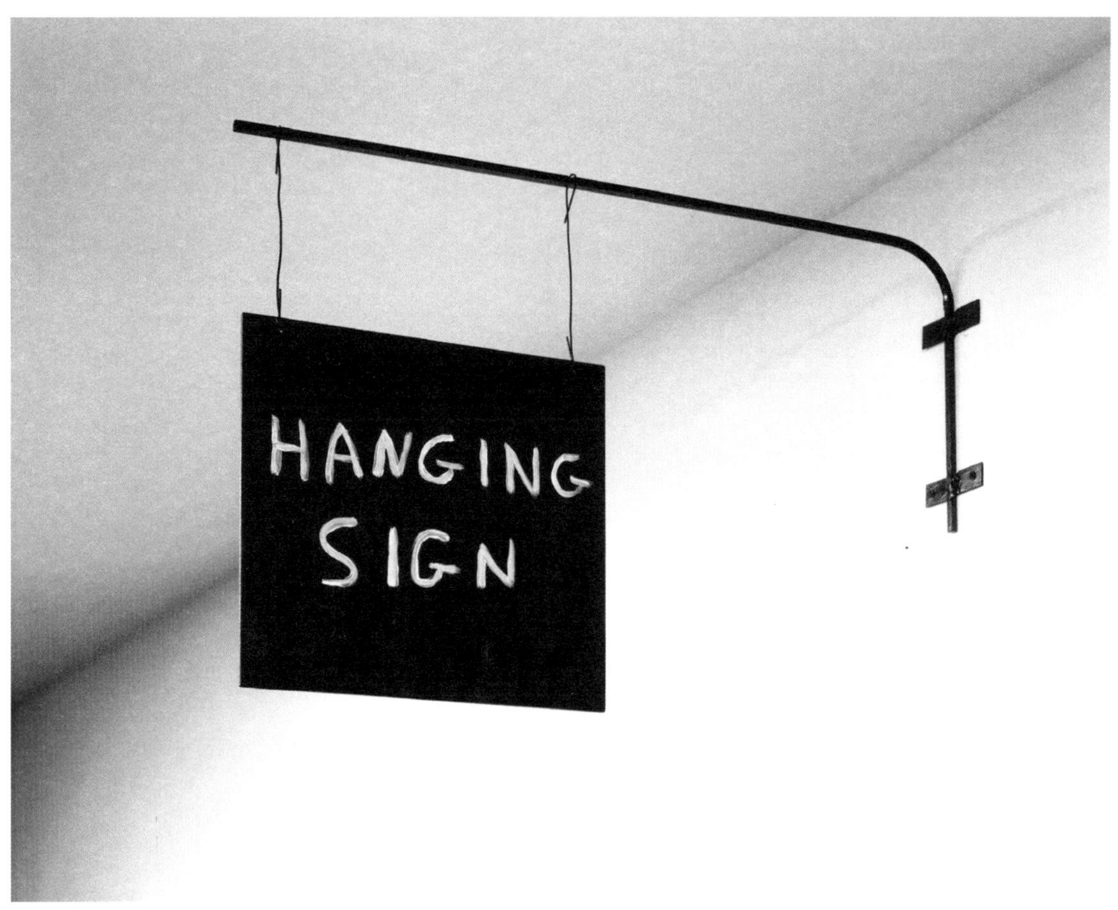

Crushed Ladder, 2008

Hanging Sign, 2007

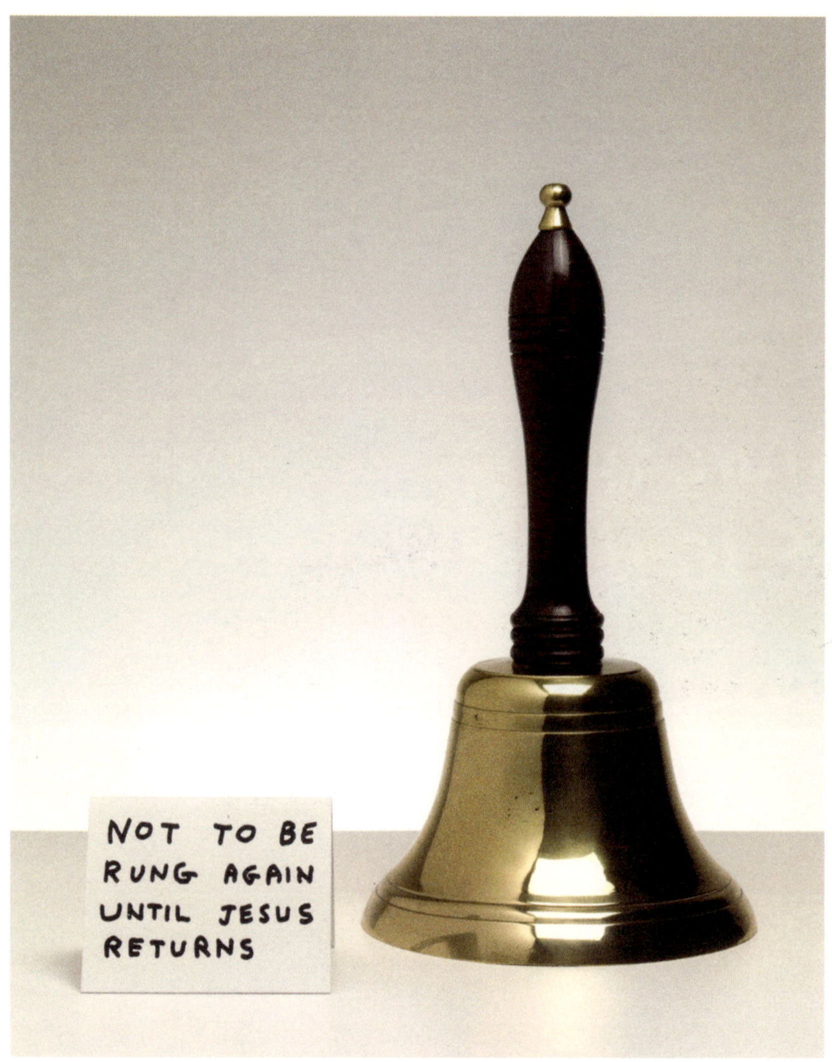

The Bell, 2007

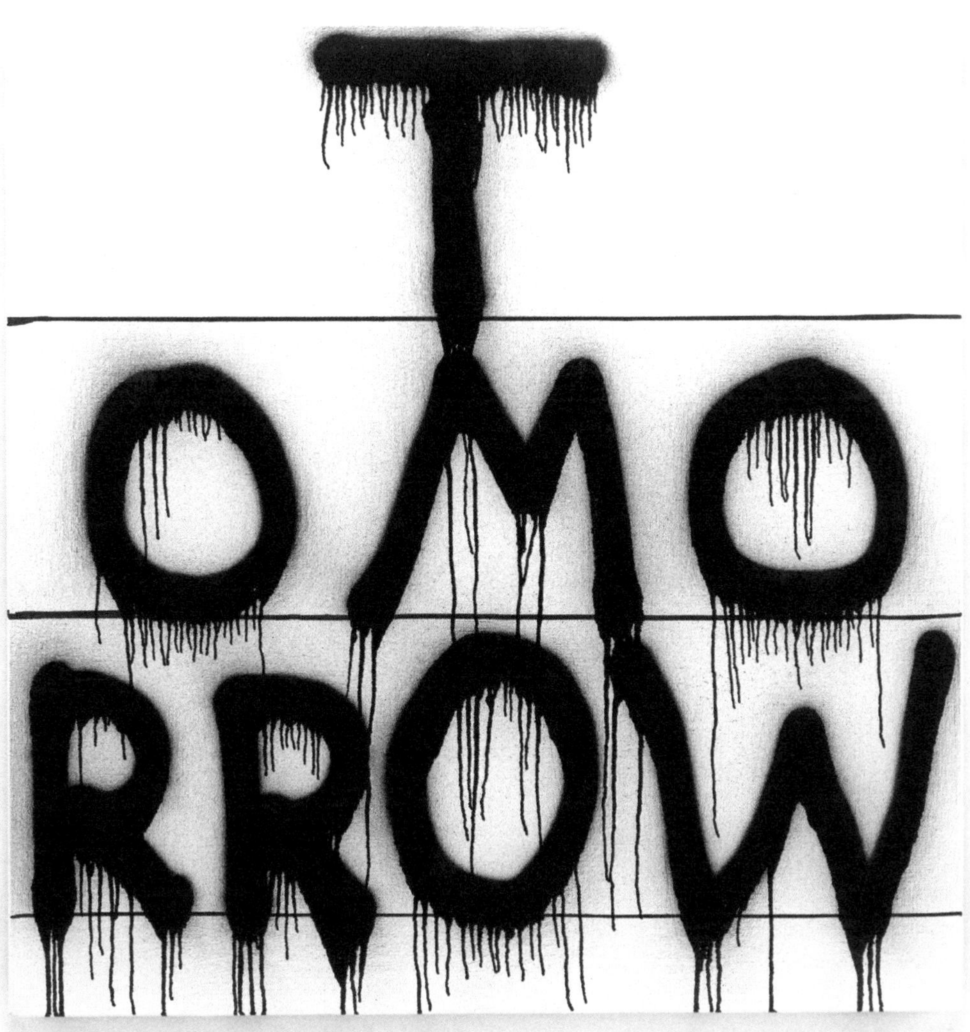

Tomorrow, 2007

Cheers, 2007

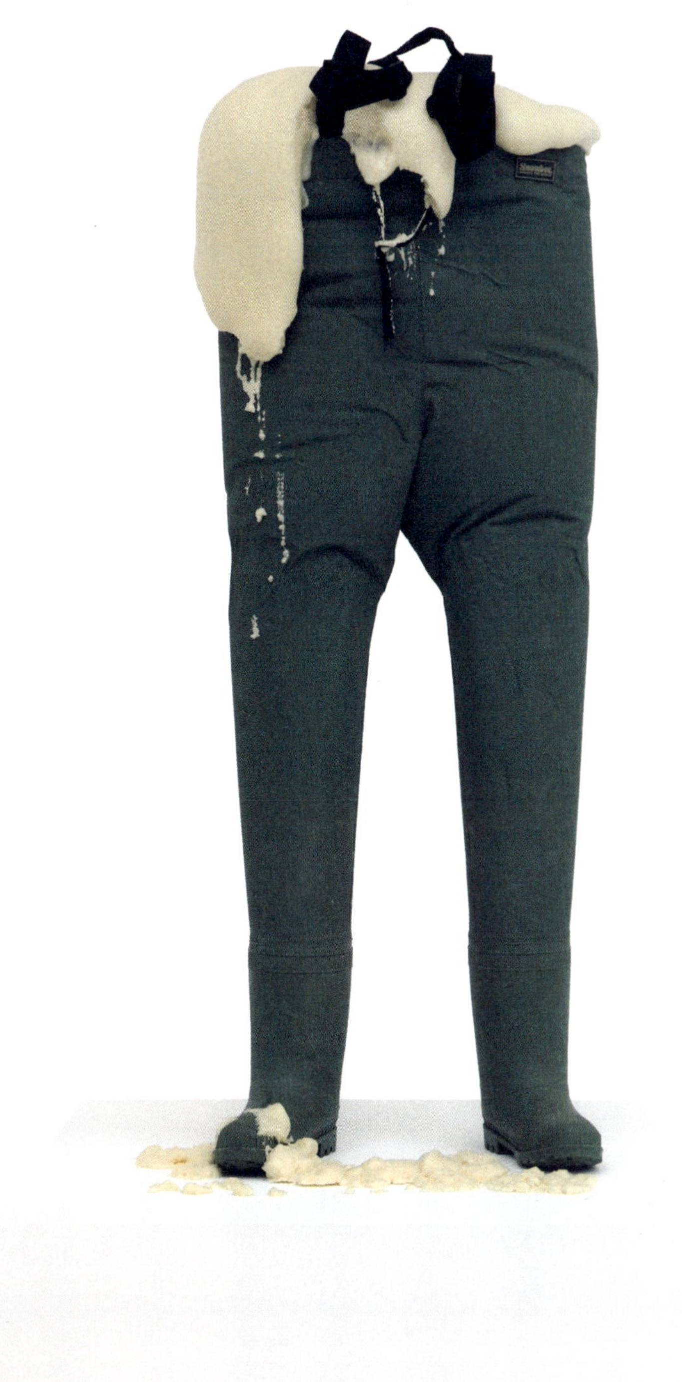

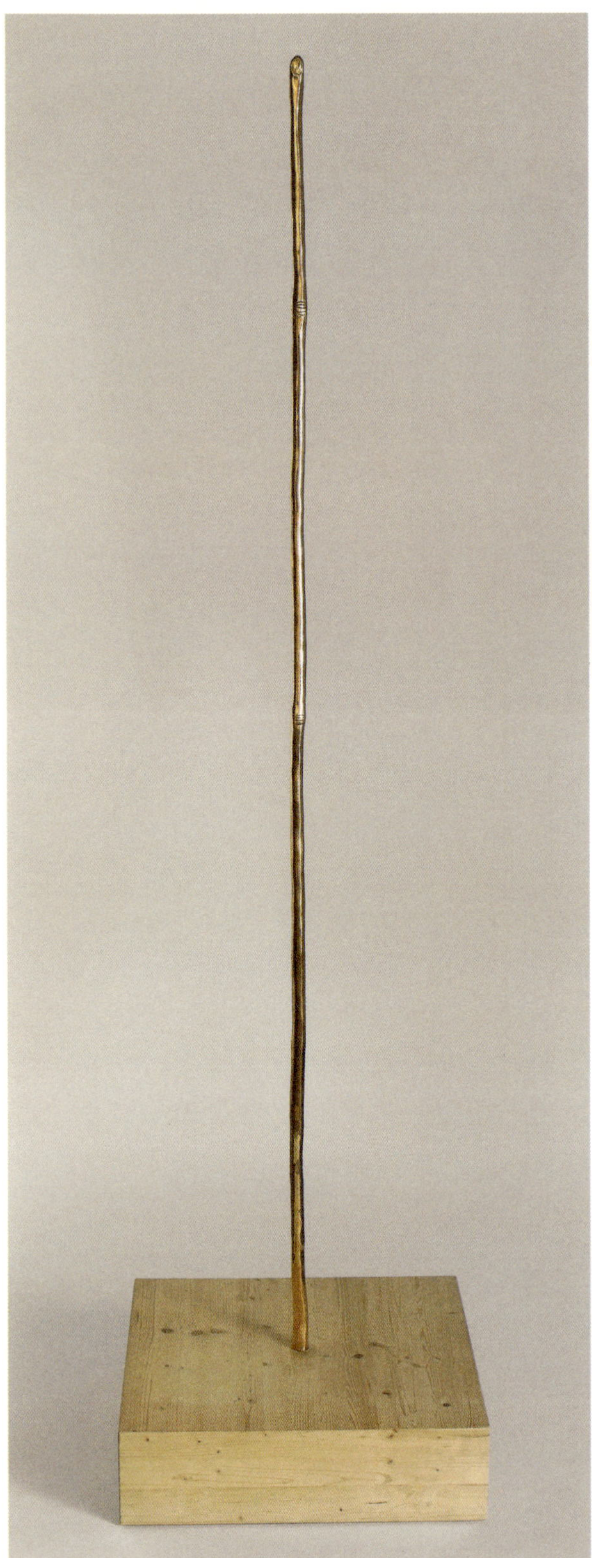

Finger, 2010

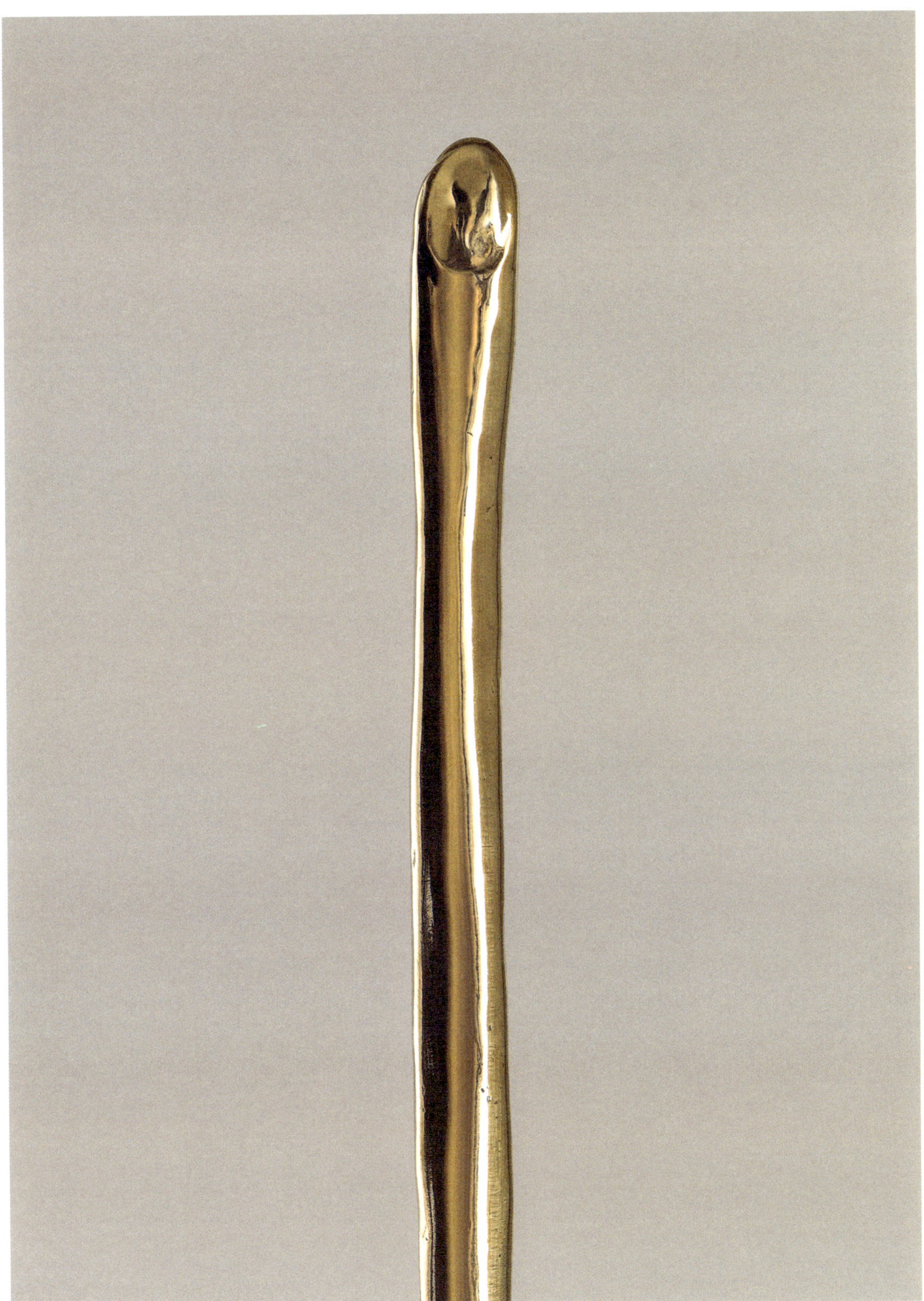

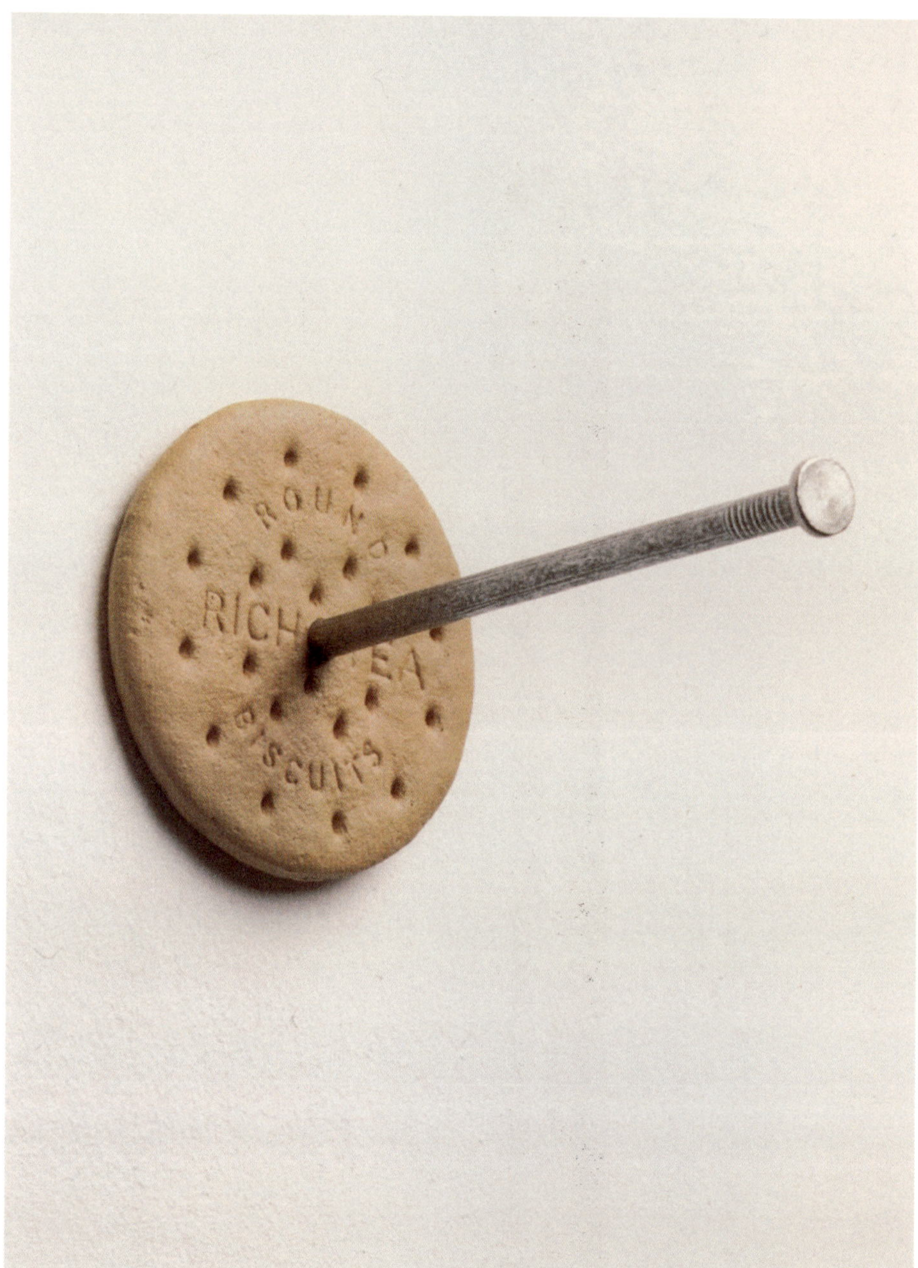

Nailed biscuit, 2001

What Decay Looks Like, 2001

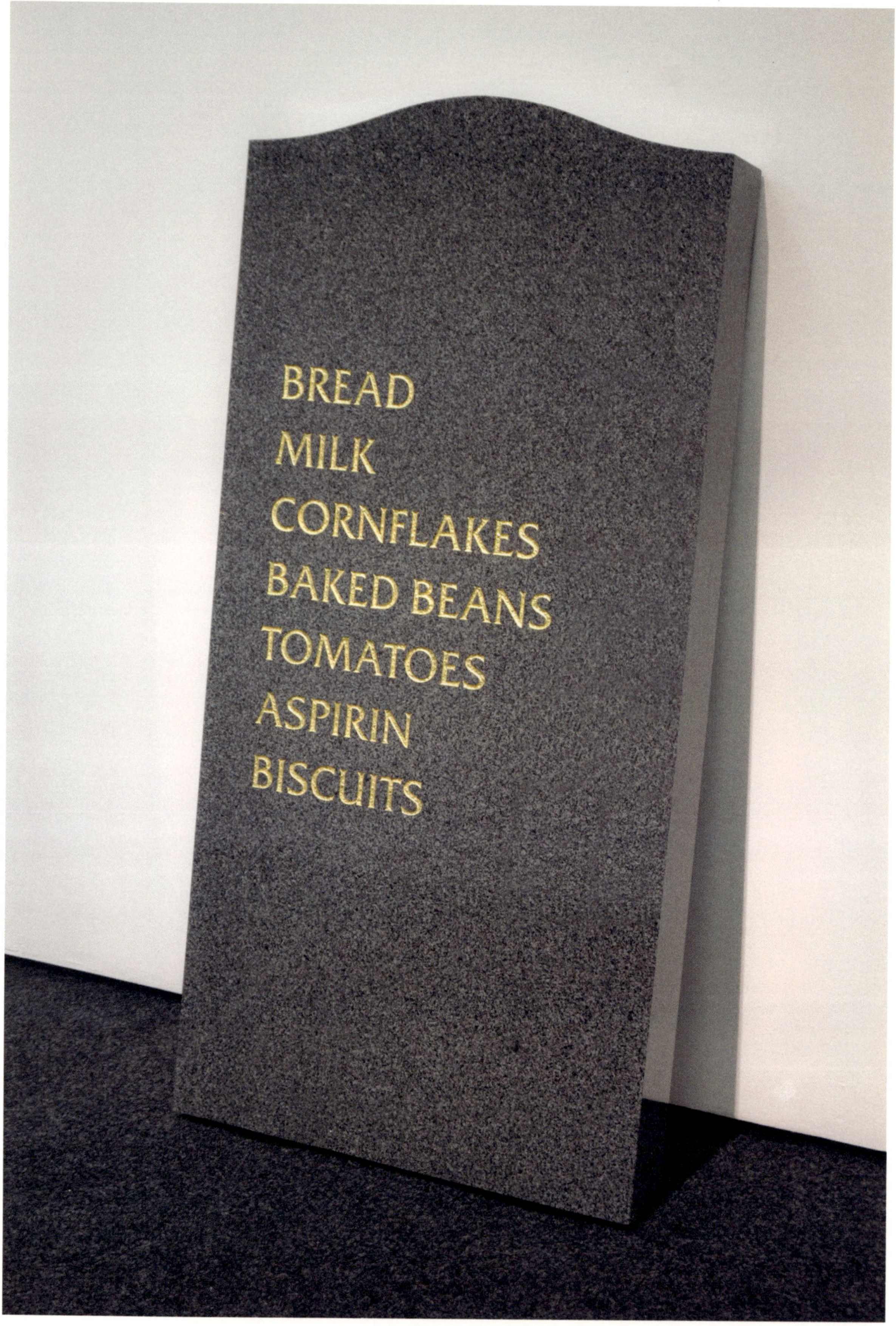

BREAD
MILK
CORNFLAKES
BAKED BEANS
TOMATOES
ASPIRIN
BISCUITS

Gravestone, 2008

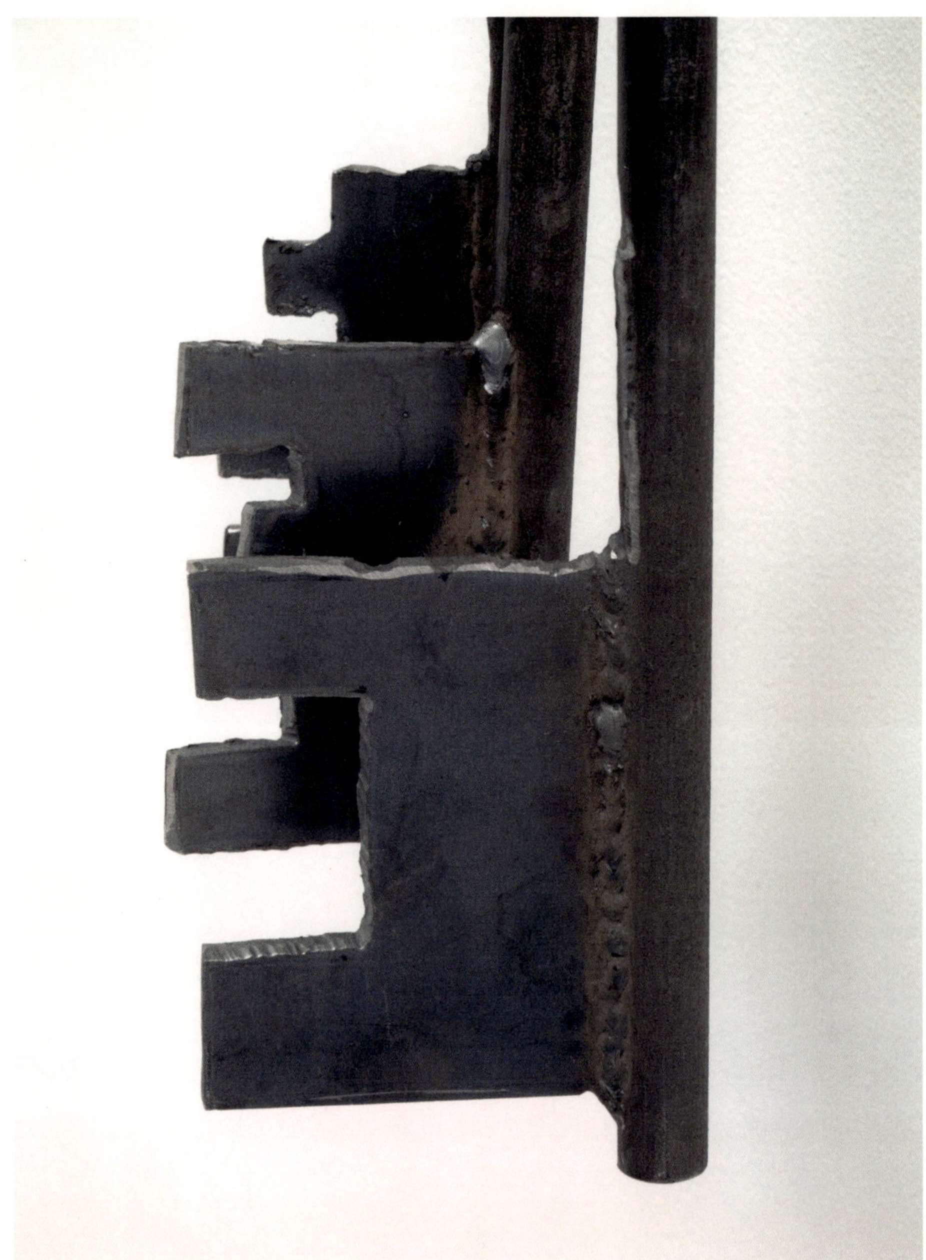

Keys, 2007

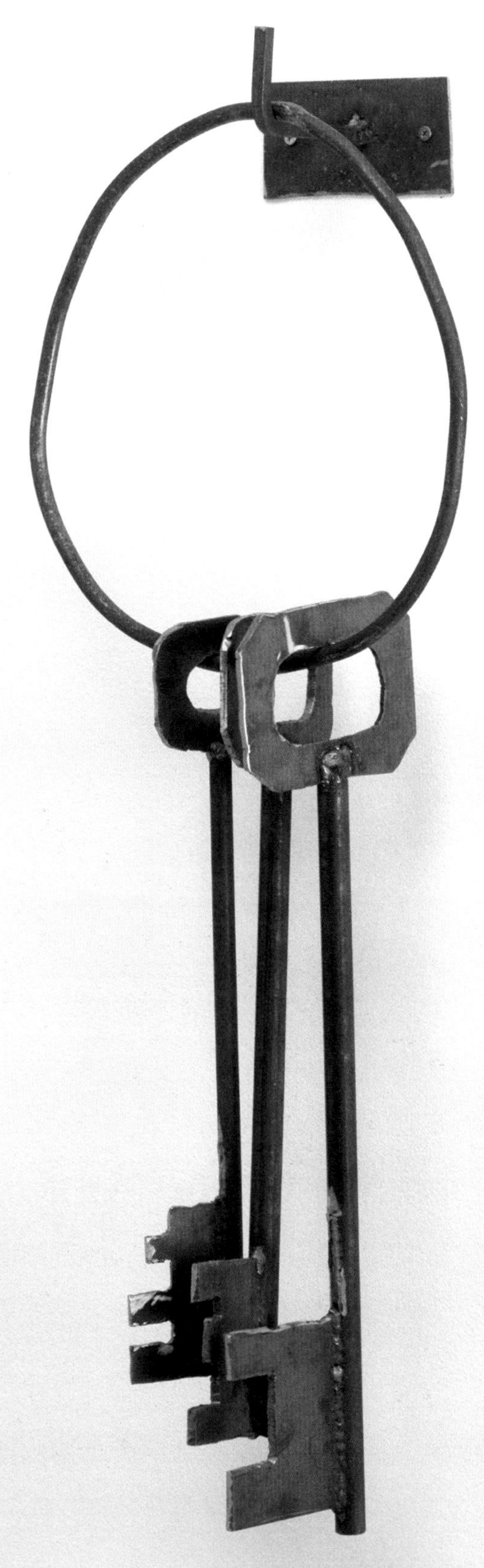

IT, 2010

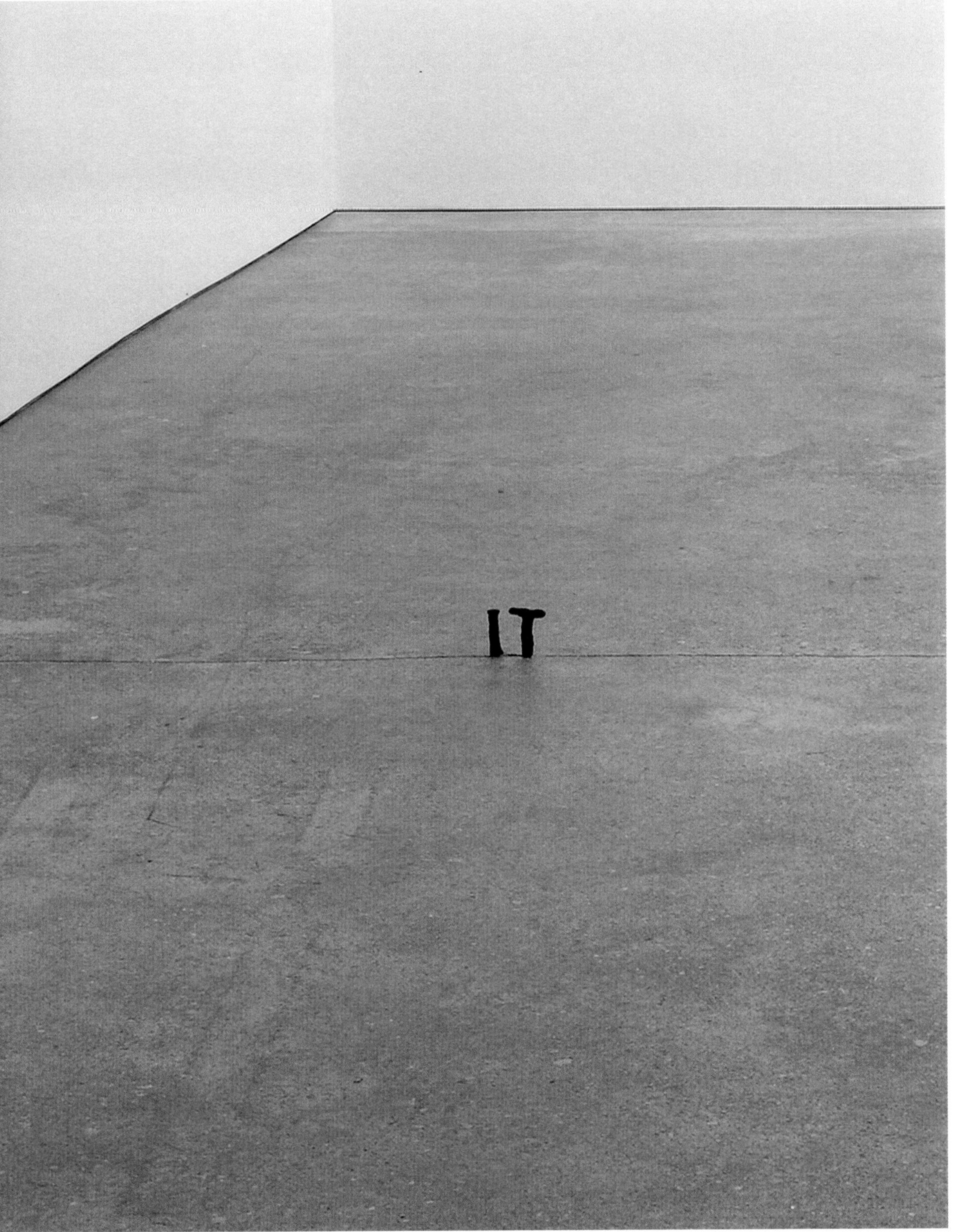

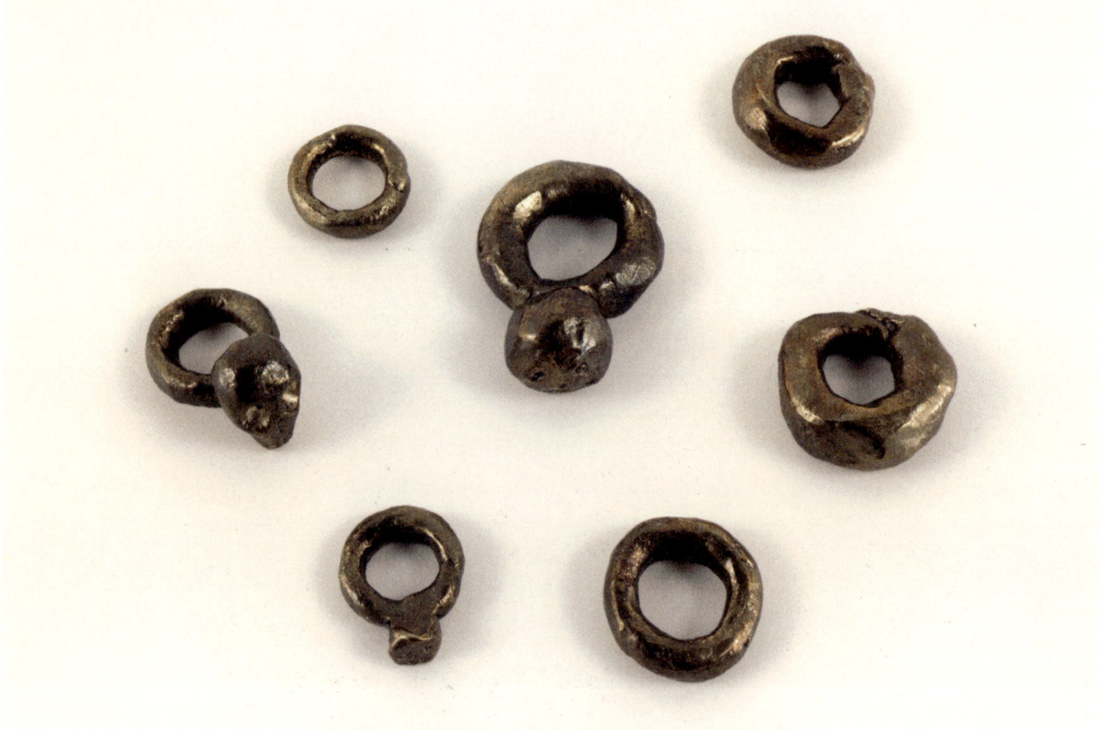

Rings, 2010

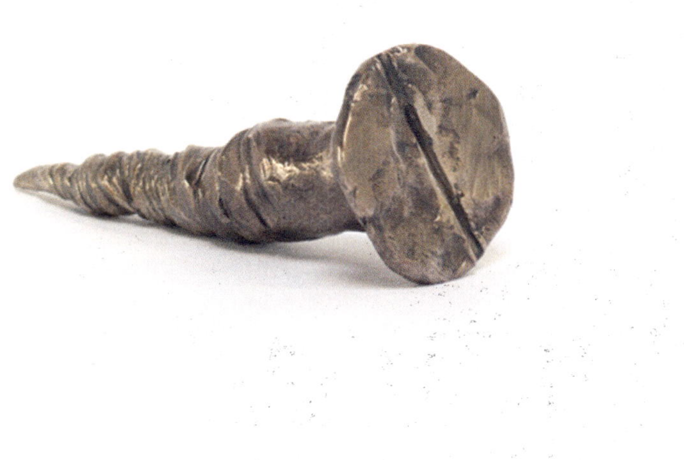

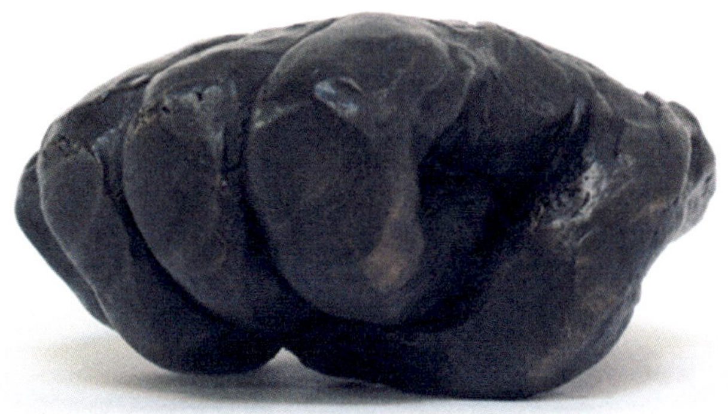

Screw, 2010

Fist, 2010

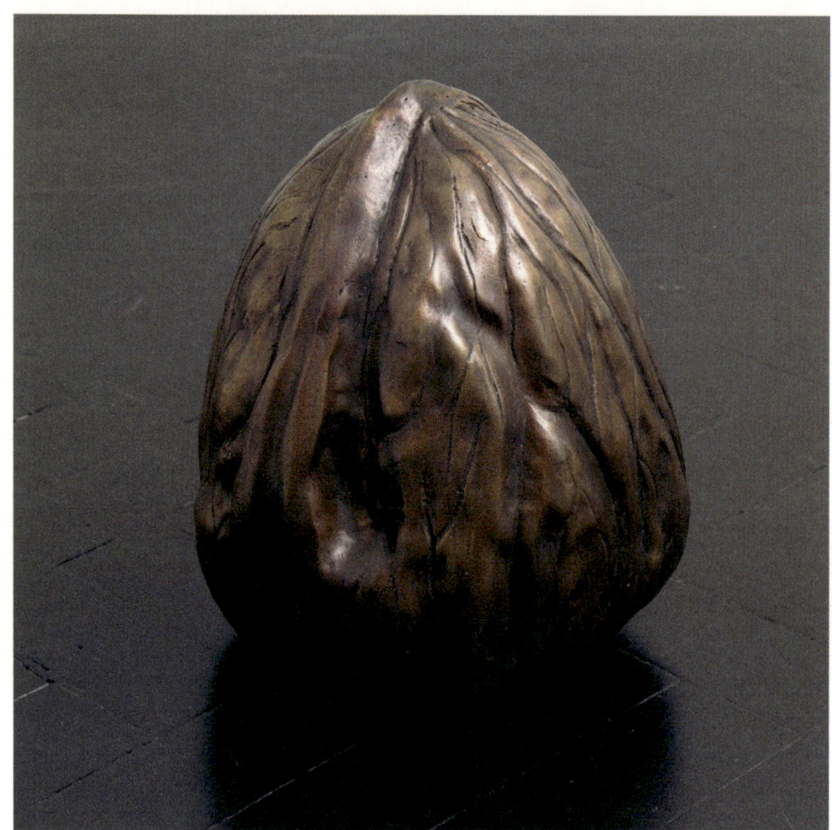

Big Nut, 1996   *Nutless*, 2002

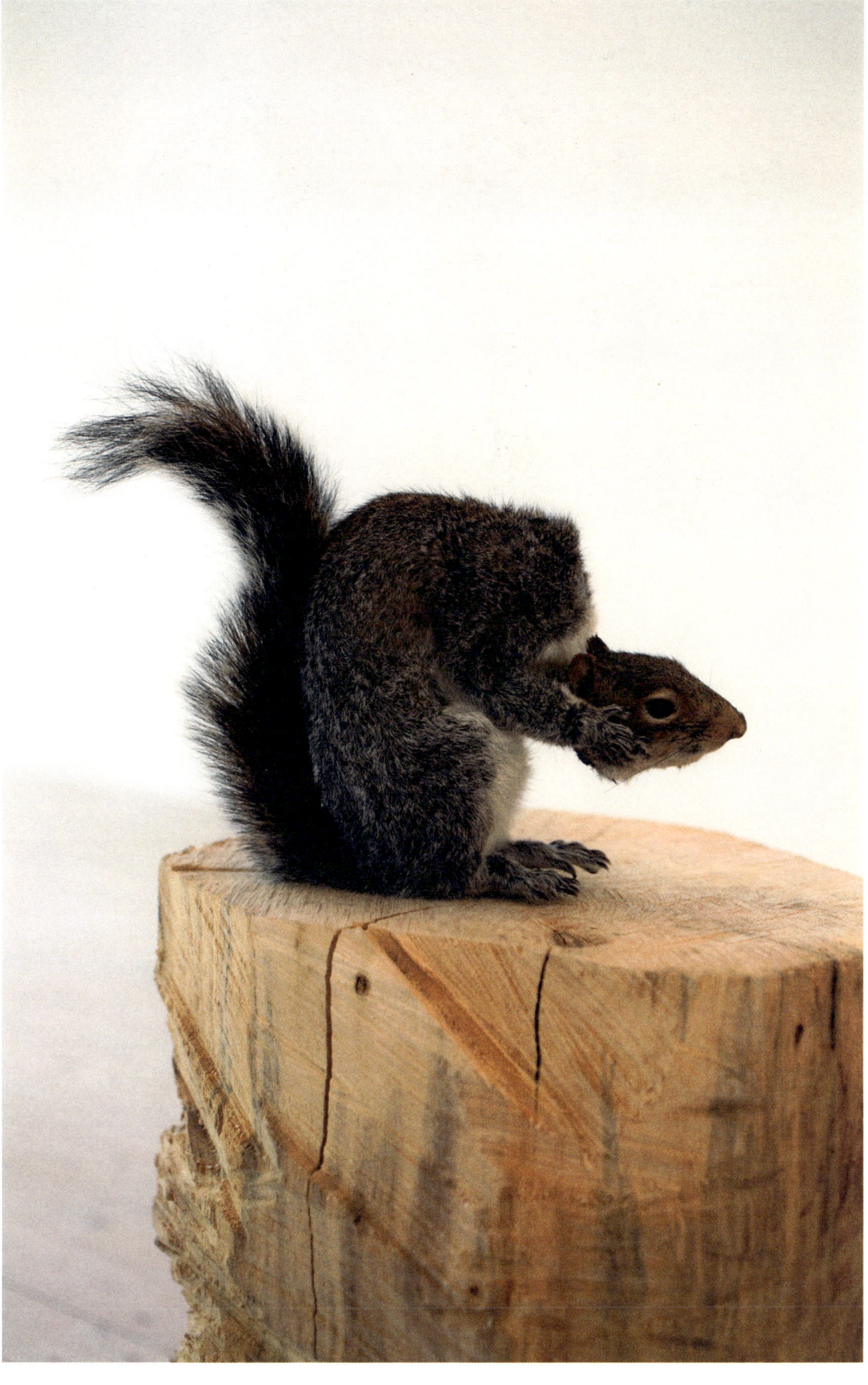

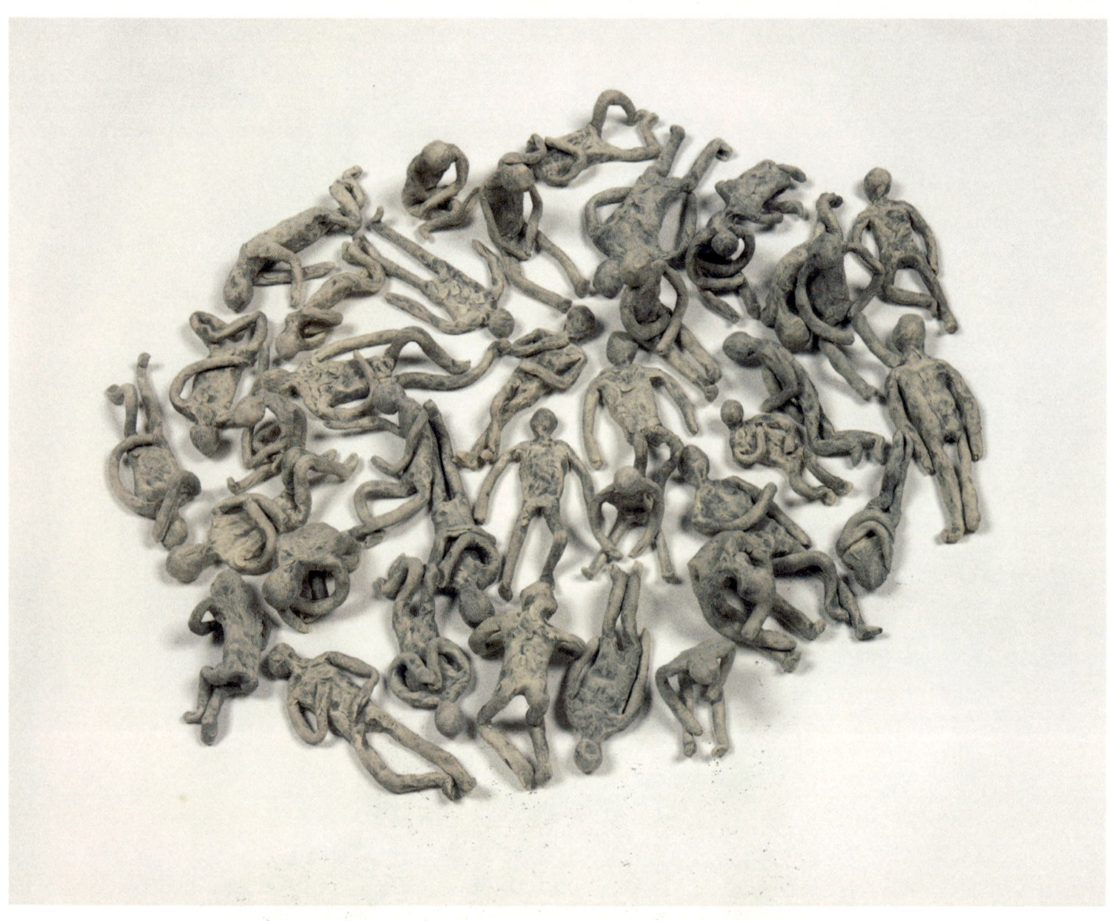

The dead and the dying, 2010

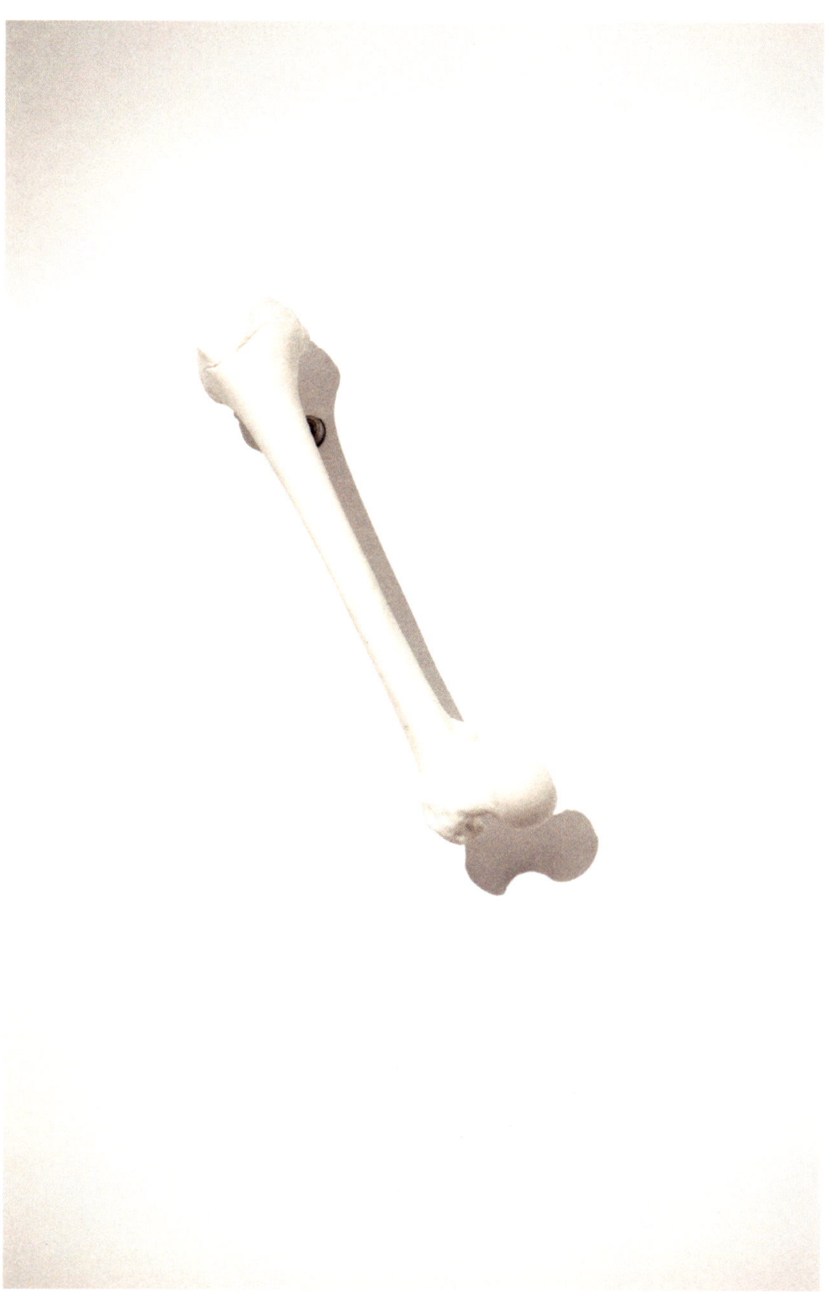

Bone Clock, 2008

I'm Dead, 2010

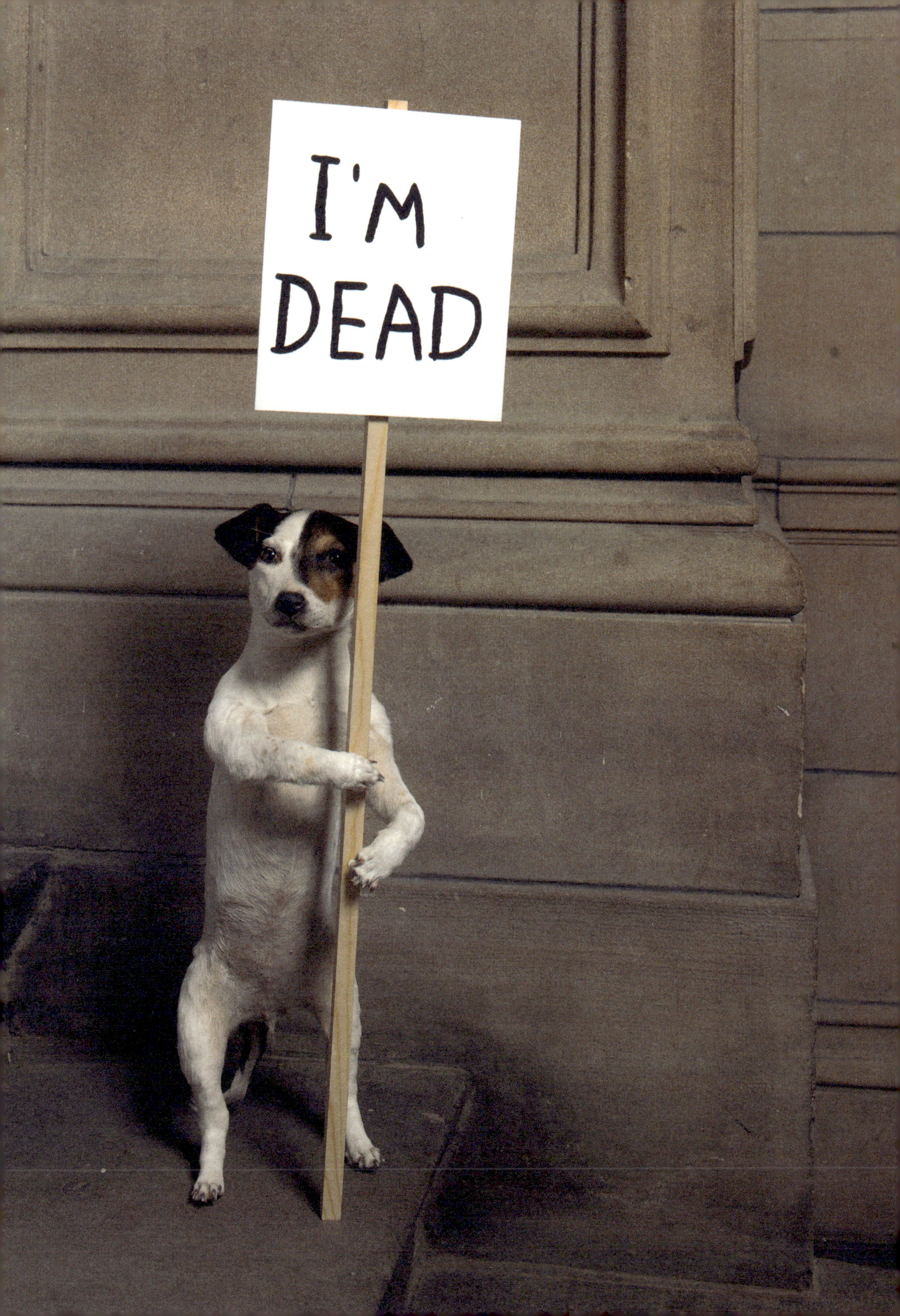

I'M
DEAD

NEW FRIENDS

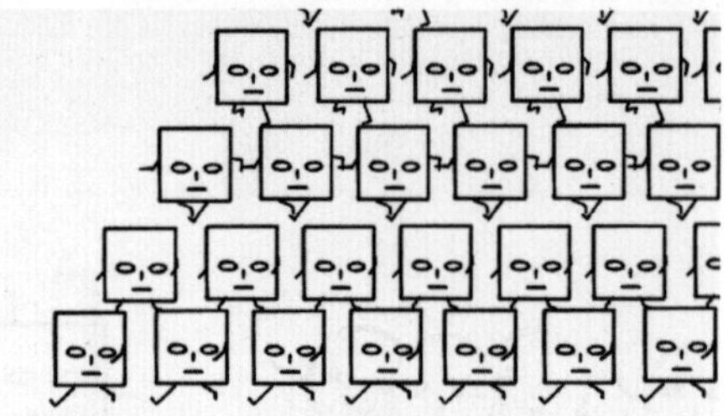

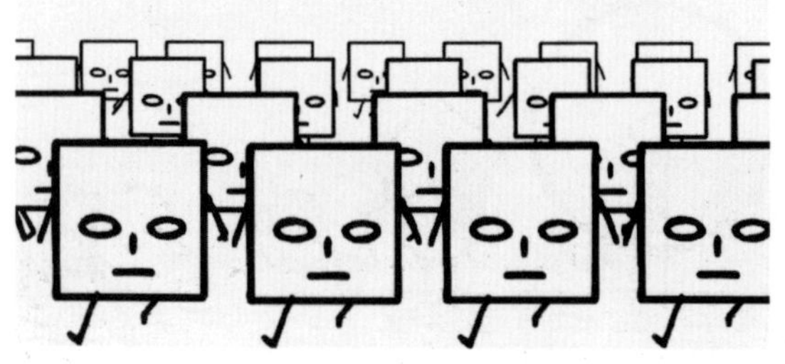

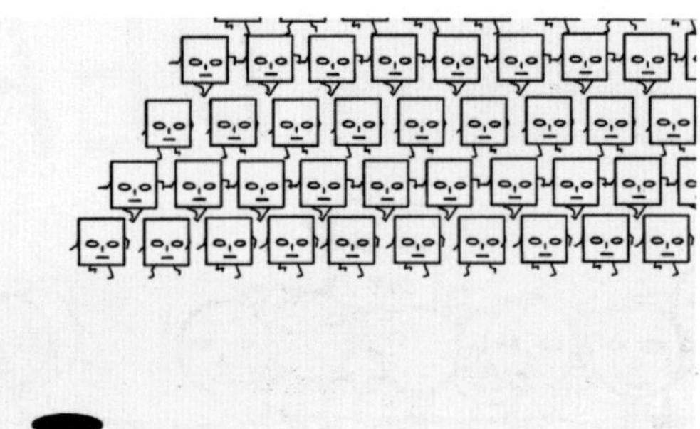

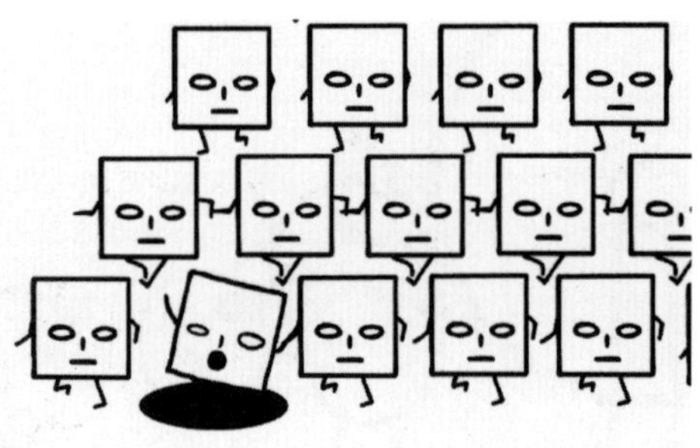

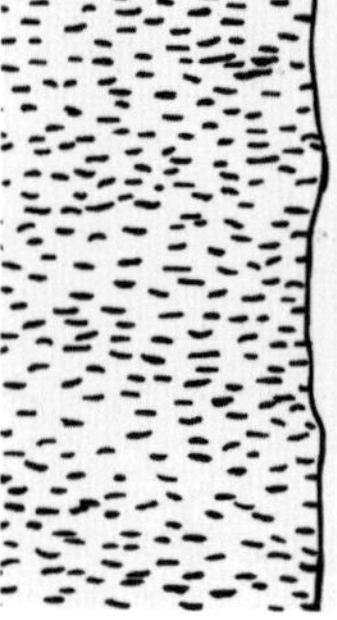

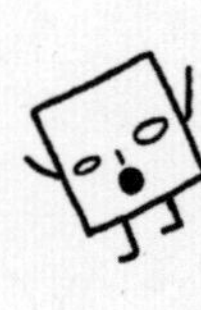

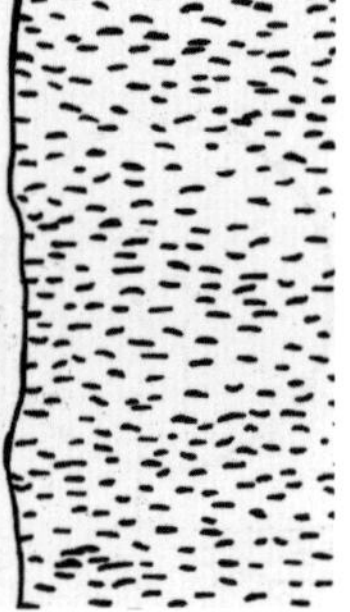

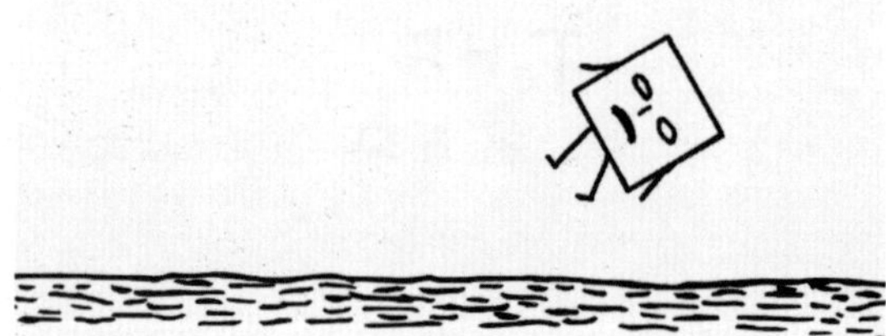

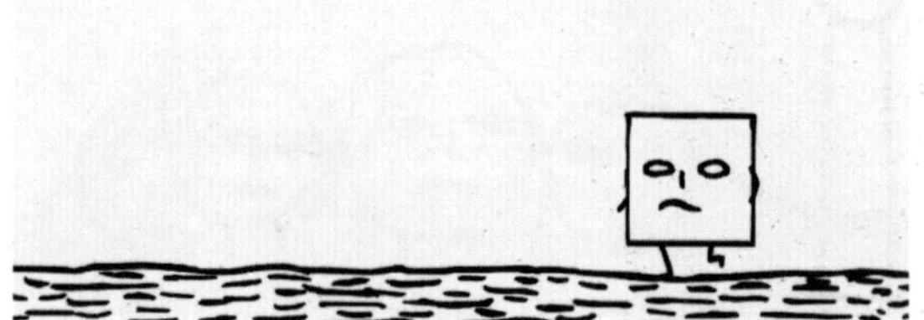

New Friends, 2006

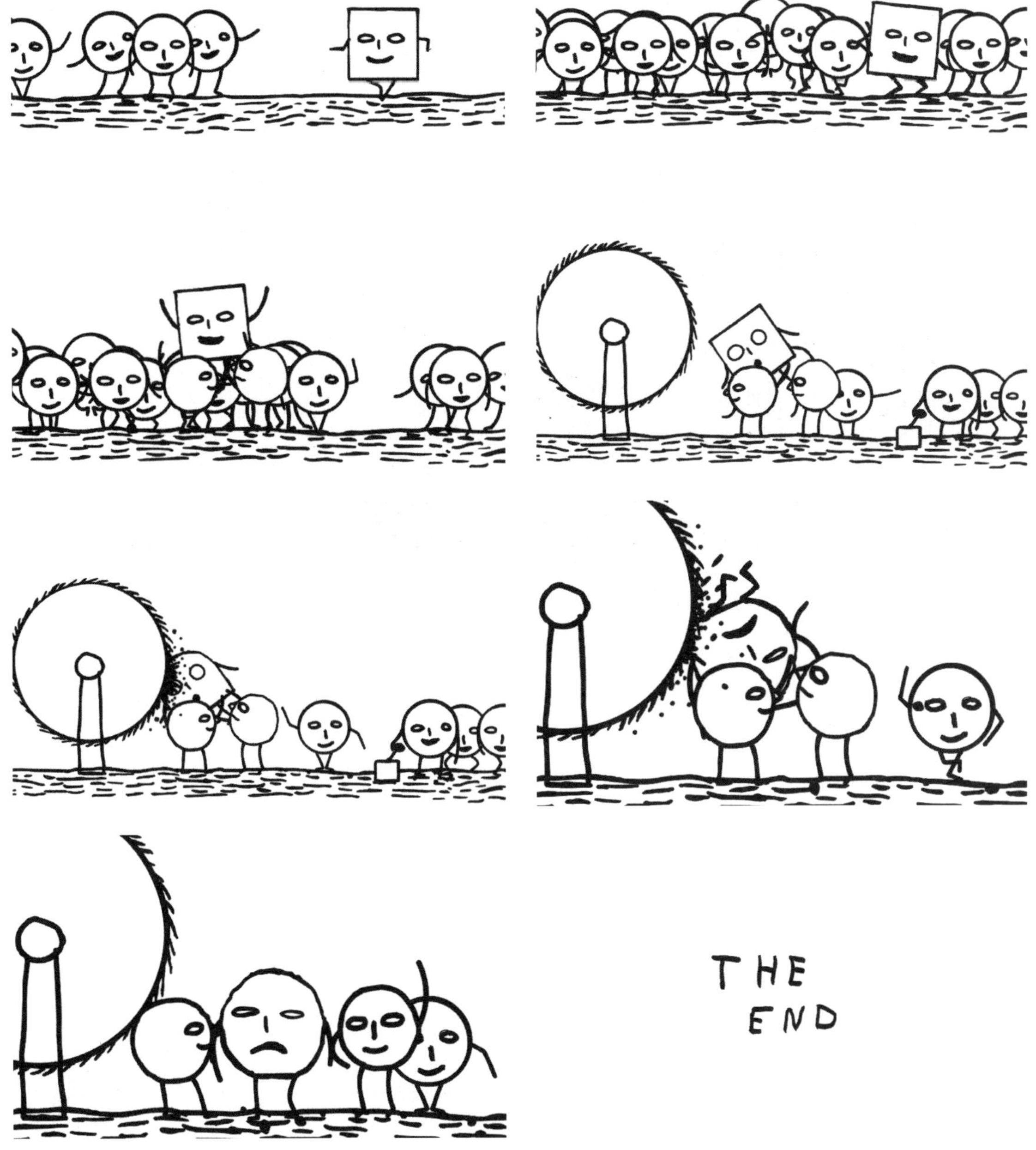

THE
END

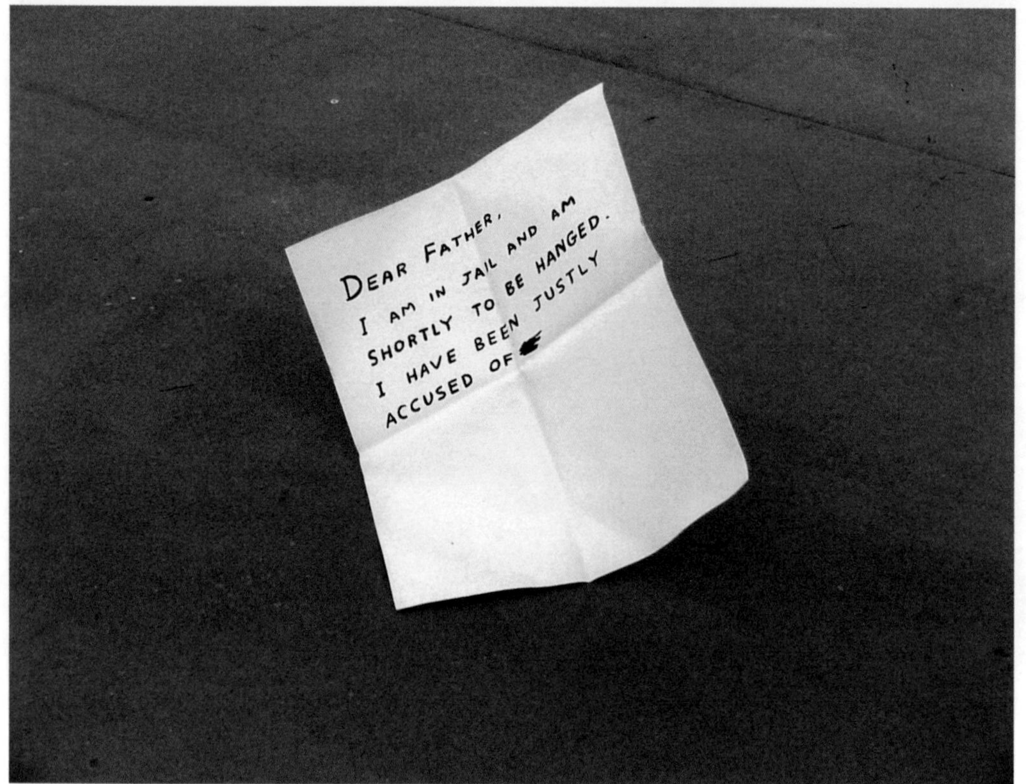

Unfinished Letter, 2003

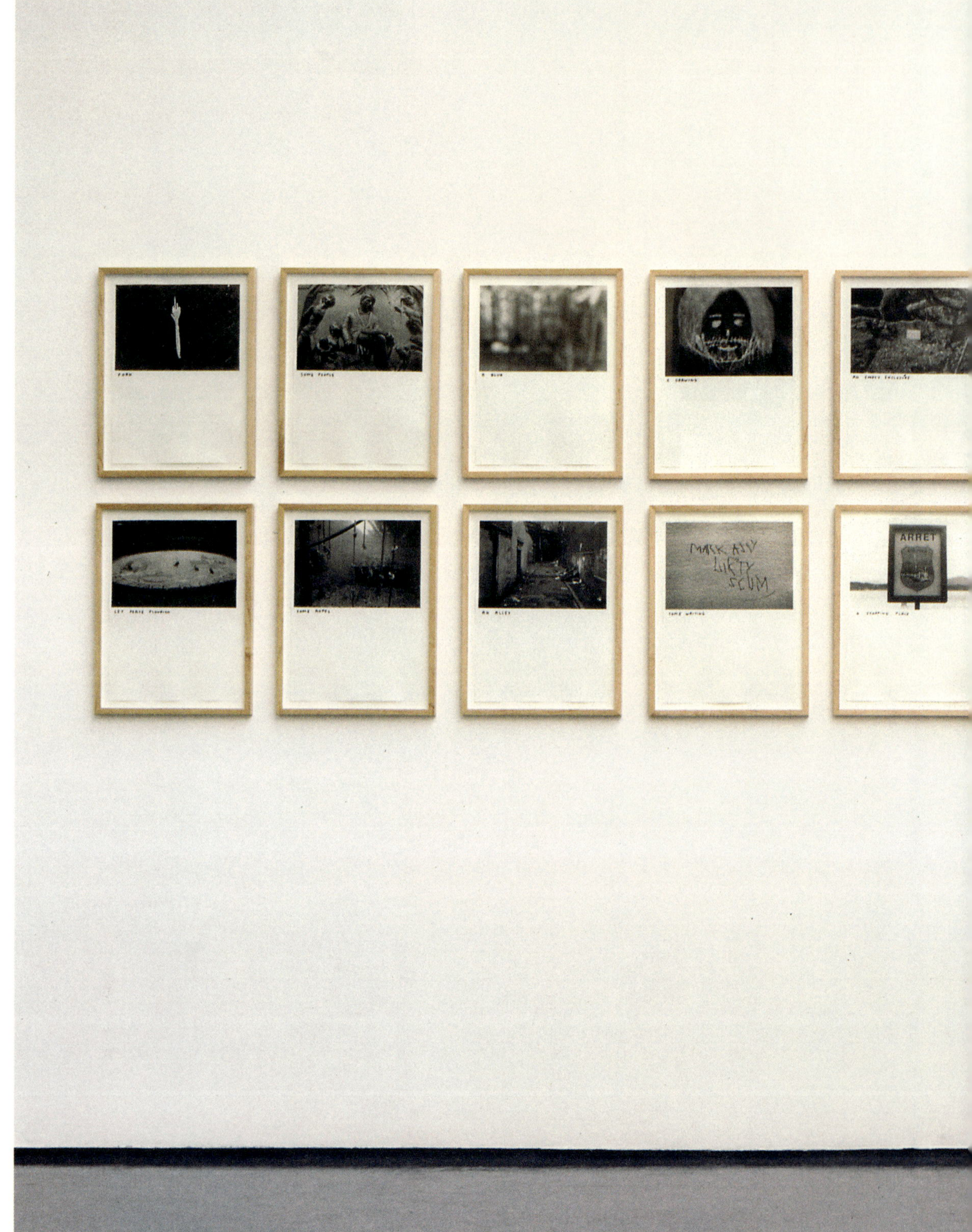

Untitled (Photographs with Text), 2005. Installation above and pp.68–77

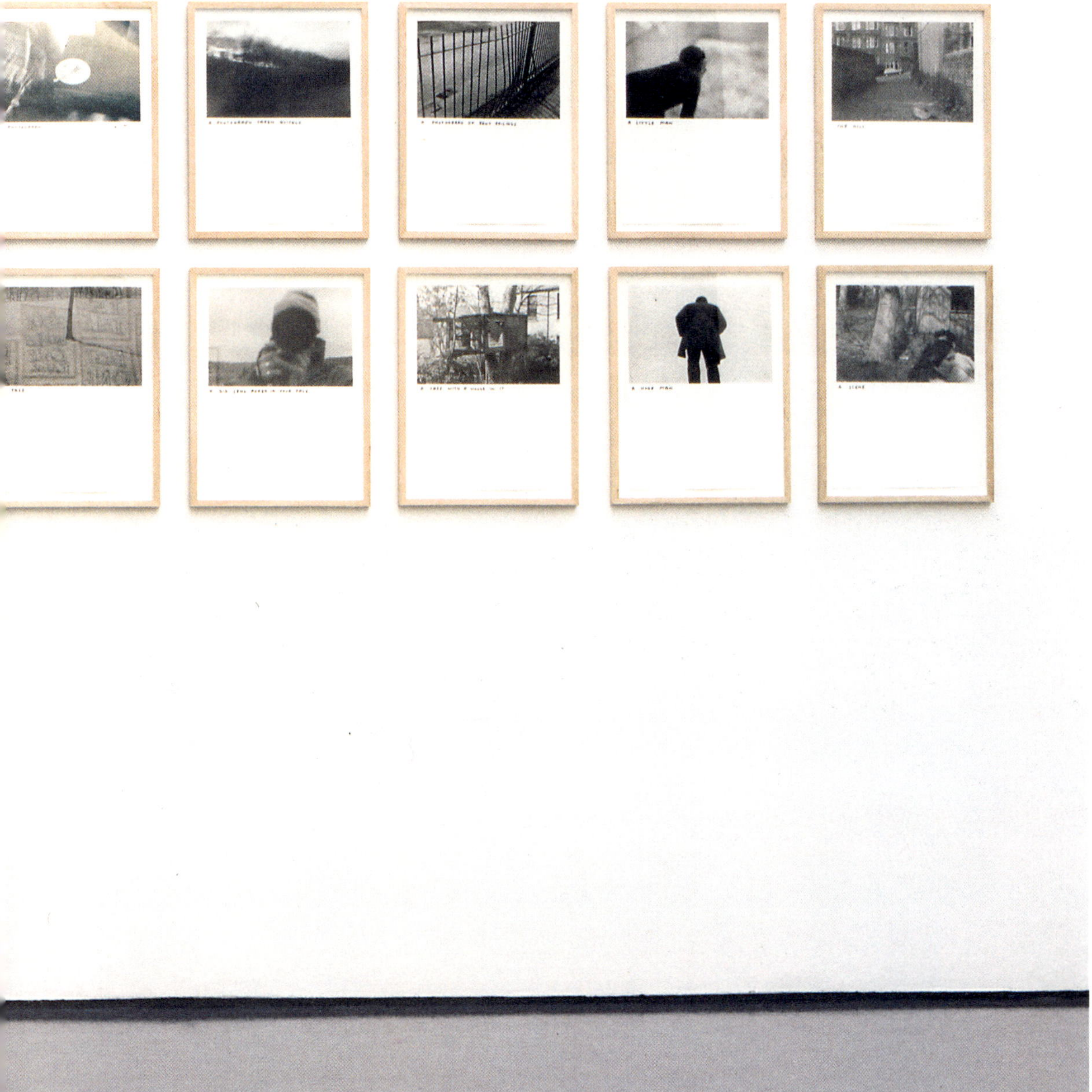

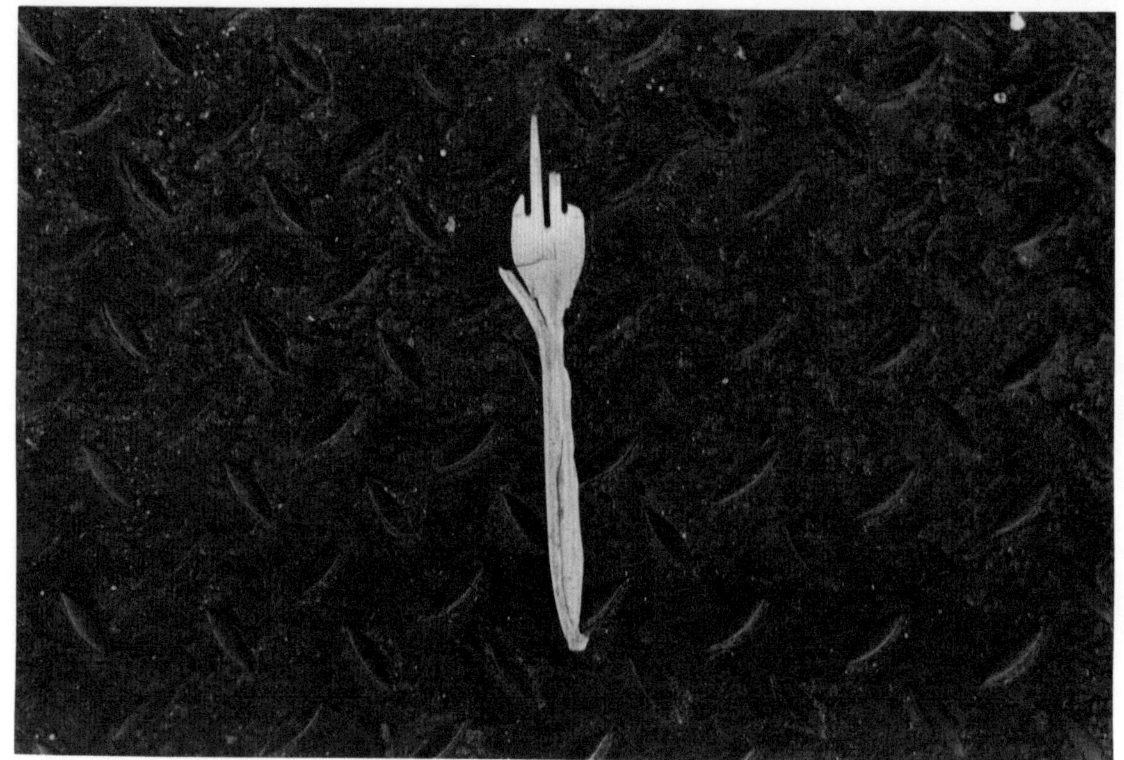

FORK

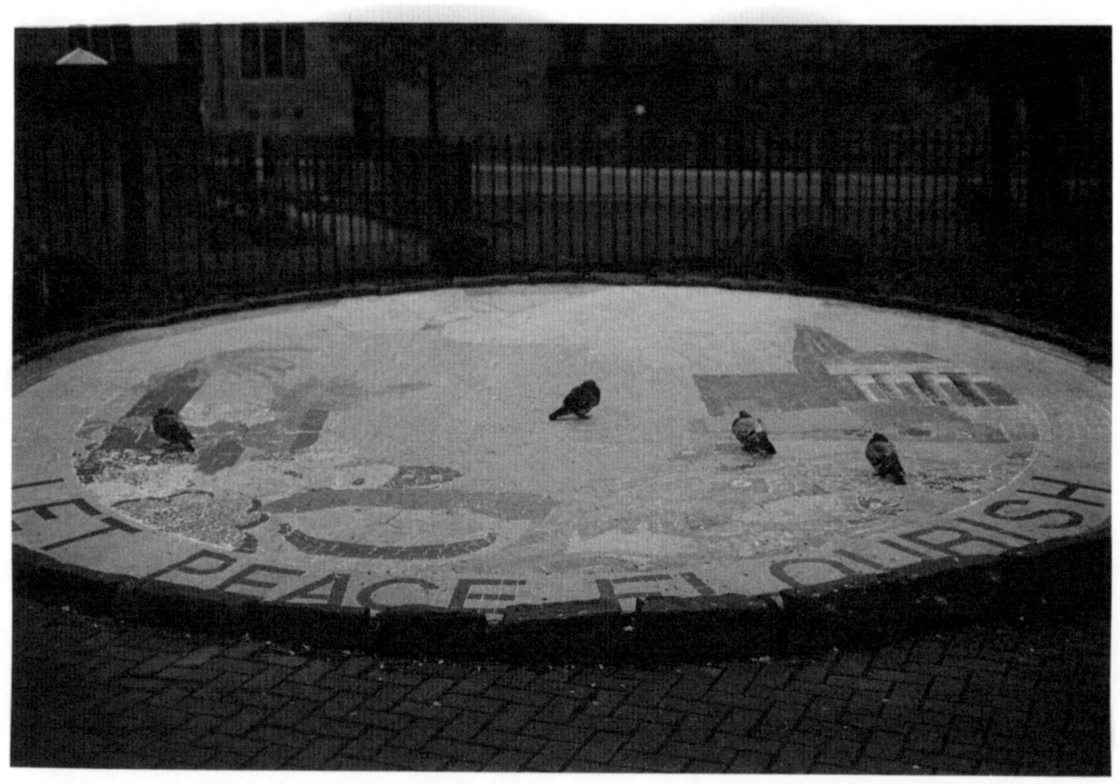

LET PEACE FLOURISH

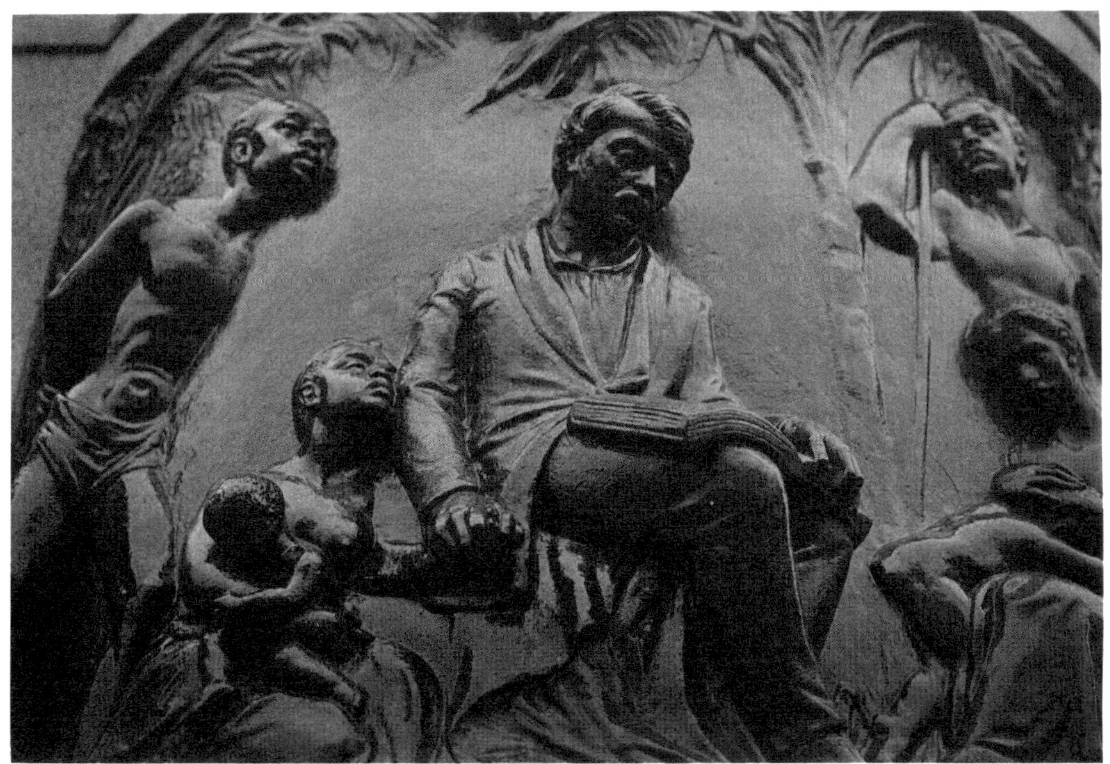

SOME PEOPLE

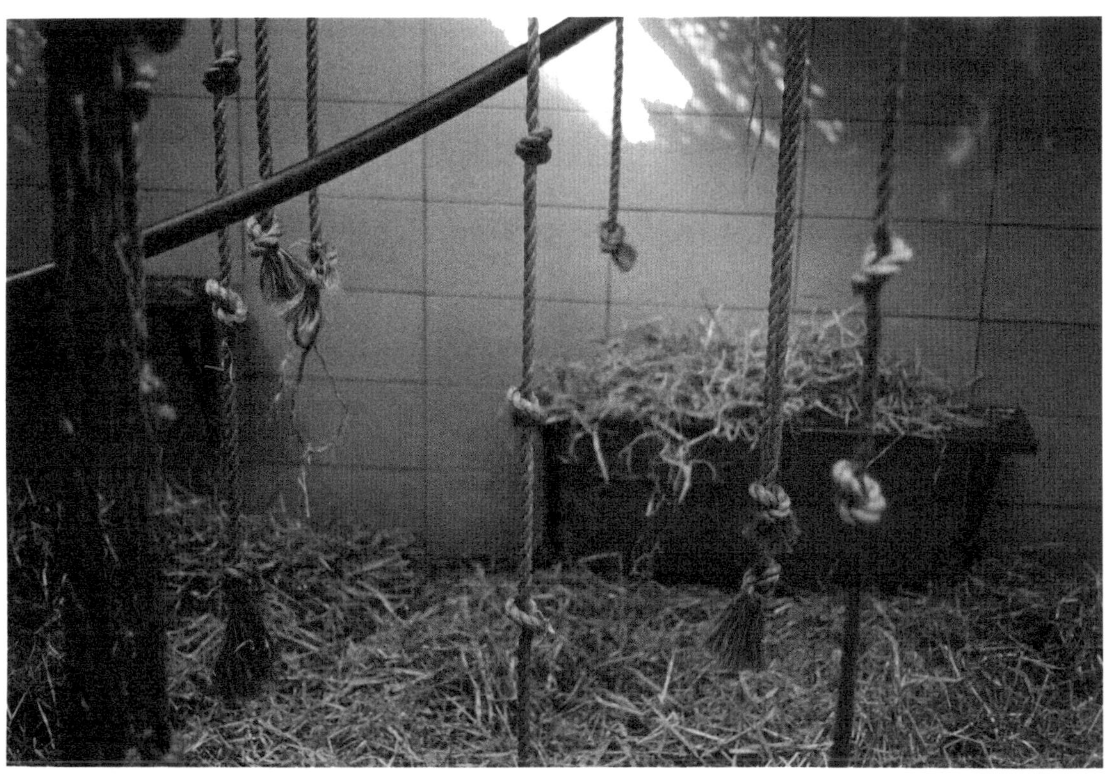

SOME ROPES

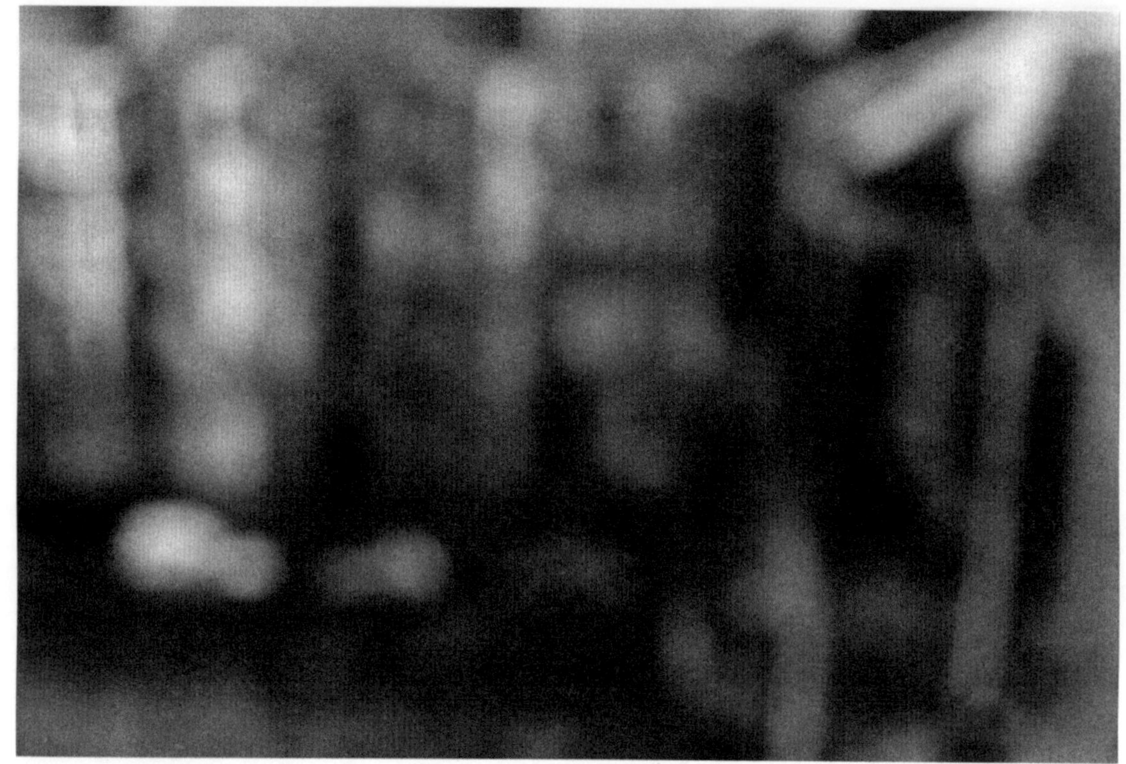

A   BLUR

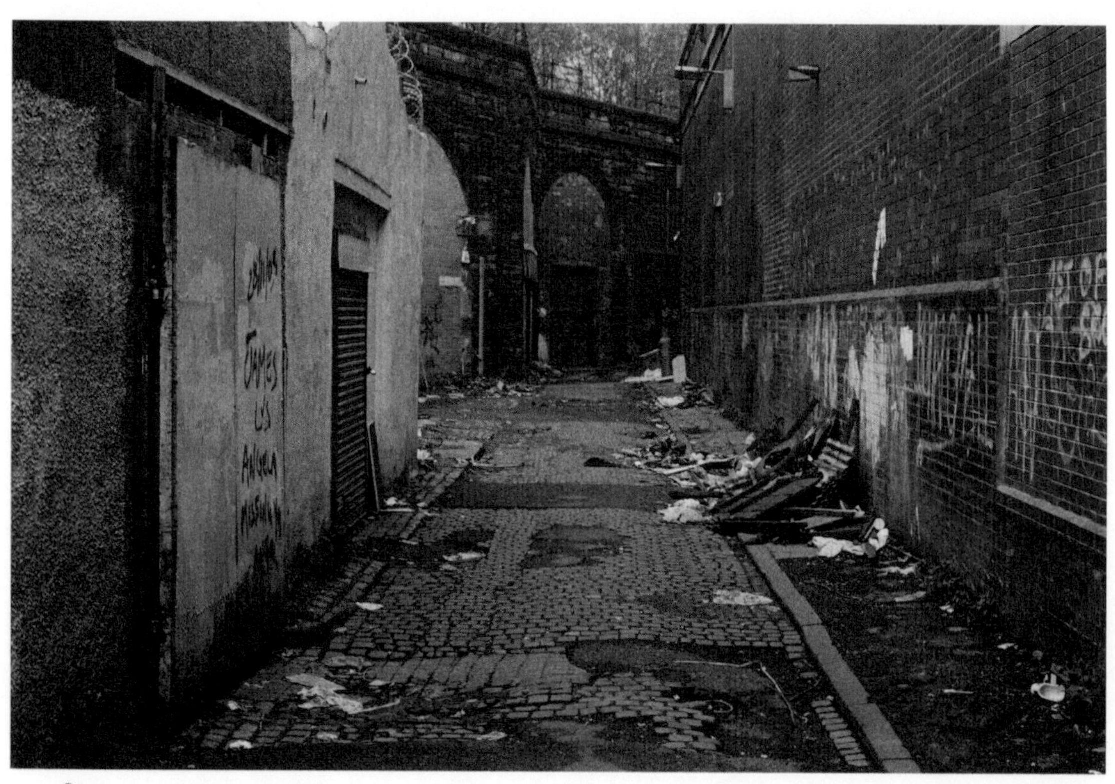

AN ALLEY

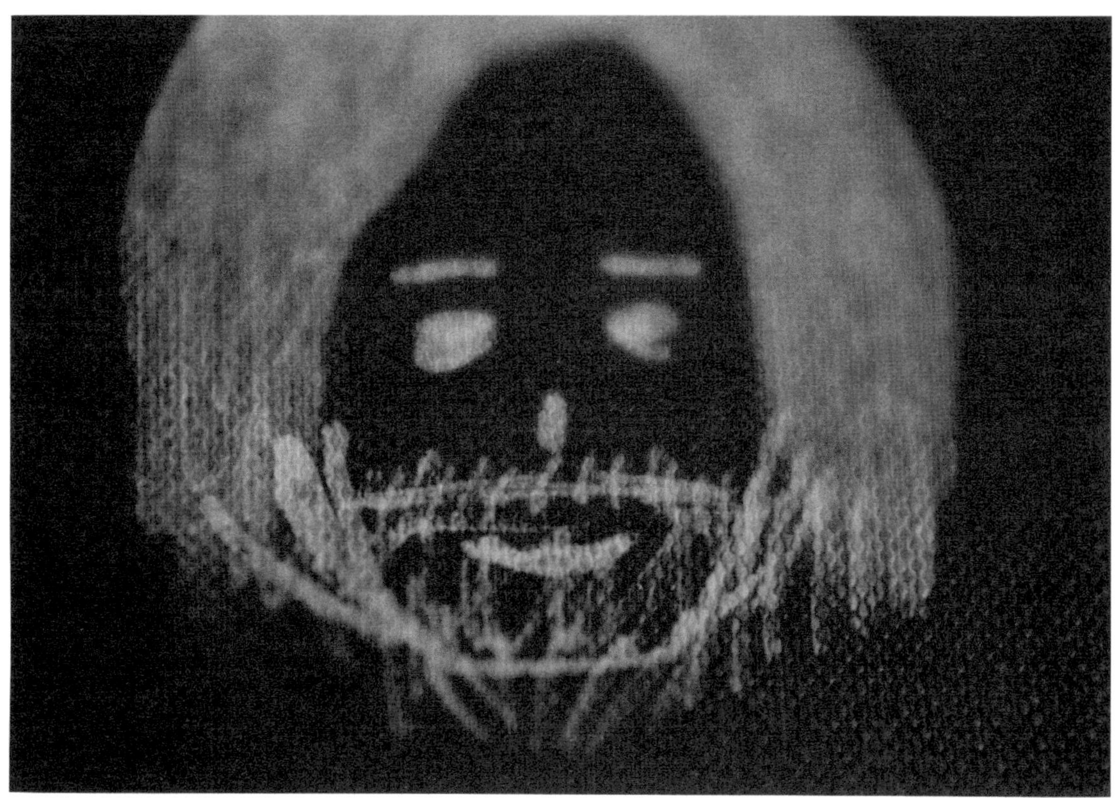

A DRAWING

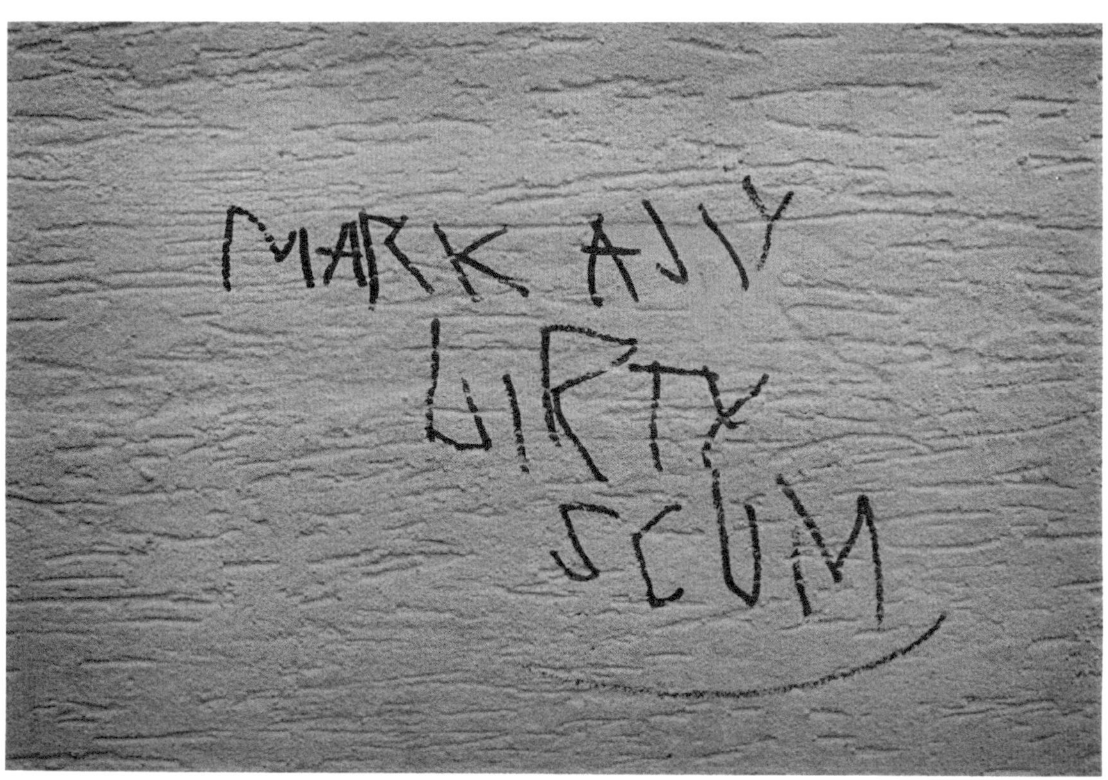

SOME WRITING

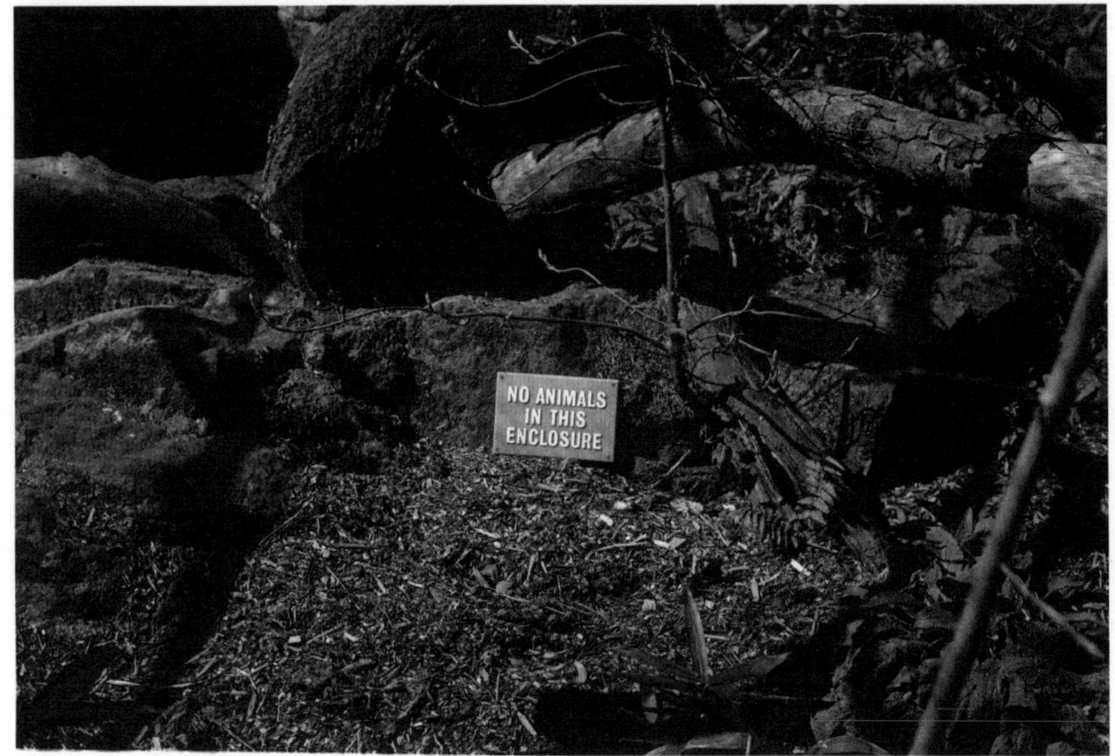

AN EMPTY ENCLOSURE

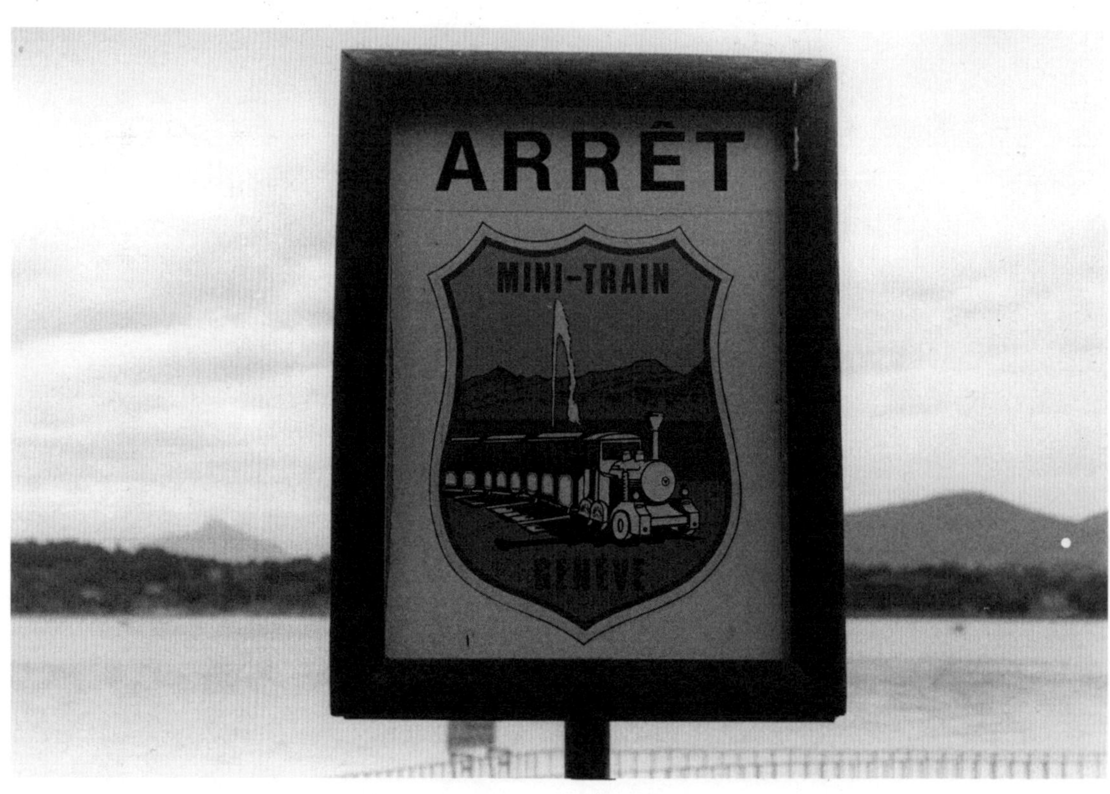

A STOPPING PLACE

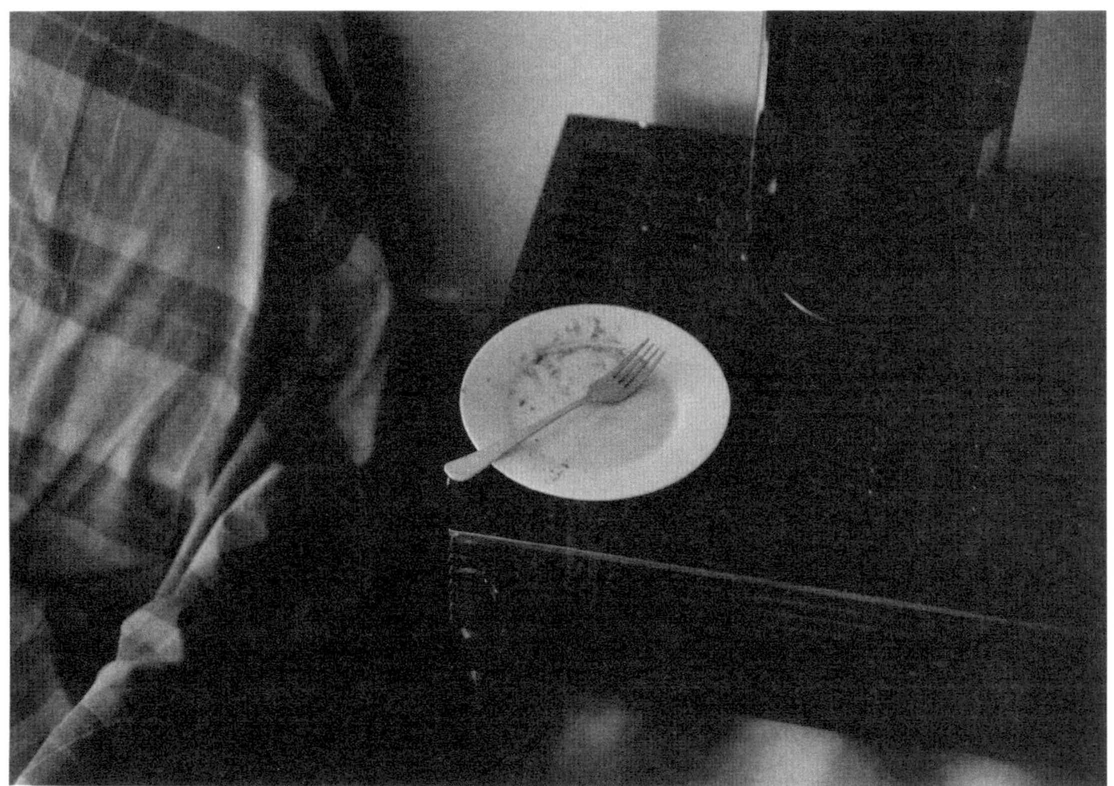

A PHOTOGRAPH

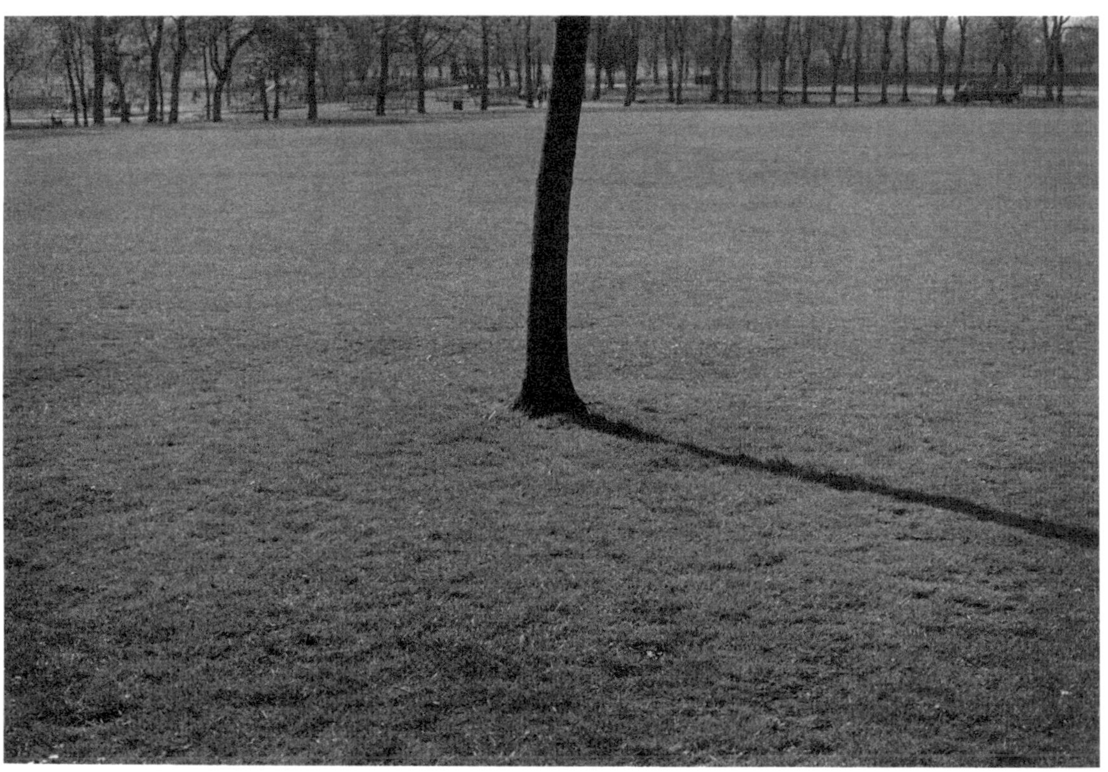

A TREE

A PHOTOGRAPH TAKEN QUICKLY

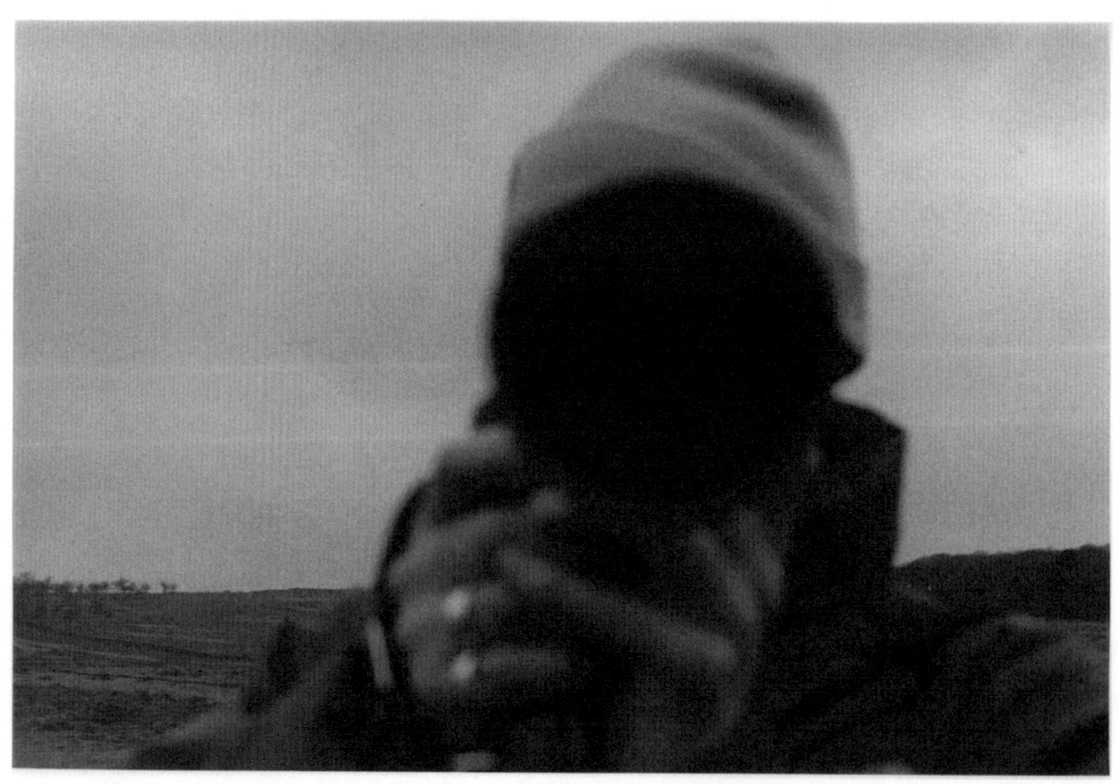

A BIG LENS POKED IN YOUR FACE

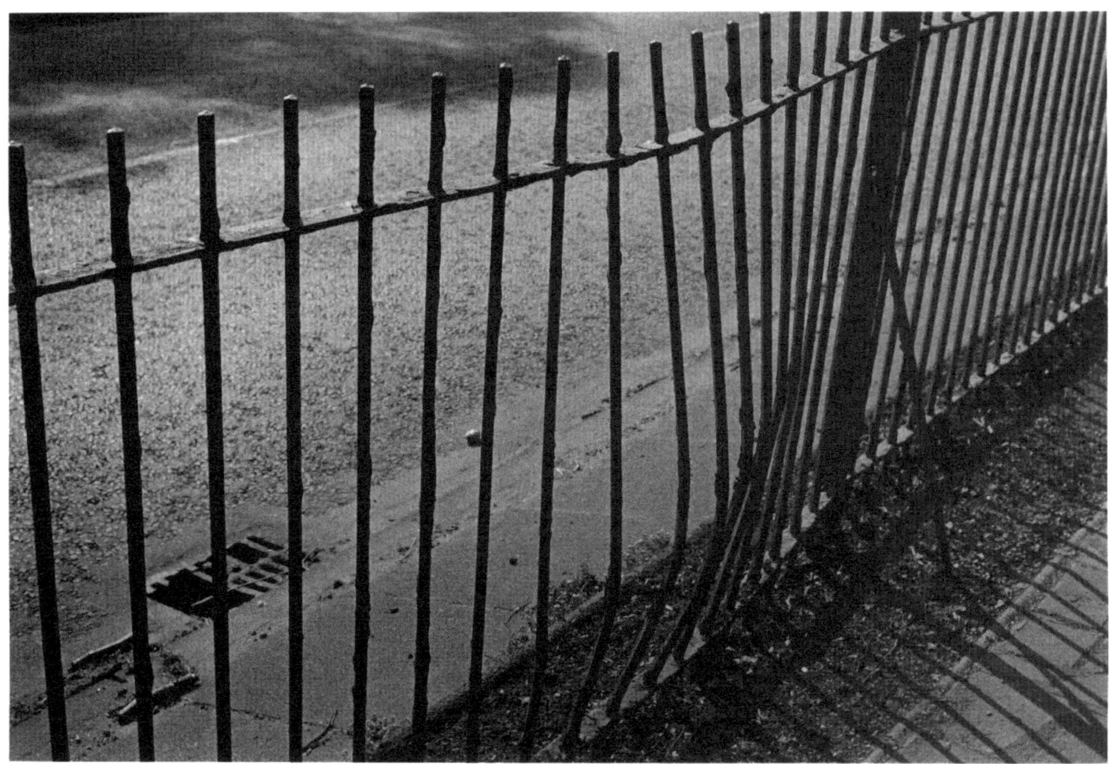

A PHOTOGRAPH OF BENT RAILINGS

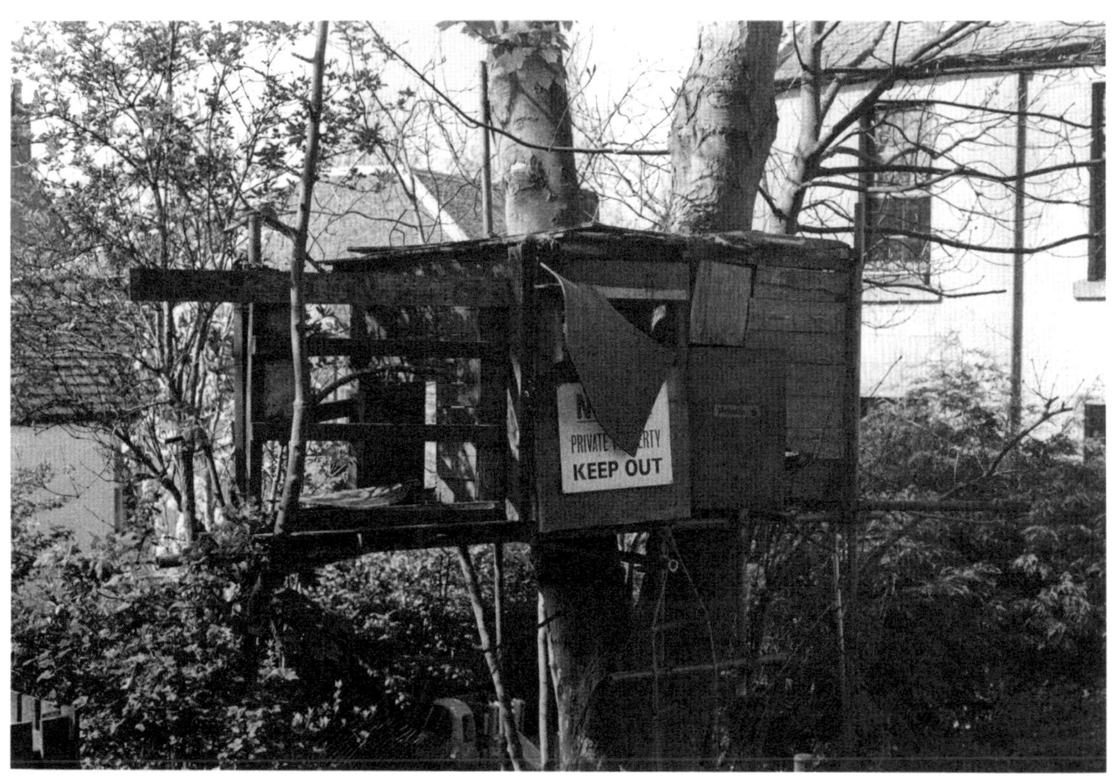

A TREE WITH A HOUSE IN IT

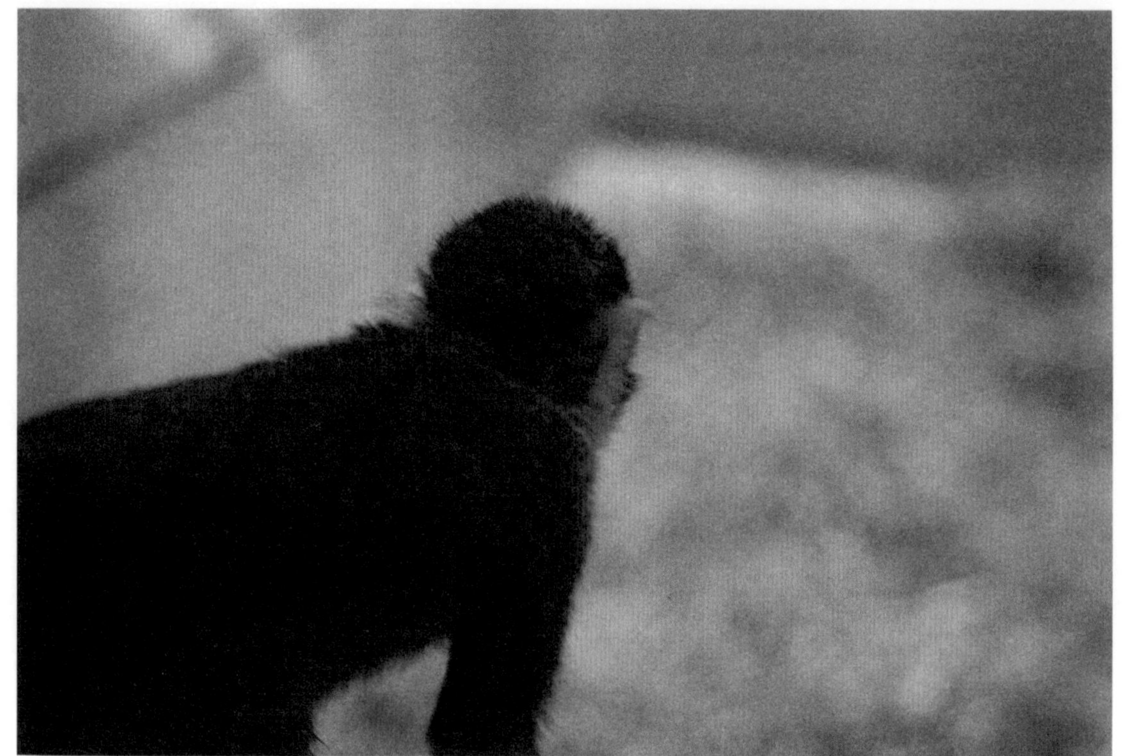

A LITTLE MAN

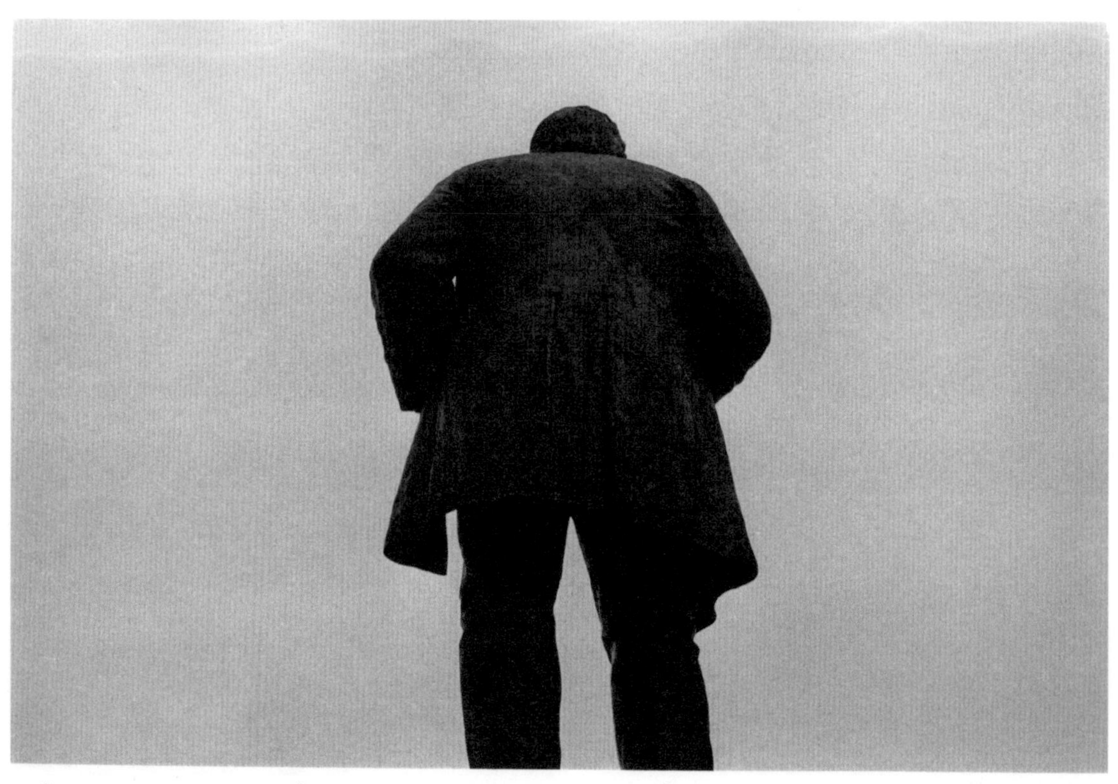

A HUGE MAN

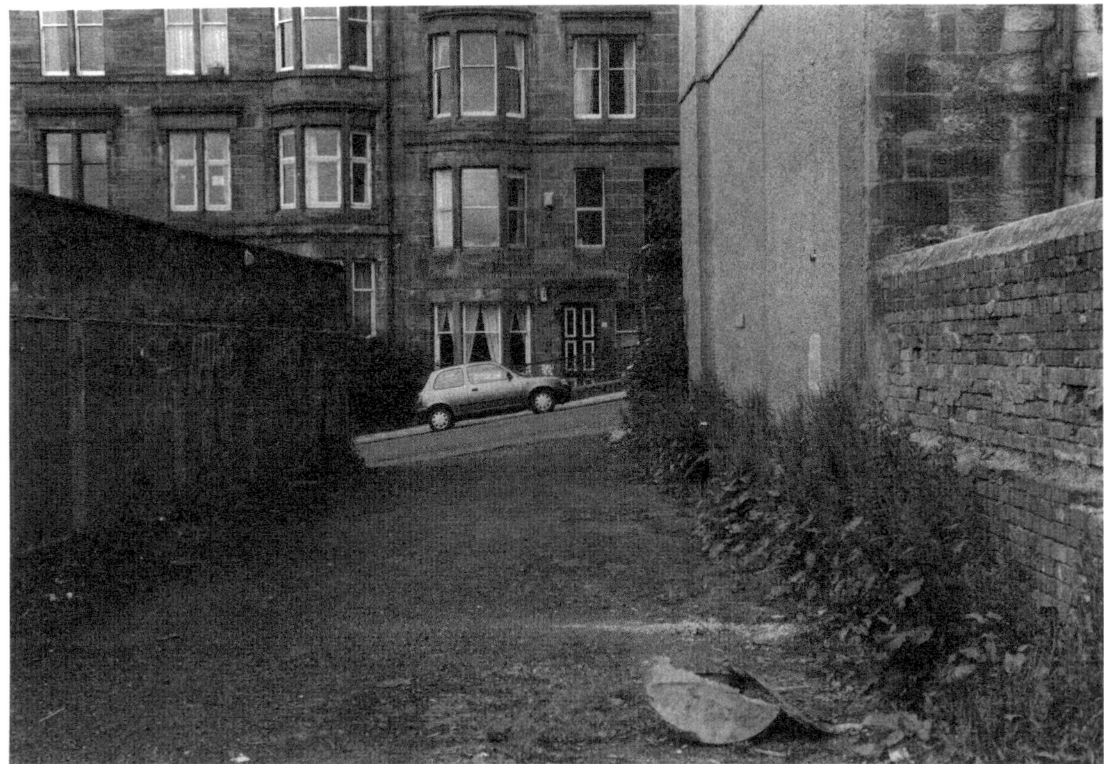

THE HILL

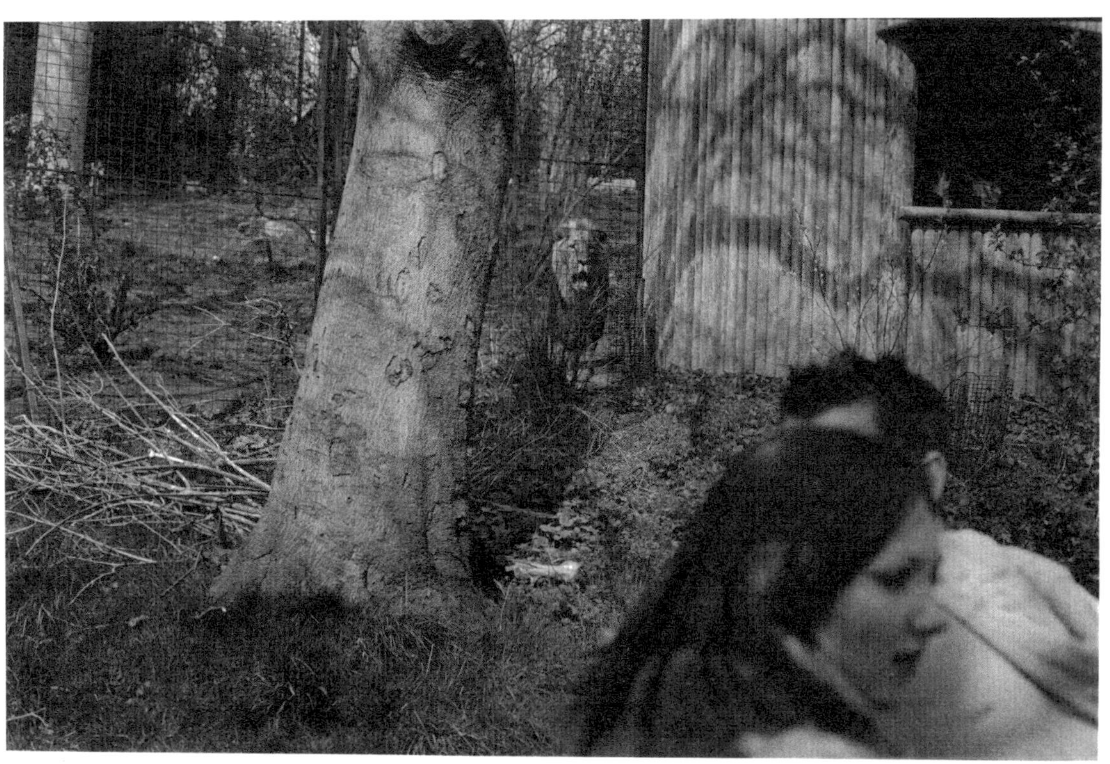

A SCENE

You Are About to Meet Yourself: Shrigley's Drawings — Martin Herbert

Two drawings, which David Shrigley placed side by side in a book published in 2010, offer a quietly eloquent *entrée* to his art. In the first, one misshapen rabbit tells another of a nearby land in which 'RABBITS LIVE IN HARMONY WITH ALL OTHER CREATURES'; his companion responds that 'THAT'S A COMPLETE LOAD OF SHIT AND YOU KNOW IT' (for all drawings mentioned in the text, but not illustrated here, see pp.102–103). The second drawing is a scruffily inked approximation of some kind of blast, at the centre of which is the sentence 'EXPLOSION INSIDE YOUR HEAD MAKES ALMOST NO SOUND'. A clandestine cortical flash – let's ignore, for now, the niggling kink of that 'almost', although the mental itch that it creates is characteristic – this, and its potential relation to the cottontails' dispute, is a manageable place to start with Shrigley. It's the inner event that nucleates his art, a reflexive defensive rejoinder to a world full of discord, illogic, idiocy and fatality. And just such an invisible paroxysm, presumably, has preceded each of the drawings, sculptures, photographs, prints, musical compositions and animtions that together make up the Shrigley *œuvre* – a heaving complex of embodied reactions whose present dimensions might be daunting if its individual facets weren't so darkly pleasurable, if these bitter pills didn't go down so sweetly.

As even a cursory acquaintance with his work will clarify, Shrigley is one of life's second rabbits, a nay-sayer to the Pollyannas and Panglosses of this world. His rabbits can't even live in harmony with each other, never mind 'other creatures'. By the lights of Shrigley's art, day-to-day life is merely a prequel to extinction, edged by quiet desperation – or so one might surmise from *Gravestone* (2008, see p.48),

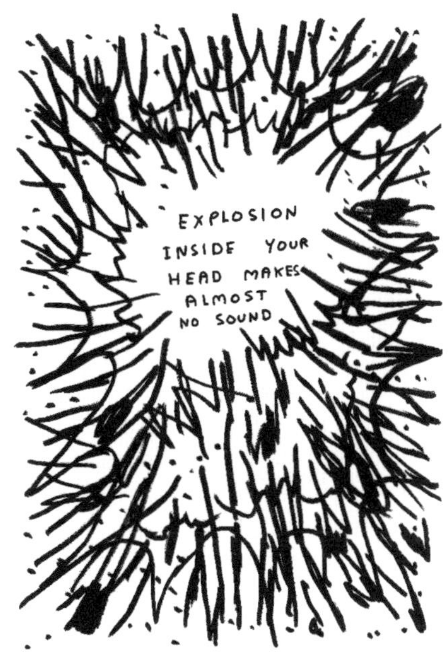

David Shrigley
Untitled (Explosion Inside Your Head...), 2006

a sculpted tombstone carved with a gold-lettered shopping list: 'BREAD / MILK / CORNFLAKES / BAKED BEANS / TOMATOES / ASPRIN / BISCUITS'. Can't take it? There are options, though desperate ones.

In one of the pseudo-psychotic, all-caps texts in the book *Kill Your Pets* (2004), Shrigley announces that 'THE HEROIN IS UNDERNEATH THE ASPRINS [sic]'. The title of the snapshot-style photograph *Anti-Depressants* (2002, see p.22) is written on a bucket-sized receptacle sitting in an artist's studio. A drawing in *Human Achievement*, from the same year, simply consists of the underlined word 'DRUGS' – name your own poison below. A recurring motif is a headless animal or human: see, for example, *Nutless* (2002, see p.57), *Cat with no Head* (2006) or the instantaneous joke of the head-burying *Ostrich* (2009, see p.35). These are not exactly unhappy images. To a citizen of the world as Shrigley presents it, being unable to think might be a merciful release.

Relief is needed, since in Shrigley's world we face insurmountable odds as a matter of course. No one is going to find the 'PIDGEON' that the artist, according to the 'LOST' notice he taped to a tree in Glasgow, nominally seeks: 'NORMAL SIZE. A BIT MANGY-LOOKING. DOES NOT HAVE A NAME' (*Lost*, 1996, see p.20). No one is going to solve the doleful sum he sets in the book *Human Achievement* (2002): 'EXPRESS AS A FRACTION: ALL PHOTOGRAPHS IN THE WORLD THAT YOU APPEAR IN (NUMERATOR); ALL PHOTOGRAPHS IN THE WORLD (DENOMINATOR)'. Shrigley will begin offering detailed instructions – on how some important charts work, for example – and then render part of the instruction illegible: hopes offered, hopes dashed. Salvation is not at hand. GOD IS IDLE, according to one 2007 wall drawing in barbed Dr Seuss-like lettering (*Untitled*, 2006), and you wouldn't be surprised if *The Bell* (2007, see p.40) – with its hand-written note, 'NOT TO BE RUNG AGAIN UNTIL JESUS RETURNS' – doesn't actually contain a clapper. Unhitched from any grand eschatological plan, we're instead cosmically irrelevant mechanisms, tiny blips in time, statistical probabilities pointlessly engaged in hedges against oblivion: collecting five years' worth of toenail clippings in a glass sphere, for example, for a work completed in 2002 (see p.113). Or, as Shrigley puts it, 'THERE IS NOTHING / THERE IS NOTHING / THERE IS NOTHING [repeats a dozen times] / THEN THERE IS SOMETHING / FOR A BRIEF MOMENT / THEN THERE IS NOTHING AGAIN.' Um, ha ha.

And yet, of course, this is funny (and very faintly miraculous, and a condensation of human or cosmic existence just as surely as the arguing rabbits are cast as believer vs atheist). A lugubrious, rather overcast, arguably very British style of humour is, with Shrigley, frequently our way in, or one way in; another is the generous accessibility of his work. That his primary medium is drawing is central to this, as it is to various other potencies of his art. Shrigley's work has transcended the environs of the art world for various reasons (such as an inclusive, freewheeling approach to format: the lost pigeon work is now a greetings card, for example, and he's also produced books of postcards), but foremost among them is the emphatically democratic, sociable tenor of his draughtsmanship. His drawings, denuded of technical skill, are not far removed – just funnier, more surreally estranged and slyly profound – from something we ourselves might doodle on a Post-it note (indeed, Shrigley has made this link himself, via the one yellow page in the square-format book *Kill Your Pets*: 'POST-IT NOTE', it reads). Accordingly they speak of Everyman frustrations; they broadcast rather than narrowcast. The inner voice ventriloquised by them is perpetually a detailing of, or itself a cartoon of, what passes for the collective unconscious: e.g. 'WHAT REALLY TROUBLES ME ABOUT HIM IS THAT I ACTUALLY THINK HE MIGHT BE A BETTER PERSON THAN I AM', written under a popeyed head scarred with worry lines (2006).

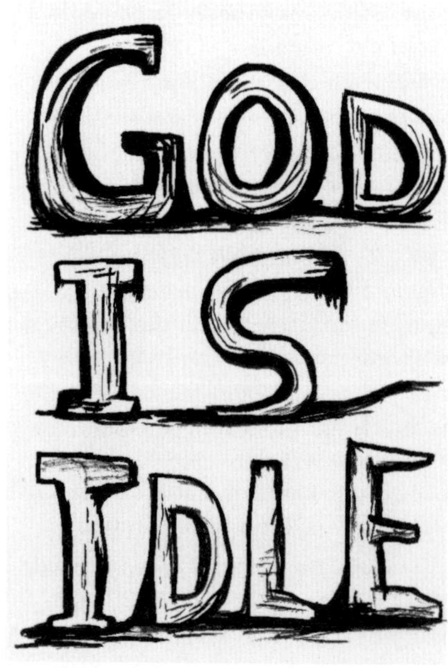

David Shrigley
Untitled (God is Idle), 2006

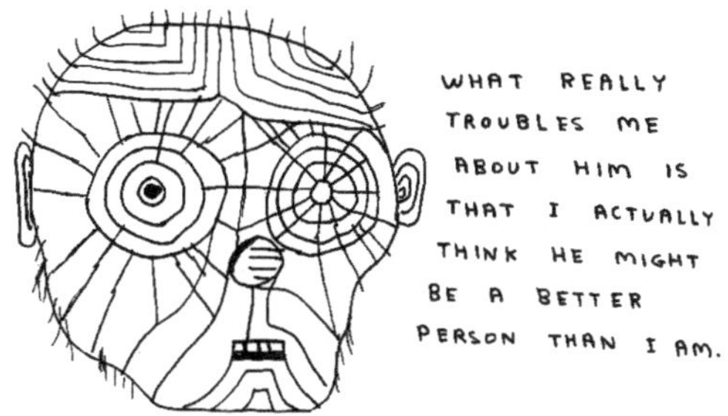

David Shrigley
Untitled (What Really Troubles Me…), 2006

Nevertheless, the drawings are not quite immediate, not quite personal in the sense that they might be construed as fully autobiographical. Underwriting this effect is a particular formal and emotional quality of pragmatic remove. When Shrigley draws – he puts in an eight-hour shift daily, produces a ton of drawings, discards a lot, puts the successes in a box to be looked at later, and then ruthlessly edits those – he produces, each time, an individual handmade image. But what appears on the page of one of his books is, of course, a reproduction. And this can even be the case (though he does show framed originals too) with works shown in galleries, a strategy developed for keeping in circulation drawings whose originals are now scattered across the globe. When this happens the result feels gratifyingly clean. It's technologically stripped of the confessional immediacy of the artist's hand – though Shrigley has already begun the divesting of angst via his approachable drawing style – and is, therefore, marginally though appreciably distanced from us, just as the tensions that thrum through the drawings have been held at bay or neutered or part-cleansed in the antic expression, (for now: according to the frantic, neurotic image Shrigley cultivates of himself within the work, the tension is already building again and the releasing must start again, ASAP)

This, one might think, is what his audience is responding to: the push-pull of accessing dark themes and yet feeling them safely held at bay, via one gambit or another. One might consider the drawing

of a 'LADDER USED FOR VIEWING ATROCITY', in Shrigley's early book *Err* (1996), to represent, more broadly, the casually inked sardonic humour that places artist and viewer slightly above the fray. Certainly it's notable that the effect is consistent across his art, with his sculptures also frequently feeling assertively detached. His scatters of shiny, painted steel peas (*Peas*, 2007) or glossily fake slices of cake (*Black Forest Gateaux*, 2001, see p.112) or the giant cavity-dotted tooth before a large mirror meant, cheerlessly given the work's title, to accommodate the whole viewer (*What Decay Looks Like*, 2001, see p.47), all feel genealogically linked to the page: they're like sculptures of cartoons or cartoons of sculpture.

But Shrigley's art is not broadly cherished solely for the fact that it allows the viewer vicarious, trauma-free access to dark cognitive territories. It's also because he has actively given it wings in terms of the media he uses, in a manner – fairly uncommon among contemporary artists – that also relates to the primacy of drawing in his art. If recent years have seen a progressive dissolving of the boundaries between fine art and the mainstream media, then Shrigley is part of this, consciously or unconsciously; trained in Environmental Art, he has taken a side-long route to being a 'public' artist (in terms of art that circulates in the public sphere). However, that's what he has become. If other artists inveigle themselves omnivorously into the worlds of fashion, music (Shrigley, with his T-shirts and record-cover art and music videos and 2007 *Worried Noodles* album, for which numerous major musicians set his lyrics to music, has form in this department) and cinema, then he has evidently mobilised the egalitarian language of humour-laced drawing to push his art towards broader audiences. For an artist who uses drawing primarily, there isn't much precedent for this. If anyone, the levelling practitioner he most reminds me of is an artist of a rather less compulsively boundary-blurring era: Saul Steinberg, who originally produced his highly philosophical, very funny 'art' as a cartoonist for magazines, yet whose work is modulated by context. Lift it from the page and put it in a gallery and there's no question that it is art; put it back, and it can work in other ways.

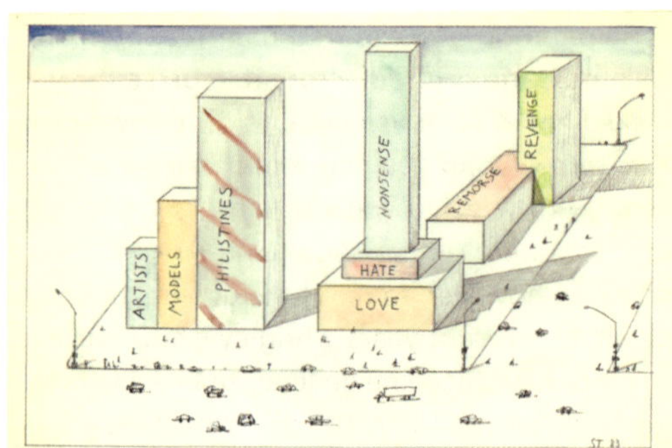

Saul Steinberg
Untitled, 1983

Shrigley, who has titled one exhibition *Everything-Must Have a Name* (2007), appears slightly ambivalent about his work being designated as art. In interviews he asserts himself as an artist, yet at the same time relishes the fact that his work sends its ideational spores beyond white cubes (considering the problems that bookshops have when deciding what section to put his books in – art? humour? – he says he thinks they're meant to go next to the till) and might even blindside and reach viewers for whom learning that an ambiguous thing encountered in the world was intended as 'art' is actively debilitating. 'High art' is a floating signifier in Shrigley's world. See his various doodled parodies of Hirst and Modernist abstraction; see the drawing of a man watching a dripping tap on-screen (shorthand for Structuralist cinema) labelled 'AVANT-GARDE FILMS DIRECT TO YOUR T.V. / VIA CABLE OR SATELLITE / UNLESS YOU STOP MASTURBATING'. But see also the affectionate nod to the work of an artist Shrigley avowedly likes, Martin Creed, in his 2007 animation *Light Switch* (an initially uncertain hand turns a light switch on and off, see pp.128–29), and the forthright yet funny animation he produced recently for the 'Save the Arts' campaign against UK government cuts to arts funding.

Is this indecisiveness? It's more like an advantage. To be high-falutin about it, Shrigley's work effectively vexes the art/not-art dialectic, functioning as a kind of rogue interstitial category. Insouciantly modular in form and effect, it can be dipped into and flicked through, or considered in depth as a

corpus veined with mordant and morbid themes. Shrigley, who tends to resist bracketing himself within a cartoon tradition, has said that the one artist he's had a long-running interest in is Philip Guston. This seems instructive, in terms of how Shrigley has fused languages and high and low forms. The American artist's work, from the late 1960s onwards, has comic strips in its DNA (Guston's love of *Krazy Kat* creator George Herriman is strongly apparent in his outlines), yet improbably compounds the graphic velocity of cartooning and the potential profundity and complexity of art. Looking back, Guston emerges as an early instigator of this kind of mix of graphic and fine art: influencing the work of younger North American artists such as Chris Johanson and Marcel Dzama, which filters the languages of comic-book art and illustration into galleries, while a parallel trend of treating cartoonists as fine artists has developed apace over the past decade.

Shrigley's art, which has both benefited from and helped drive this progression, might stand as the deepest interpenetration of these 'two worlds' in contemporary art, simply because he's able to act legitimately within both of them. At the same time, one might see his very visible, drawing-driven practice as playing an active role within a larger development: the increased recognition of the medium as a major one in contemporary art. In his

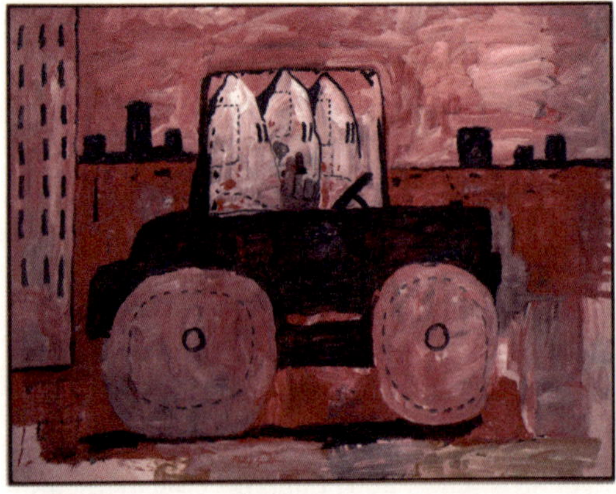

Philip Guston
City Limits, 1969

hands, it's a format that can partake of both the greatest levity and an unexpected profundity, which, in an unexpected way, parallels Guston's braiding of comic aesthetics with bleakness.

And so sometimes humour barely registers in it, overwhelmed by what it typically militates against. A drawing headed 'BIRD ON A WIRE GETTING ELECTRO-CUTED' is split on the horizontal: above is the dying animal, the current killing seen as concentric lines radiating through its body; below are six panels labelled 'PREVIOUSLY IN THE BIRDS [sic] LIFE'. Here she is in the egg, then being fed by her mother in the nest, learning to fly, meeting a mate, warming her own eggs and, finally, it seems, flying off in search of food for her brood. Very little art makes me well up; this, to my own consternation, does. It's heart-rending in its compression, particularly if we imag-ine that the bird has died while retrieving food for her young, and not least because of the carefully artless way in which Shrigley has drawn it (another use for casual draughtsmanship). *You, Your Wee Sister, Your Parents and the Social Services* (a sculp-ture from 2001; 'YOU' and 'YOUR WEE SISTER' written on ping-pong balls, 'YOUR PARENTS' and 'THE SOCIAL SERVICES' on wooden bats) similarly emphasises the 'tragi' in tragicomedy.

So there are, one might say, numerous Shrigleys. Some are avowedly respectful of art, some are comparatively cavalier; some can face the day, some can't so easily. He's fond of reversals or can't help them: the artist who declared that 'everything must have a name' also made the ambiguous plaster sculpture (with paradoxical identifying label) *Object Without A Name* (2008). Sometimes he's a boldfaced nihilist, as in a painting of a woman with the self-descriptive caption 'STAMP ON THE EGGS BEFORE THEY HATCH' (compare with the elegiac electrocuted-bird scenario). Sometimes he poses as such a champion sourpuss that one assumes ironic self-parody, as in a painting of a light bulb in a grey space captioned 'LIGHT IN THE GLOOM / SPOILING THE GLOOM', or an image of a splashy bit of geometry labelled 'WORLD'S LARGEST DIAMOND / OBSTRUCTING MY VIEW'. This deso-late view of reality reaches some kind of acme/nadir in *Untitled (Coffee from a Cracked Pot)* (2001),

a gnarly painting of a fissured blue teapot with a bleak message printed across it: 'COFFEE FROM A CRACKED POT & POISONED BISCUITS ON DIRTY CROCK-ERY SERVED BY A MAD OLD WOMAN IN A FILTHY HOUSE IN A BAD PART OF TOWN WHEN IT IS RAINING ON A MONDAY MORNING AND NO SUGAR AND MILK IS SOUR'. It's possible, however, to make the general obser-vation that, in recent years, Shrigley's humour has modulated. It has become generally more abstract, less immediate, moodier. This shift towards a less end-directed, optimistic humour operates under the formless sign of the polyurethane foam leaking from tents (*Tent*, 2007) and trousers (*Cheers*, 2007, see p.43) and sleeping bags (*Sleeping Bag #2* (*Green*), 2007), which feels like a kind of shorthand for the inevitability of entropy. It has become tautological, as in a hanging sign labelled HANGING SIGN (2007, see p.39), and a belligerent, interrogative voice has crept in – one that feels less like Shrigley's own (assuming we know what that is) than that of a badgering disembodied authority. In big imageless works, it announces that 'YOU CANNOT HELP LOOKING AT THIS' or orders us not to look out of the window. Words are pushy, resistible things; witness *Word Gate* (2009), a steel gate made up of the word 'WORDS' repe-ated ten times in a vertical stack (hello, Wittgenstein?).

A work like *Swords and Daggers* (2010, see p.158), a menacing circular array of bronze weaponry, is all violent heraldic tone: no language and no comedic pay-off at all. This does feel like it could have origi-nated in a fast drawing – sprung, that is, sidelong from Shrigley's cerebellum during one of his ex-tended stints at the drafting table (he has a history of drawing swords). The relation of his process to automatic drawing, though, is a cloudy one. Shrigley's art is far more controlled and self-audited than the spontaneous eruptive sketches of André Breton *et al*; the indecorous nature of the worldview on show makes Shrigley's drawings feel like a relatively direct transmission from the id – compared to much contemporary art, anyway – yet we don't know how finessed the almost-silent explosion has been in its journey to the page. The drawings flirt with a confessional style, but don't actually settle on one. Again, in terms of allowing viewers to feel that

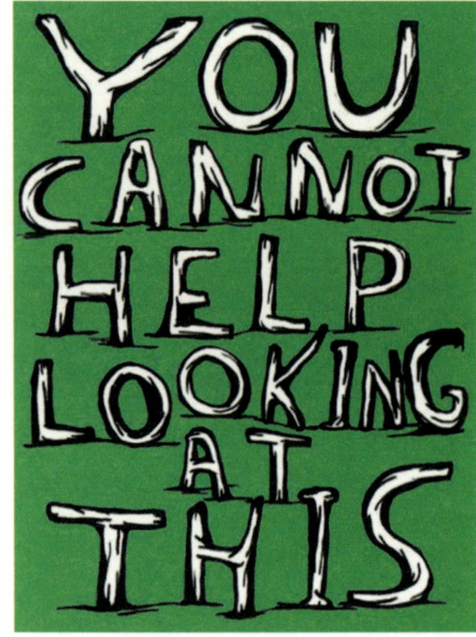

David Shrigley
Untitled (You Cannot Help Looking At This), 2006

Shrigley's articulations of widespread frustration and fear etc. are their thoughts too, it's a vacillation that becomes a virtue.

What is clear is that the protean tenor of Shrigley's practice expansively models somebody's personality convulsively, perhaps therapeutically, answering a fairly senseless world and doing so, either theatrically or not, in different ways on different days. Relatedly, the aforementioned shifts in his art feel authentic in their movement towards a profounder sense of anxiety and irresolution. In the yellow painting *The Bells* (2007), the text – 'THE BELLS / DING / DONG / DING / DONG' – is fundamentally ambiguous, the chosen colour telling us nothing definite; portentousness battling brightness.

Through Shrigley's work, then, one might trace a trajectory over the last dozen years from a performative pessimism leavened by humour to an increasing evocation of psychic perplexity and an almost sullen retreat into abstraction. Couple that, too, with an oblique awareness of time ticking away, leading us towards the actuality of the ending that his art has repeatedly, safely, rehearsed on the page (witness the various types of clock that have,

with seemingly increasing frequency, punctuated his art). If this arc into real and relatively interiorised, garrulity-free anxiety isn't wholly true of Shrigley, who comes across in conversation as admirably level-headed and pragmatic, then it feels like it might be a plausible journey for the rest of us.

And if we are Shrigley's audience – misshapen rabbits, present or future high-functioning malcontents unencumbered by misty notions of an afterlife or the perfectibility of mankind – then we look upon his works, feel his wobbly drafting open the door to us, and experience the shock of recognition. It feels, though far from cosy, surprisingly inviting. One can be surprised by whom it strikes. In the British Library, where I am writing this text, the 60-something security guard at the door examines my books in case I'm trying to steal the library's property. He opens *Evil Thoughts*, Shrigley's 2002 book of postcards, and reads the first one aloud, unnervingly aloud in the scholarly hush of the library: 'SORRY I PAINTED THE WORD "TWAT" ON YOUR GARAGE DOOR'. He laughs. 'What is this?' he asks me. 'Art', I say, though he has already returned to the postcards, flipping through, declaiming more. As this happens, Shrigley's art is doing precisely what it was designed to: making its way out into the world, and simultaneously emphasising and resisting the pains of being human.

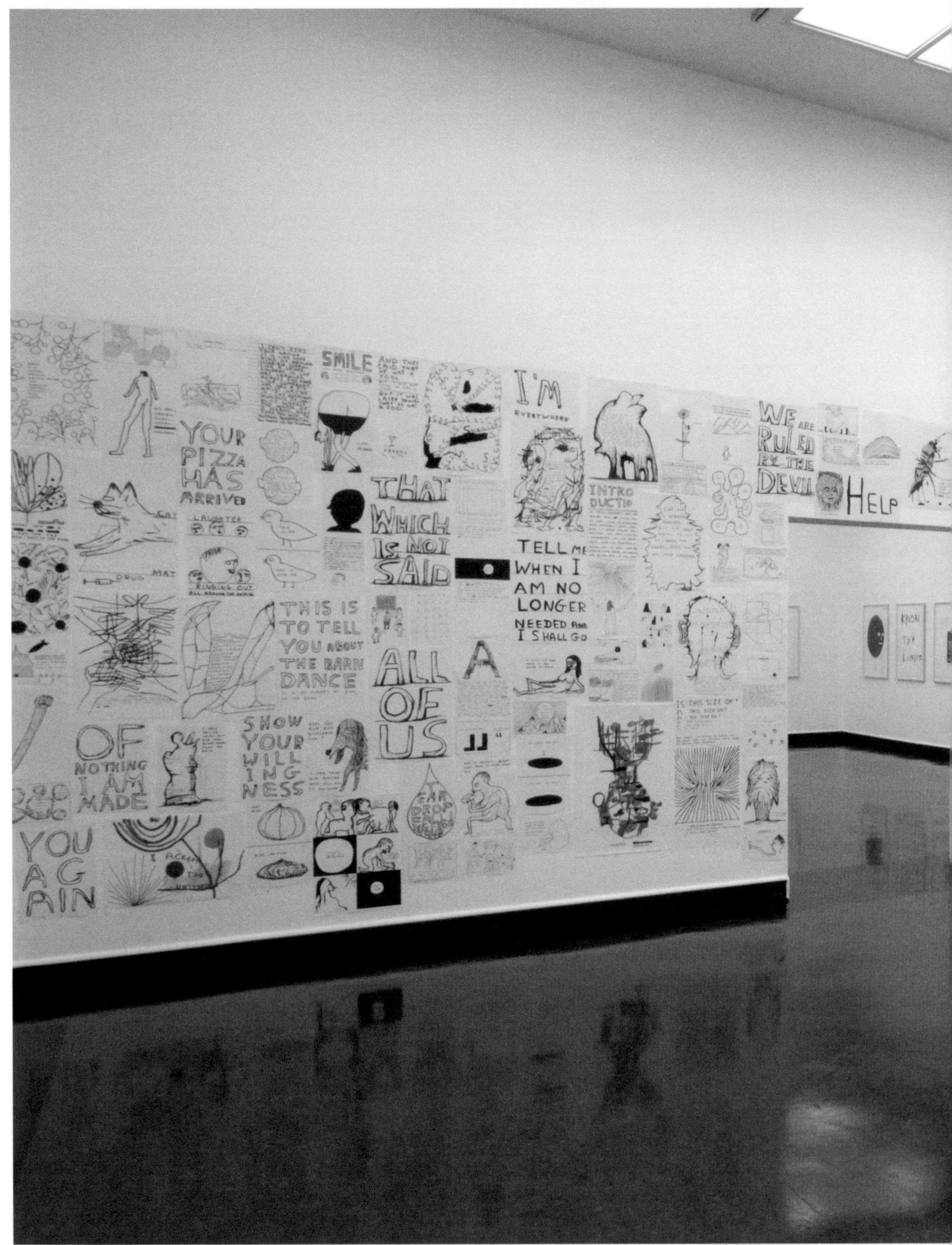

Untitled, Installation at Bergen Kunsthall, 2009

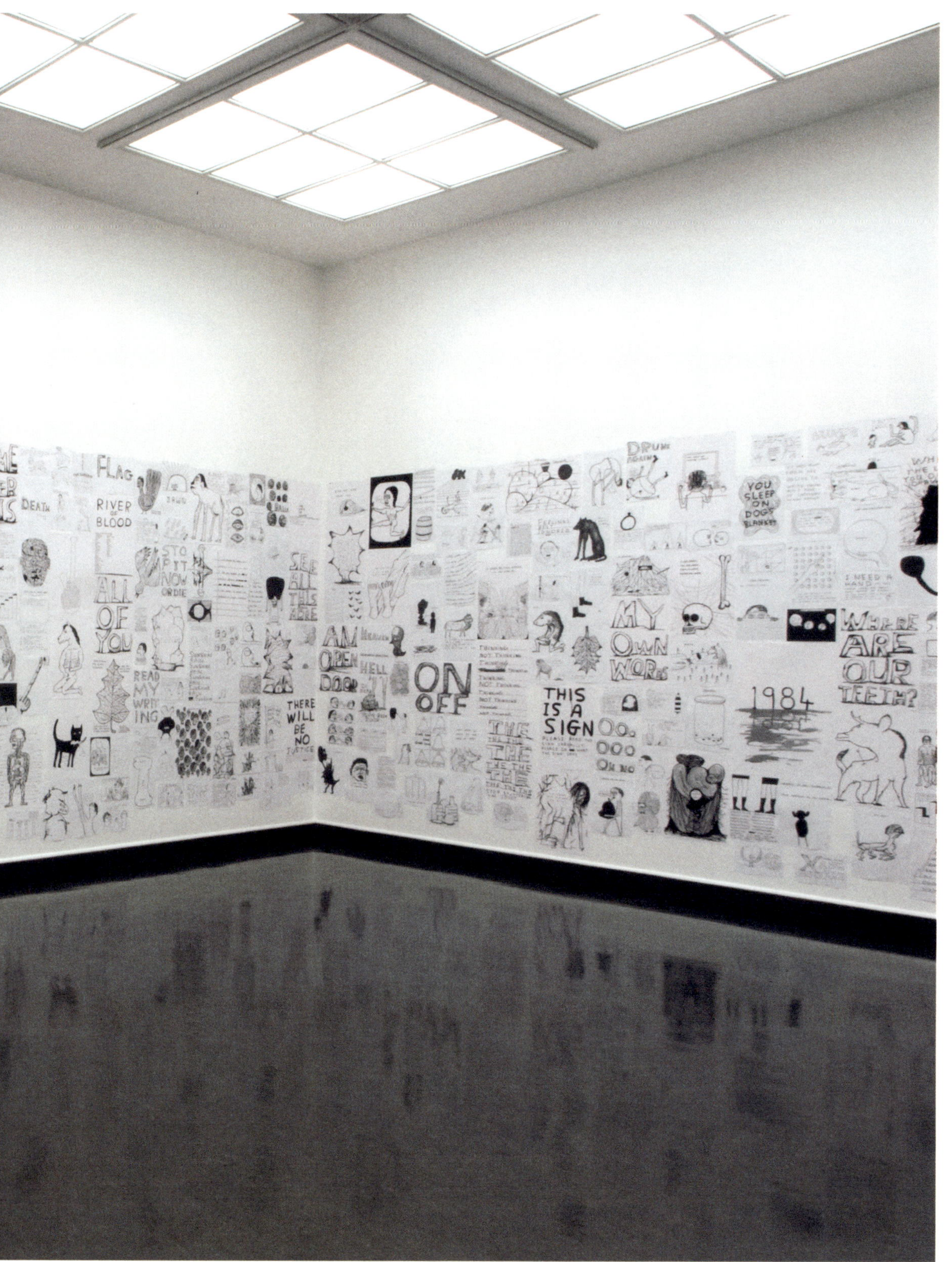

Selected drawings, 2011 (pp.89–104)

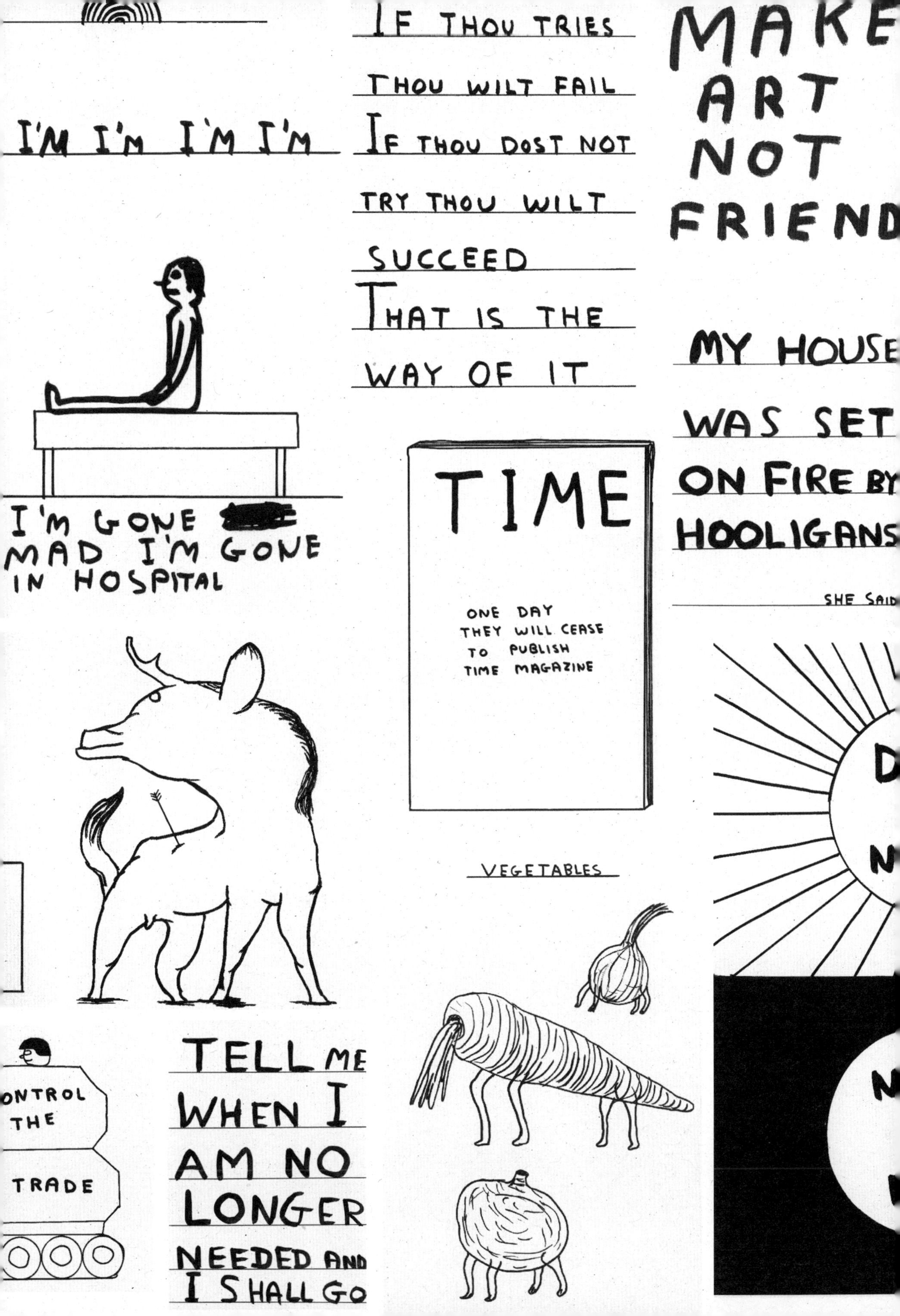

I'M I'M I'M I'M
I'M GONE MAD I'M GONE IN HOSPITAL
IF THOU TRIES THOU WILT FAIL
IF THOU DOST NOT TRY THOU WILT SUCCEED
THAT IS THE WAY OF IT
TIME
ONE DAY THEY WILL CEASE TO PUBLISH TIME MAGAZINE
VEGETABLES
MAKE ART NOT FRIEND
MY HOUSE WAS SET ON FIRE BY HOOLIGANS
SHE SAID
CONTROL THE TRADE
TELL ME WHEN I AM NO LONGER NEEDED AND I SHALL GO

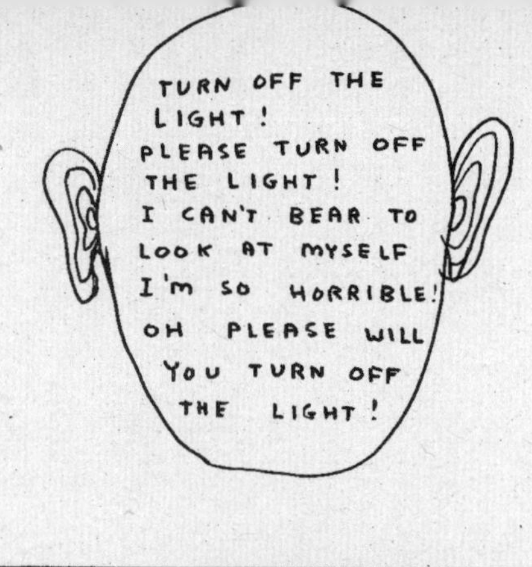

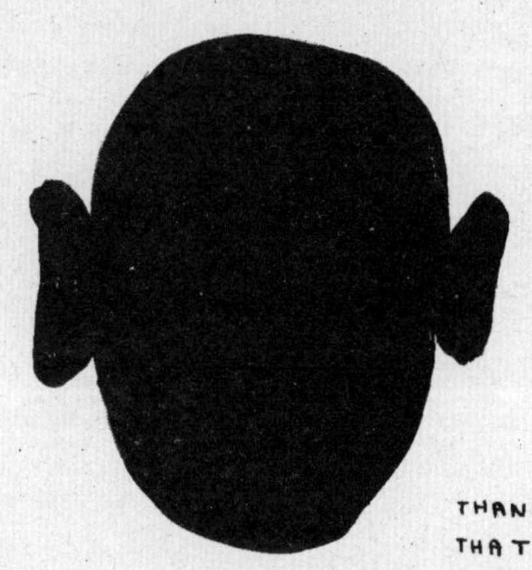

VIDEO GAME

THINKING
NOT THINKING
THINKING
NOT
THINKING
THINKING
NOT THINKING
THINKING
NOT THINKING
THINKING
NOT THINKING

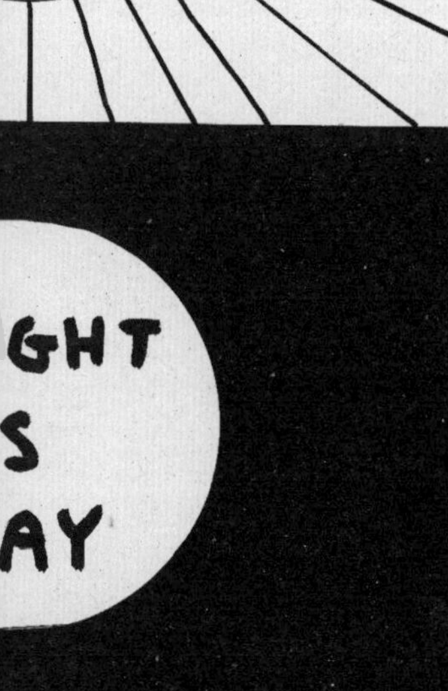

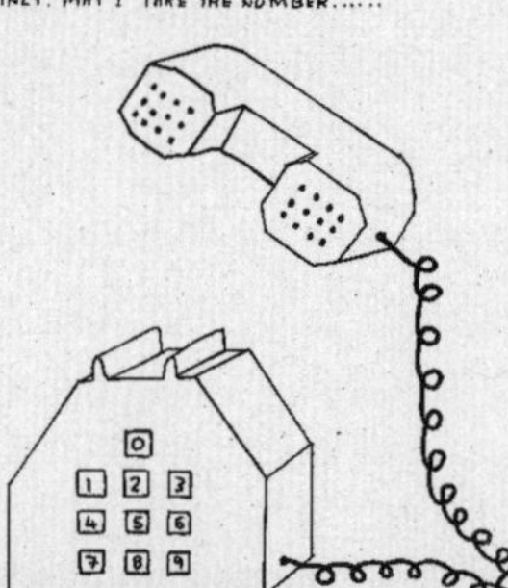

GRAFFITI

JOHN IS A BASTARD
CAROL IS A BITCH
ENGLAND IS SHIT
JANE IS A WHORE
BOOKS ARE SHIT
PETER IS SHIT

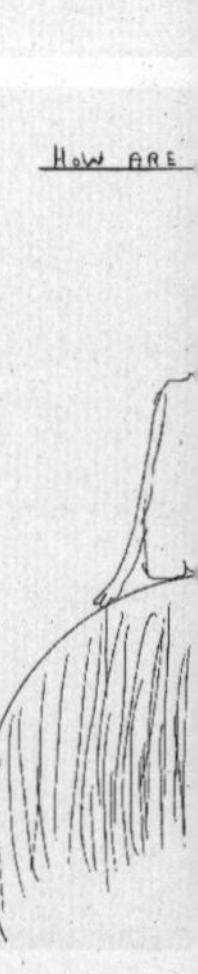

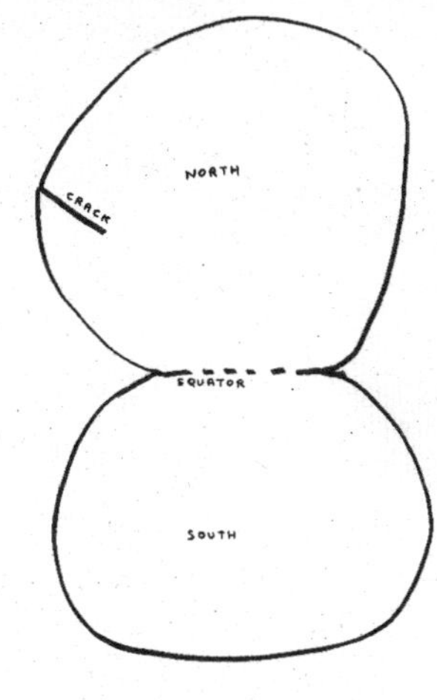

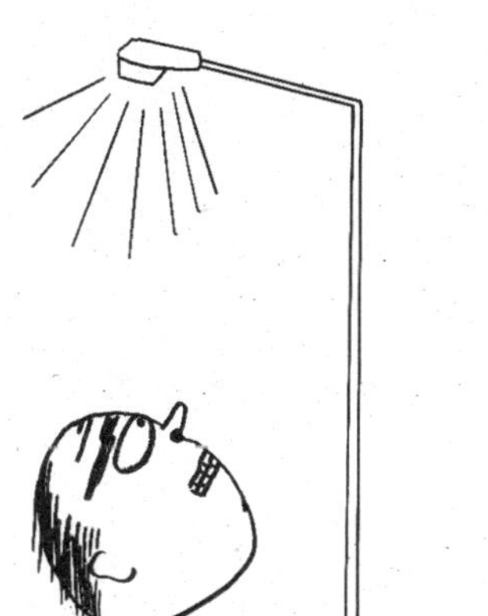

FOOTPRINT

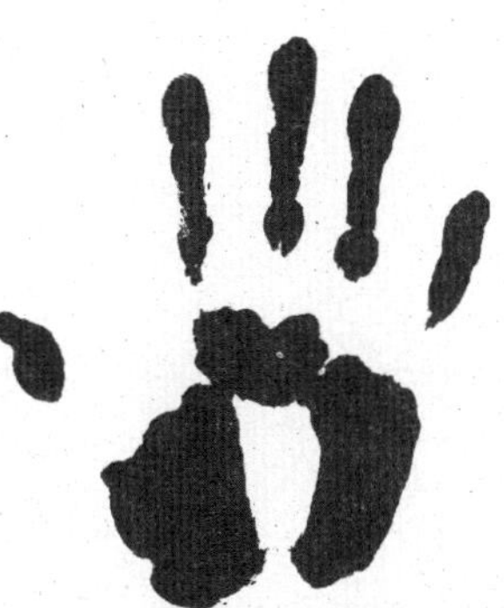

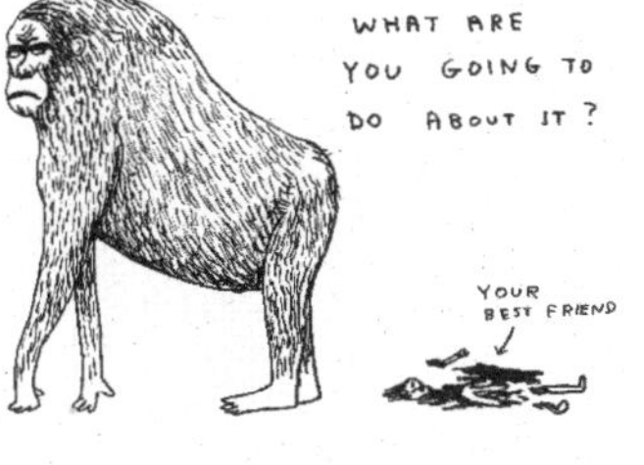

WIN BACK
YOUR DIGNITY

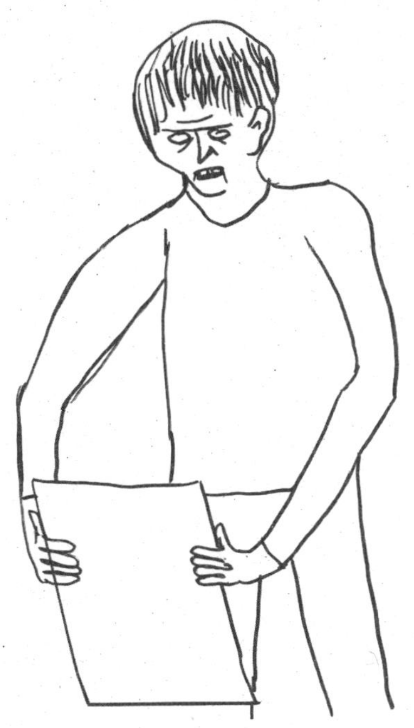

BUNK BEDS

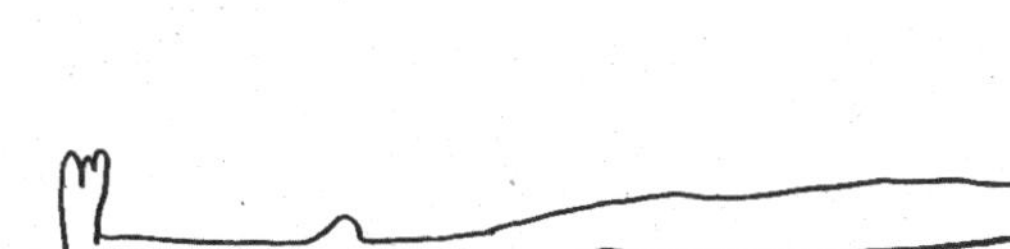

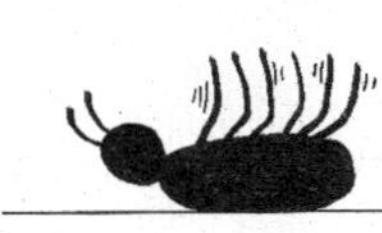

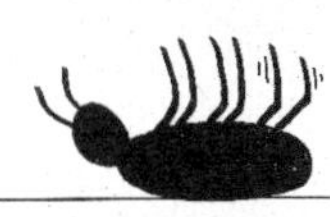

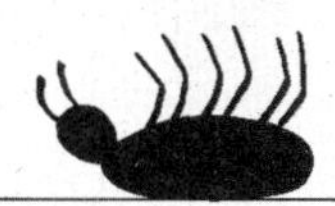

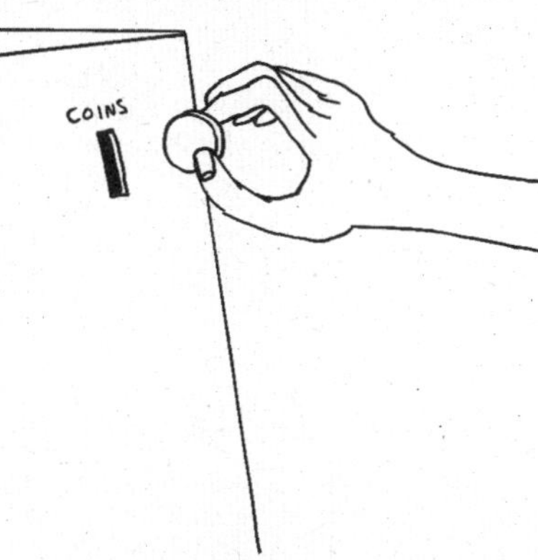

ALL HOLES LEAD TO HELL

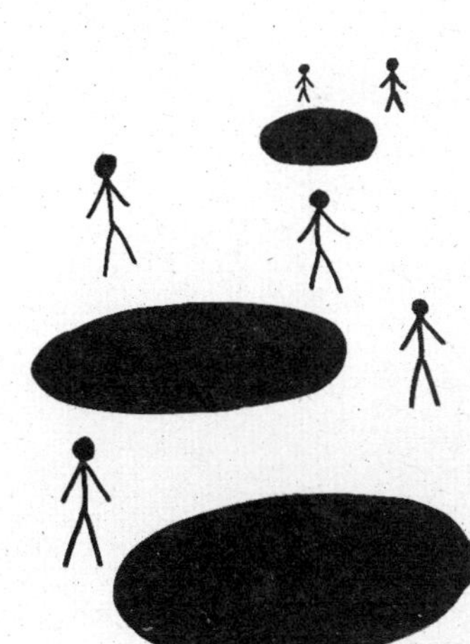

MY
IAS
TO
PAG

YOU

BEEN

IT HAS ALWAYS
BEEN MY
DESIRE TO
WRITE POETRY
BUT I FIND
IT INCREDIBLY
FUCKING DIFFICULT

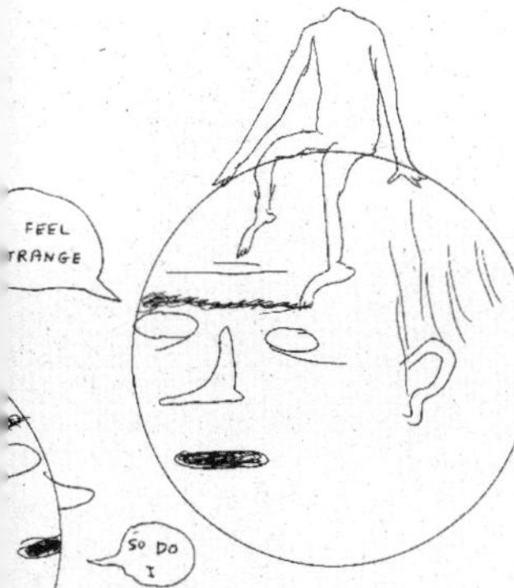

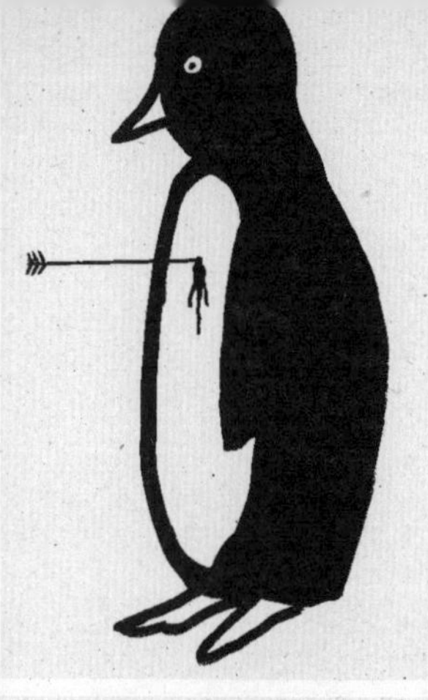

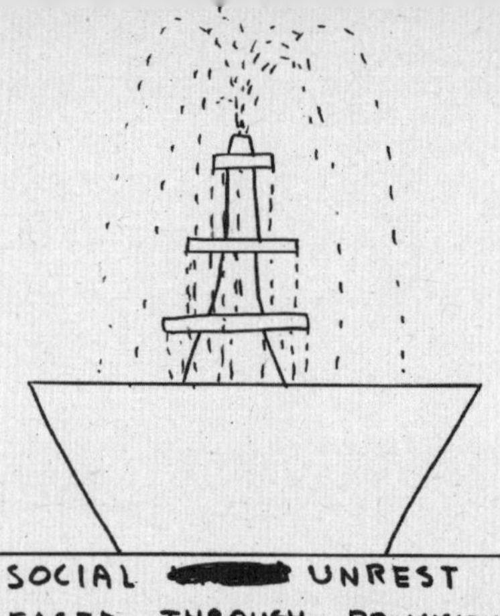

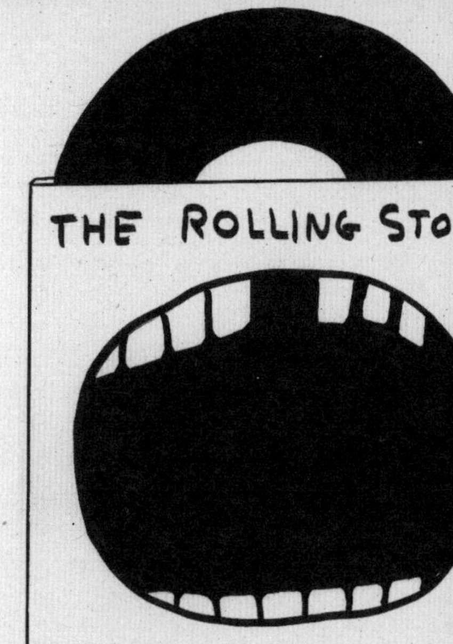

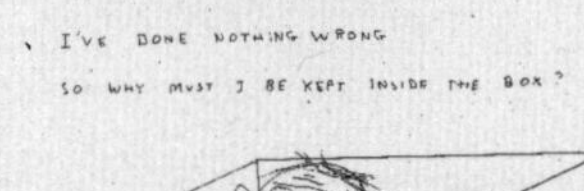

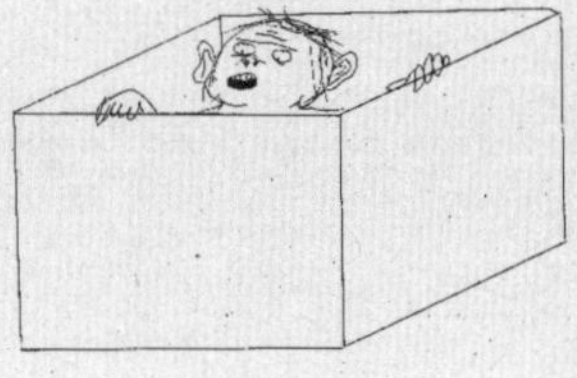

I WAS SUFFERING
THEN MY SUFFERING
ENDED
THEN MY SUFFERING
BEGAN ANEW
AND IT WAS AWFUL
AND IT WAS HARD
THEN MY SUFFERING
ENDED AGAIN
AND MY LIFE WAS GOOD
AND I WAS HAPPY
AND THEN ONE DAY
MY LIFE ENDED
AND THAT WAS THAT.

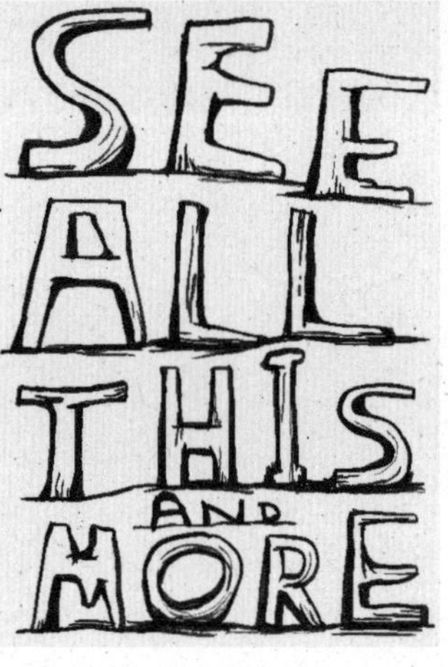

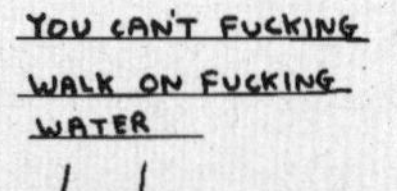

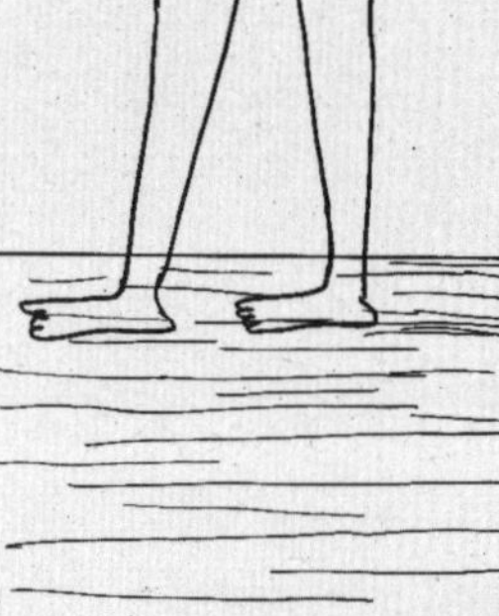

ONLY

IS

FILL THE

HAVE NOT

IVEN A TASK

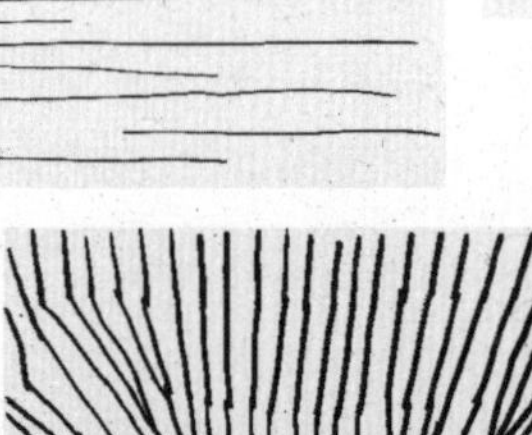

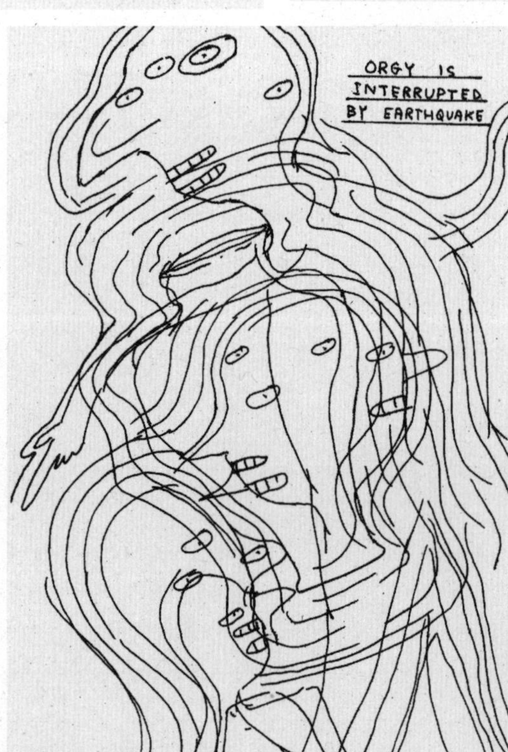
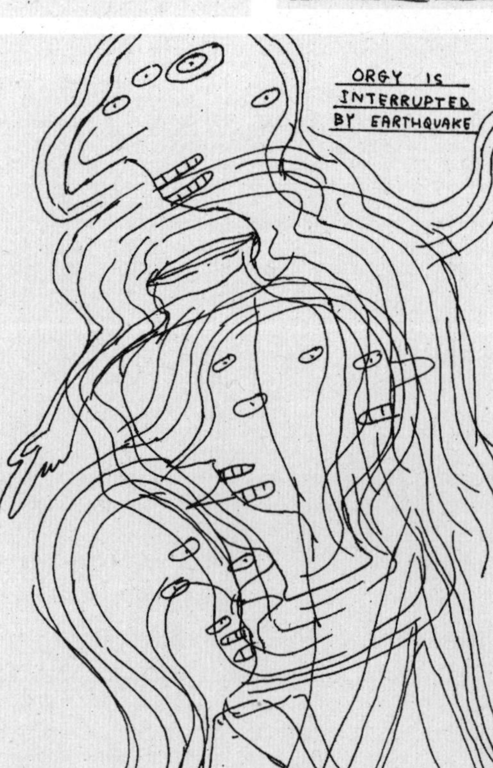

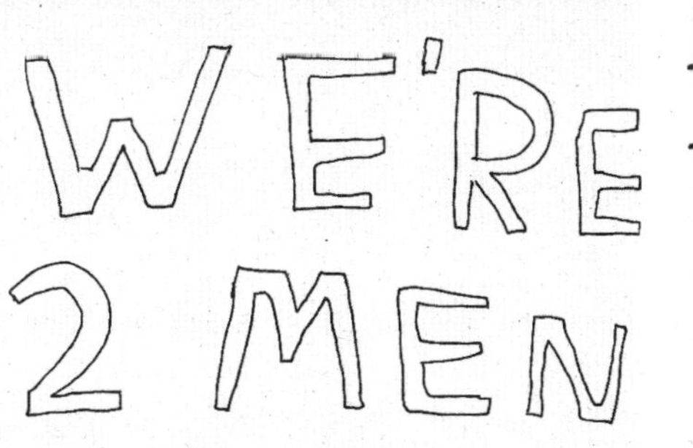

AND WE ARE UNABLE TO MOVE.
MUCH AS WE WOULD LIKE TO MOVE
WE WERE DOING SOMETHING WICKED
AND WE GOT FROZEN

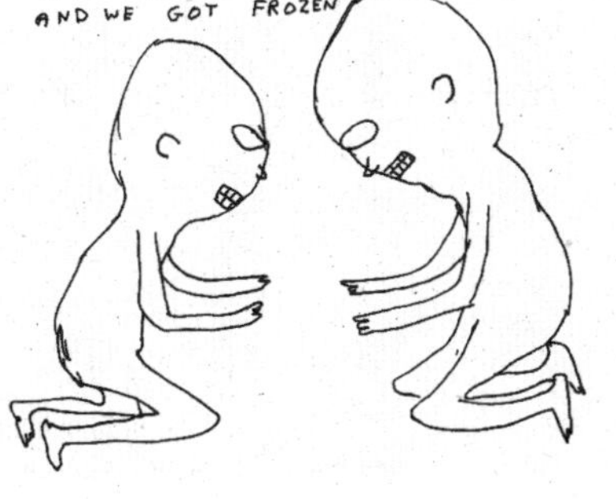

FIND A
PICK IT
ALL DAY
WILL BRI

W

THE HOLE

DON'T GO DOWN THE HOLE.
THERE IS AN ALBINO DOWN THERE
AND HE WILL FRIGHTEN YOU.
HE ALWAYS FRIGHTENS PEOPLE
WHO GO DOWN THE HOLE.

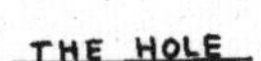

I AM A CAT-
WALK MODEL

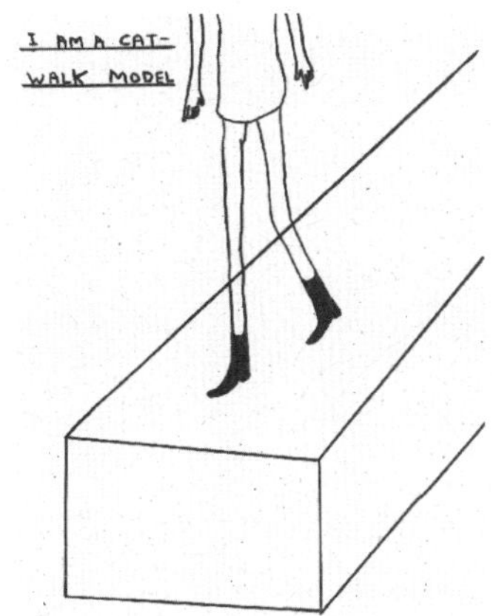

I AM VERY UGLY BUT NOONE SEEMS TO NOTICE

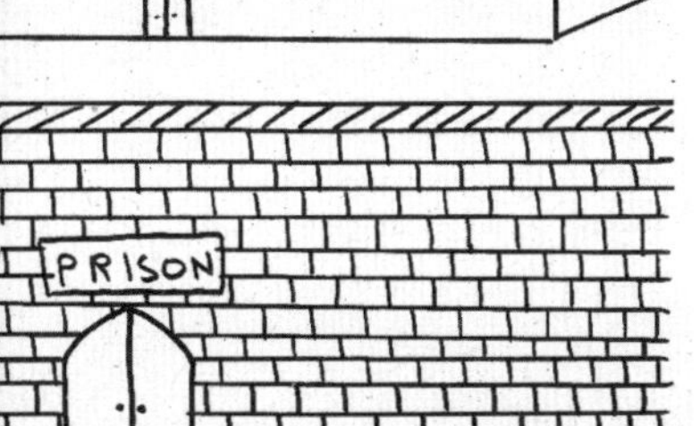

PRISON

ENOUGH

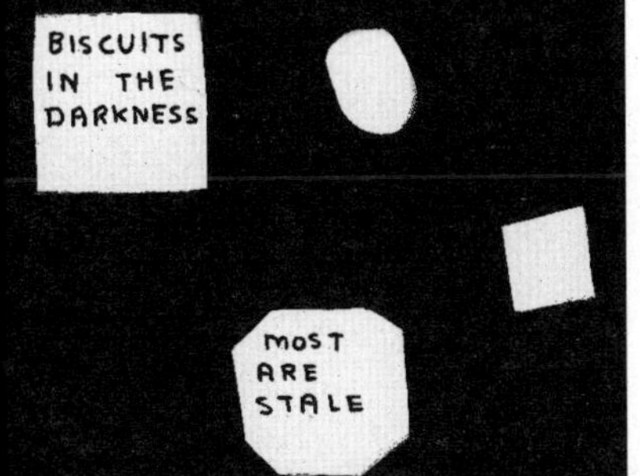

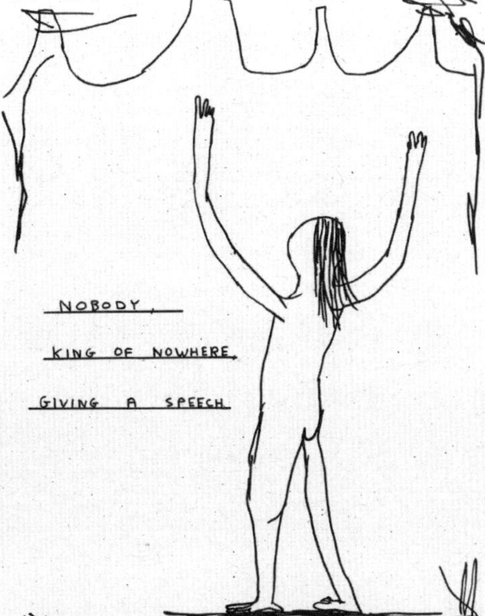

NOBODY,

KING OF NOWHERE,

GIVING A SPEECH

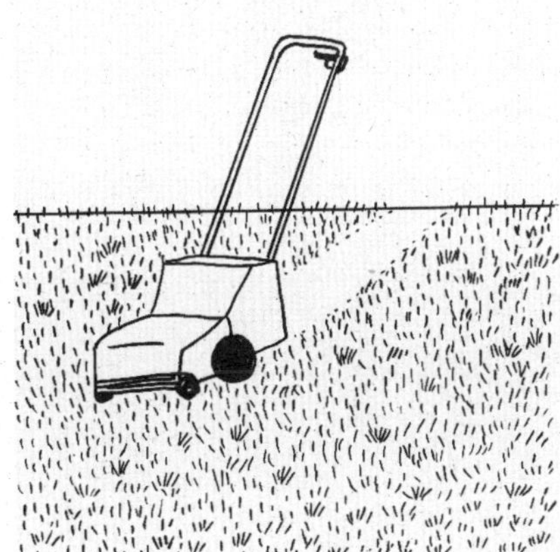

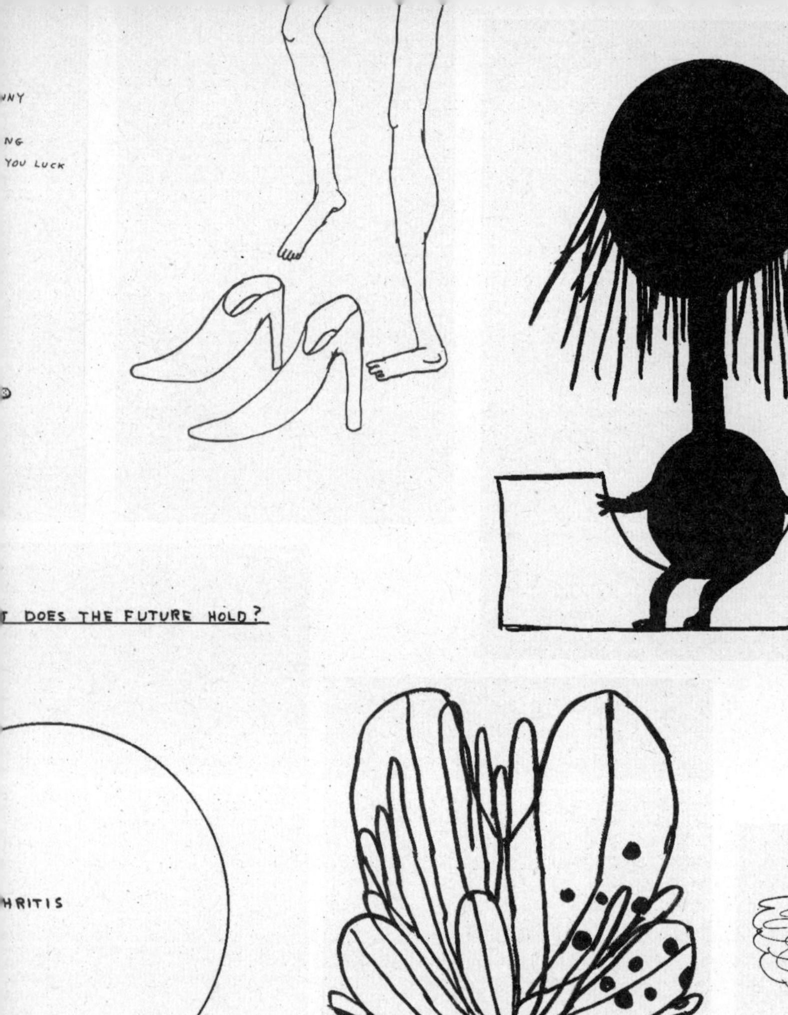

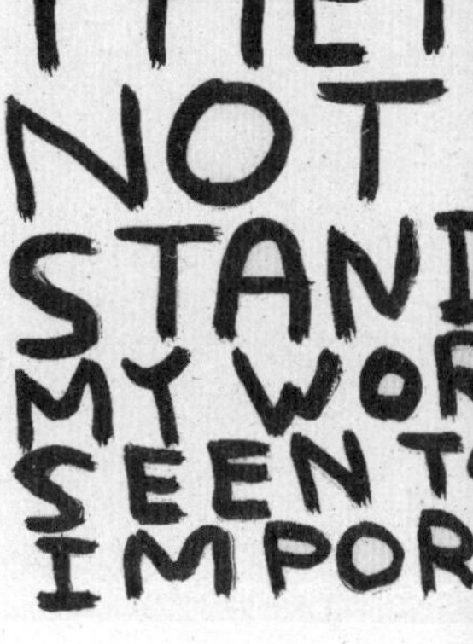

T DOES THE FUTURE HOLD?

HRITIS

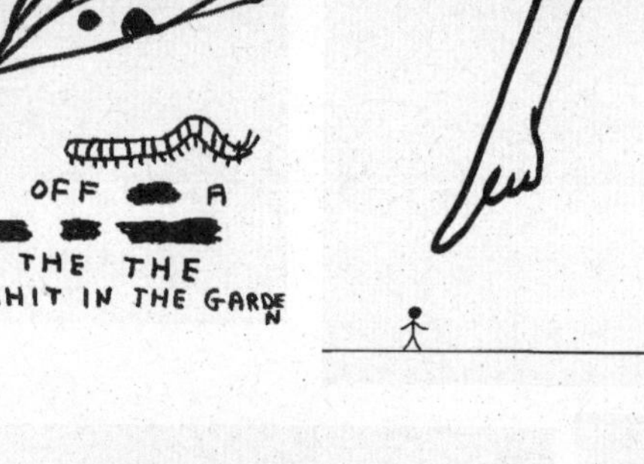

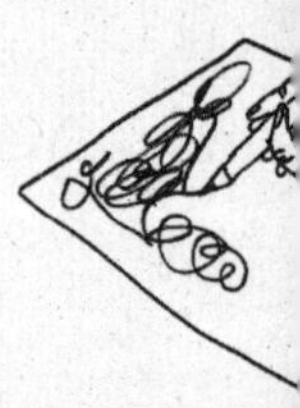

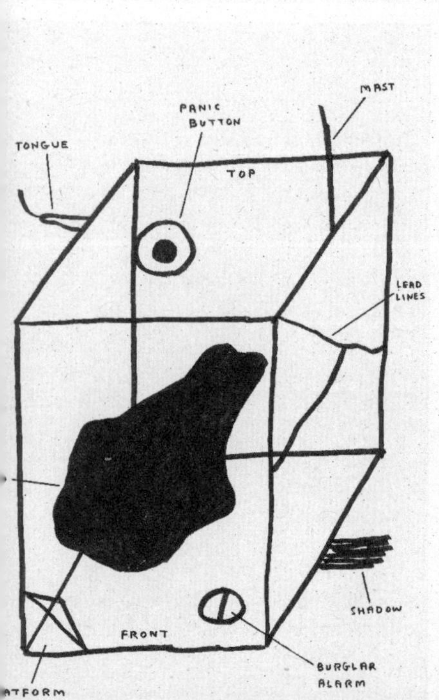

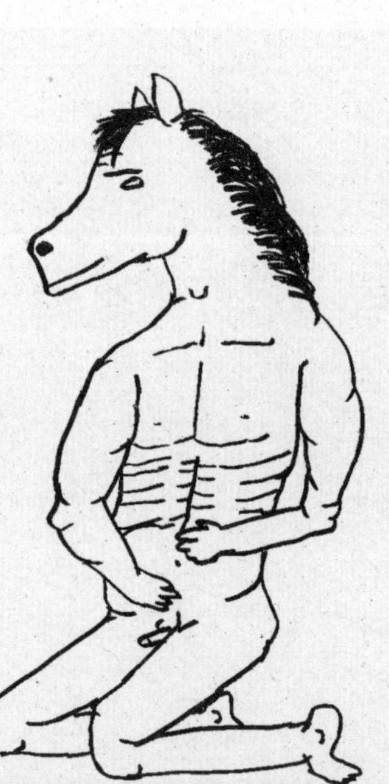

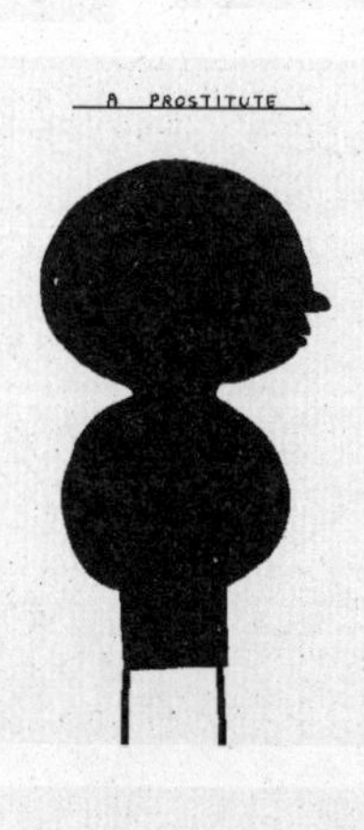

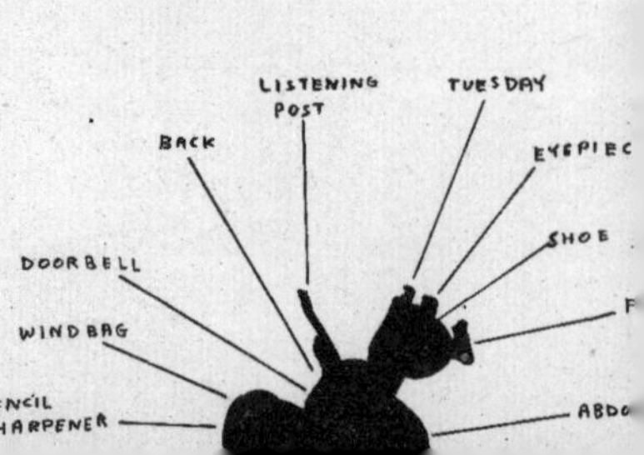

OLLECT ON THE SURFACE
M WITH MY SHARP FINGER

SEPTEMBER

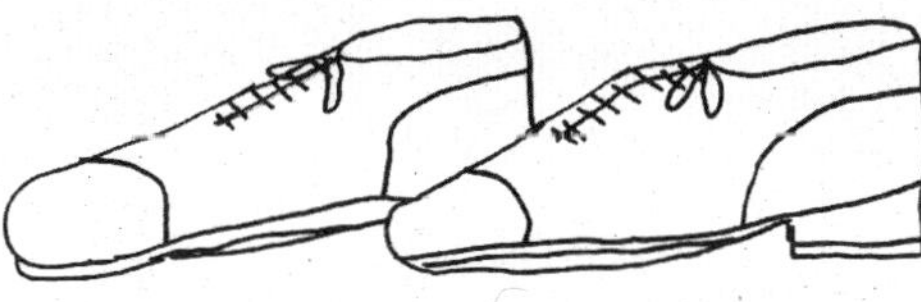

I HAVE GONE SWIMMING IN THE SEA
PLEASE POLISH MY SHOES WHILE I AM GONE
IF I DO NOT COME BACK
TELL EVERYONE I WAS A GOOD PERSON

APRIL

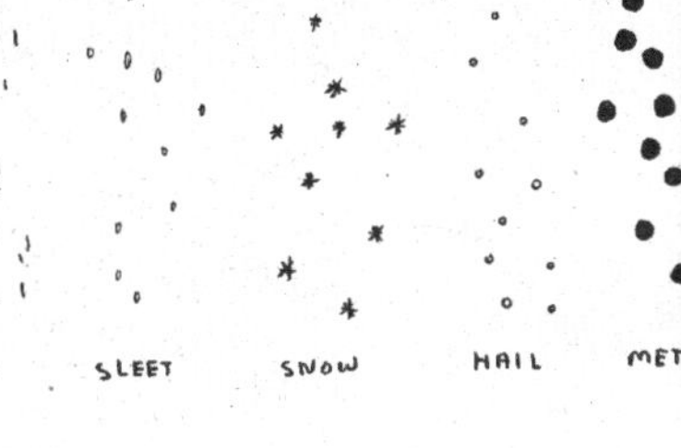

RAIN   SLEET   SNOW   HAIL   META

O
NDER
WHY
ARE
SO
N

JARY

H OF THE YEAR
AURY I WRITE
S THAT I MUST DO.

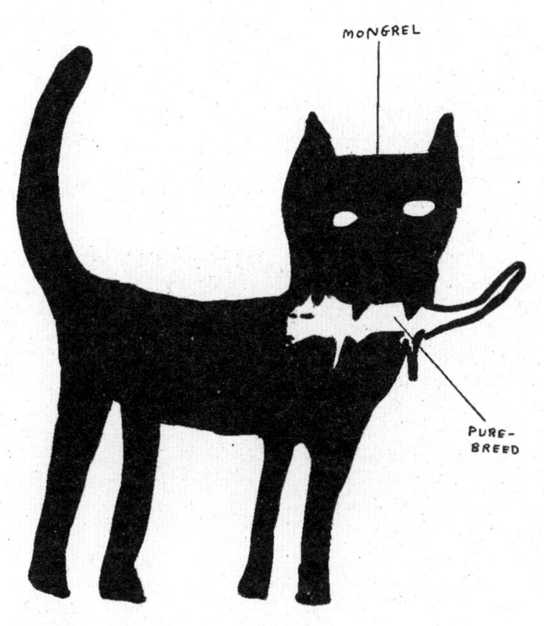

MONGREL
PURE-
BREED

PORN

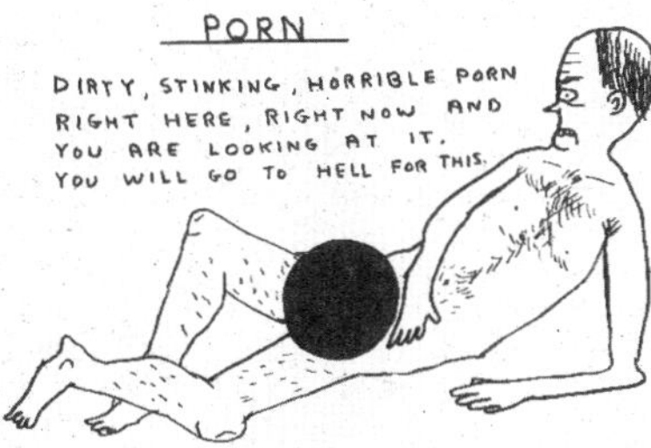

DIRTY, STINKING, HORRIBLE PORN
RIGHT HERE, RIGHT NOW AND
YOU ARE LOOKING AT IT.
YOU WILL GO TO HELL FOR THIS.

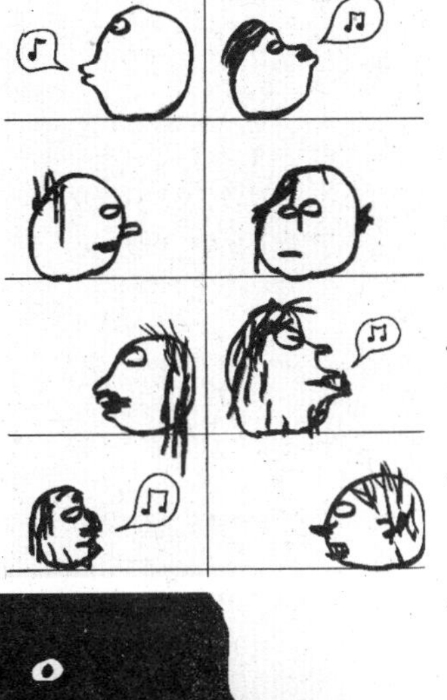

SOME WHISTLE SOME DON'T

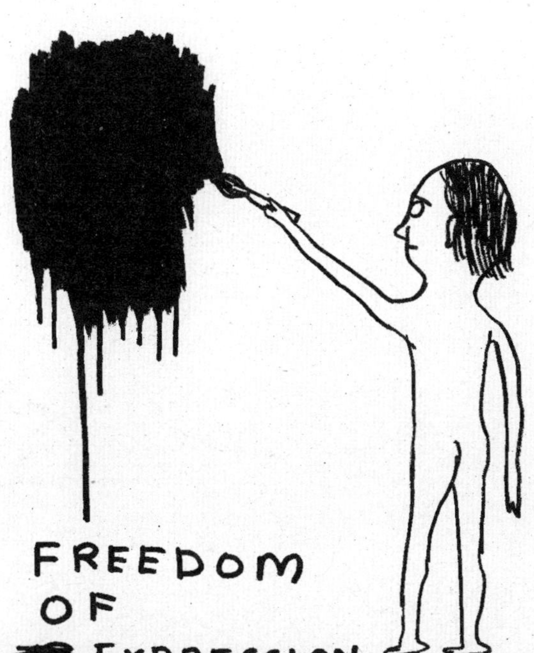

FREEDOM
OF
EXPRESSION

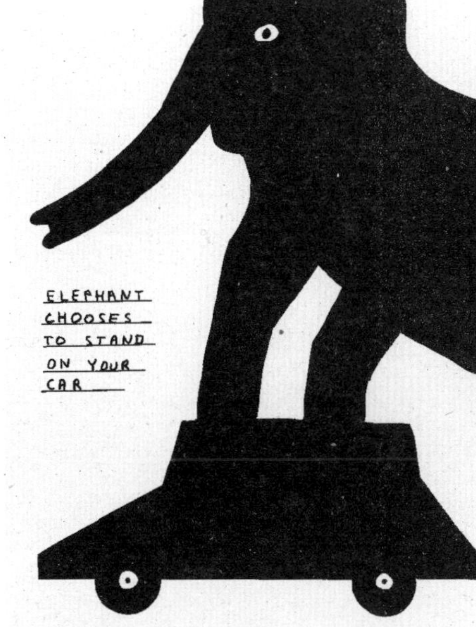

ELEPHANT
CHOOSES
TO STAND
ON YOUR
CAR

OUR HO
AIR
MUM
WARMTH

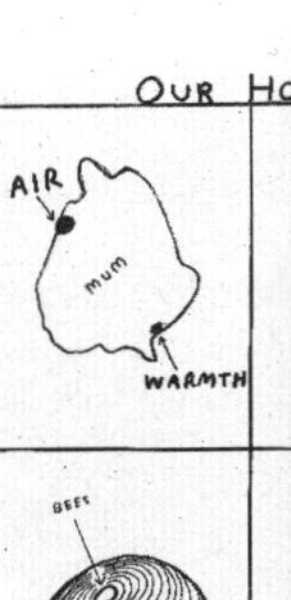

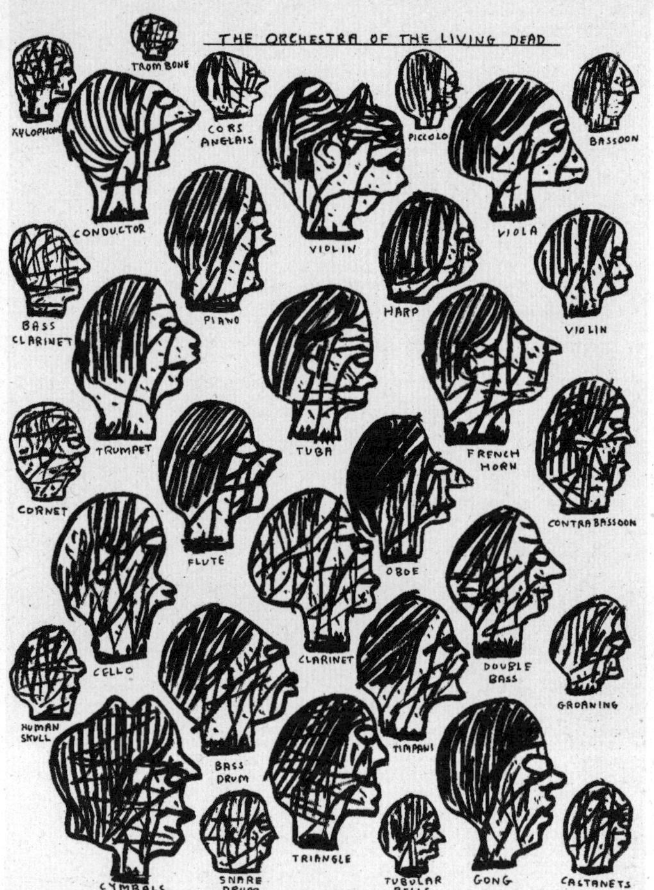

THE ORCHESTRA OF THE LIVING DEAD
TROMBONE
XYLOPHONE
CORS ANGLAIS
PICCOLO
BASSOON
CONDUCTOR
VIOLIN
VIOLA
BASS CLARINET
PIANO
HARP
VIOLIN
TRUMPET
TUBA
FRENCH HORN
CORNET
CONTRABASSOON
FLUTE
OBOE
CELLO
CLARINET
DOUBLE BASS
GROANING
HUMAN SKULL
BASS DRUM
TIMPANI
CYMBALS
SNARE DRUM
TRIANGLE
TUBULAR BELLS
GONG
CASTANETS

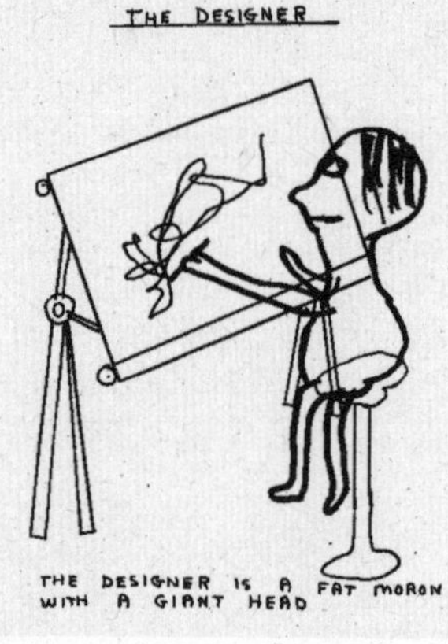

THE DESIGNER
THE DESIGNER IS A FAT MORON WITH A GIANT HEAD

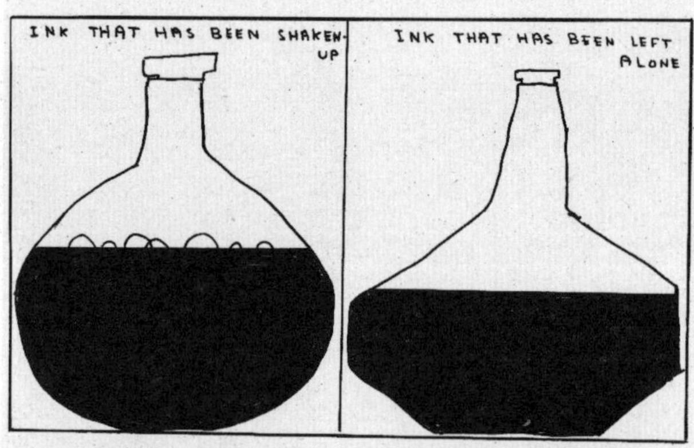

INK THAT HAS BEEN SHAKEN-UP
INK THAT HAS BEEN LEFT ALONE

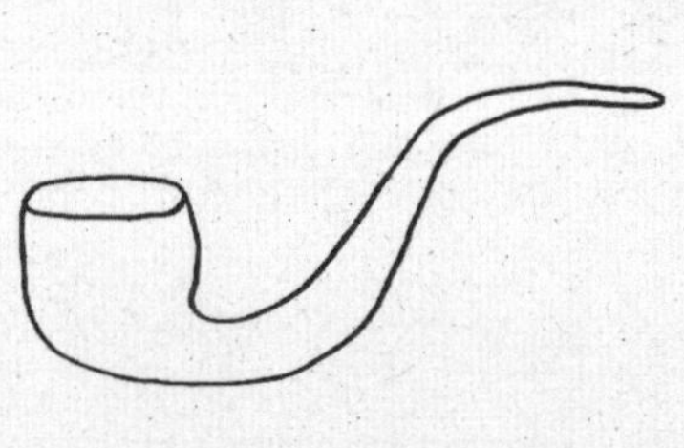

THIS IS NOTHING

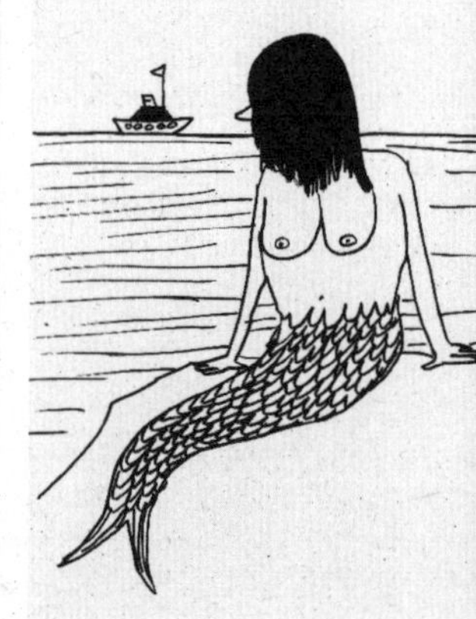

BITCH

RE YOU
ATE AT
IGHT OR
RE YOU
ARLY IN
HE MORN ?

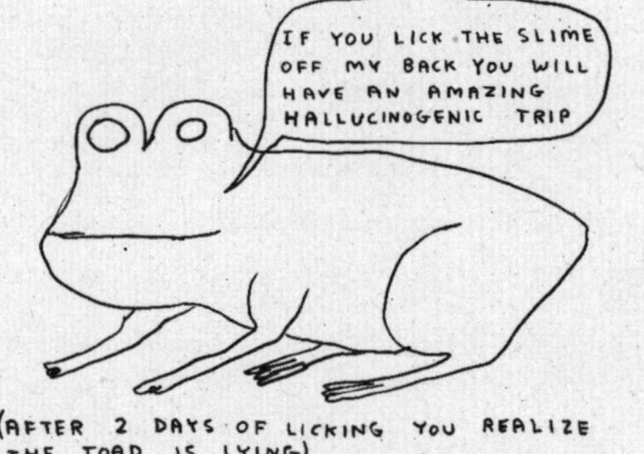

IF YOU LICK THE SLIME OFF MY BACK YOU WILL HAVE AN AMAZING HALLUCINOGENIC TRIP

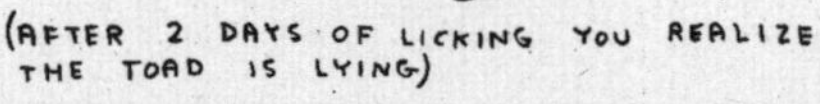

(AFTER 2 DAYS OF LICKING YOU REALIZE THE TOAD IS LYING)

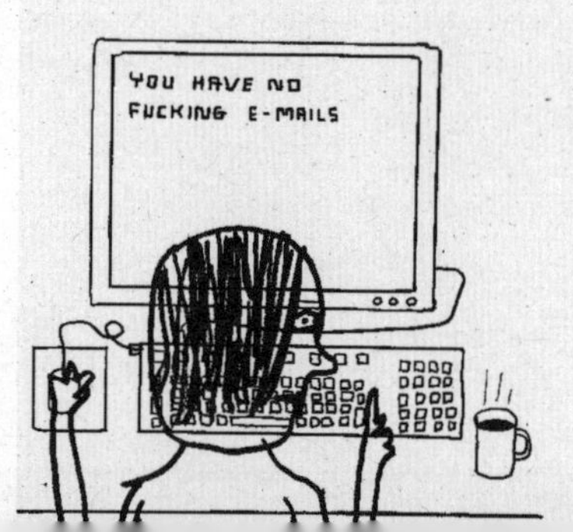

YOU HAVE NO FUCKING E-MAILS

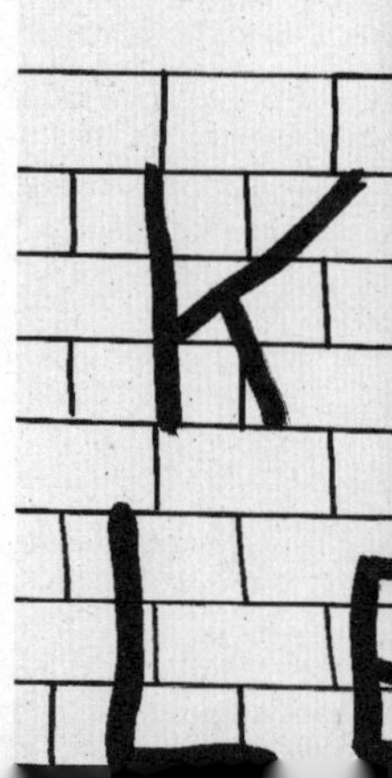

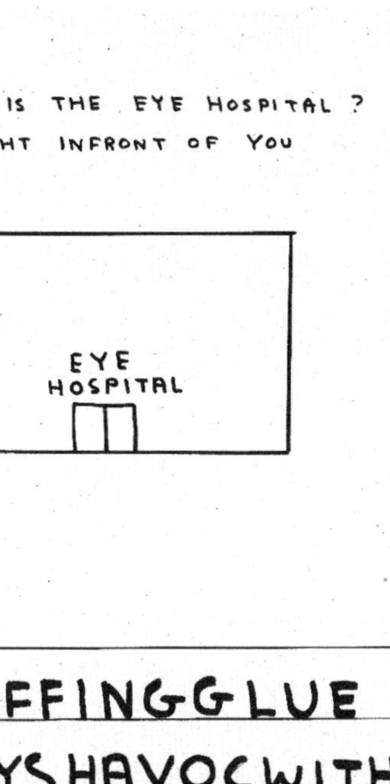

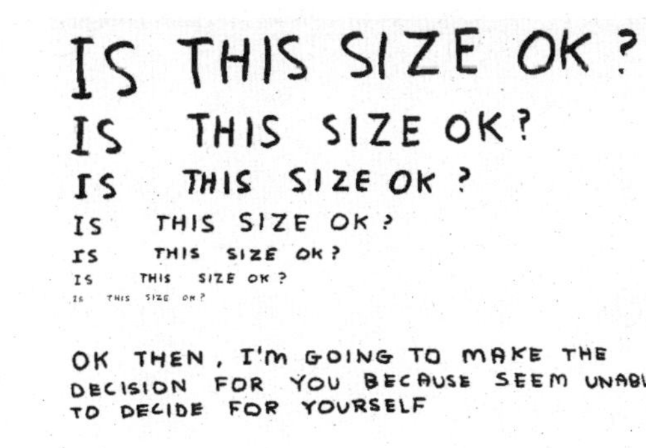

IFFINGGLUE
YSHAVOCWITH
ESABILITYTOUN
RSTANDTHEWRIT
N WORD

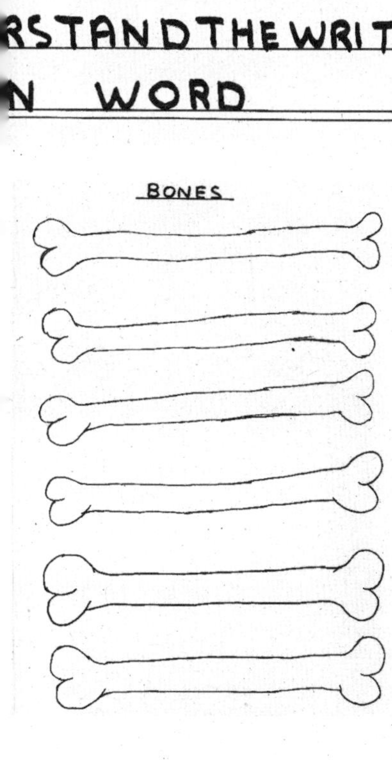

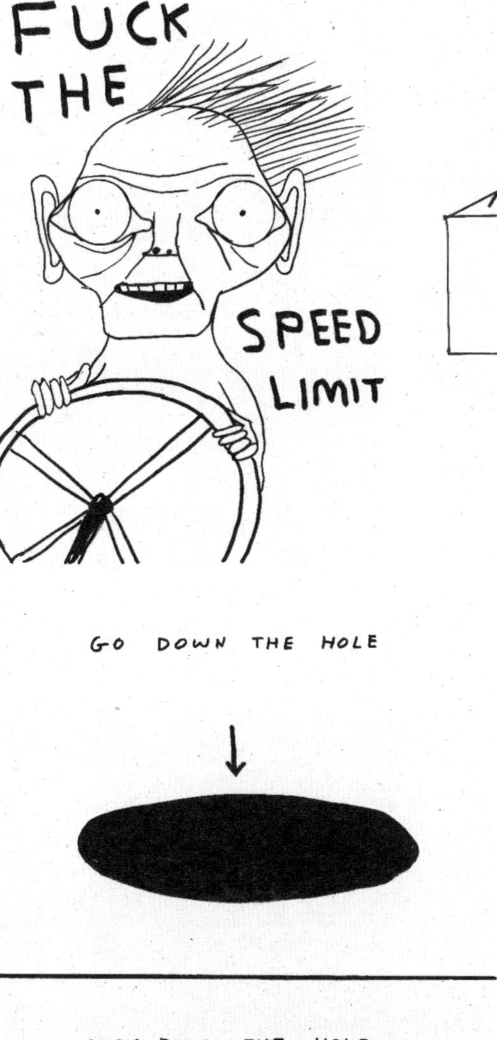

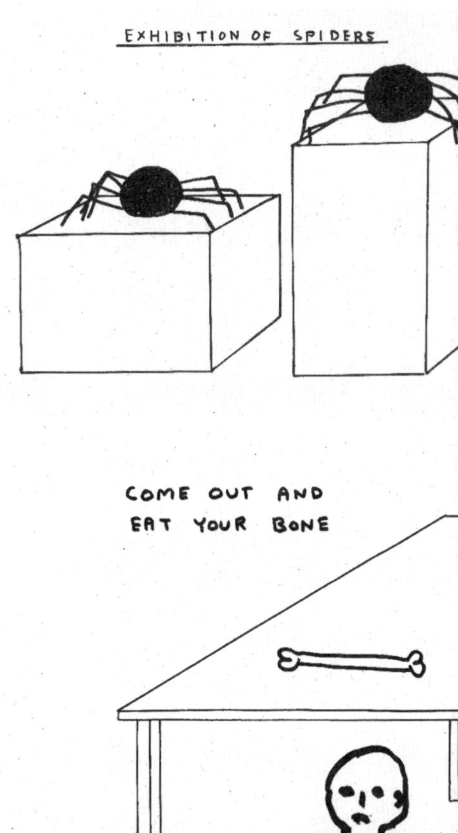

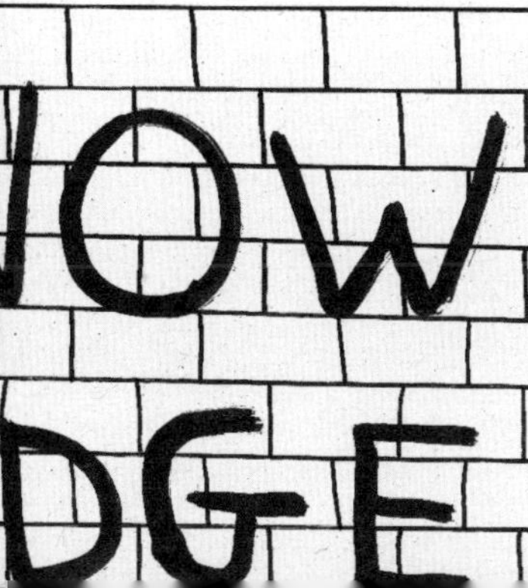

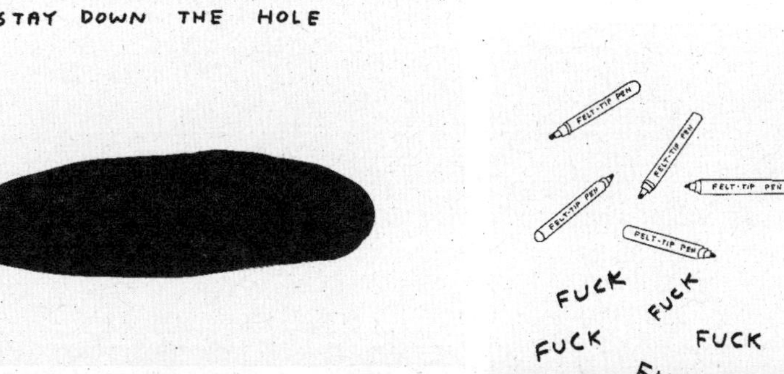

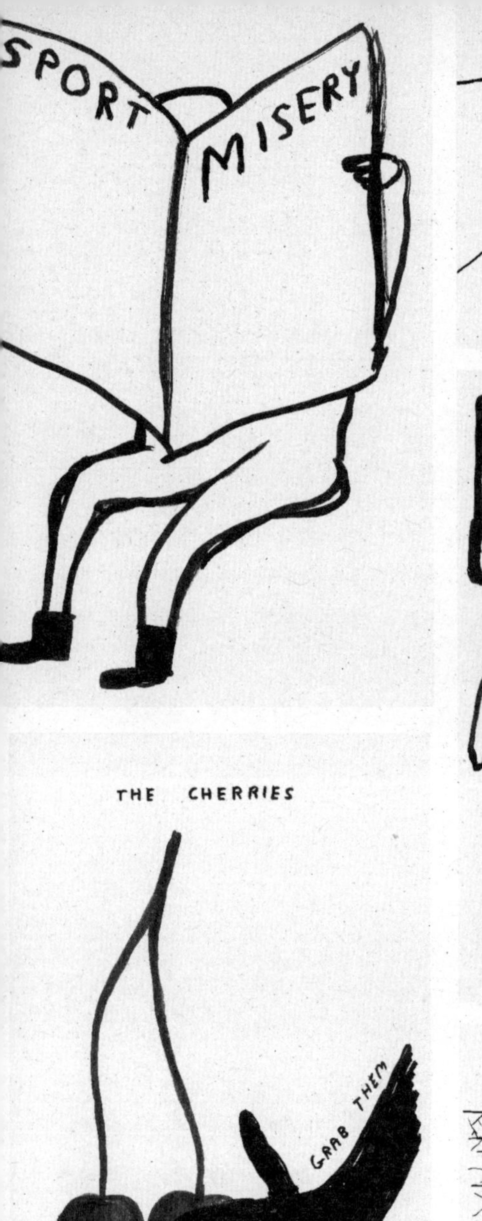

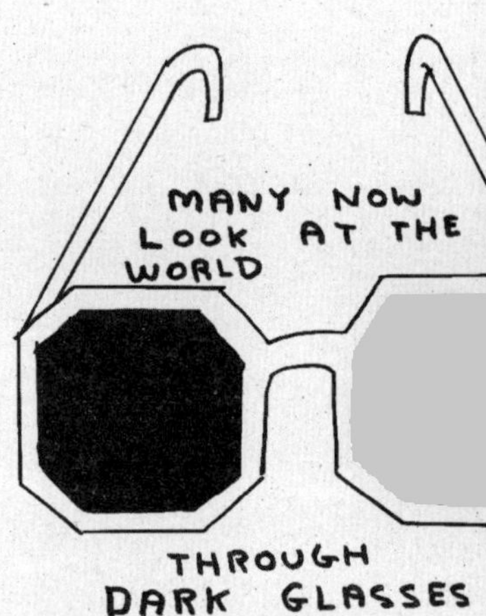

THE CHERRIES

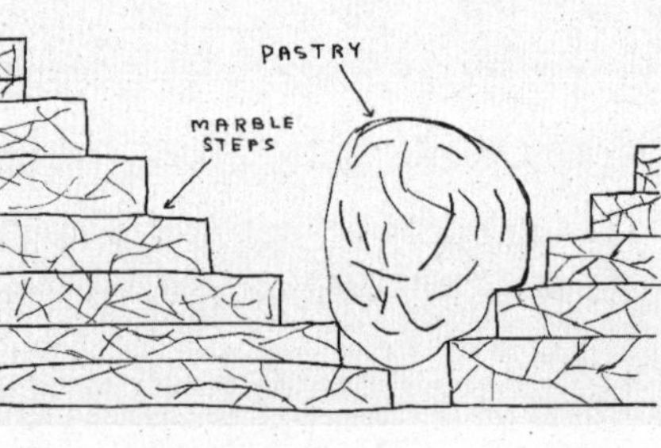

ALLOW ME TO DANCE
FOR YOU

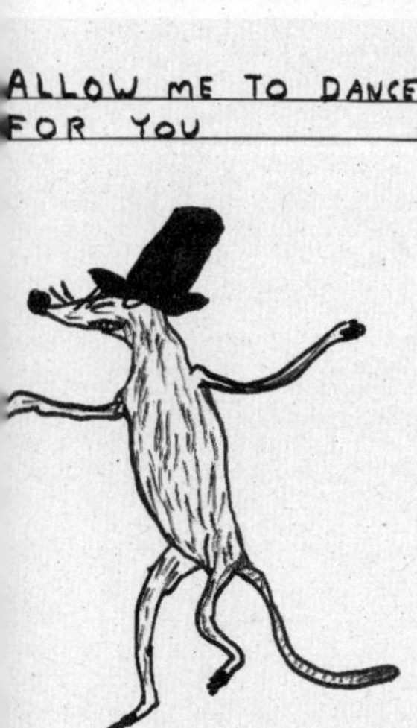

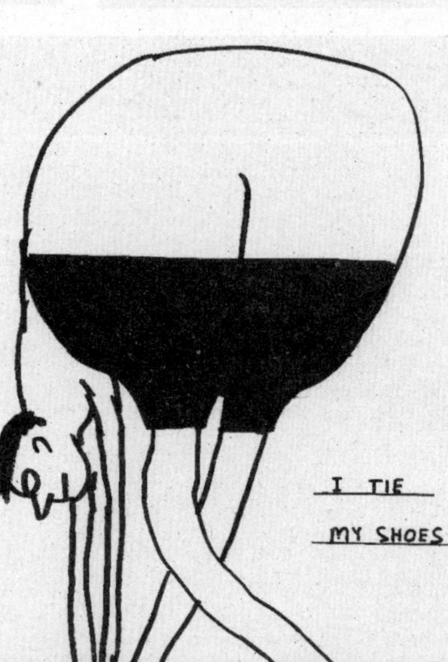

I'm
LEAV

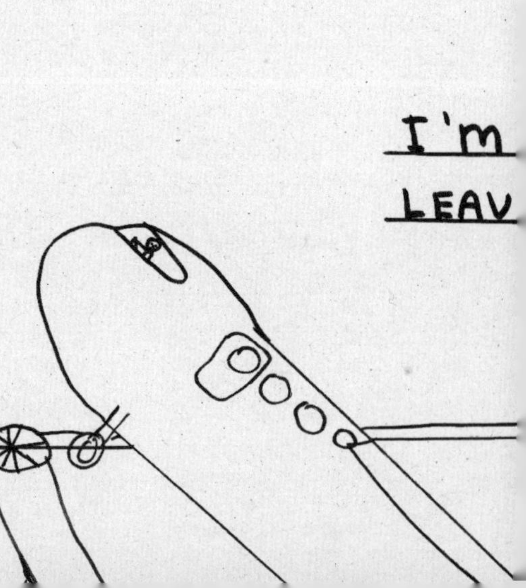

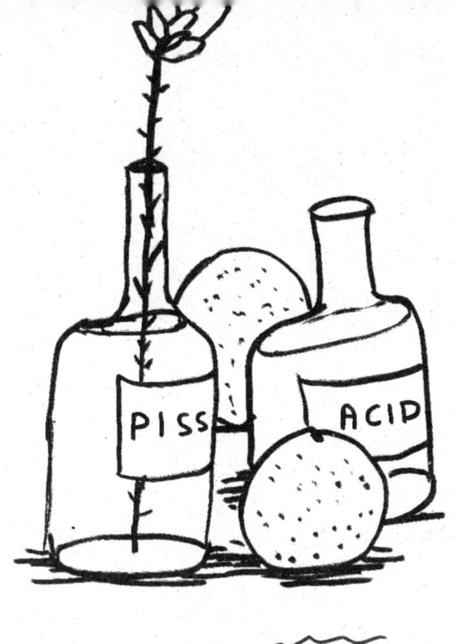

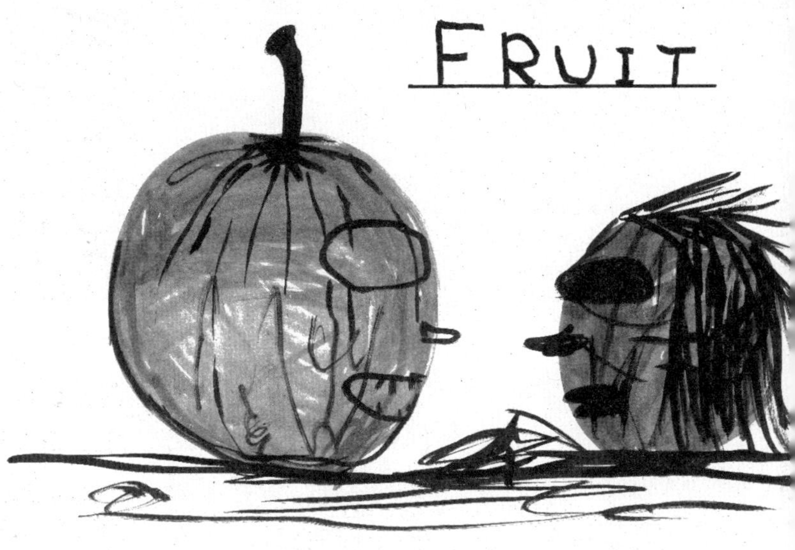

FRUIT

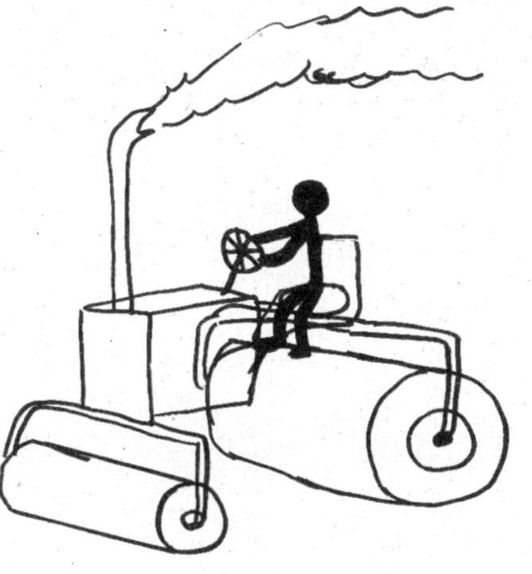

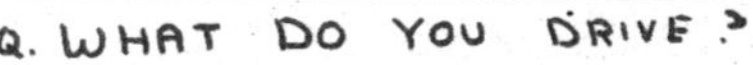

Q. WHAT DO YOU DRIVE?
A. I DRIVE A STEAM ROLLER
Q. WHERE DO YOU PARK IT?
A. I PARK IT WHEREVER I
   FUCKING LIKE.

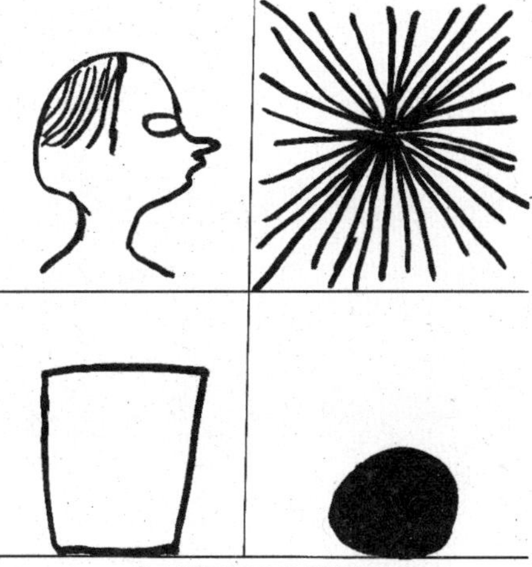

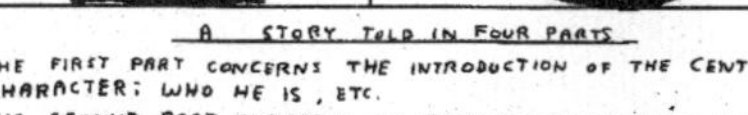

A STORY TOLD IN FOUR PARTS

THE FIRST PART CONCERNS THE INTRODUCTION OF THE CENTRAL
CHARACTER; WHO HE IS, ETC.
THE SECOND PART CONCERNS AN ▬▬ EXTRAORDINARY EVENT
THAT BEFALLS THE CENTRAL CHARACTER.
THE THIRD PART CONCERNS HOW THE CENTRAL CHARACTER
DEALS WITH THE EXTRAORDINARY EVENT THROUGH SUBSTANCE
ABUSE.
THE FORTH PART IS THE CONCLUSION ▬▬▬ ▬▬▬ WHICH,
WHILST IT PROVIDES CLOSURE, LEAVES ROOM FOR A
CONTINUATION OF THE STORY.

HELP

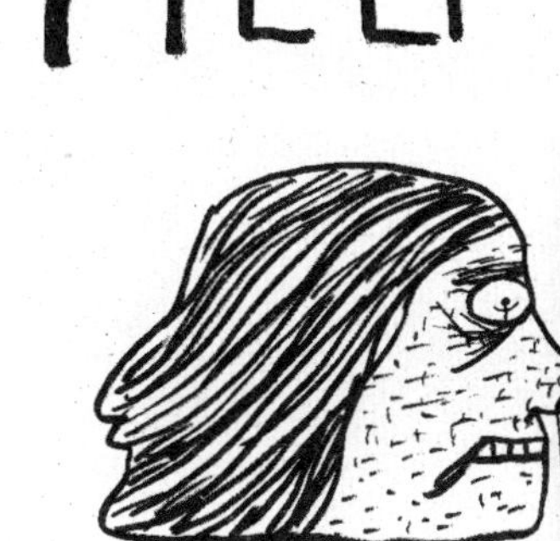

GO A

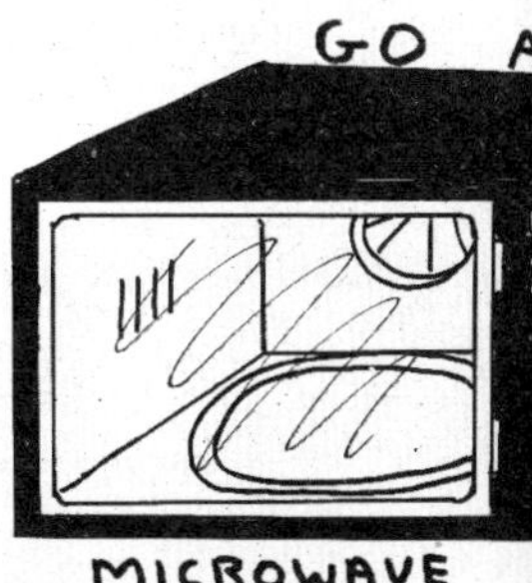

MICROWAVE
YOURSELF

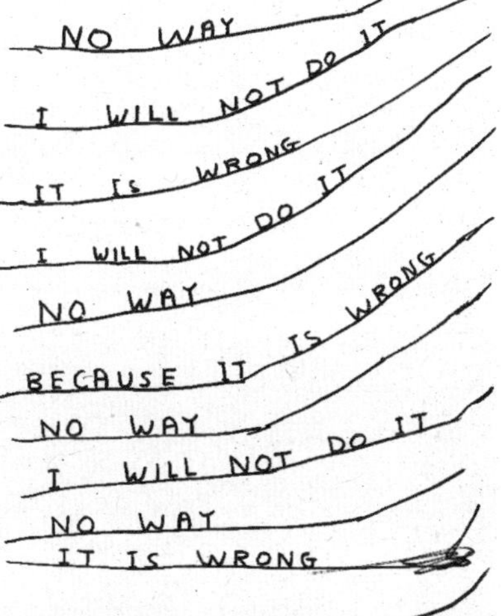

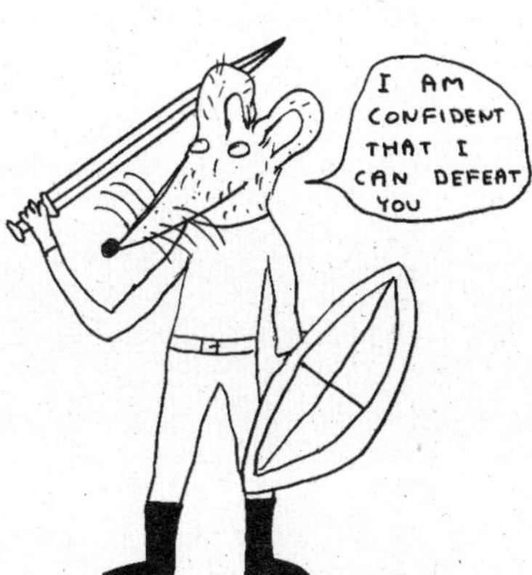

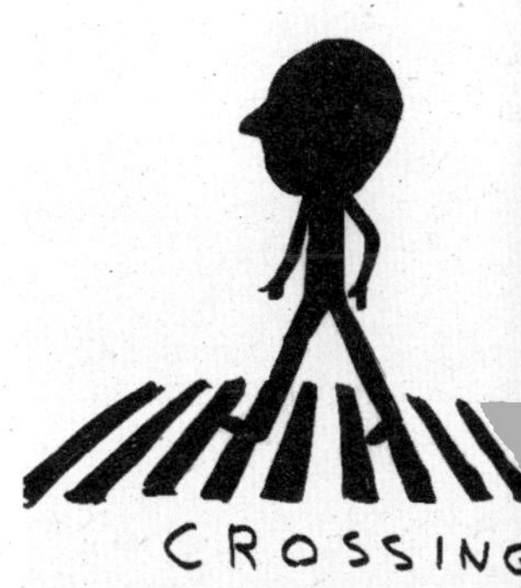

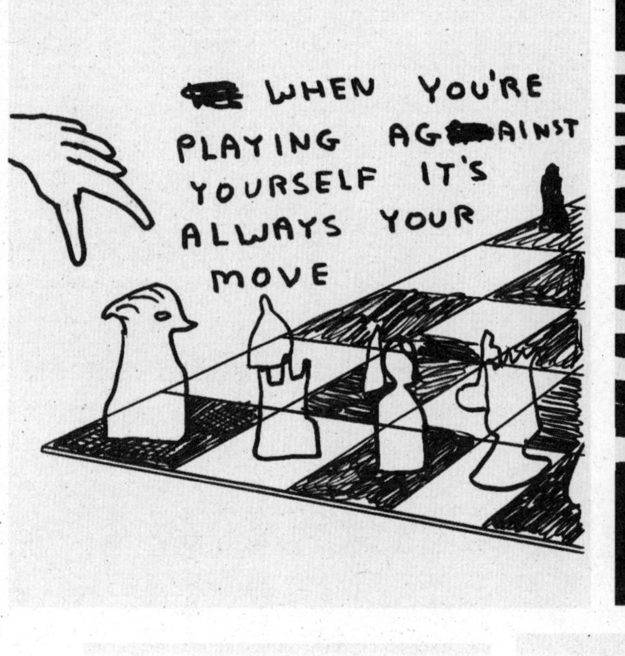

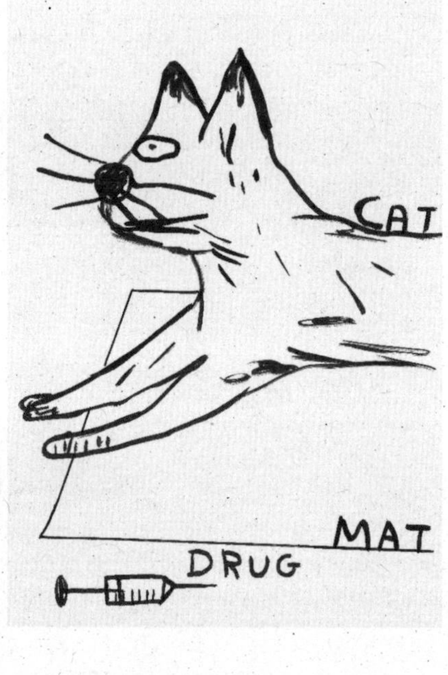

FEEL
MY
INK

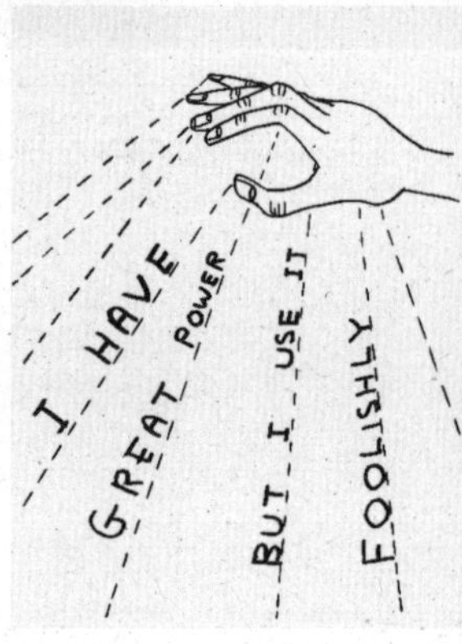

YOU BUILD BRIDGES

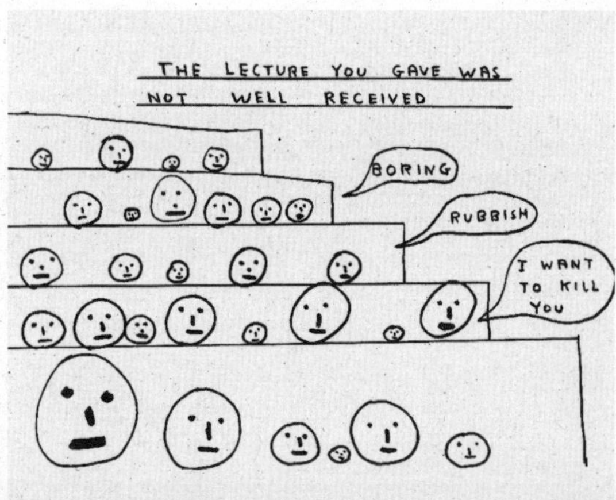

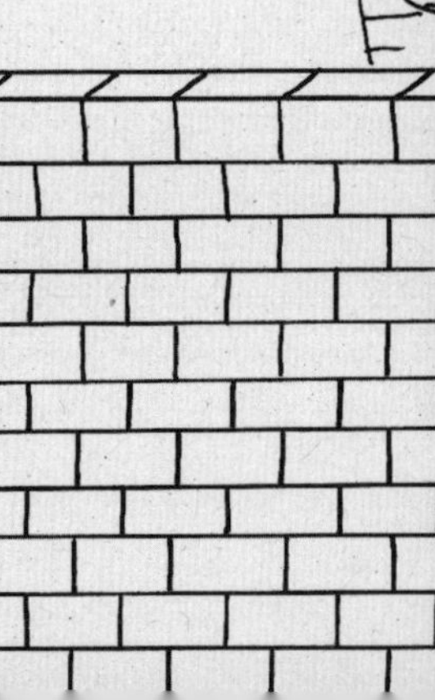

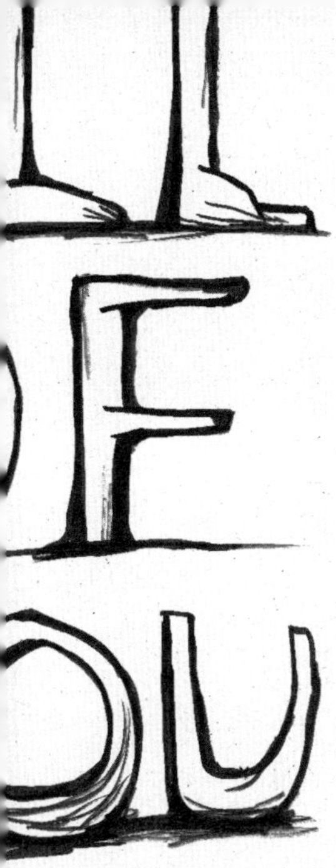

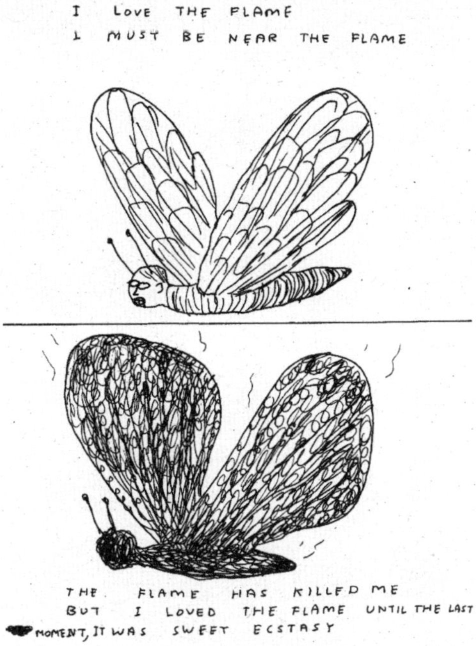

OF
OU

I LOVE THE FLAME
I MUST BE NEAR THE FLAME

THE FLAME HAS KILLED ME
BUT I LOVED THE FLAME UNTIL THE LAST
MOMENT, IT WAS SWEET ECSTASY

<u>IT'S OK</u>
<u>I'M OK</u>

Y CAMPING HOLIDAY
HAVE TO HAVE SEPARATE
BECAUSE WE ALL

ILD WALLS

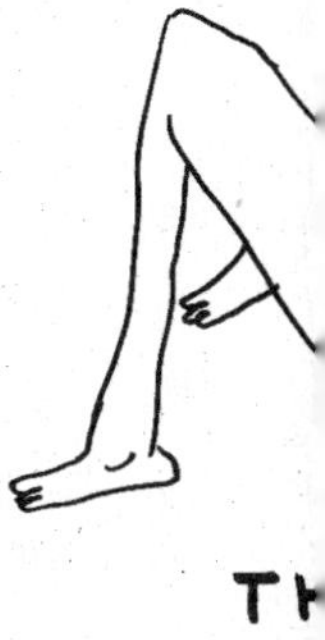

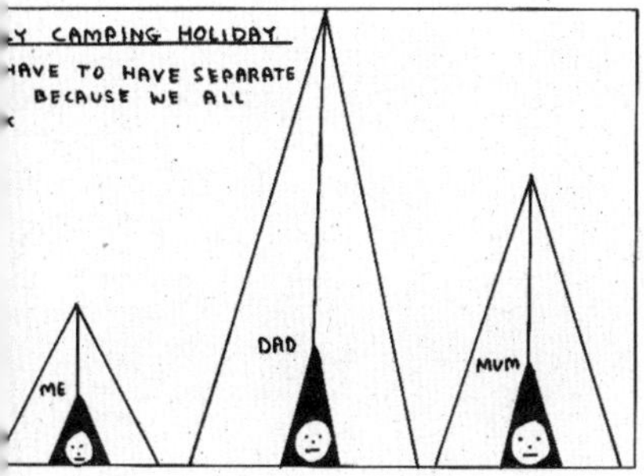

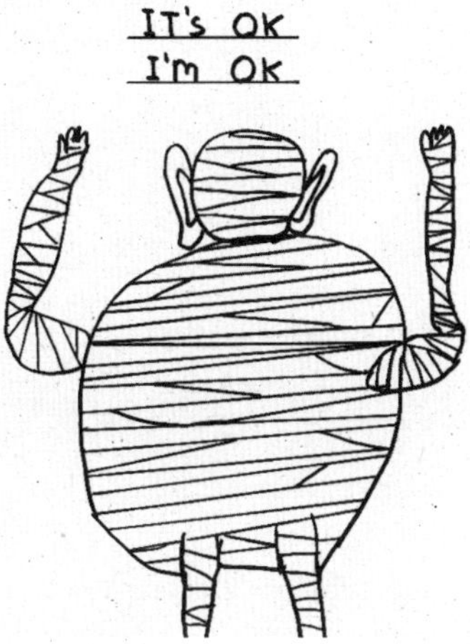

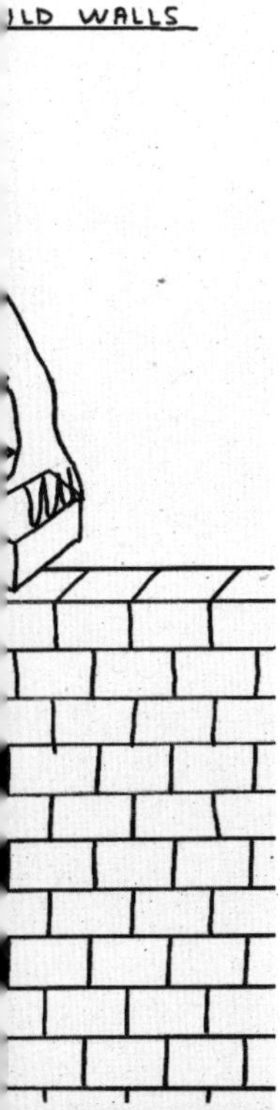

THIS IS TO TELL YOU ABOUT THE BARN DANCE

IT IS ON SUNDAY AT 8PM
IN THE BARN

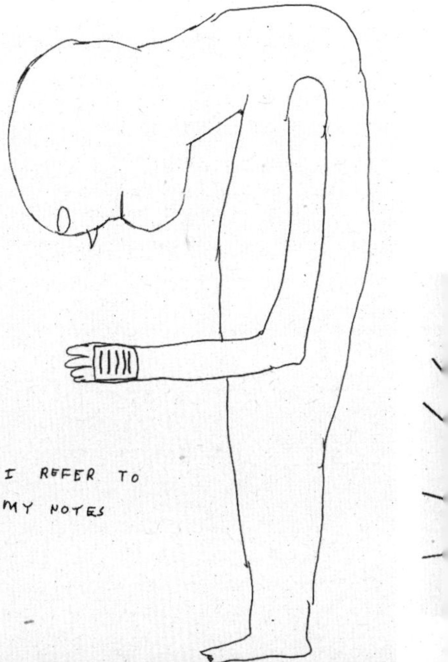

CHANGE

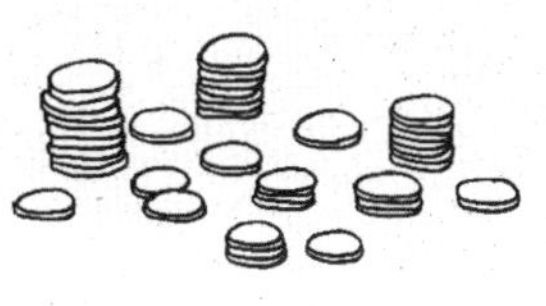

PLOYS HOLP ME

TH

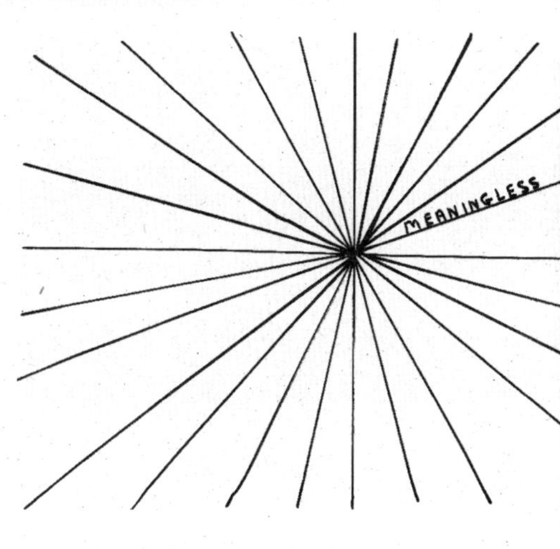

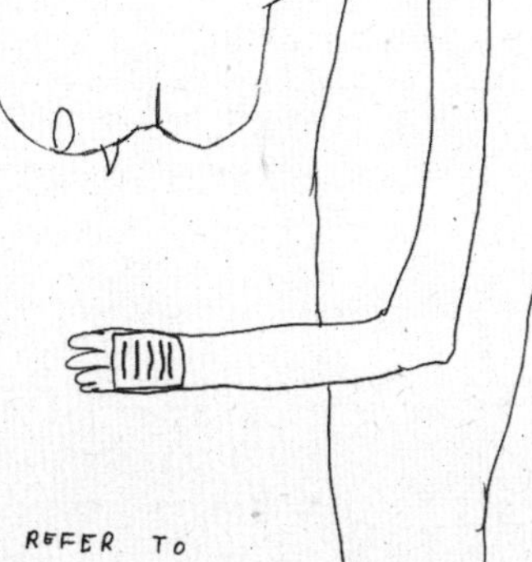

I REFER TO
MY NOTES

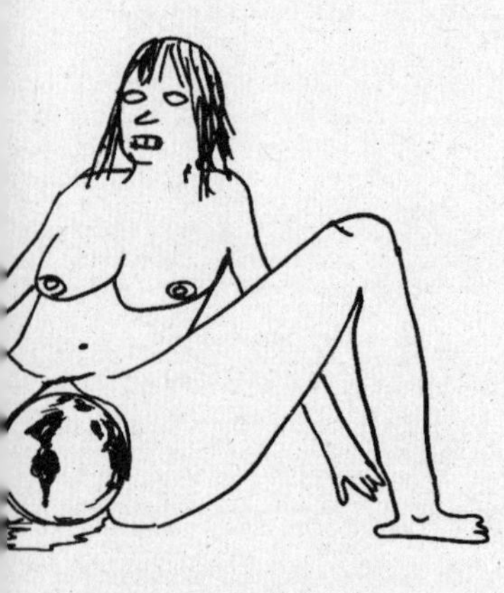

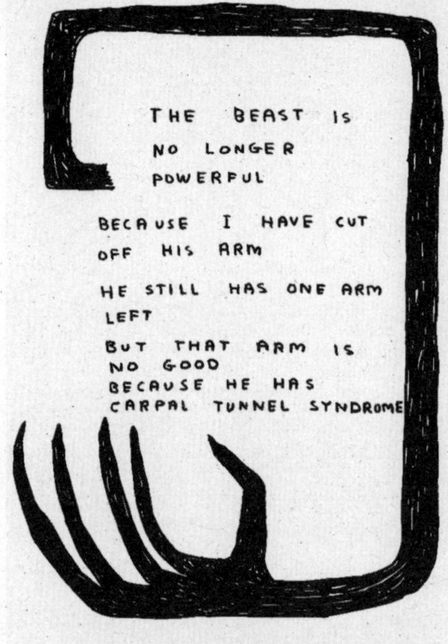

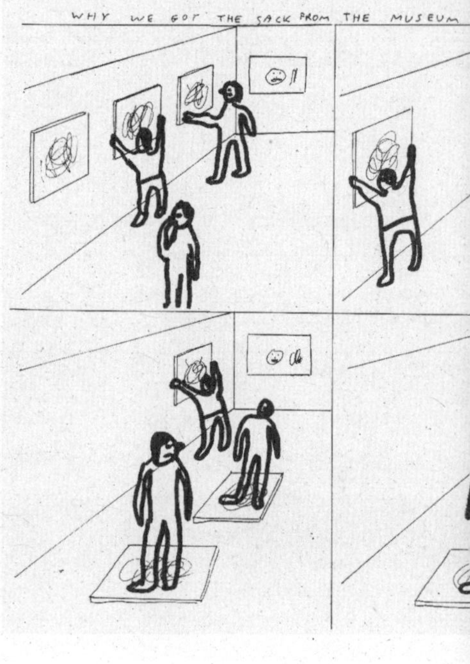

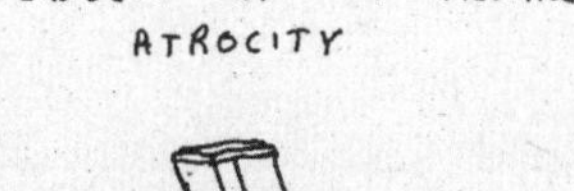

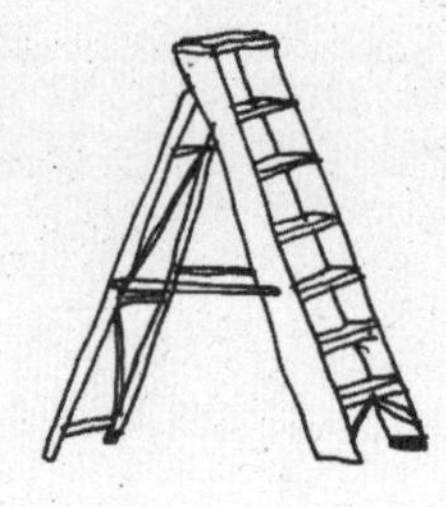

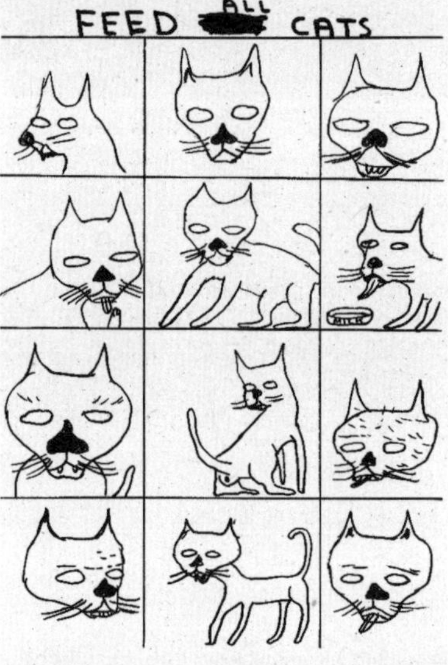

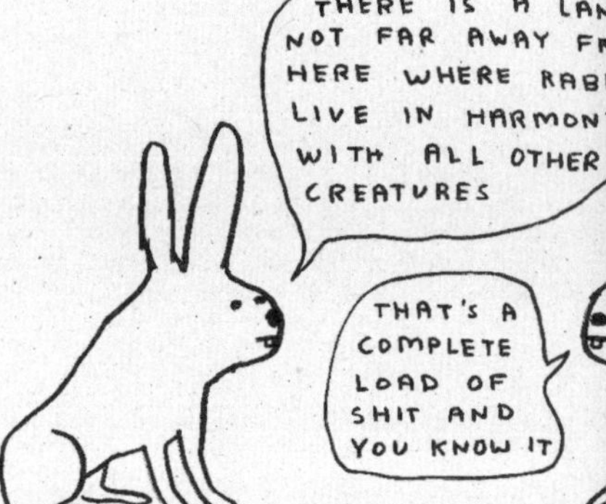

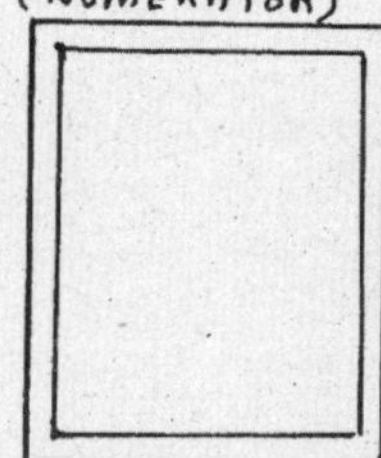

THE
HER
IS U
-NEAT
ASPR

AVANT-GARDE FILMS DIRECT TO YOUR T.V.
VIA CABLE OR SATELLITE
UNLESS YOU STOP MASTURBATING

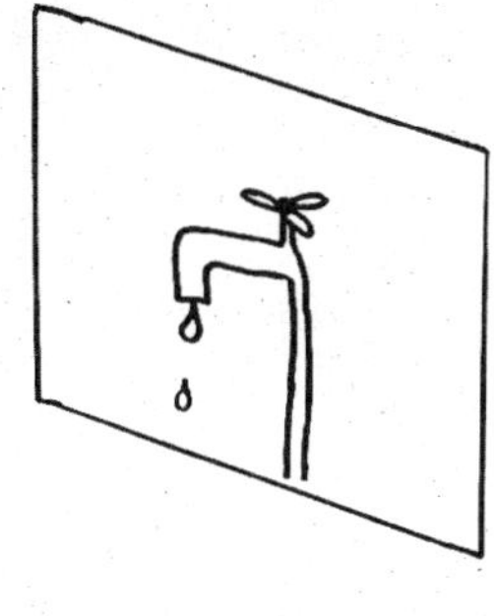

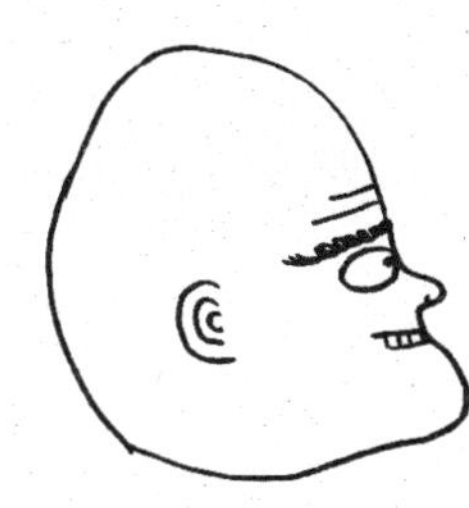

DRUGS

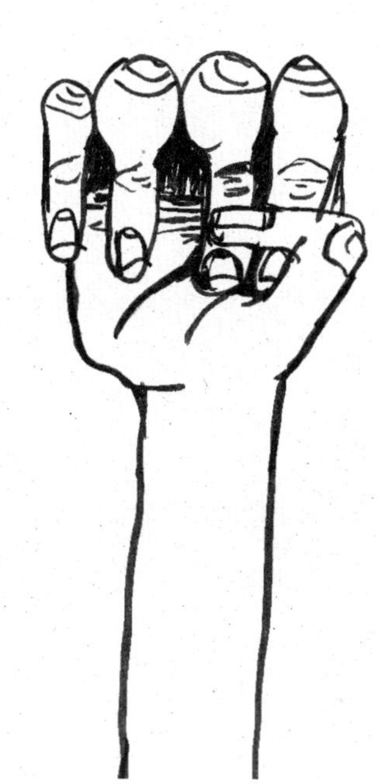

YOU CANNOT HELP LOOKING AT THIS

BIRD ON A WIRE GETTING ELECTROCUTED

IN
DER
THE
IS

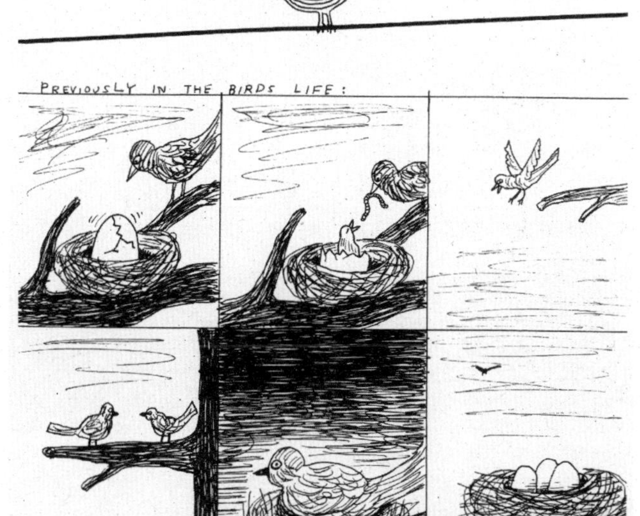

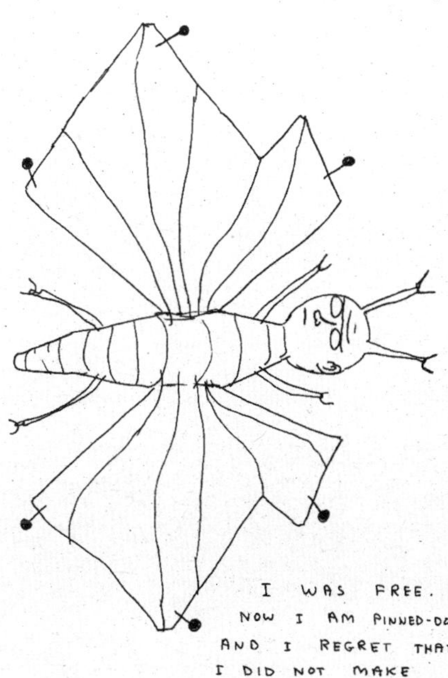

I WAS FREE.
NOW I AM PINNED-DOWN
AND I REGRET THAT
I DID NOT MAKE
MORE OF MY FREEDOM

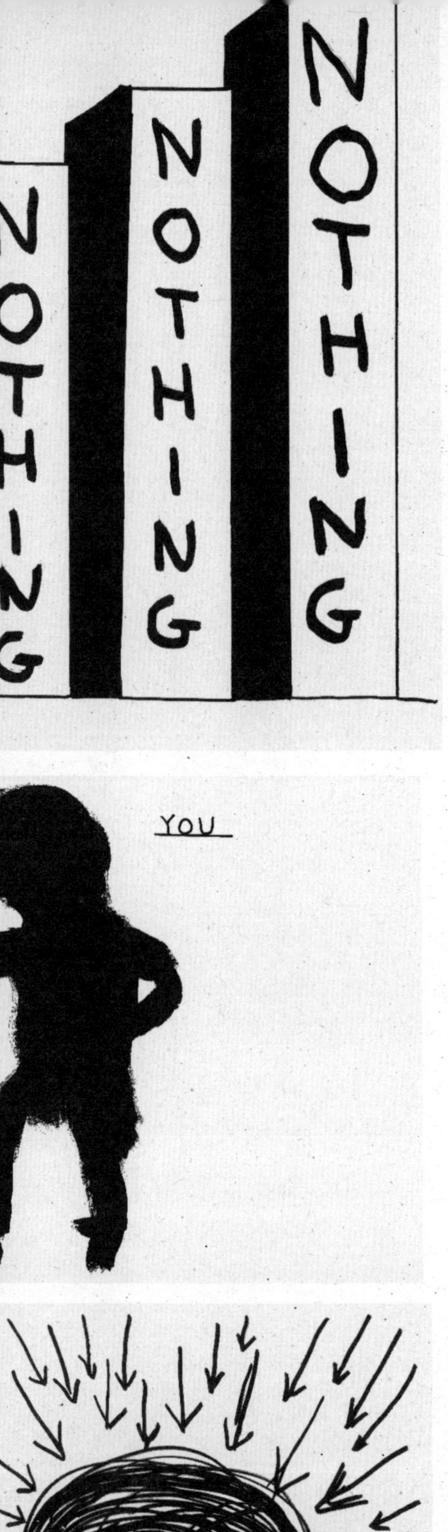

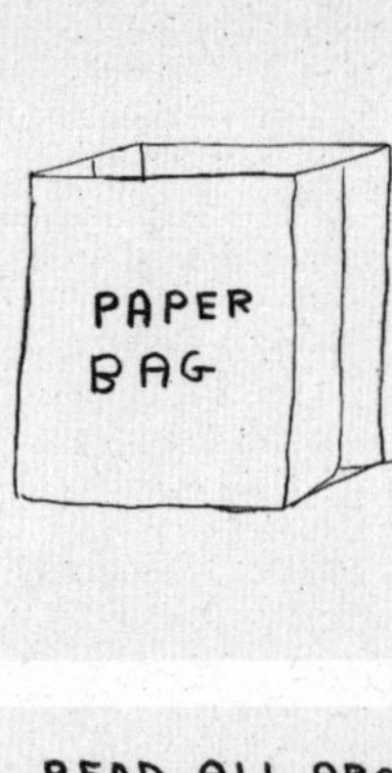

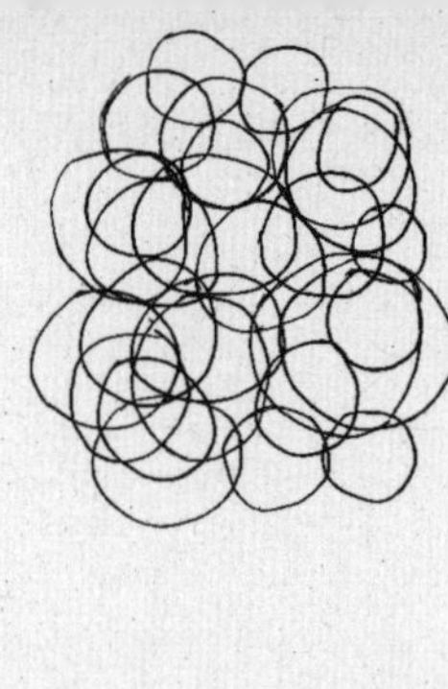

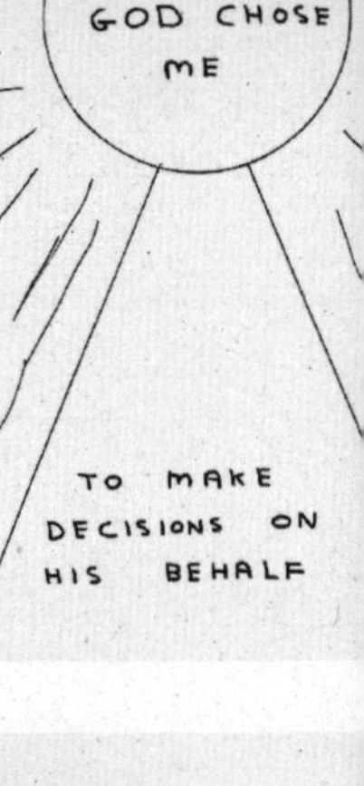

READ ALL ABOUT IT

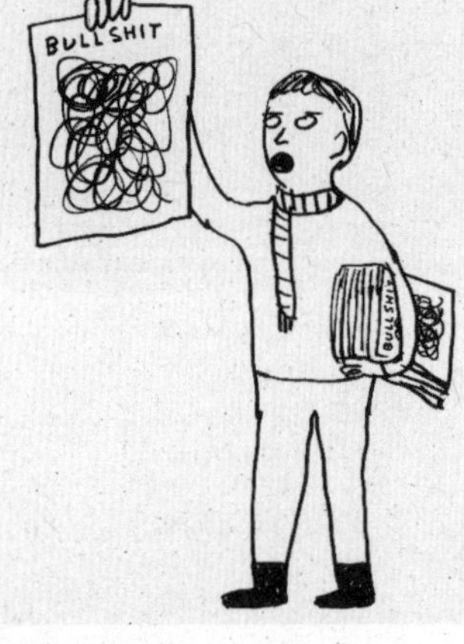

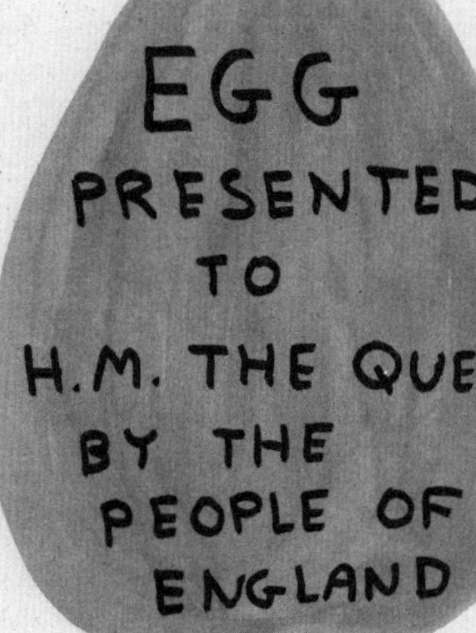

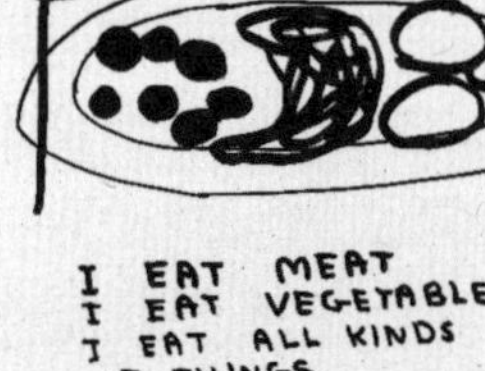

A HOUSE

AWNING

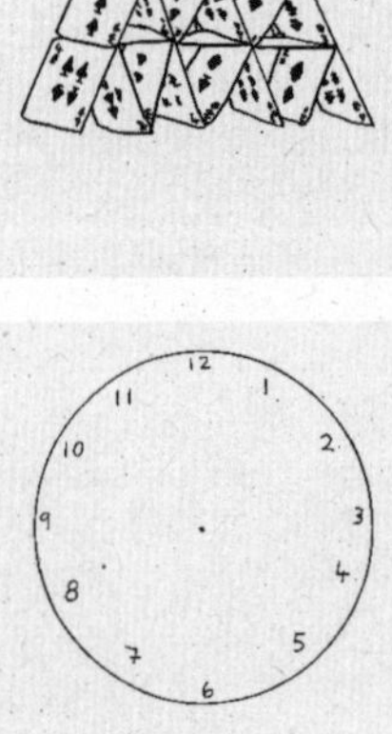
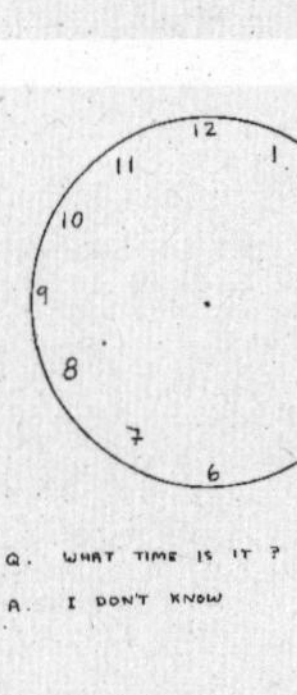
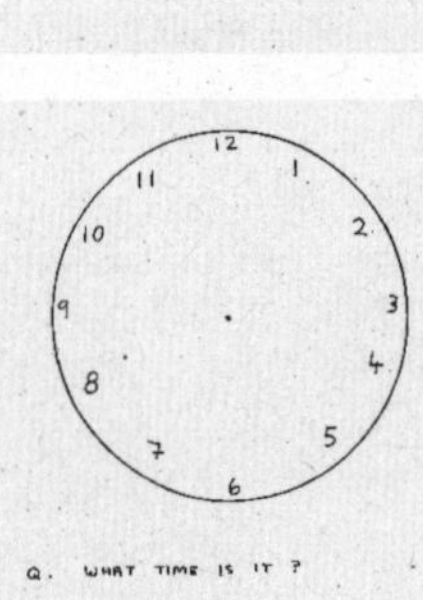
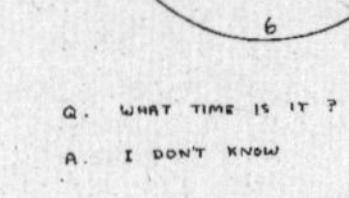

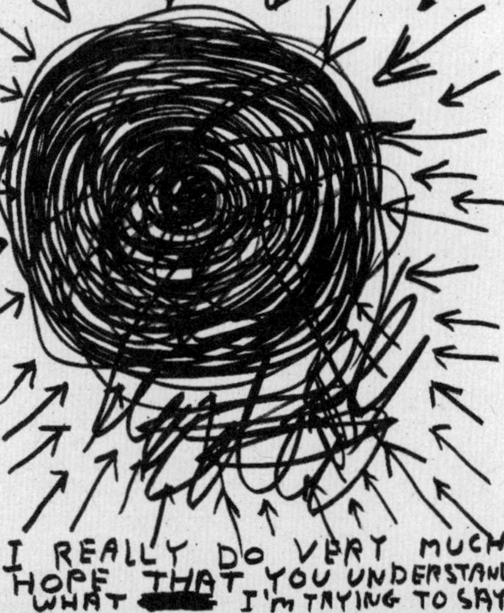

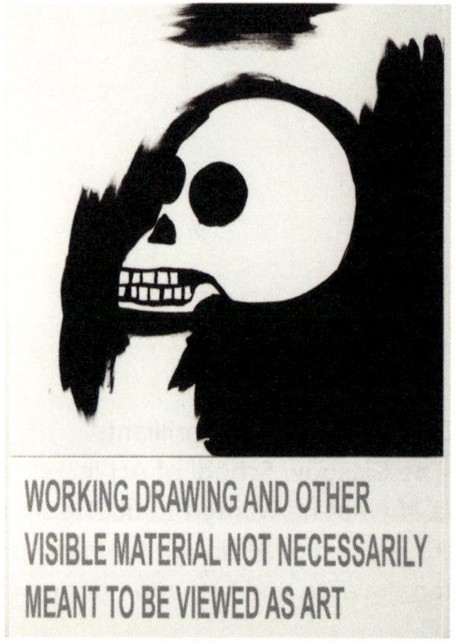

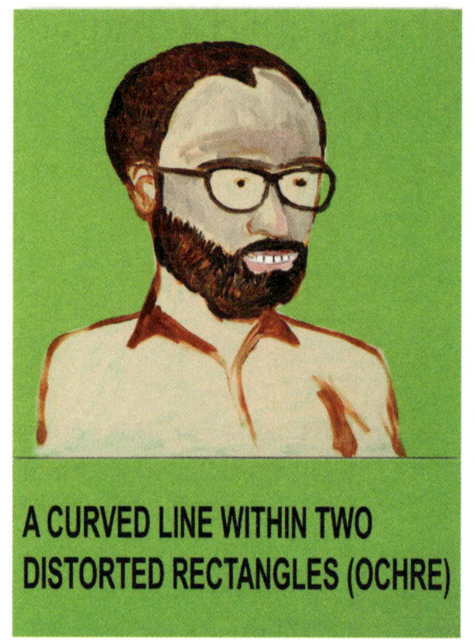

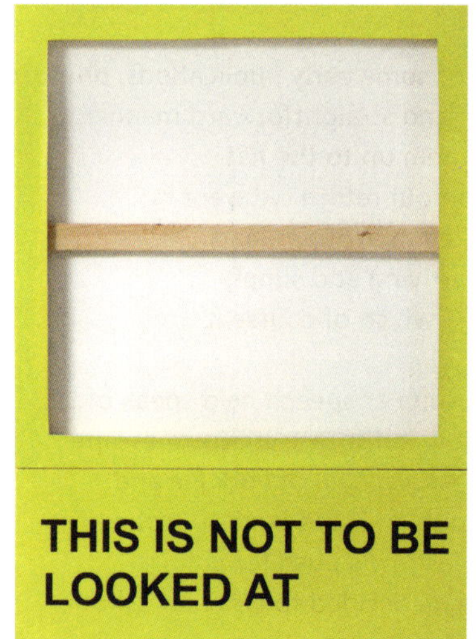

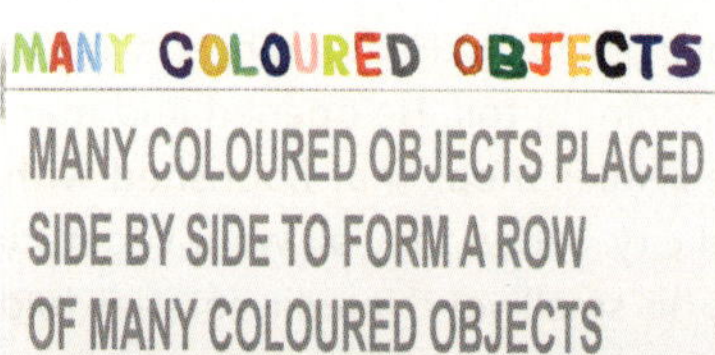

Working Drawing and Other Visible Materials, 2008. *A Curved Line Within Two Distorted Rectangles (Ochre),* 2008. *This Is Not To Be Looked At,* 2008. *Many Coloured Objects,* 2008. From a series of collaborative paintings by Jonathan Monk and David Shrigley.

Notes, Nowts and Owts
— Jonathan Monk

I think it is probably impossible to copy Mr Shrigley. Which is both crap and brilliant.

When David graduated from The Glasgow School of Art in 1991, it seemed
clear that he had a rough idea of what he wanted to do. He signed on to the
dole and lived the high life, like we all did. Although I think he soon realised
this was not for him. He started drawing and he hadn't done much of this
at art school.
These drawings did lead to other things... firstly to books and then to...
(a long list of David Shrigley works is available at the back of this publication
– width follows height).
I was involved in the piecing together of some early publications, photocopies
carefully collated and bound in a clean and straightforward manner.

One book edition arrived boxed – David proudly carried them up to the flat
from the waiting taxi. A celebratory drink followed and on our return we were
shocked to discover our front door had been brutally kicked in. Nothing had
been taken. The robbers had observed the boxed books arriving and simply
assumed something of value had entered the apartment – which of course it
had... I suppose it's how you look at it.

David was always very entertaining. In one after-dinner speech he'd speak of
his move up north. He'd say he walked to Glasgow in the late 1980s to escape
a life of mining toil. He opened and managed a small chain of Pork Pie and
Bicycle Wheel Shops that flourished within the pub and club land of Scotland's
second city. When they all went vegetarian in Glasgow's push for cultural
status, his small yet dynamic eateries folded and he decided to enter art school.
The rest, as we say, is history, depending on your viewpoint... David is very tall.

When David and I lived together, we watched a lot of TV. Perhaps too much,
but we'll never know.
On the odd occasion we forgot to switch the telly on there was always an
odd deathly silence.
Communication often went via a TV presenter or actor – sometimes it is easier
speaking via Pat Butcher or Des Lynam.
We invented little songs to accompany our favourite programmes...
What do we want?
Darts!
When do we want them?
Darts!

We also quoted a number of overly-watched films.
You are halfway to becoming a household name. And don't look at me,
I'm not washed.
An evening would finish with – 'If we don't laugh in the next ten minutes
it's off' –
It is impossible for me to write about David's work in a detached subjective
manner. We grew up together. Although I'm not sure we really grew up.
We met as teenagers. It was a barmy summer evening. We were both young
fighters. Boxing is a noble art. When we met, we had just attended a series of
long and drawn out philosophy lectures. We agreed to disagree. Belief in the
impossible is a shared goal.

David retained a positive attitude when Glasgow's famously depressing winters
turned everything to a grey brown sludge. I think he had a belief within
himself that all would be well in the end or before the end. He worked on his
work, kept things slowly trudging forwards until the sun came out. I feel that
the ups and downs within his work are always present and everyone (perhaps
not those who easily take offence) can relate in some way to David's output.
The work allows for uncomfortable laughter...
But maybe this is just me?
An American friend of mine recently noted that those who do not like Shrigley must
be lacking something. What is there not to like? I suppose it's how you look at it.
David is very hard working.
And a daily studio routine is very important to him. David doesn't like change.
He is a slave to routine. For him art is a job. It is not a very romantic thing.
It is not only about fancy expensive dinners and distinguished guests, although
this is clearly a big part of it. I think a lot of people have a preconceived idea
of what an artist might do or not do and perhaps it is better to keep it like this.
He just makes it look easy.
It isn't easy.
It just looks like it might be.
He is both unique and in edition... multiplied throughout the world in
one way or another.
The conceptual side of David's practice is often hidden within his working method.
We can't see the wood for the trees. He is a dedicated Nottingham Forest fan.
Please compare, if you will –
On Kawara's early telegraphed work, *I am still alive*, with Shrigley's taxidermy
cat holding a small placard displaying the message 'I Am Dead'.
And imagine David's texts written on a circa 1967 typewriter.
Perhaps it is time to reorganise your library.
David can draw.
He can actually draw quite well.
Figure drawing was his passion... light and shade dancing over naked Scottish skin.
David moved away from his struggle with the naked figure on health grounds.
His doctor felt it was the only way to release him from the curse that had possessed him
from a very early age. Even now the smell of oil paint and turpentine can make him bad.

His own child-like hand took over and a new life was formed from the
ashes of study.
There is even a font on my computer called 'Shrigley Pro Ext'.
It is hidden, but most new computers have it.
Words words words...
Only words.
But it really depends on how they are used.
Some small and some long but all of them aimed at David Shrigley.
'One hundred and eighty' cried in an East Midlands accent.
I love darts, me... see above. Language is important to David Shrigley.
As a student he would find new words in his much-used thesaurus.
He would learn these words and put them to use.
Now he continues to use them and many others. Some rude words have
entered into David's vocabulary but I'm not sure he means to be rude,
so please don't take offense.
A more direct route within communicating an idea is generally considered
less poetic.
But it really depends on where you are standing.
We are all in the gutter, but some of us are looking at the stars.

CONVEYER BELT

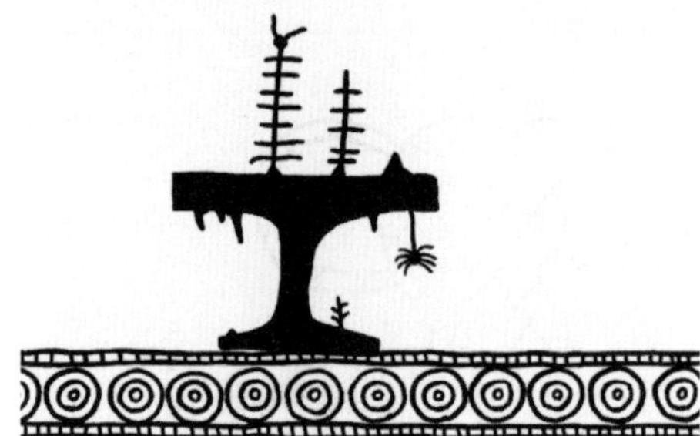

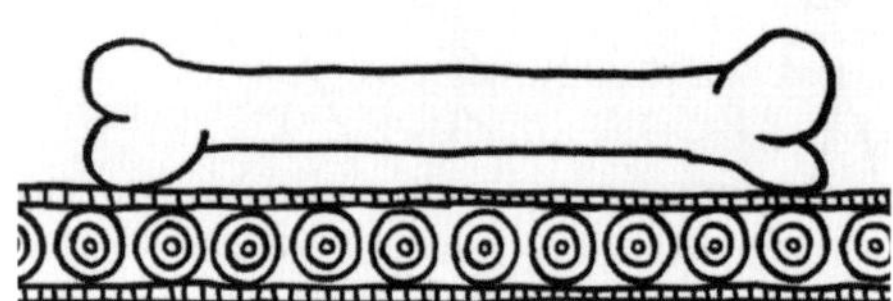

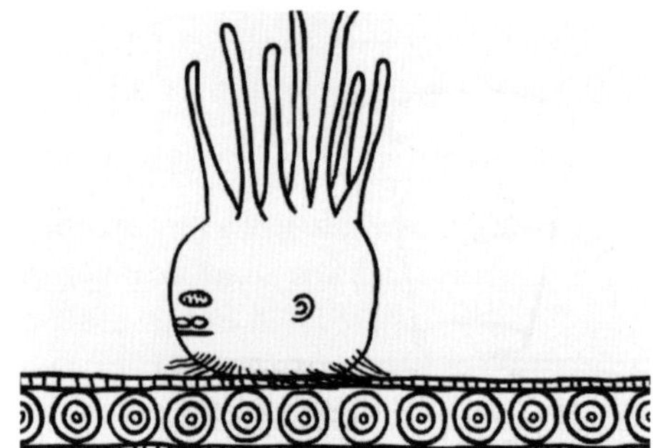

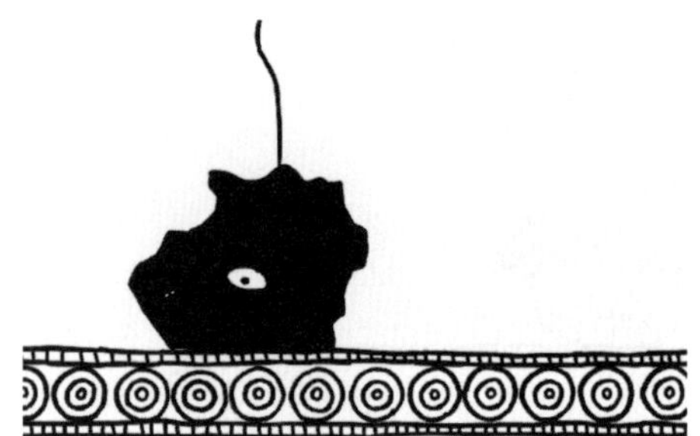

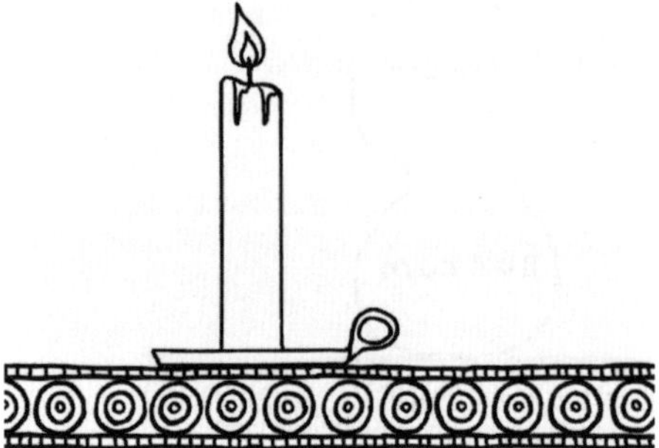

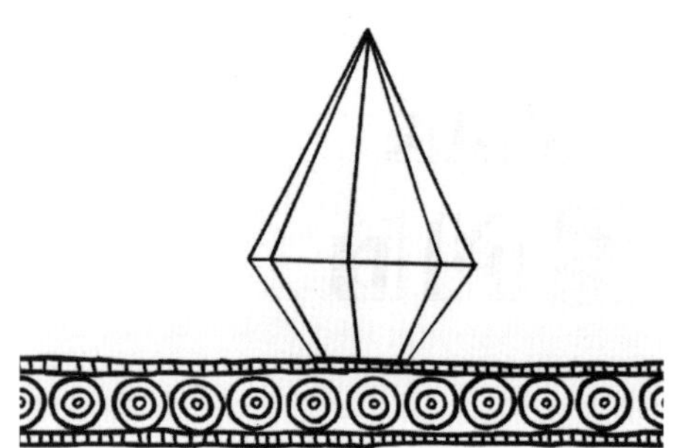

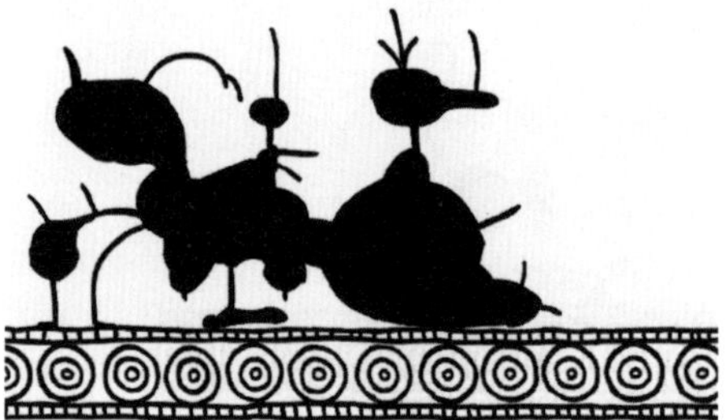

Conveyor Belt, 2008

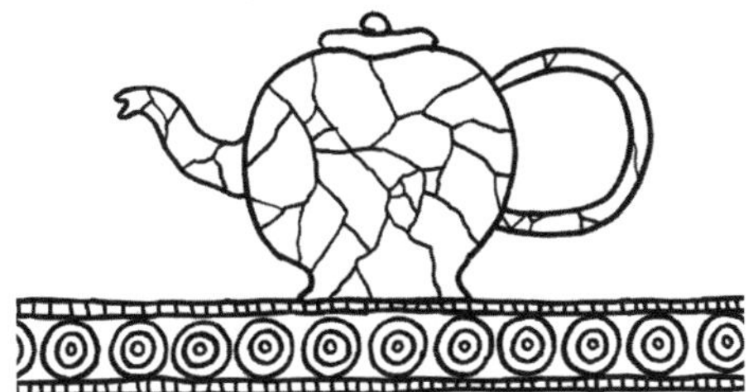

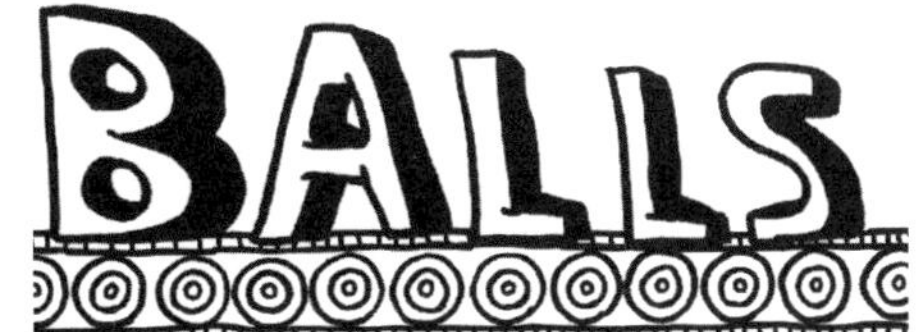

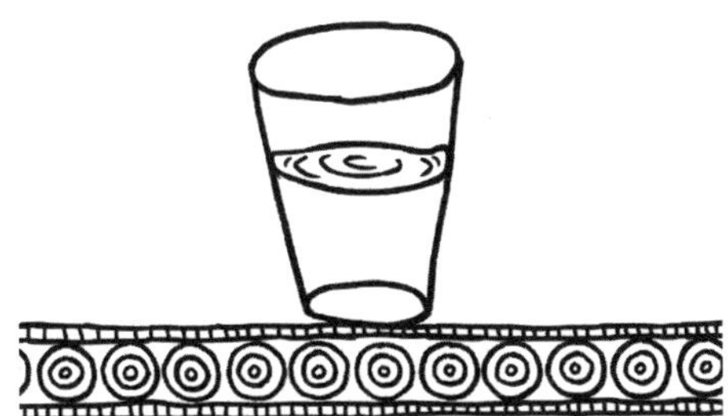

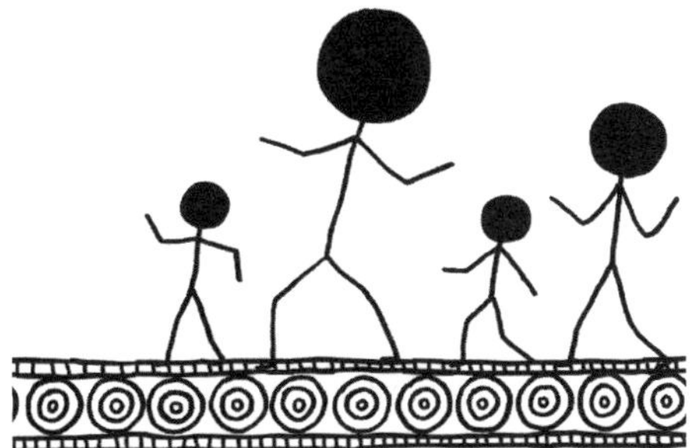

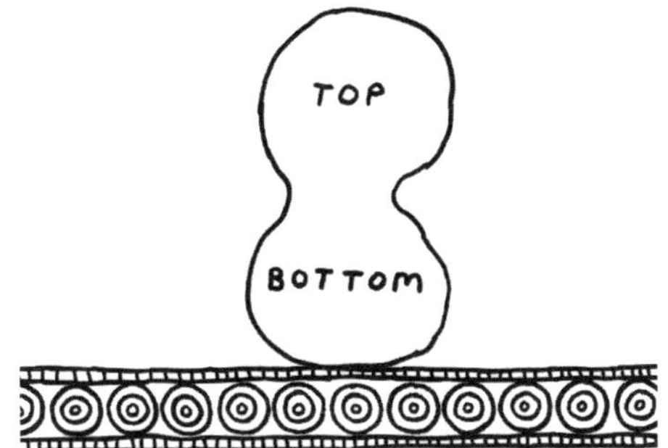

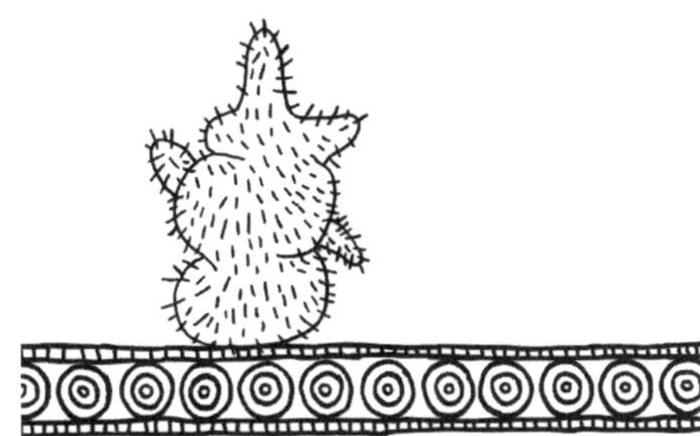

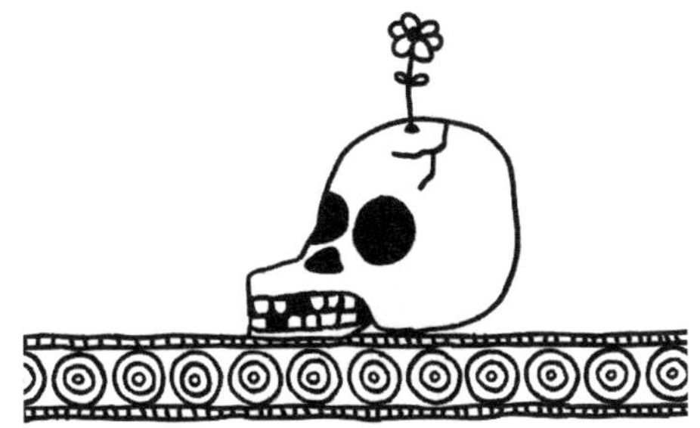

THE
END

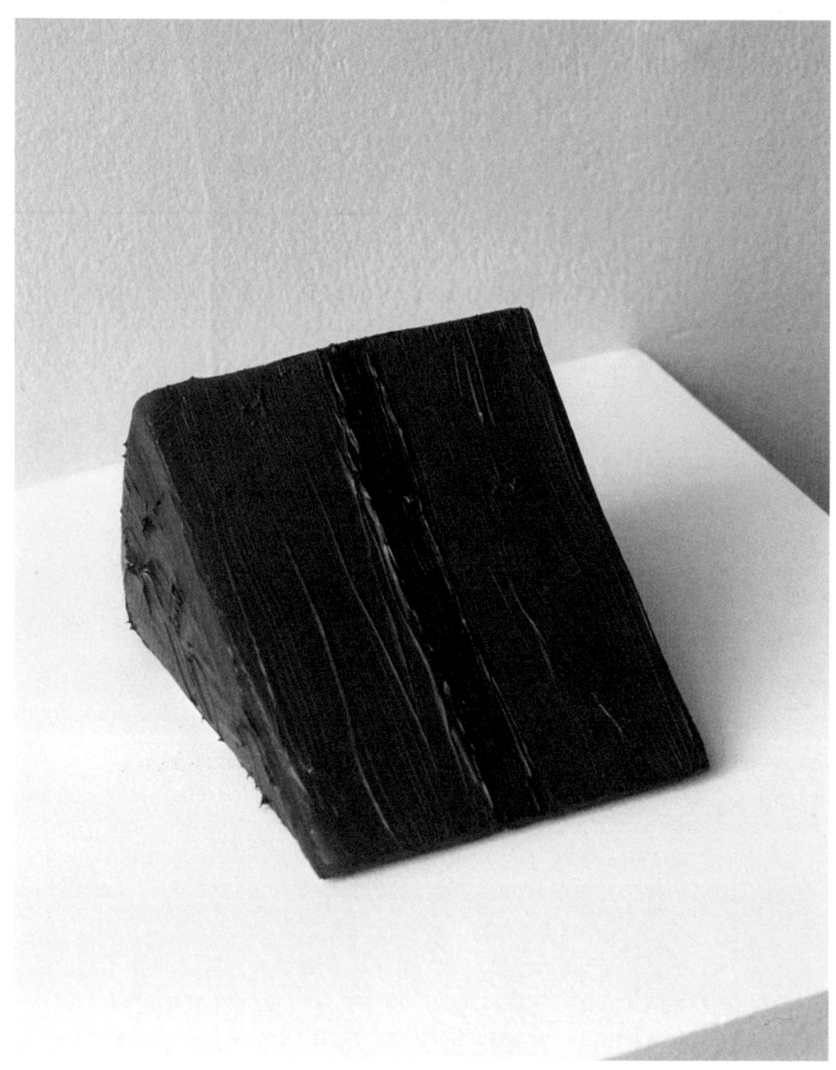

Black Forest Gateaux, 2001

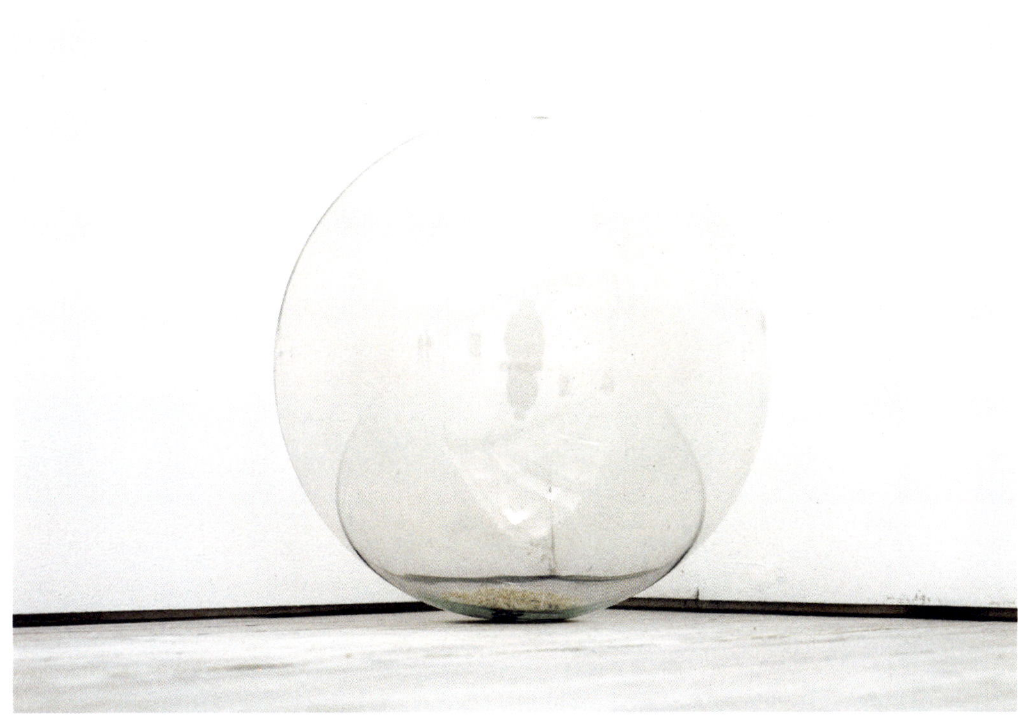

Five years of Toenail clippings, 2002

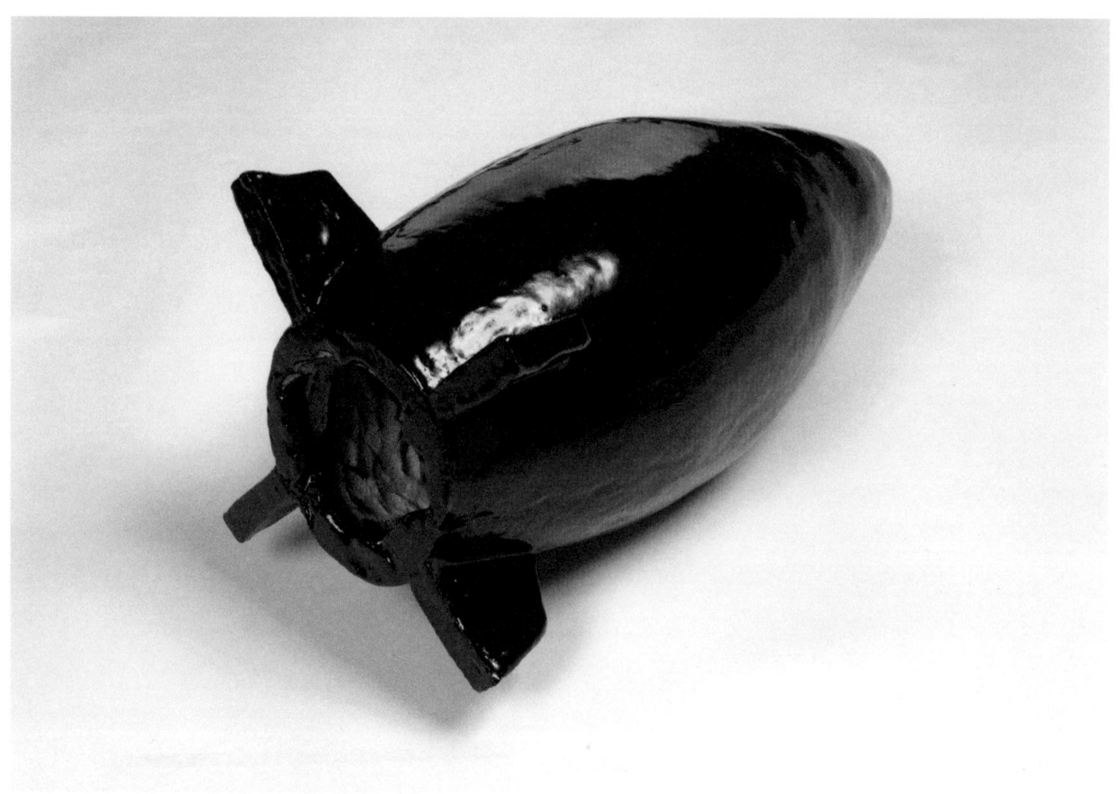

Bomb, 2010

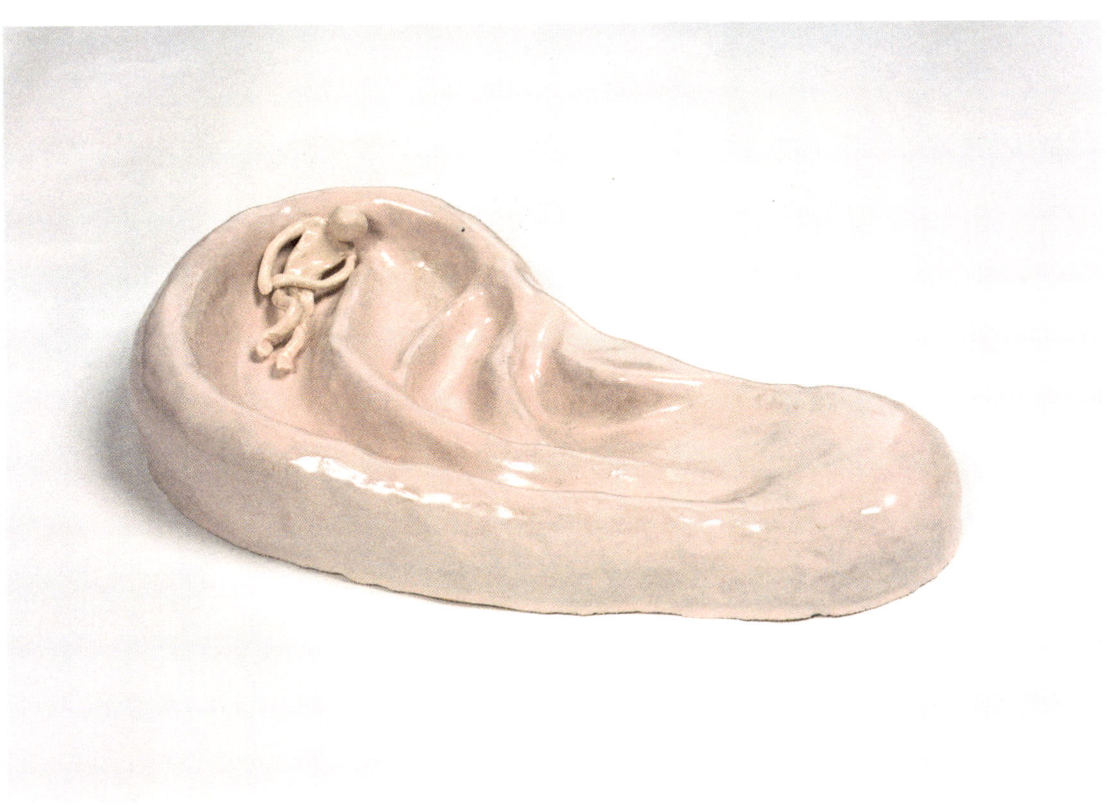

Ceramic Ear, 2010

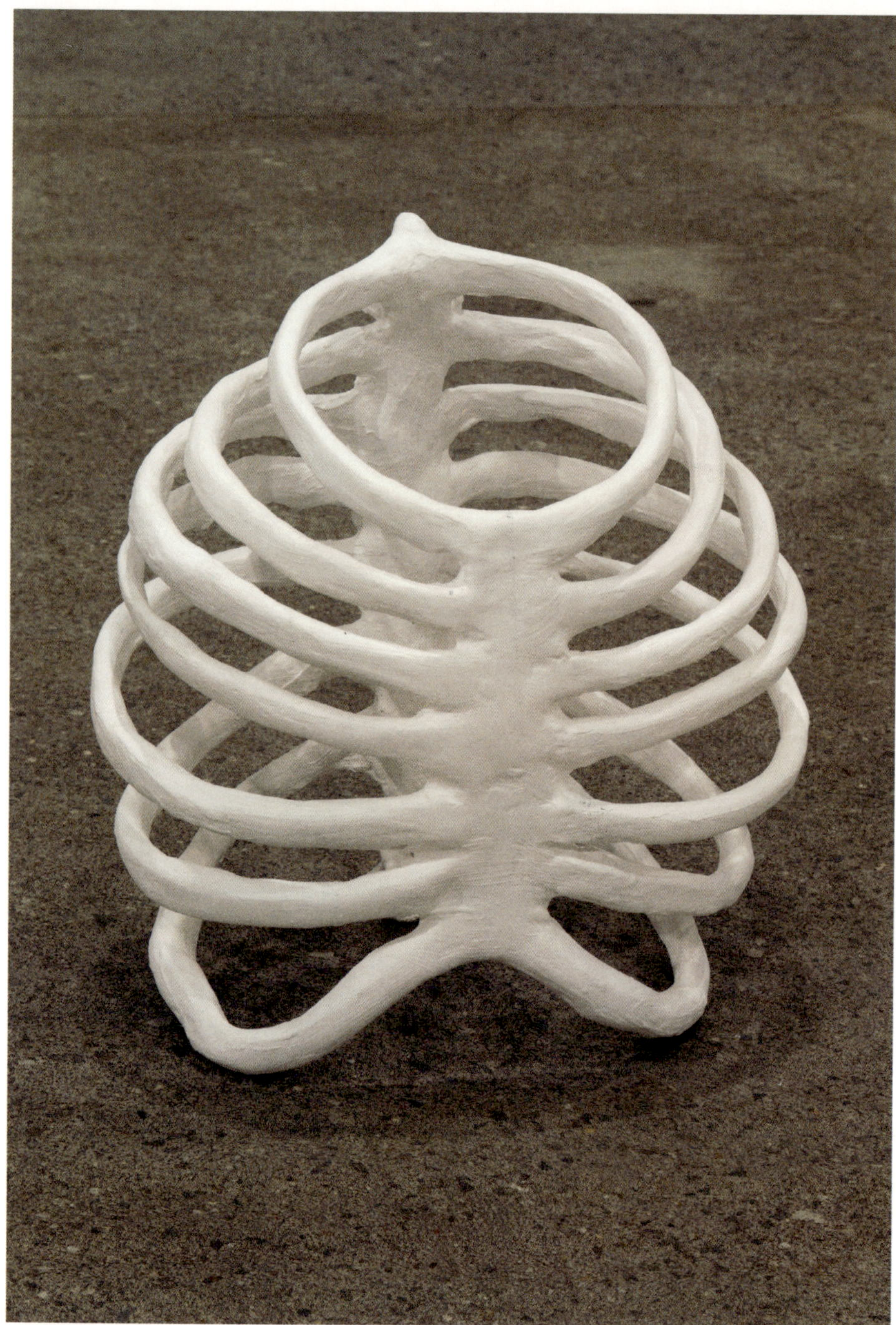

Rib Cage, 2010

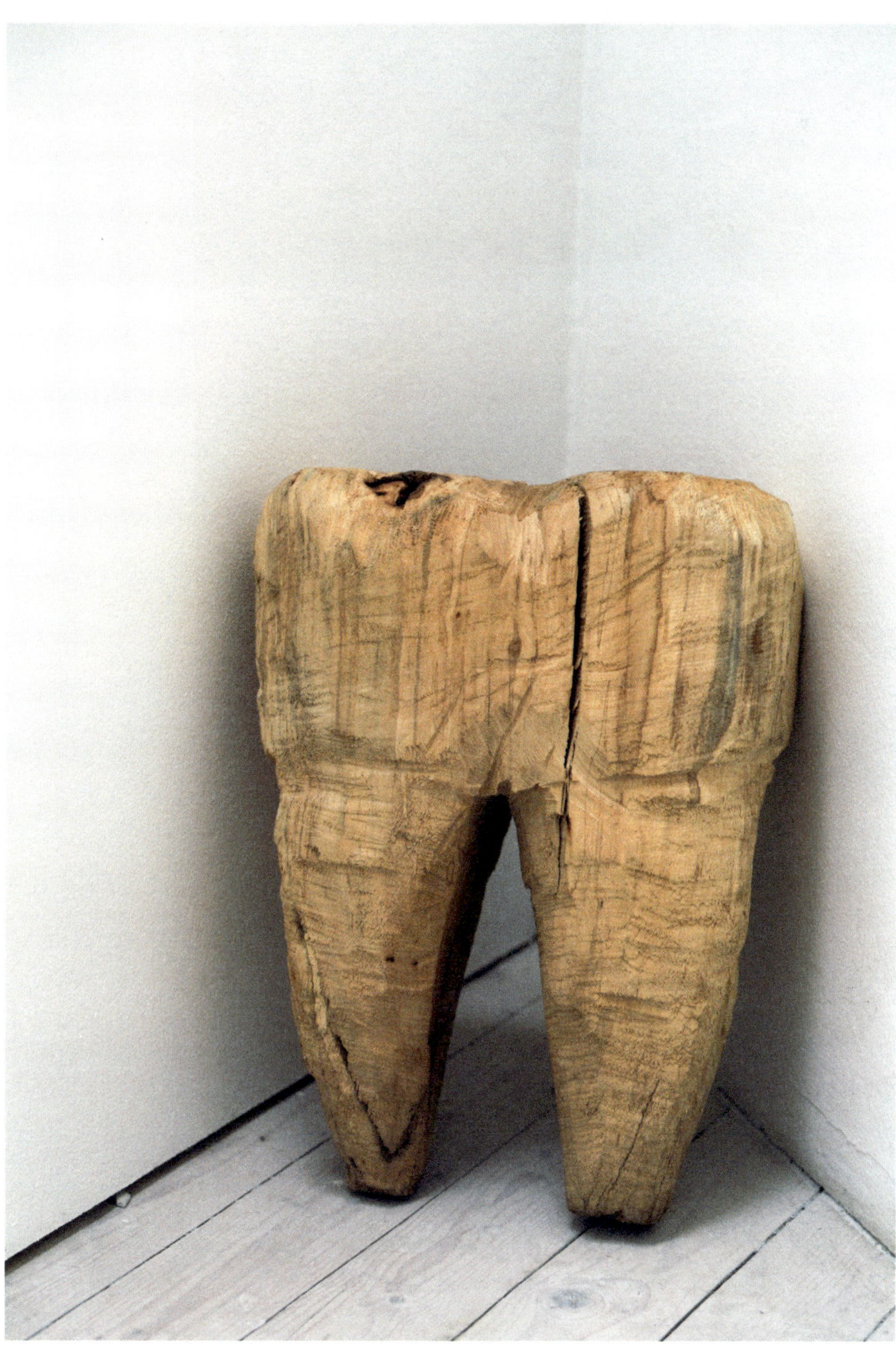

Wooden Tooth, 2003

The Philosopher, 2008

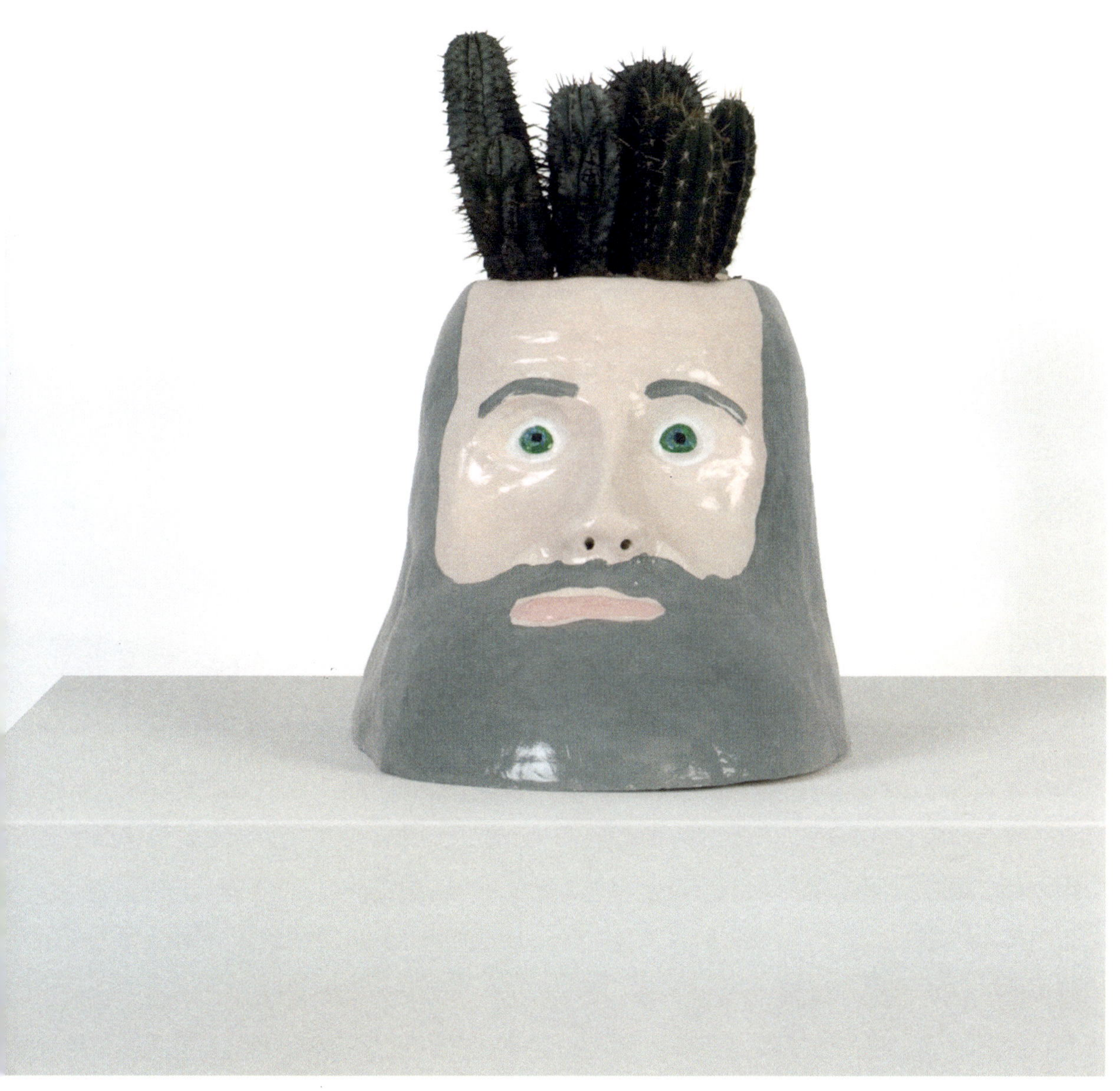

pp.120–23: *Untitled*, 2009–. Installation at Bergen Kunsthall, 2009

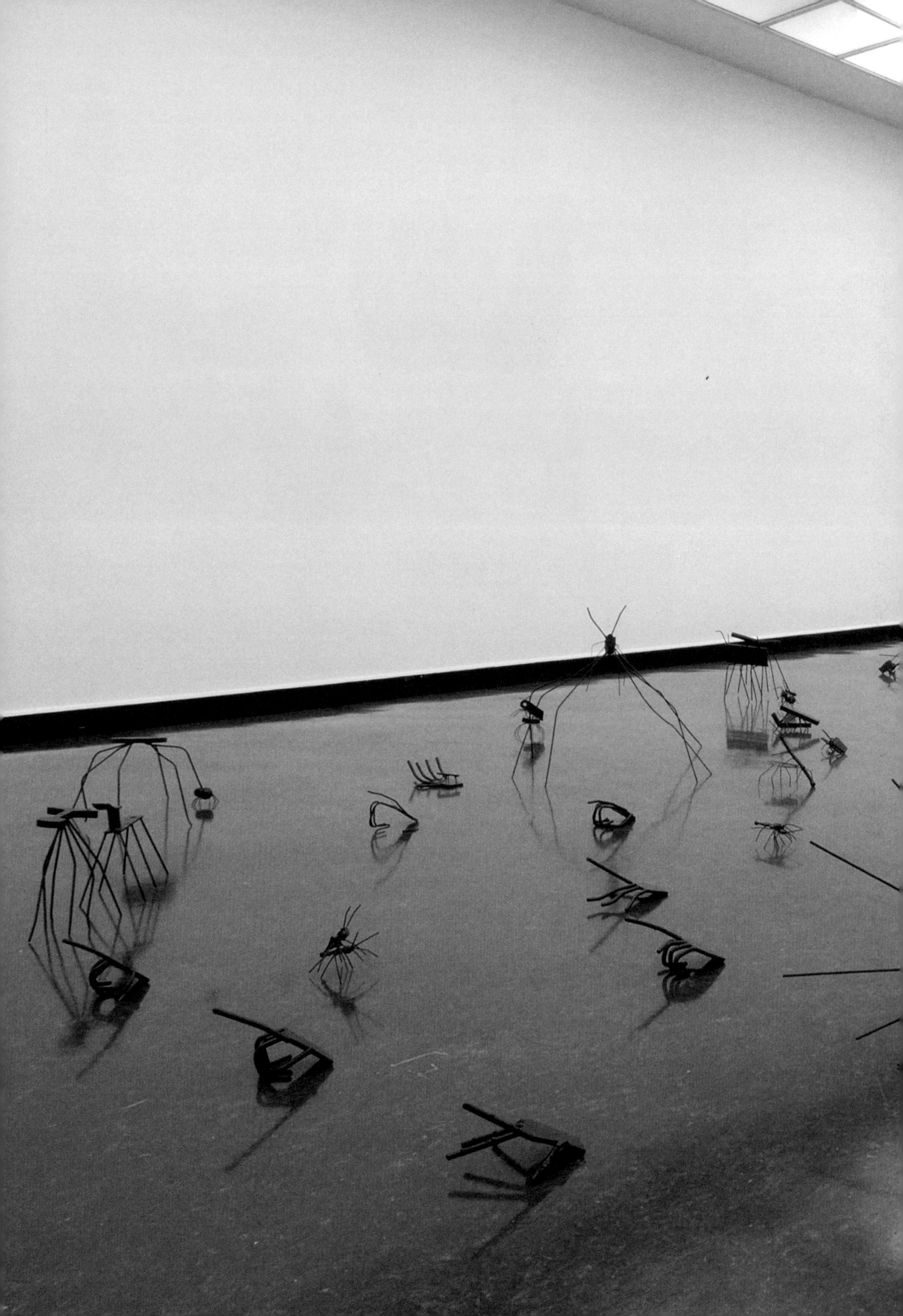

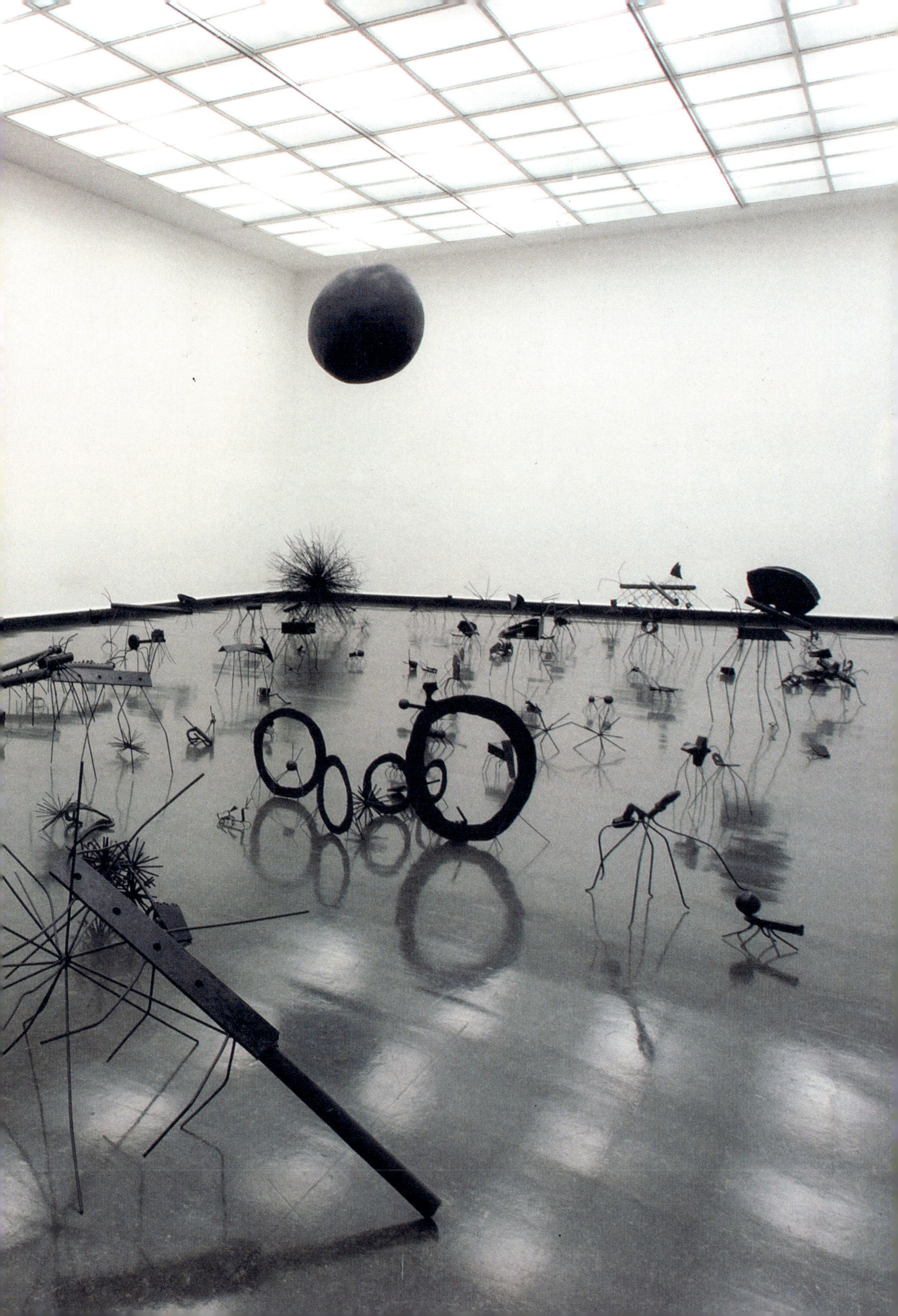

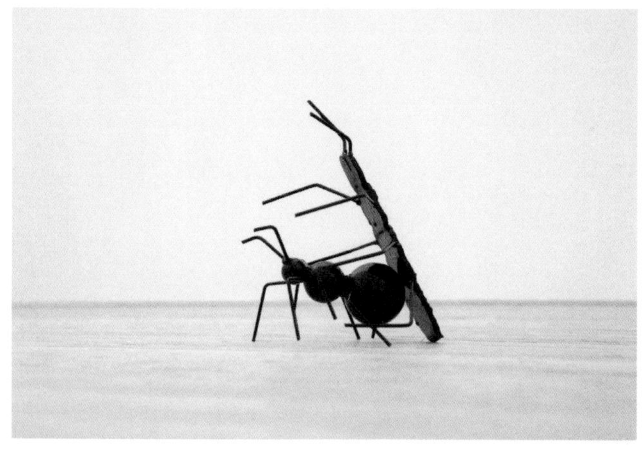

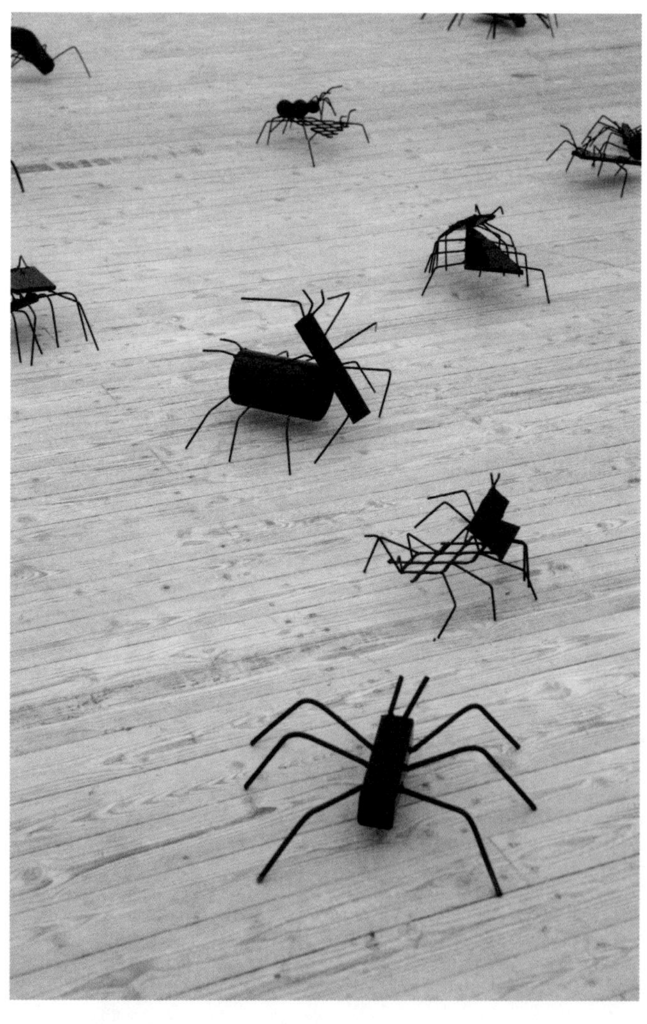

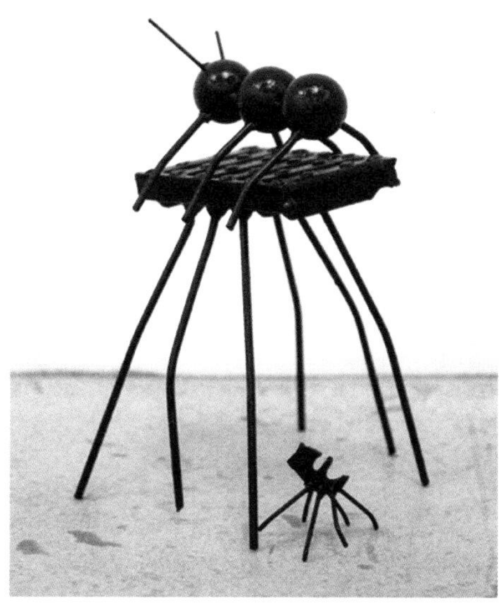

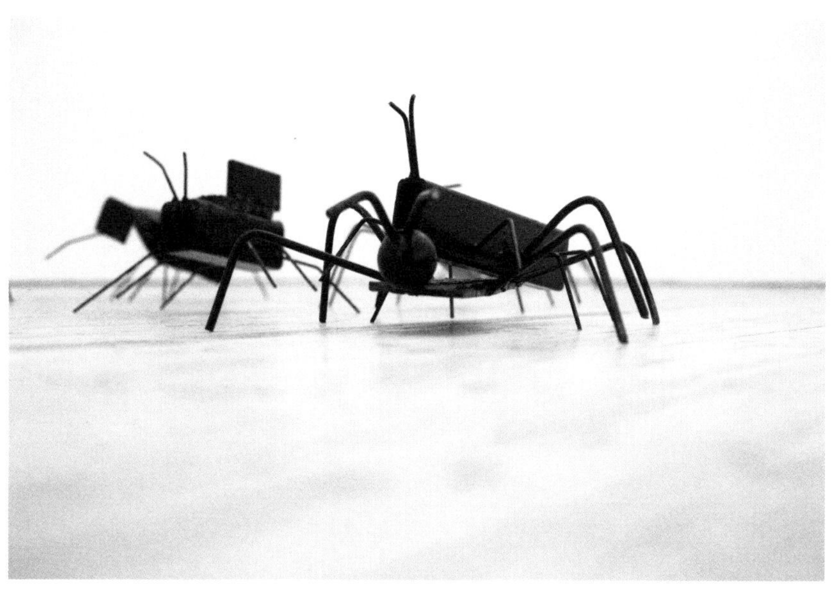

Stick figures having sex on car hood, 2007

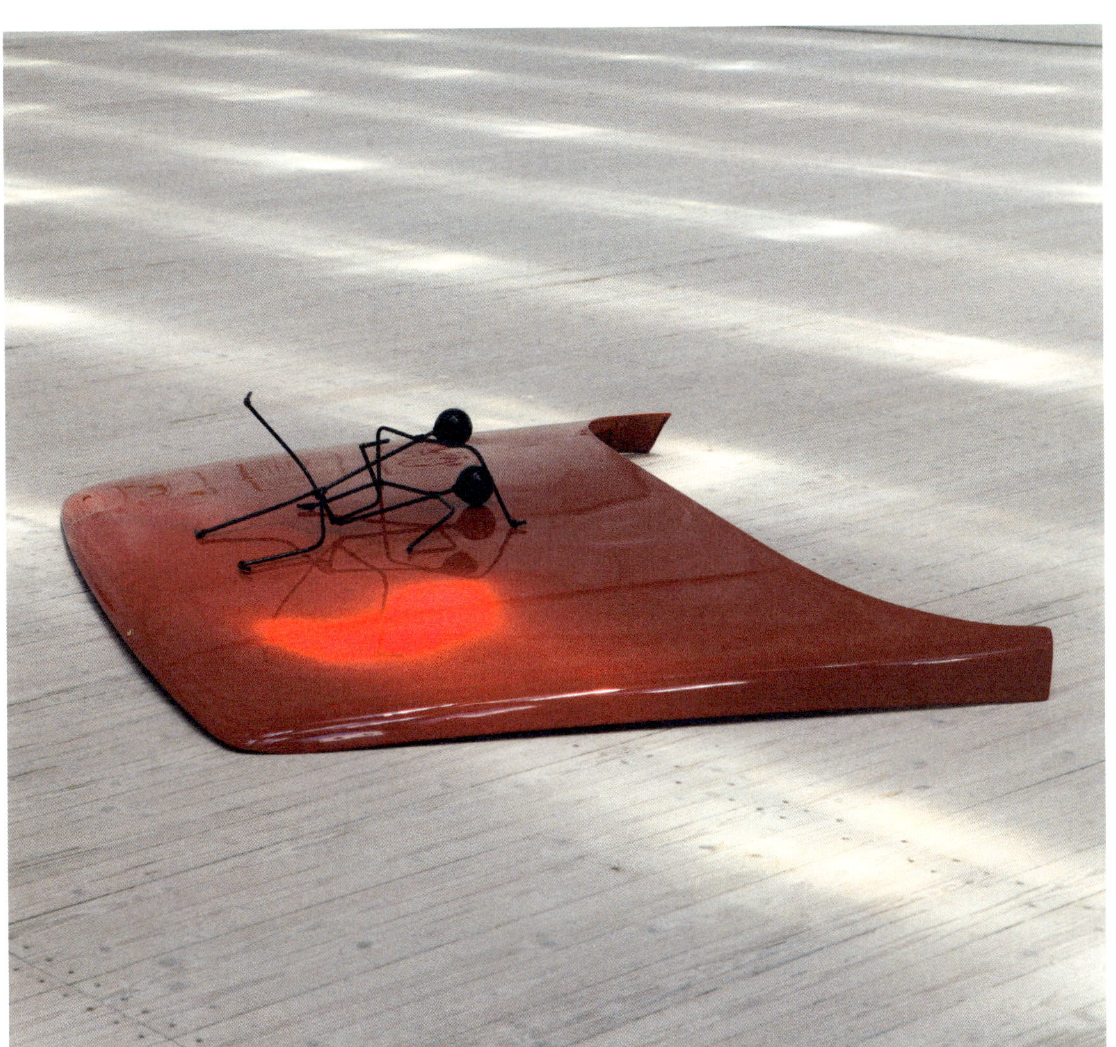

ONES

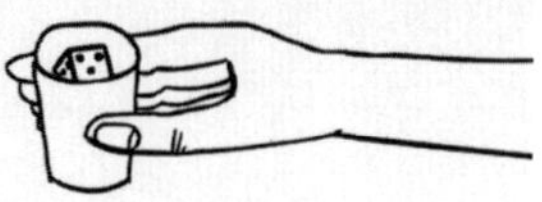

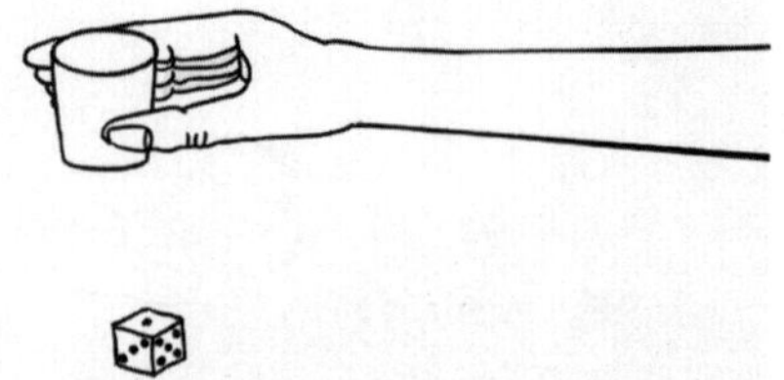

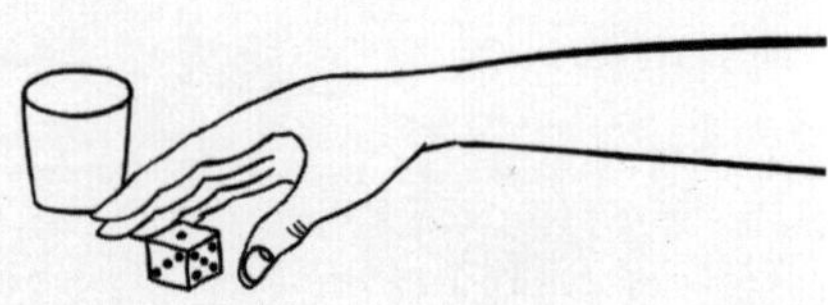

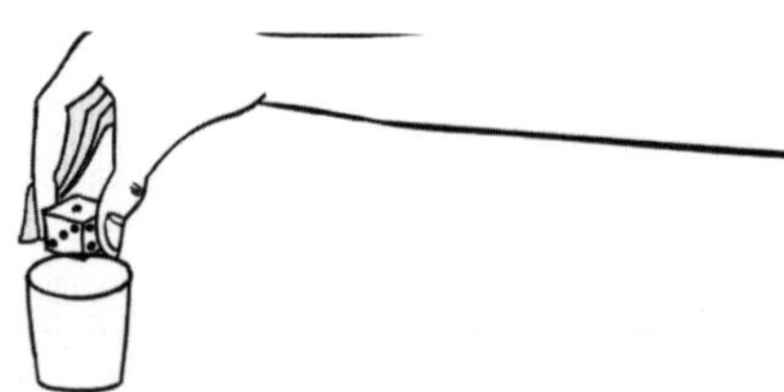

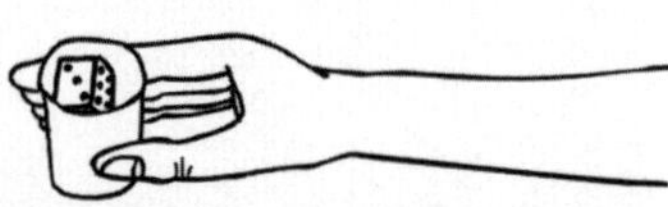

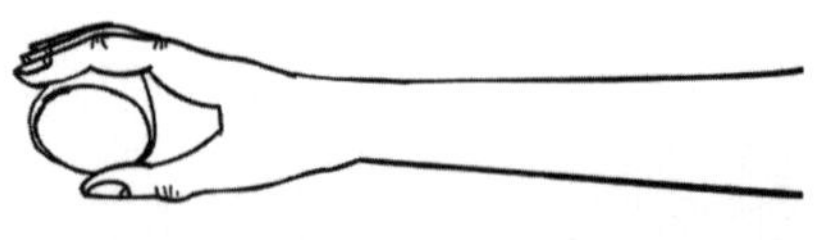

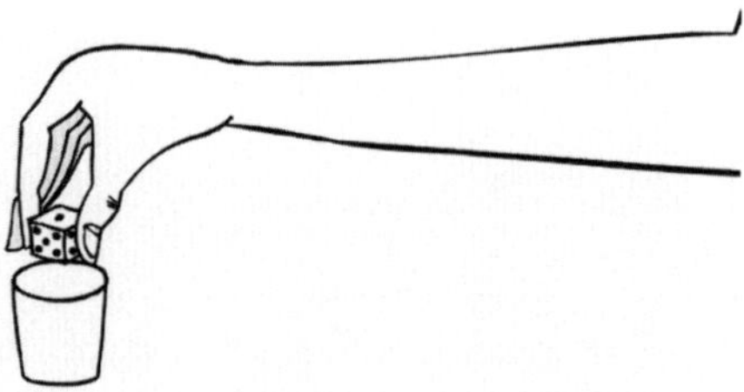

Ones, 2009

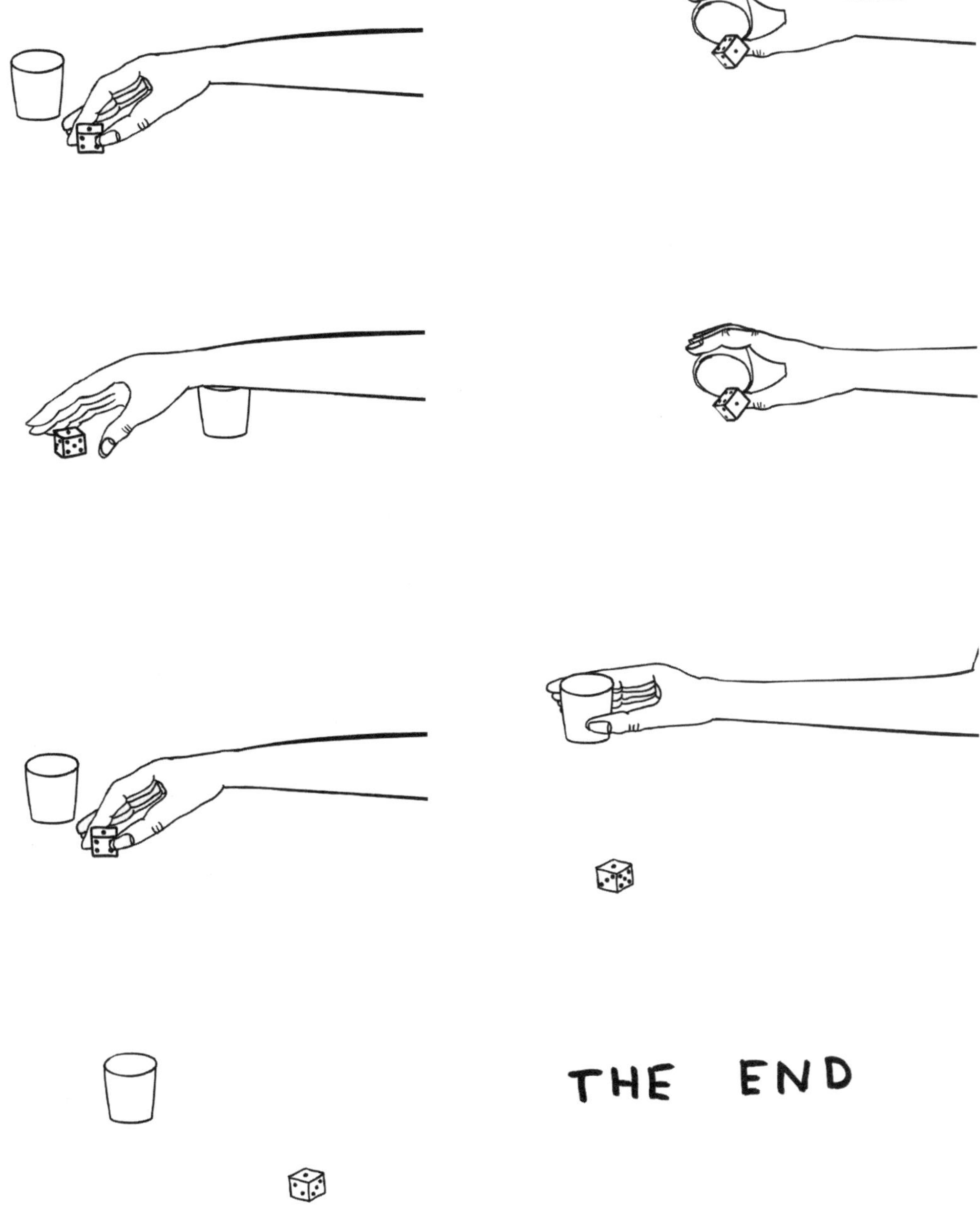

THE END

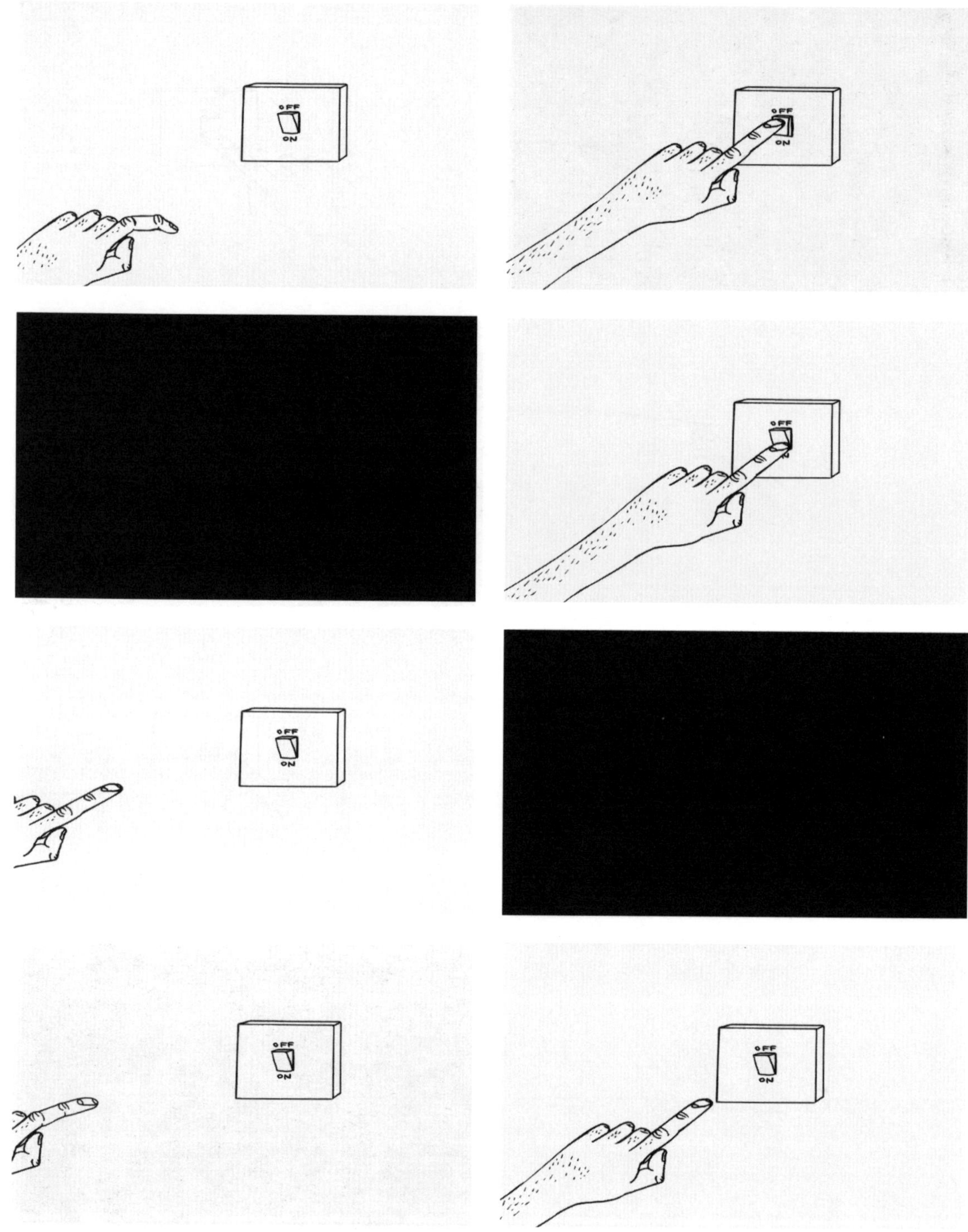

Light Switch, 2007

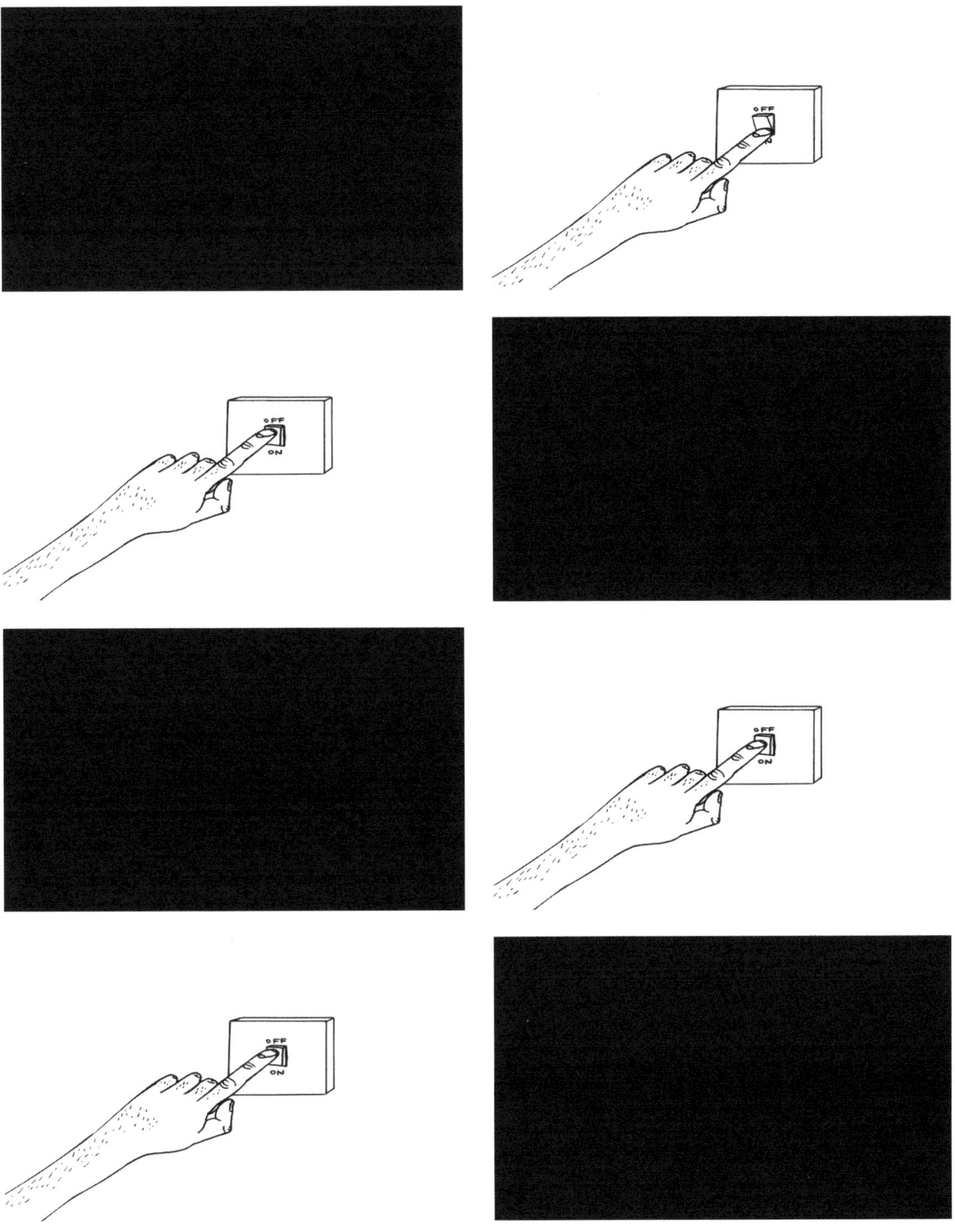
OFF
ON
OFF
ON
OFF
ON
OFF
ON

Do Not Linger At The Gate, 2008

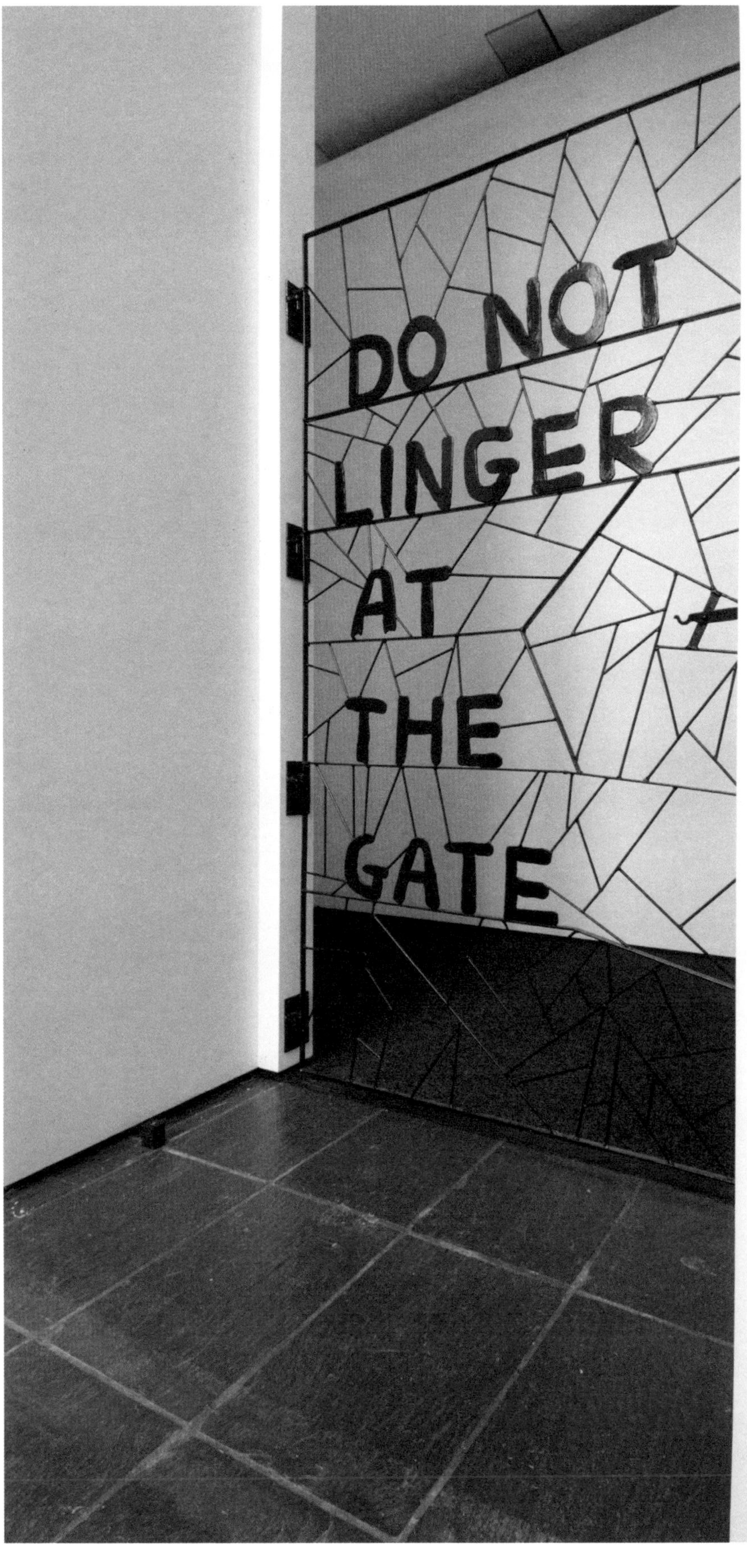
DO NOT
LINGER
AT
THE
GATE

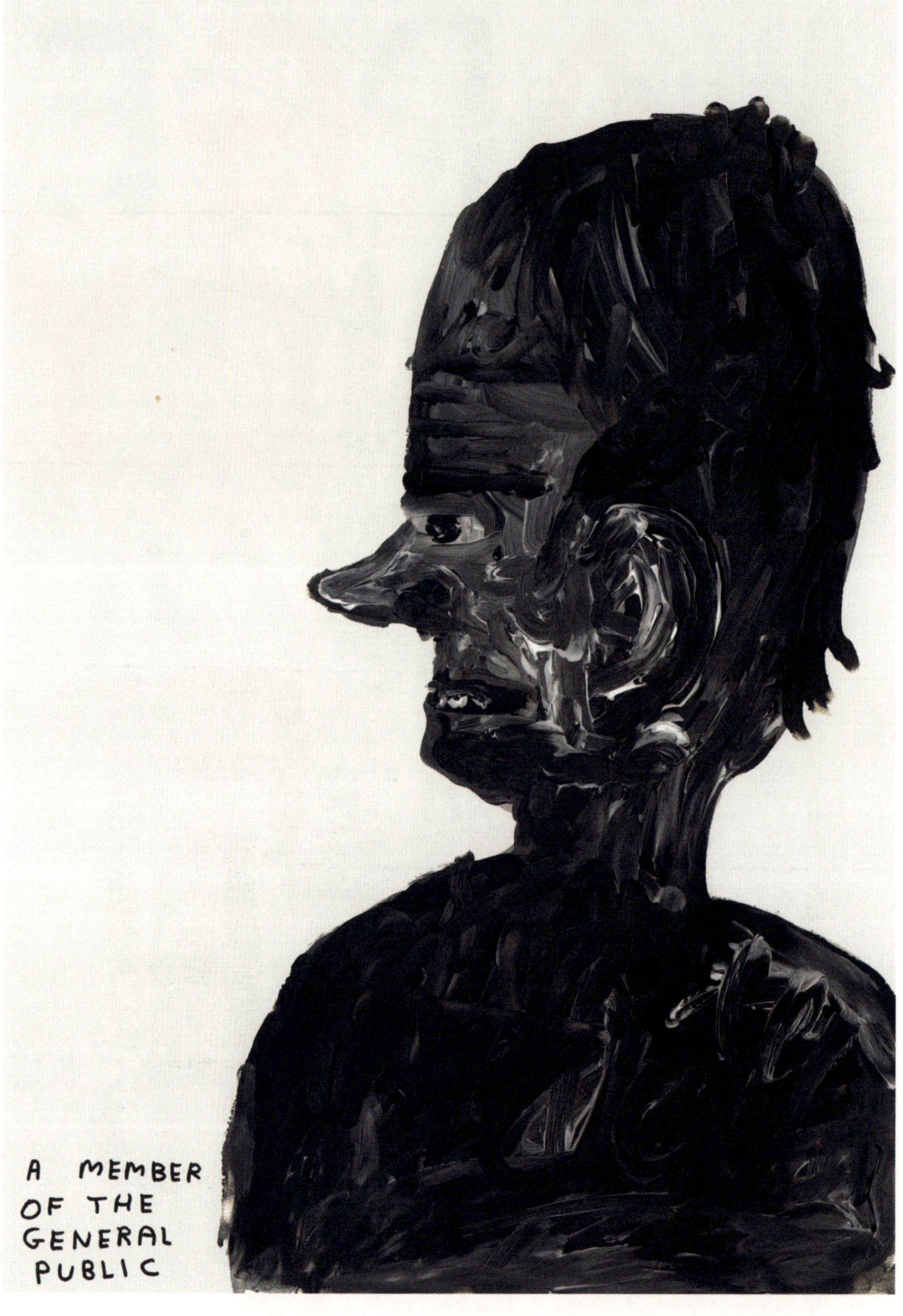

Untitled, 2010

LARGE
FANCY
ROOM
FILLED
WITH
CRAP

Untitled, 2010

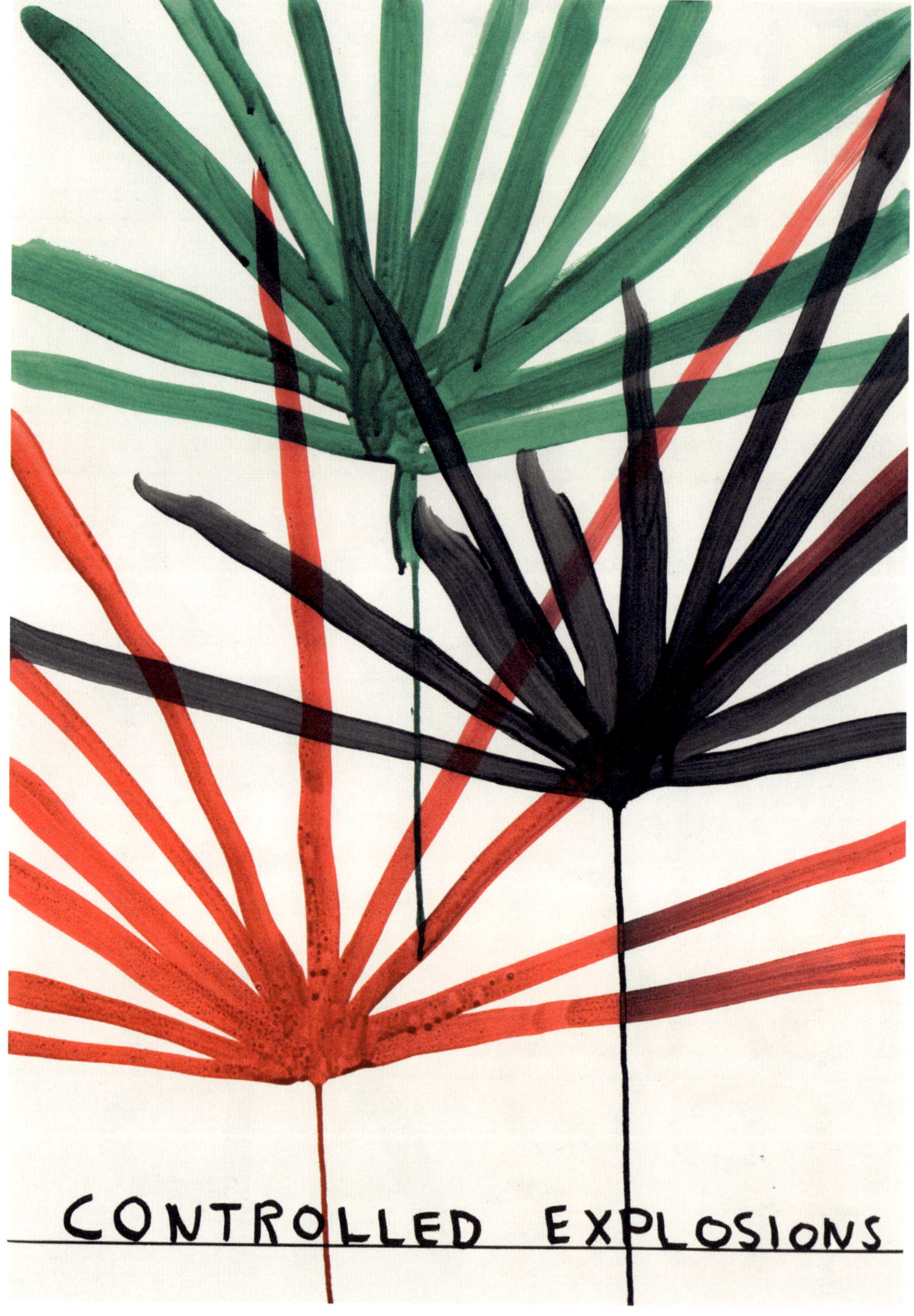

Untitled, 2010

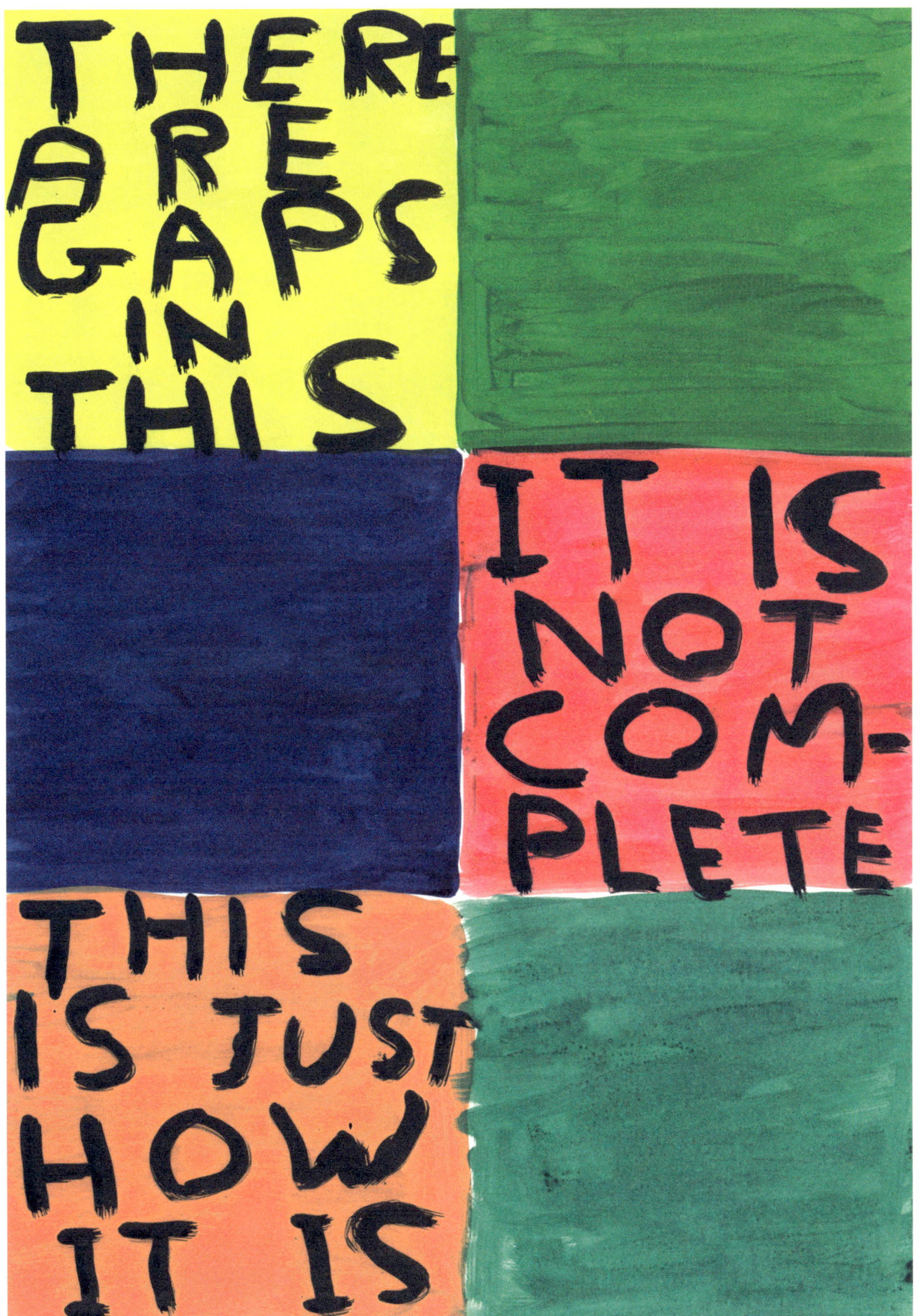

Untitled, 2010

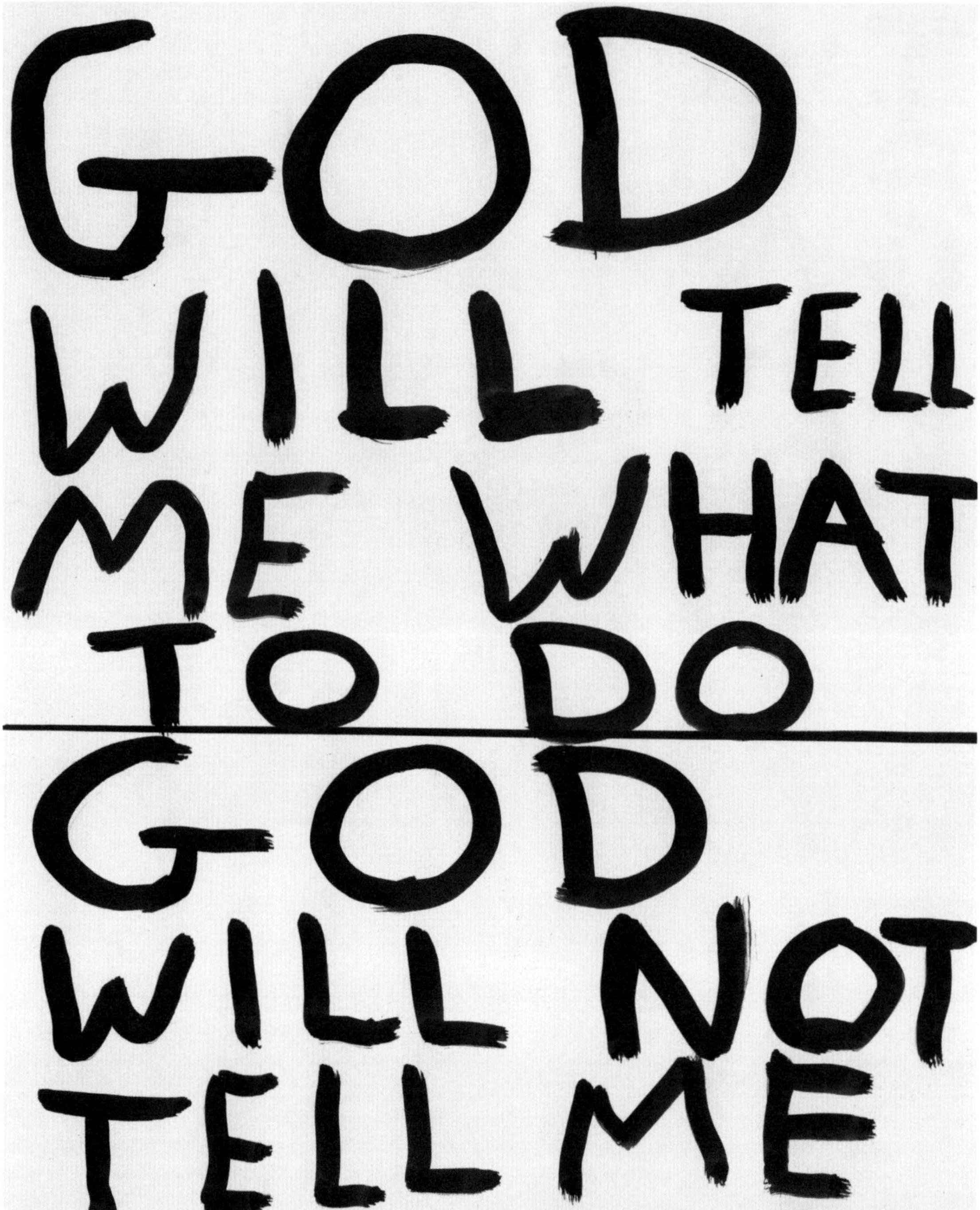

GOD WILL TELL ME WHAT TO DO

GOD WILL NOT TELL ME WHAT TO DO

Untitled, 2010

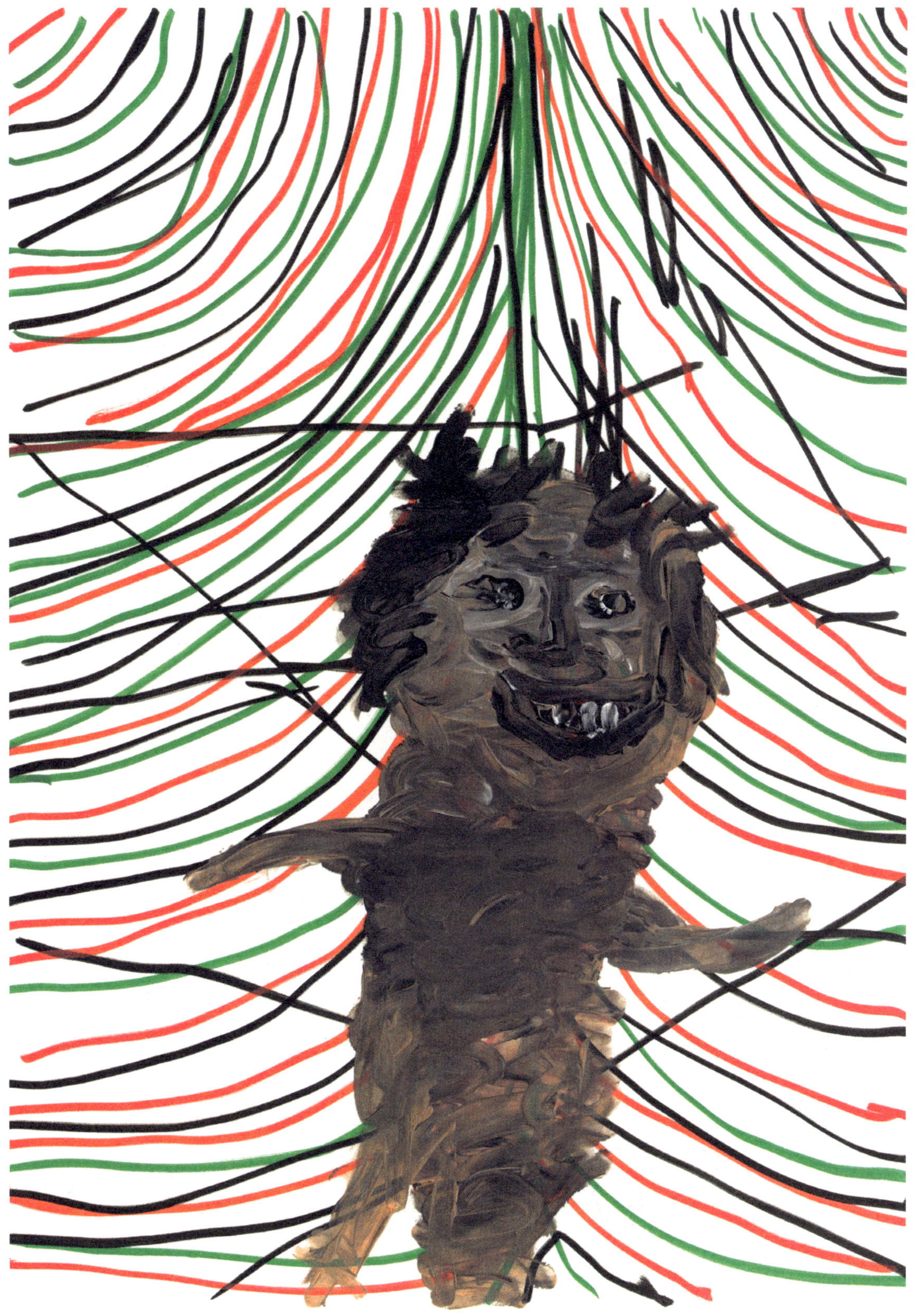

Untitled, 2010

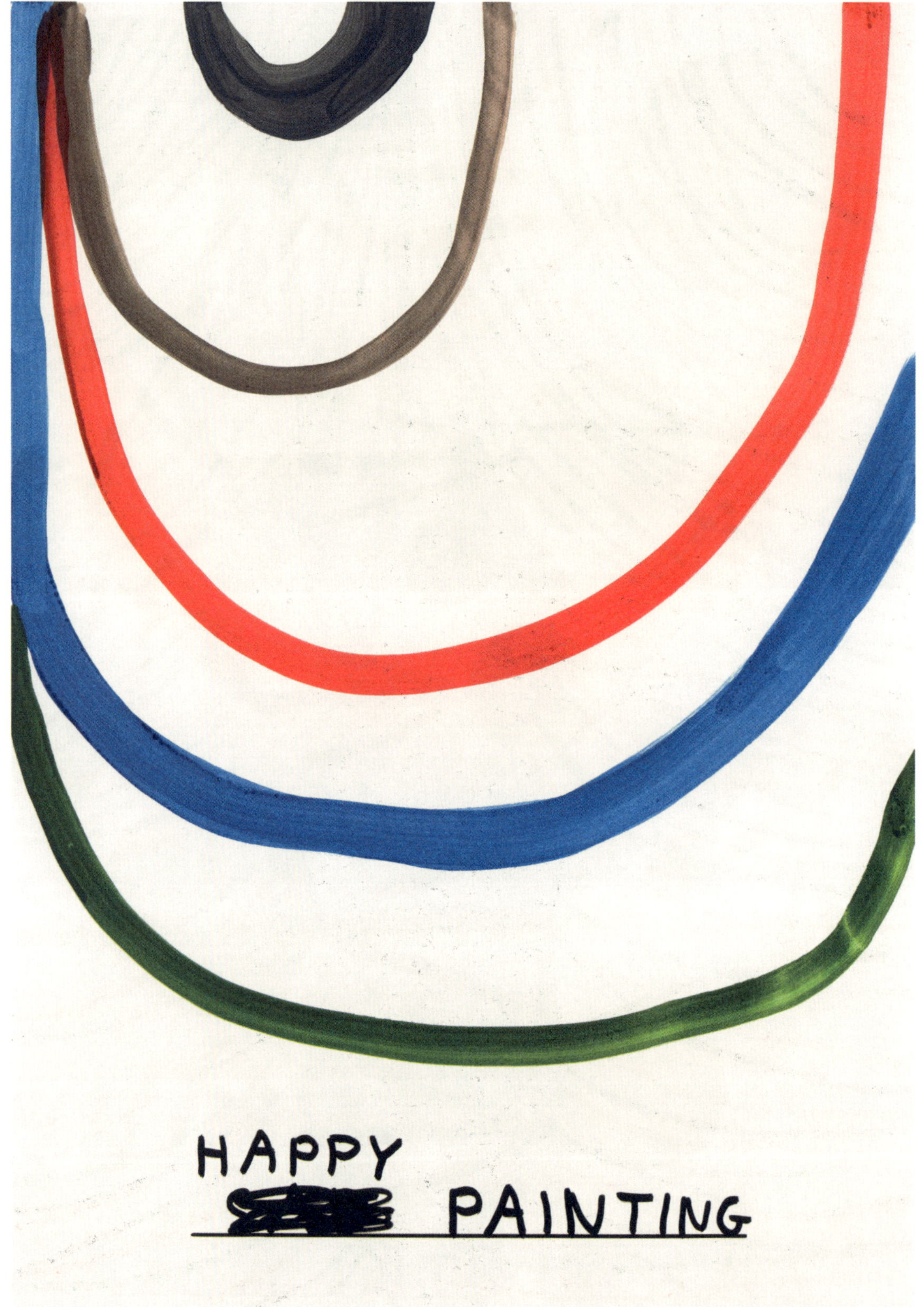

Untitled, 2010

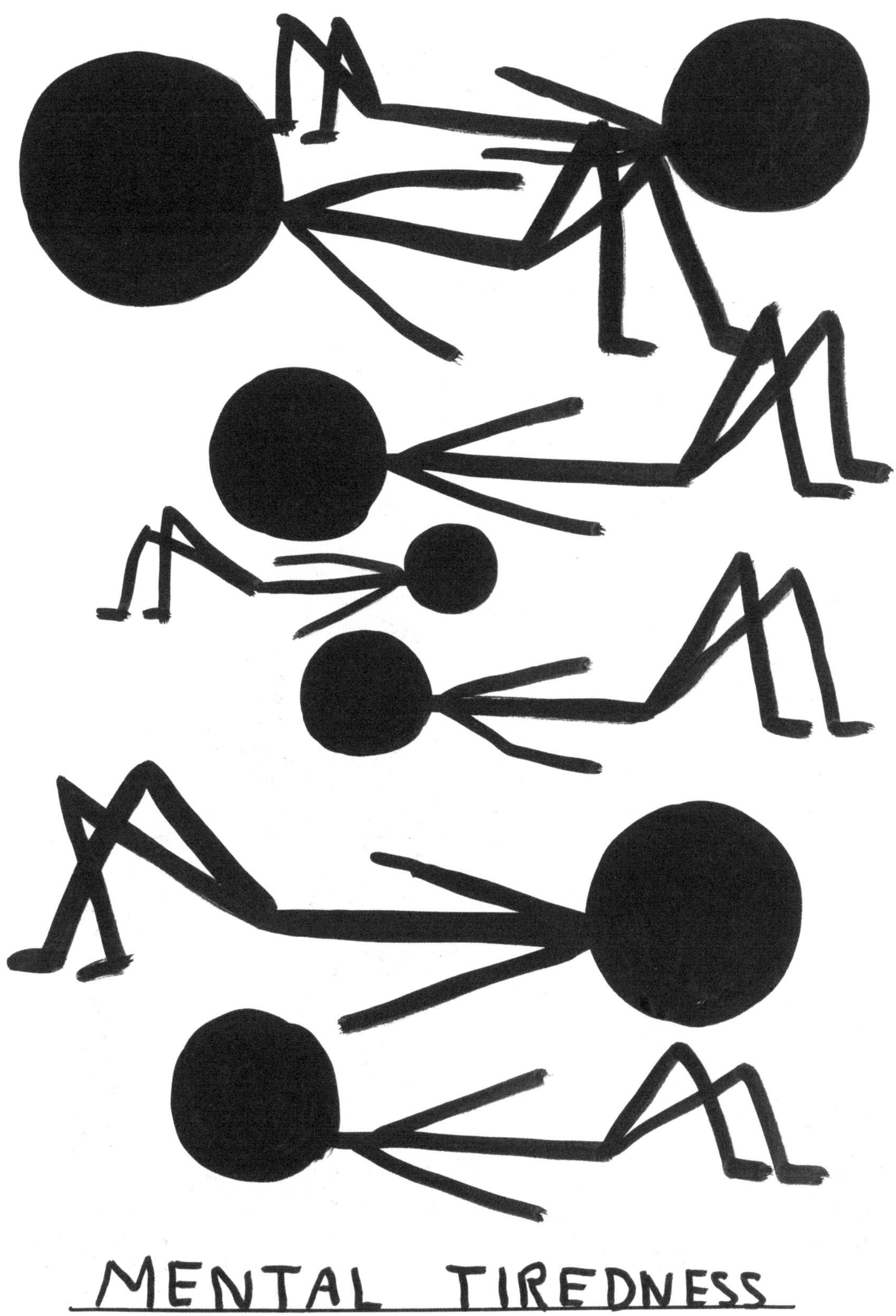

Untitled, 2010

PIG DRAWING

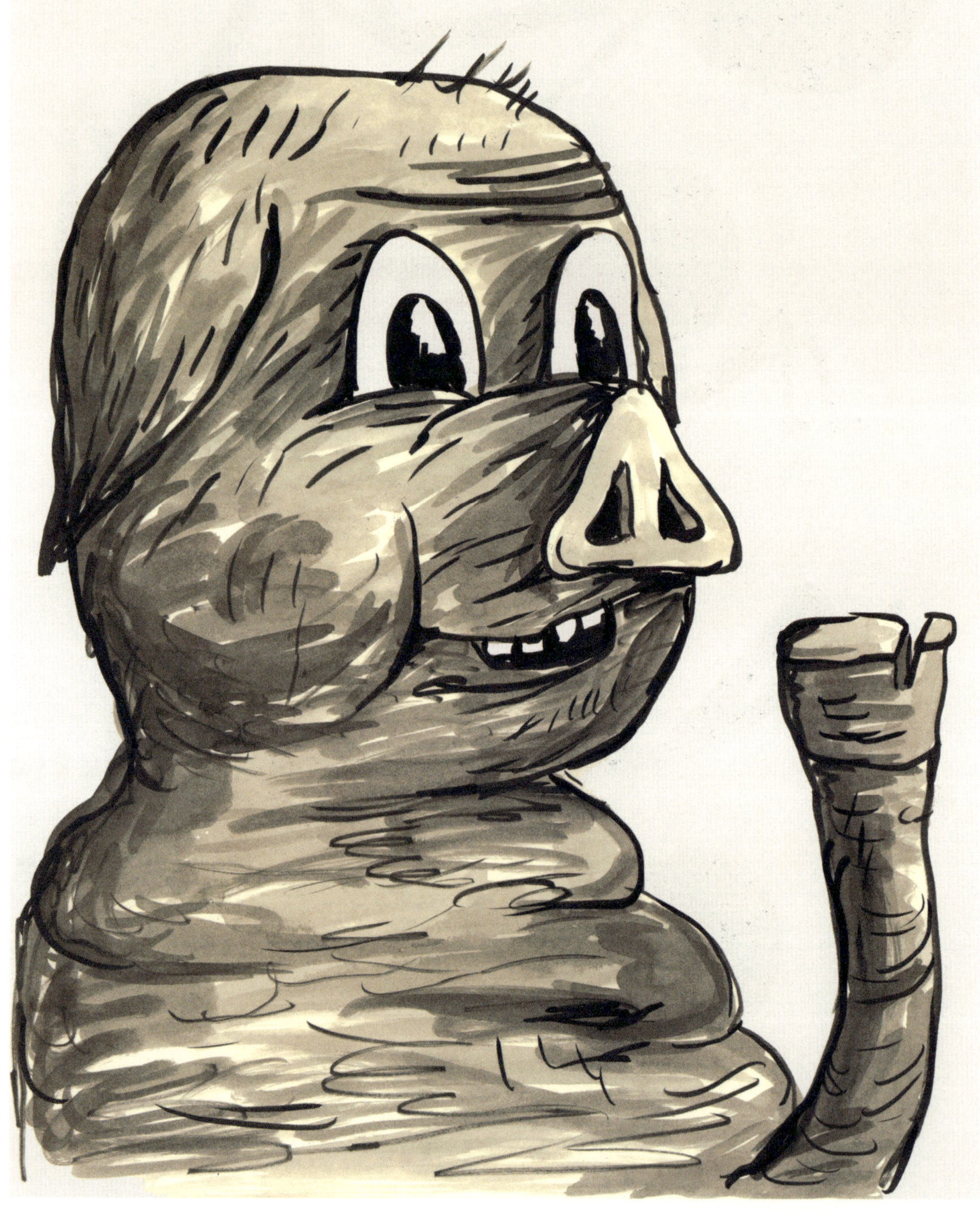

Untitled, 2010

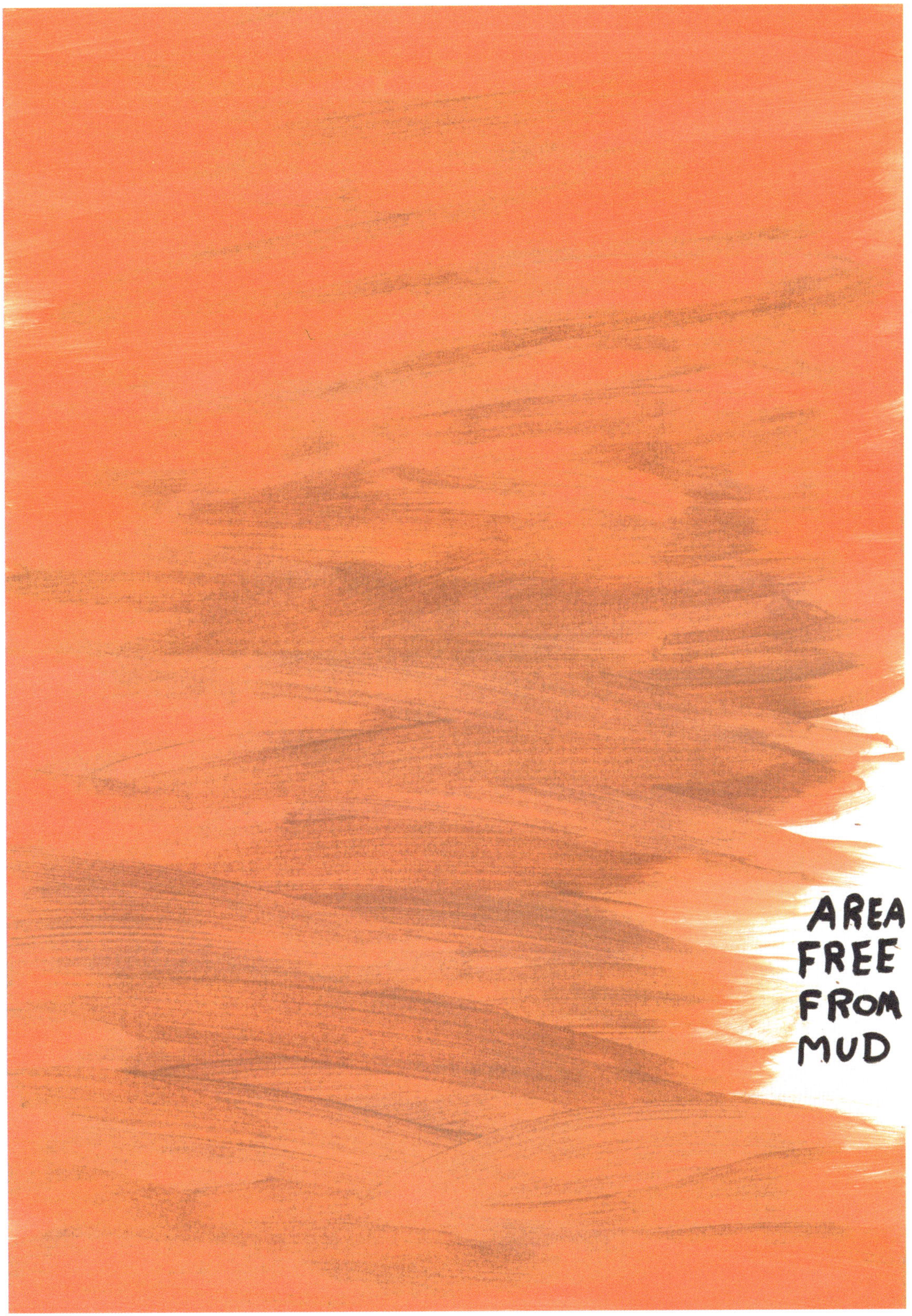

Untitled, 2010

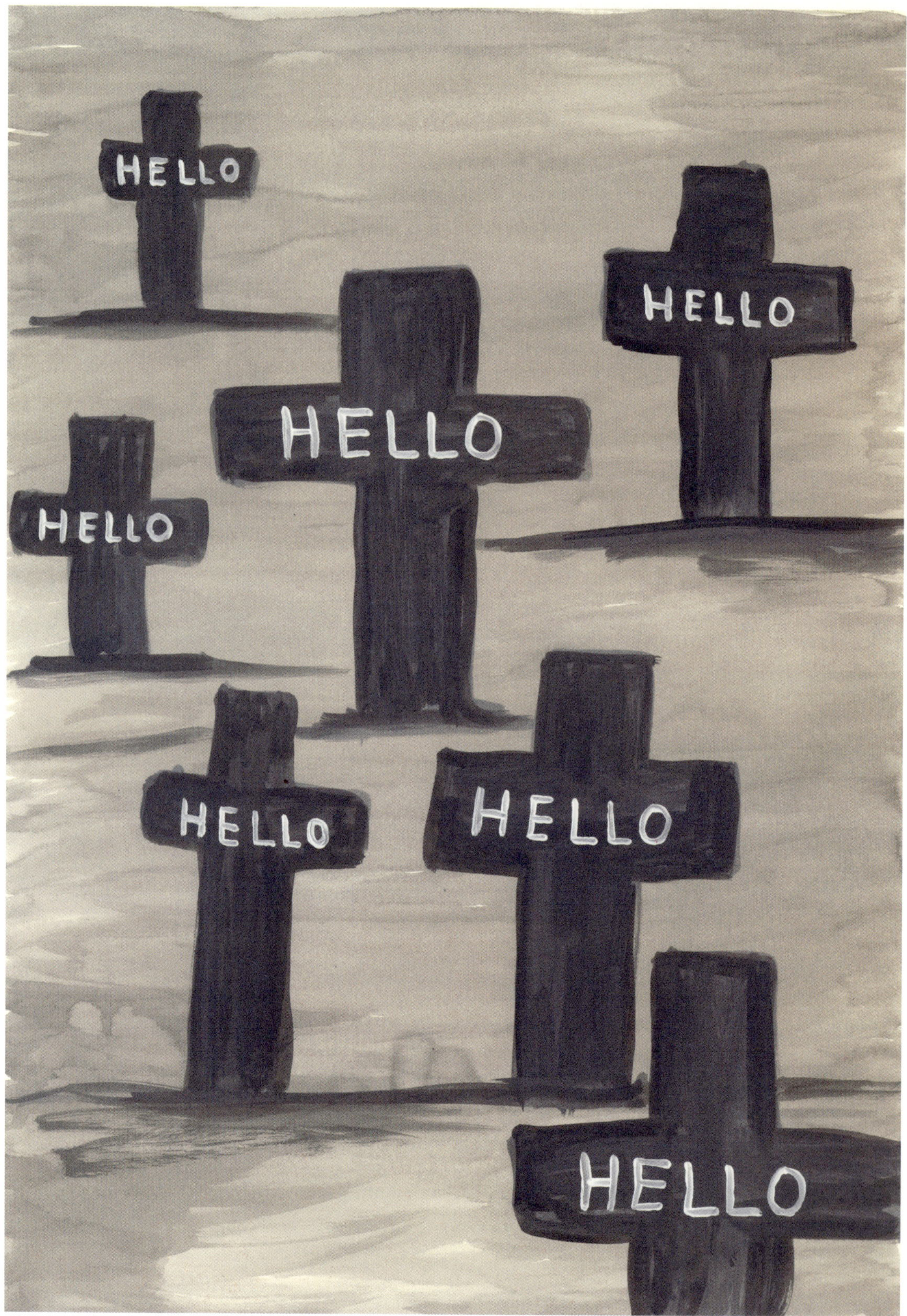

Untitled, 2010

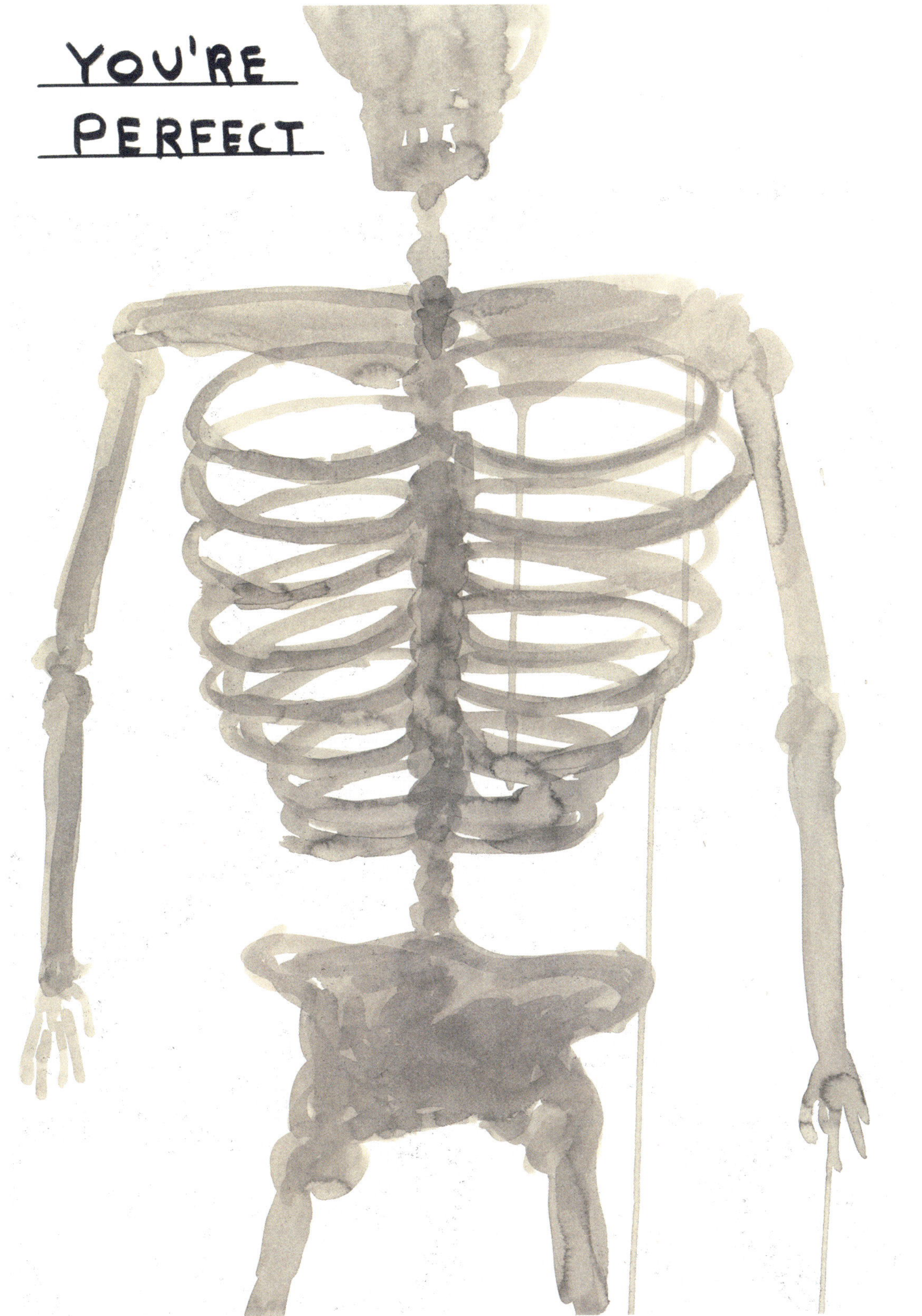

Untitled, 2010

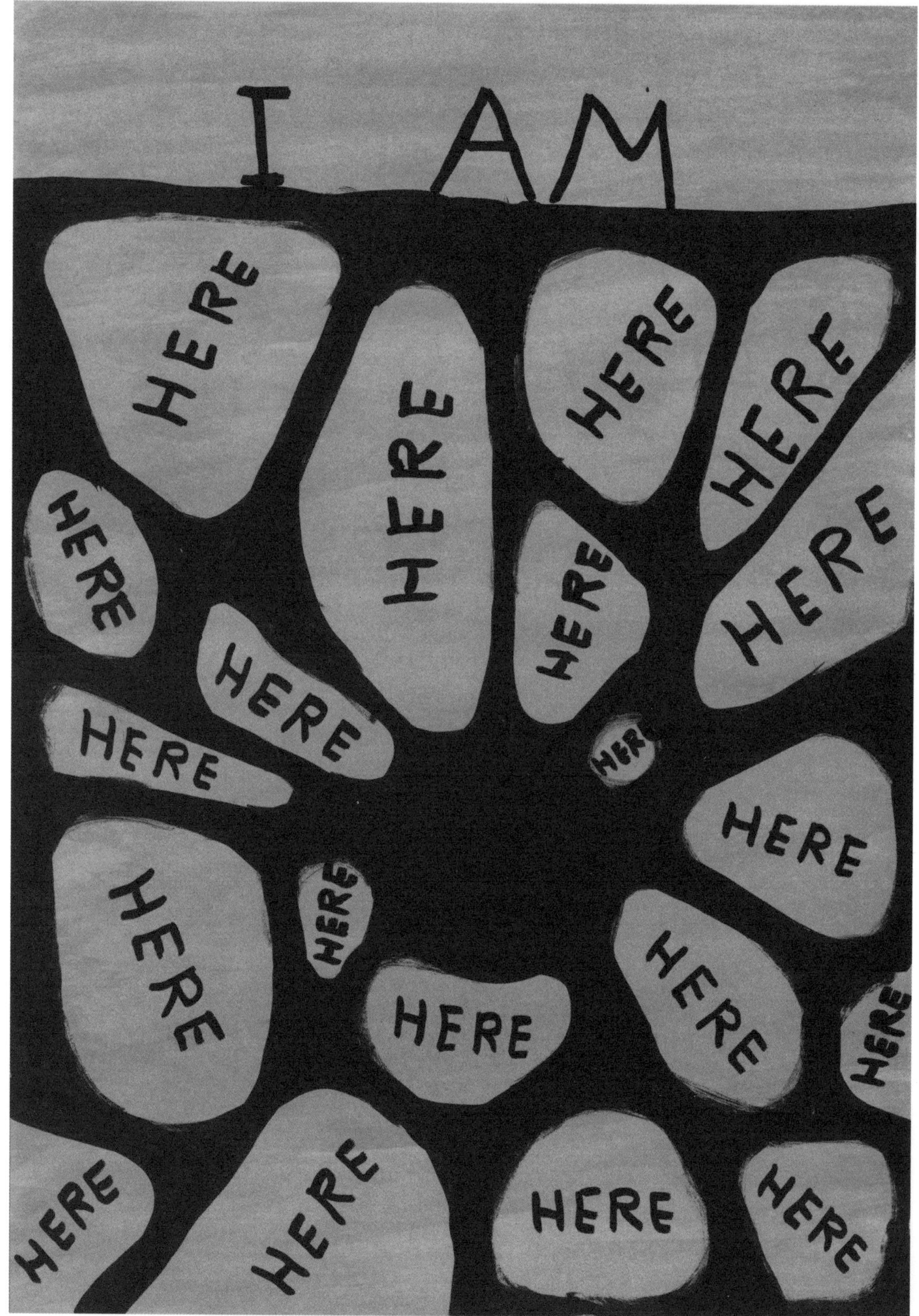

Untitled, 2010

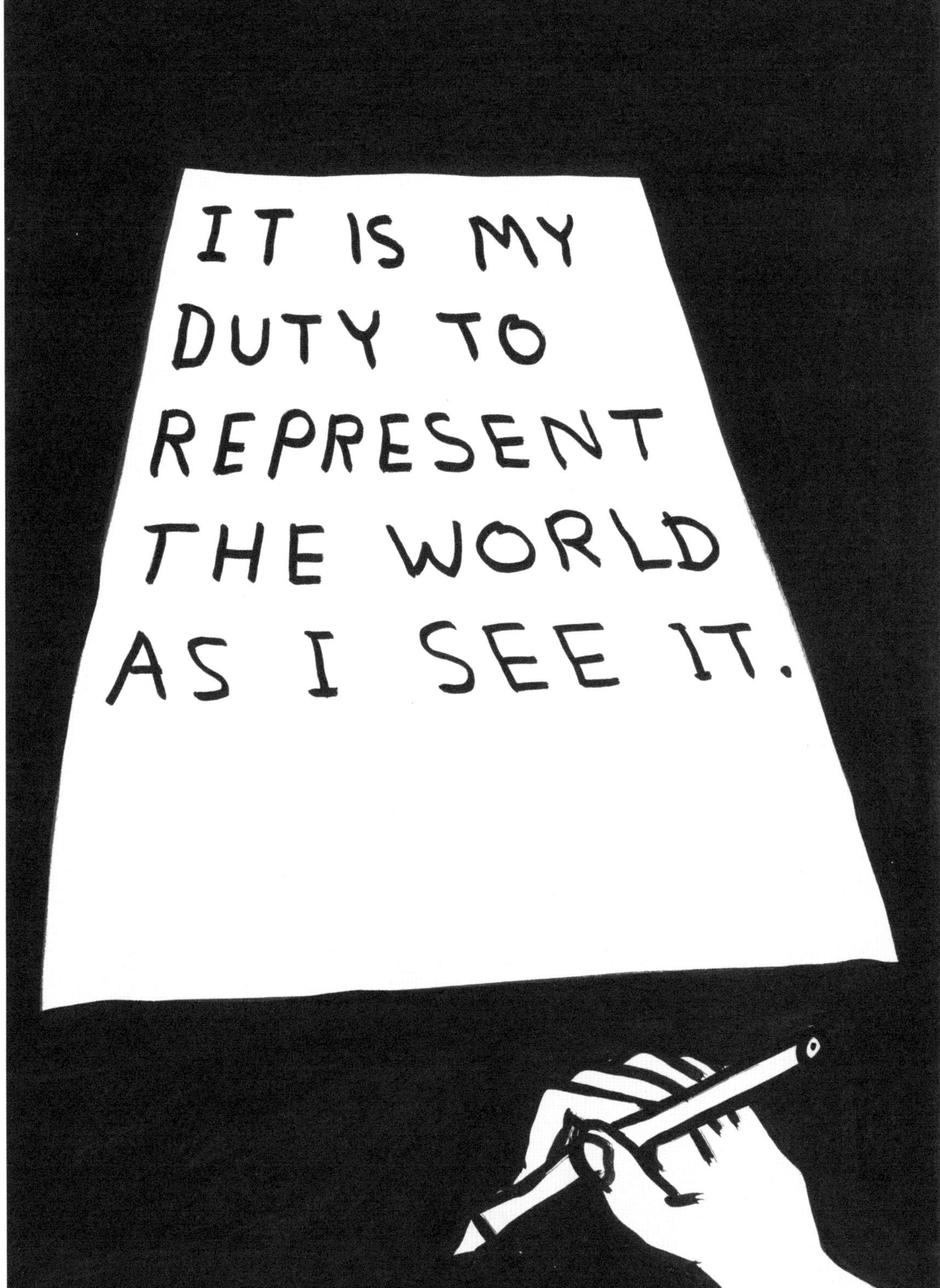

Untitled, 2010

Door, 2007

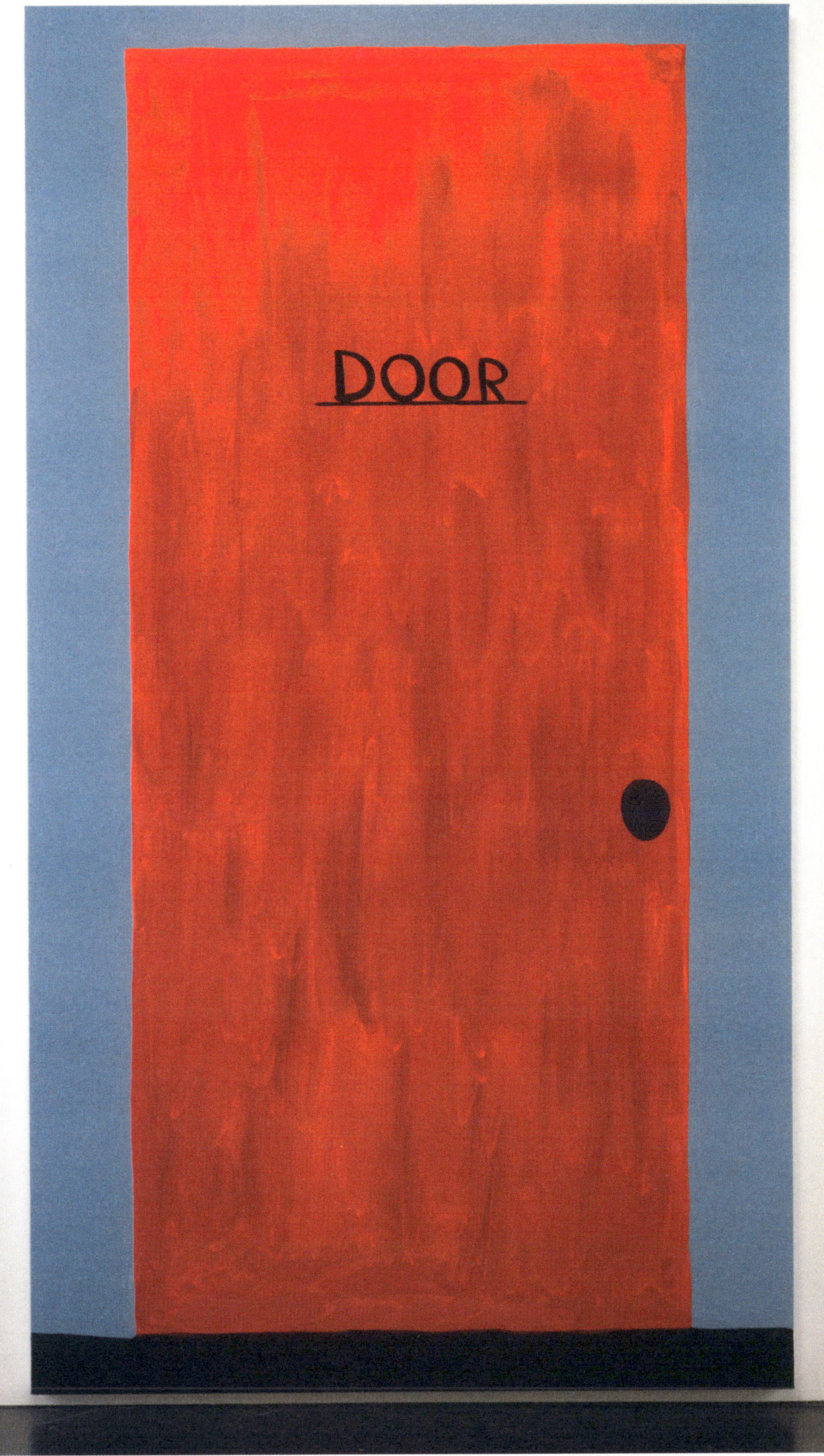
DOOR

A Long-Distance Conversation between Dave Eggers and David Shrigley

The following talk occurred on 27 September, 2011. It was conducted via Skype and was the third time I had ever used that technology. I was surprised by how well it worked, and was also surprised that David Shrigley appeared so clean-cut and sane. Like most people who have loved his art, I assumed he was a much more bizarre and unhinged man. But he proved to be very presentable and polite. – **Dave Eggers**

I don't think Dave really knows how to use Skype. He perhaps didn't realise that I could see him as well as him seeing me: he had the camera pointing at an odd angle so I could only see the top half of his head and the wall behind him for most of the conversation. Anyway, it was nice to talk to him.
– **David Shrigley**

    DE: Are you in Glasgow?
DS: Yeah, I'm in my office.
    DE: What's that screen behind you?
DS: That's my drawing board.
    DE: You draw on a vertical surface like that?
DS: Yeah, it's an ergonomic prescription. I have a back problem.
    DE: I do, too. What part of the back is it for you? Let's talk about our back problems.
DS: Well, I have a lower back problem. I have ergonomic furniture as part of my treatment. Part of the furniture is this drawing board, which is at a good angle, and I have this chair I'm sitting on there, which is kind of high up, and I've got a computer which is really high up. And I do yoga.
    DE: That is hugely surprising to me.

DS: I was there today, doing yoga. Sweating and grunting. And you know, I go on yoga holidays with my wife.
    DE: See, between your clean-cut appearance and the yoga, my perceptions have been totally upended. I thought you'd be doing this interview from a bar somewhere, where you'd be in the corner, drunk and filthy. One would presume it's much more of a fringe personality who is creating the artwork you create. The person responsible for your drawings is not necessarily the person that's doing yoga.
DS: Yeah, yeah. When I'm talking about doing yoga, I feel like I'm talking about somebody else anyway. When people are talking about you, and writing about you and your work, it seems like they're writing about somebody else. So I suppose it's only right and proper that I should be writing from the point of view of somebody else as well. And also, I don't really understand why anybody is really that interested in me either. I think the parts that I create are more interesting. They generally are kind of, you know, slightly psychotic, dysfunctional, sociopaths.
    DE: You've said before that when you're drawing, you're taking on a role. That is, that there's a persona, almost, that you've generated who is behind your work. That's something that not everyone knows about or assumes – that the artist is often shaping a persona that's different than the artist's everyday self. But I wonder how you get to the place where you create. The drawings, at their best, I think, have a desperateness to them that I like to assume

you're only reaching after drinking heavily,
or being depressed, or being alone at 4 a.m.
DS: Well, I'm quite disciplined about the way that
I go about using my brain in that light. I'm always
totally sober. There's a specific amount of caffeine
and sugar and nutrition and work at a certain time,
I suppose, to get stuff done. But yeah it's kind of
late in the evening I tend to get quite a lot of stuff
done, and also earlier in the day. As well as, you get
to your 40s and suddenly you realise you've got to
eat stuff otherwise you get really grumpy. There's
a certain zone that you get into that you're kind
of almost not really thinking anymore, but it just
feels like it's all pouring out of you like water out of
a jug. But it's not necessarily any good. Sometimes
it's terrible. But yeah, I do have those moments. But
I'm also quite a type B person in the sense that if
I had a glass of wine, that's it, game over. I'm going
upstairs to watch *CSI: Miami.*

> **DE:** I think, though, that the viewer gets
> the experience that you are having fun, and
> that's fairly rare. I think it's what the viewer
> responds to with your stuff. It seems like a
> train of thought that actually reflects what
> goes through our minds, and that you're not
> self censoring. But you must edit.

DS: I guess there's only 25 per cent of the stuff that
I make that makes it, that doesn't go in the garbage
or the recycling. I throw a lot away. My attitude
towards it is very free, because I know there's only
a one-in-four chance that I'll keep the drawing in
question. And at that point you're not really worried
too much about making a mess of it.

> **DE:** But the mess of it is part of what works
> with what you do. The drawings are
> somehow funnier because of the awkward-
> ness or the crudeness, and the crossings-
> out. You can't improve upon how sort of
> perfect that mix is, between the text and
> these awkward figures, with their terrible
> hair, and their bones that don't go in the
> right direction, the overlapping lines.
> Do you remember the moment when
> you arrived at your style?

DS: I've always sort of drawn in that way, and that's
just my handwriting, that kind of drawing. That's
kind of the drawing that you use just to describe
something to somebody. You say 'I saw somebody
that looked a bit like this' and you just do a drawing.
It's not the kind of drawing where you're trying
to get their eyes in the right place, you're just trying
to tell somebody something as directly as possible.
I guess that's what that kind of drawing is, it's
kind of a non-drawing, in a way. It's somewhere
between handwriting and drawing. At a certain point
I realised that I just wasn't interested in objective
drawing. I think my work has become quite stylised
and I'm only interested in a certain thing. But then
again there are also certain rules to what I do,
like I'm not allowed to re-draw or anything, it just
is what it is. It's not like I'm trying to consciously
achieve a style, I guess, although I'm sure there is
some kind of manner to it.

> **DE:** Between the casualness of the work,
> and the fact that it's funny – these are art
> world no-nos.

DS: I know a lot of people still don't see my work
as serious, because it's funny. But then again, I've
come to realise that the opposite of seriousness is
not humour. The opposite of seriousness is incom-
petence. It's somebody who isn't really engaged
with what they're doing. And the opposite of
humour is maybe sadness.

> **DE:** The art world does tend to attract a
> very self-serious type of person. I noticed
> that when I was in art school myself,
> and then when I worked at an art gallery.
> I tend to think that there's a fear of
> acknowledging the inherent absurdity of,
> say, sticking a urinal on a plinth and calling
> it art. Duchamp knew it was absurd, and
> very funny, but I've been around a lot
> of art-world people who treat Duchamp
> with great seriousness, when that's sort
> of the opposite of his purpose as an artist.
> It's as if to crack a smile would be to
> diminish the importance of the work.

DS: For me, humour is kind of volatile. I don't think
you'd ever judge a writer any differently according to

the humour in their work, but they do that with fine artists. Quite obviously I don't really agree with that.

DE: It's a weird no-humour zone, right? It's a strange thing to remove humour completely from all visual art, but it has been removed from 95 per cent of it, as if humour was some very tangential or superfluous part of the human experience as opposed to being very central.

DS: I agree. I guess the odd thing for me is that I am kind of a real cartoonist, as well as being a real fine artist, in the sense that my work is filed under humour in the bookshop, sometimes as well as being filed under art. And also a lot of people who look at the work think I'm just one of those comic-book type dudes. Which is nice, but I guess I've got a foot in either camp, as it were. To be honest, in terms of the way my work is received, I feel like I'm taken far more seriously than I should be anyway.

DE: In your last few books, though, there's a real mix of the outright funny stuff and then a lot of stuff that's I think much more pained and political. Humour that I like comes from a place of anger, exasperation. I was re-reading a lot of Vonnegut recently, and then I was looking through your drawings and there was a similar sense of humour – a dark humour that comes from a place of frustration, of wanting better for humanity.

DS: Well, I suppose it's a cathartic thing. It enables you to say what you want to say, and vent your anger about just the lunatic, idiot world we live in. I think I'm a much saner person because I'm able to be an artist, or be a kind of artist that I am, where you can make work about how horrible people are, and how unacceptable it is that they are so horrible and how unacceptable it is that people accept how horrible these people are. I kind of assume that's a given for everybody, that everybody feels that there are quite a number of aspects of contemporary life in an advanced capitalist society that are really unacceptable, but what can we do to change it? Make stupid drawings I suppose.

DE: That's step one, right? In the revolutionary handbook, make stupid drawings.

DS: The thing is, I was actually given the opportunity to make political cartoons for this magazine called the *New Statesman*, in the UK, and I did straight political cartoons for 18 months. But then I stopped doing it because it became a bit contrived, because it was all too brief and I was having to draw pictures of David Cameron and Tony Blair and other politicians, and I just can't do that. I'm not a regular caricaturist. I really liked the fact that I was able to make that political commentary, but I guess the way that in my mind politics manifests itself is what I'm good at, which is not necessarily doing caricatures of… really direct and topical things. So I'd like to do things to change the world, but I'm not really quite sure what I'm supposed to do.

DE: There are some drawings in this book where I think they're going to have a punch line at the end of some kind. But then there is no punch line. Are there certain days when you're just despairing and can't bring yourself to make it funny?

DS: It's not really despairing, but more about the process of making the work. I have a discipline of making the work, and it involves just drawing every day. Sometimes they're good and sometimes they're rubbish. But the only important thing is that I did it. From that practical point of view, I don't worry. I have good days and bad days like everybody.

DE: Let's talk about art school. Was your work accepted in school? Were you encouraged? I would think we were studying art at the same time and, because I came from the cartoon world, I wasn't made very welcome.

DS: My experience of art school in Glasgow, where I studied, was that in the end, people didn't really get what I did. I think that they thought I was doing something inappropriate, or maybe that I wasn't a serious artist. Ultimately, I wasn't taken seriously at art school and wasn't seen as being a very good artist as such. I left with quite a poor mark. We get marks for our degrees, for when you study art. And I got kind of, the mark that you get for turning up.

I didn't get the mark that you get if you're actually talented. So when I left art school I was pretty pissed off with the establishment as I saw it, which was basically my teachers at art school. But I'm not really angry with them, I just think they didn't really know anything about art. But I was really quite arrogant, anyway, I think I felt that I knew better than they did. I think that's why I made the real decision to become a cartoonist I suppose, because it was quite a gesture, a game of fine art as I saw it.

> **DE:** And that interaction with the world of fine art is important in your stuff. I don't think I've seen your originals in a gallery, come to think of it. I've only seen your work in books, and was surprised when I learned you had gallery shows and all that. Do you think that the book medium sort of gets around some of the exclusivity that's inherent in the art world?

DS: I think it does. I guess everybody knows how to read a book, but not everybody knows how to walk around an art gallery. When you're in Chelsea in New York, when you're walking around the Phillips auction house, it's a really intimidating experience for people who might like art, or might want to have an appreciation of art, but they don't feel very welcomed there. Whereas, if you take a book off of a bookshelf in a bookstore then obviously you know what to do with it. You're not really sure whether you should smile or laugh in the art gallery, or whether you're allowed to rub your chin, or scratch your head, or whatever. For the likes of my sister, for example, she wouldn't feel very comfortable at some fancy gallery in New York, and wouldn't really know what to do. She'd sort of look around and look at her watch and fiddle with her Blackberry I suppose. But books are accessible.

> **DE:** But galleries are part of it for you.

DS: I guess, because that's what pays my mortgage. That's why I don't have to teach at the art school, because the original drawings sell and I don't have to have a job. I think I'd rather be judged by a book than some exhibitions. But I guess also, I make sculptural work because I have exhibitions I suppose, and if I never had any exhibitions and just made books,

I probably wouldn't make any sculptures.

> **DE:** How long have you been doing the sculptures?

DS: Ever since I was at art school. I've always made stuff for as long as I've made drawings I suppose. I've been making some ceramics in my studio, a lot of the sculpture I do is ceramic now. Like casts and push moulds, and quite primitive mould-making but with ceramics and then glazed. I guess I make ceramics because it's a bit crafty and it sort of seems to fit somehow aesthetically with my graphic work. And ceramics are somehow a little bit unsophisticated, which I sort of feel is my style.

> **DE:** That unsophisticated aspect of your work is kind of a nice place to be, I would think. It seems really liberating. I know you identify with cartoonists, but then again, cartoonists actually are expected to polish their work. Most cartoonists are very tidy, very practiced and professional.

DS: Yeah, I'm always interested in real cartoonists, and I look through their books and stuff. I identify with them I guess. Maybe it's about nihilism or something. When I meet fine artists, I never really feel like… you know, you meet people and some of them you get on with and some of them you don't. But I feel that I don't generally feel very sympathetic with gallery artists, even though I might like them. But then when I'm in a show about comic books and cartoons, I feel very sympathetic with all these people because their work is about exactly what I'm interested in, which is usually just violence and sexual beings – that kind of thing. Most times people ask 'Who are your favorite artists?' And one or two cartoonists would come to mind. But in a way, I feel like I have a lot more fun than they do, because I can do whatever I like, and it doesn't have to be anything. The rules are that I don't have to do it again, I can do it once, and in that way I am totally free. I feel lucky in that respect.

> **DE:** Do you keep a notebook? When you're out and about are you writing things down?

DS: You want to see it?

> **DE:** Yeah.

DS: Here it is. [DS shows the notebook via Skype] It's just a heading that says 'Beer'. I'm not quite sure what that means. But I have a Moleskine book like everybody else.

> **DE:** How often are you transferring ideas from the notebook as opposed to just sitting and spontaneously doing stuff?

DS: Well I guess I've got a notebook. You know, if I'm on the bus or something, I can just write stuff down. But it's not very often, to be honest, that I actually use stuff in the notebook. It's just that there are certain statements that come into your life that you just want to write down. You don't want to waste those thoughts somehow, even though I'm not really quite sure what currency they are. I think they're healthy things to have. But I don't keep a diary. And I don't do a blog. I just do Twitter, which I suppose is a bit like a diary, isn't it?

> **DE:** I didn't know you did that. I still haven't figured out how to follow those things.

DS: So you don't have a publicist who basically says, 'Do you do Twitter?'

> **DE:** No, no.

DS: And you say 'I don't want to do Twitter,' and they say, 'Well that's OK,' and then they send you this YouTube video that's basically a small infomercial about the merits of social networking, and how you're a total buffoon who doesn't have any actual kind of commercial product to sell. And so, basically that was about a year ago, and I've been doing Twitter ever since. It's just kind of rubbish, but I understand it. It's like a diary but, then again, it's also really vain and horrible in a way as well. You're just telling people stuff and I can't really respond to everything that everybody writes to me.

> **DE:** It would be a great burden.

DS: Yeah, but she's a nice lady, that publicist. She might get fired if I don't do it.

> **DE:** So you're saving someone's job. You're contributing to the economy. You're a job creator. That's very noble of you.

DS: She worked really hard to get that job and I don't want to mess it up for her.

> **DE:** It's all out of generosity and kindness that you do these things.

DS: Yeah.

> **DE:** So we should wrap up soon, and I'm thinking because we're about to say good bye, I really want to know about something. It's the way that you say goodbye. It seems like there's a new British thing, that when you say 'goodbye' on the phone, you say 'byeeeee'. You don't say just a simple quick, even-toned 'goodbye'. It's more like a long, fading 'byeeeee' – it rises up and away like a kite. And I swear this has happened in the last ten years. Every British person I know does this. Was there some sort of mandate that came down from a central office that told you all how to do it? It really seems like a recent phenomenon. At the same time that every American began calling everything 'amazing'. you guys started doing the kite flying 'byeeeee'.

DS: Yeah, I guess I do that. But I also say 'Cheerio' to people.

> **DE:** No you do not. Have you really said this?

DS: Yeah, I say 'Cheerio' to everybody. That's just the way I say goodbye to people. It's quite Scottish actually, to say 'Cheerio' or 'Cherry bye'.

> **DE:** 'Cherry bye'? What is that? What does that mean? That's terrible, that shouldn't be allowed. I thought the Scottish were prouder than that.

DS: The Scottish have no shame. I'm actually English as well. I grew up in England so, I have an English accent, as you may recognise. So I'm sort of a politically Scottish, for 23 years, but I'm ethnically English.

> **DE:** I've never heard 'ethnically English' before. I like it.

DS: I like saying it.

> **DE:** See, now we're sounding smart. This will be the best interview ever. And when we transcribe it and we'll make ourselves sound smarter.

DS: We'll get a third party to do that.

> **DE:** It will be incredible. Okay, now it's time for you to say your 'byeeeee'.

DS: Byeeeee.

> **DE:** Yup. That's how it's done. Perfect.

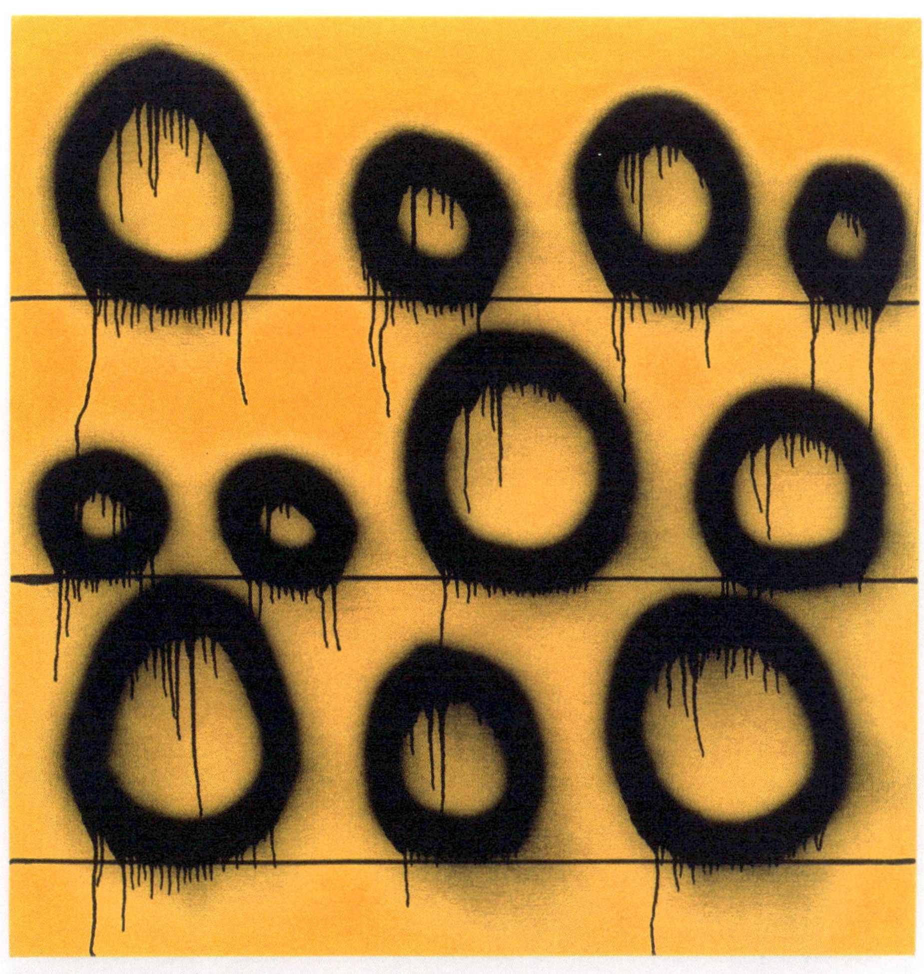

OoO…, 2007

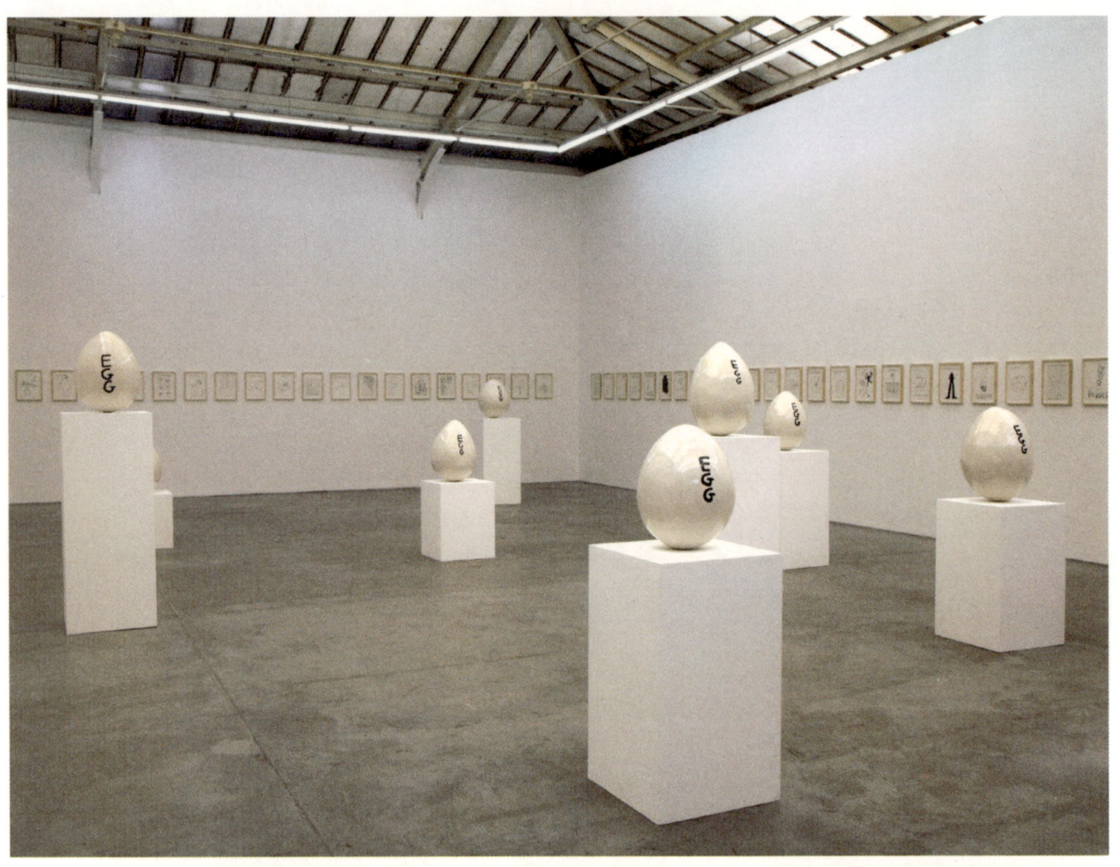

Eggs, 2011

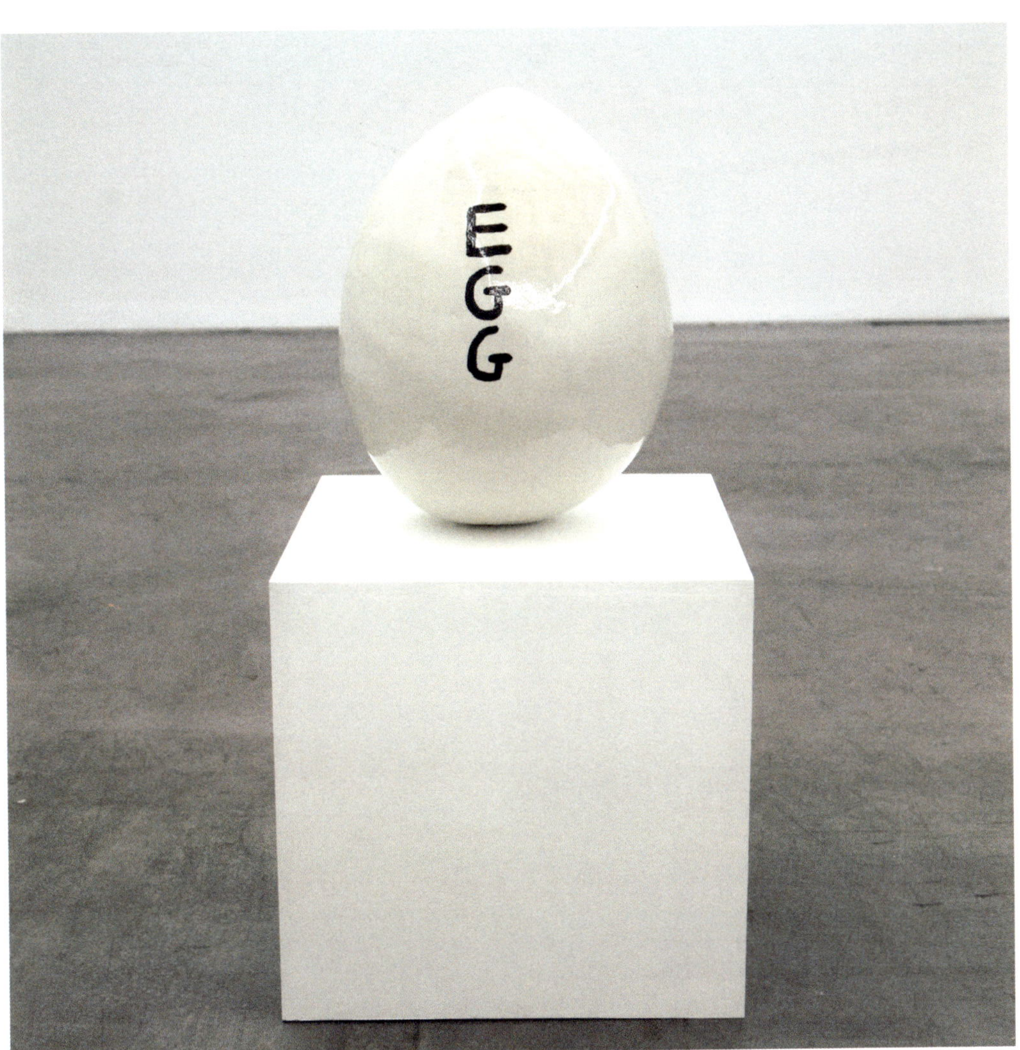
EGG

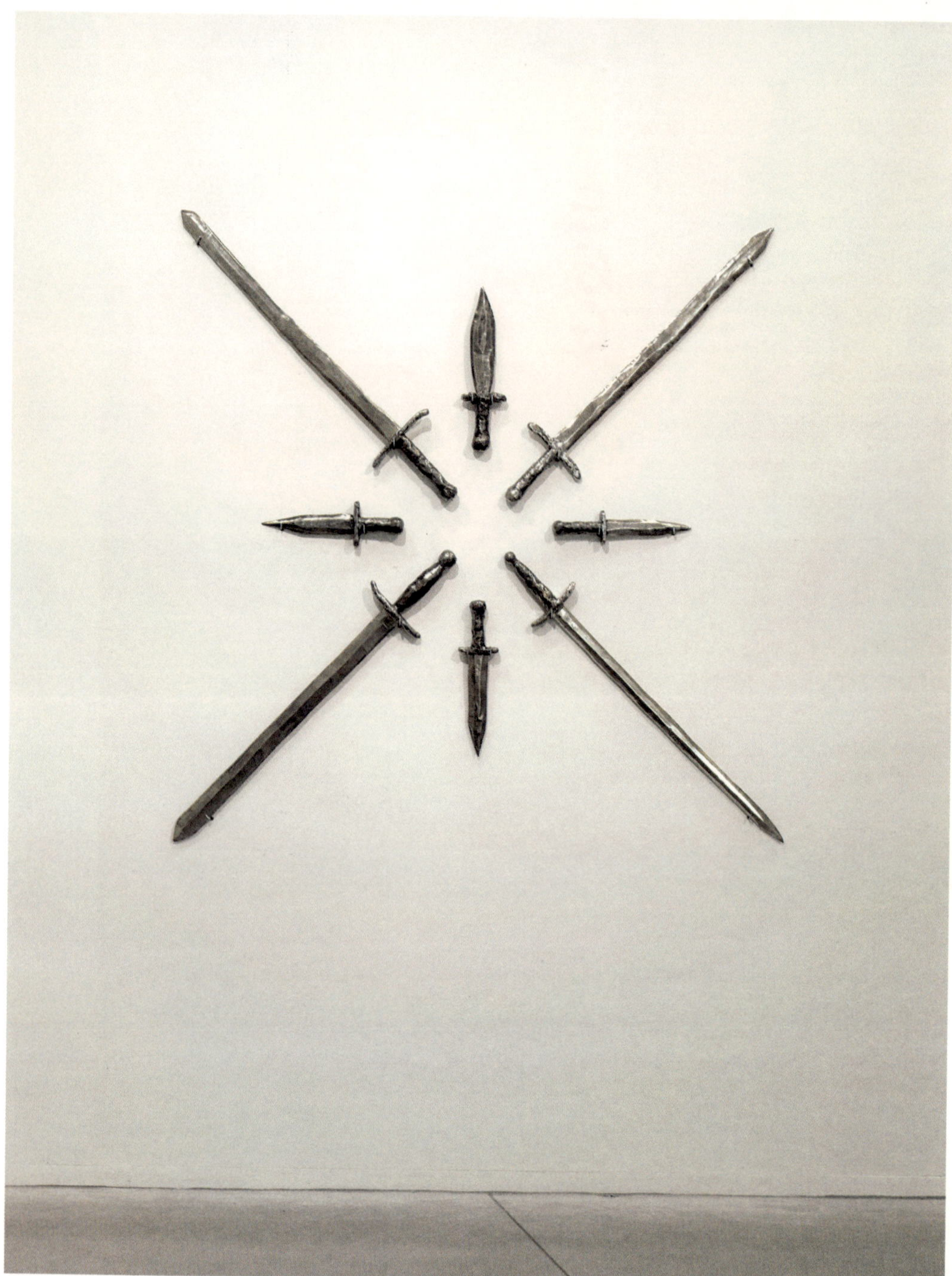

Swords and Daggers, 2010

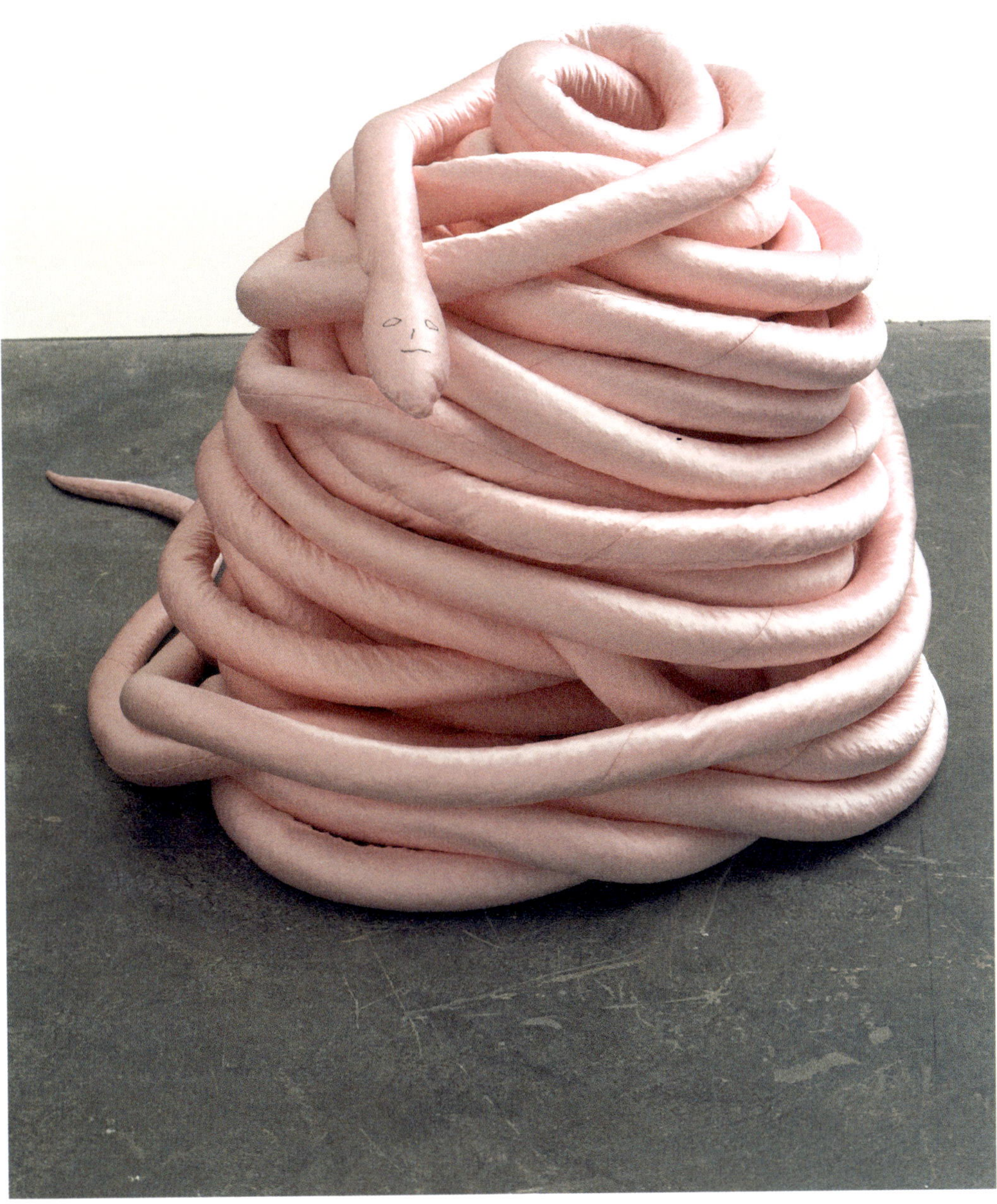

Strange Toy for Strange Child, 2002

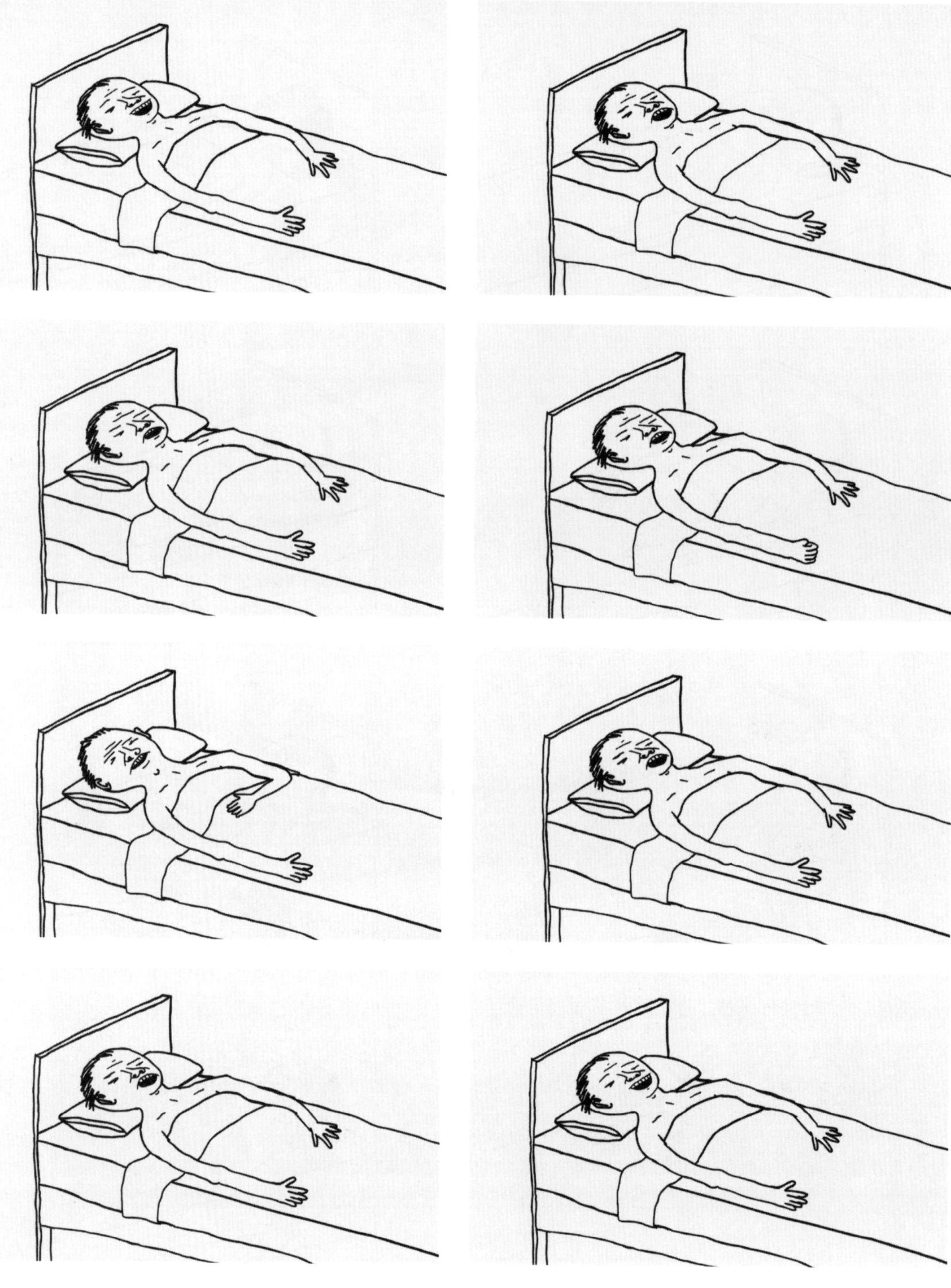

Sleep, 2008

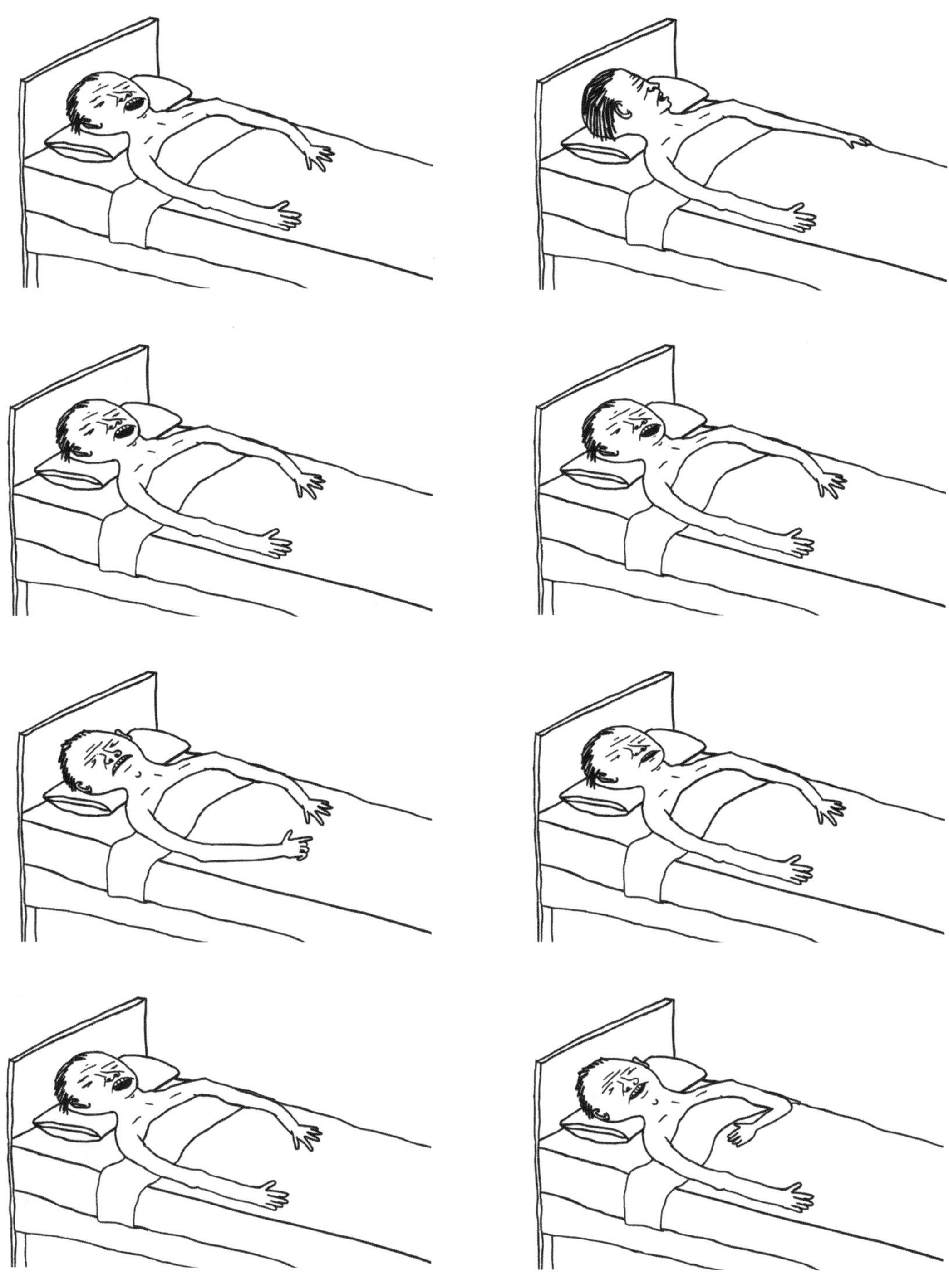

Overleaf: *God is Idle,* 2007. Wall painting at Malmö Konsthall

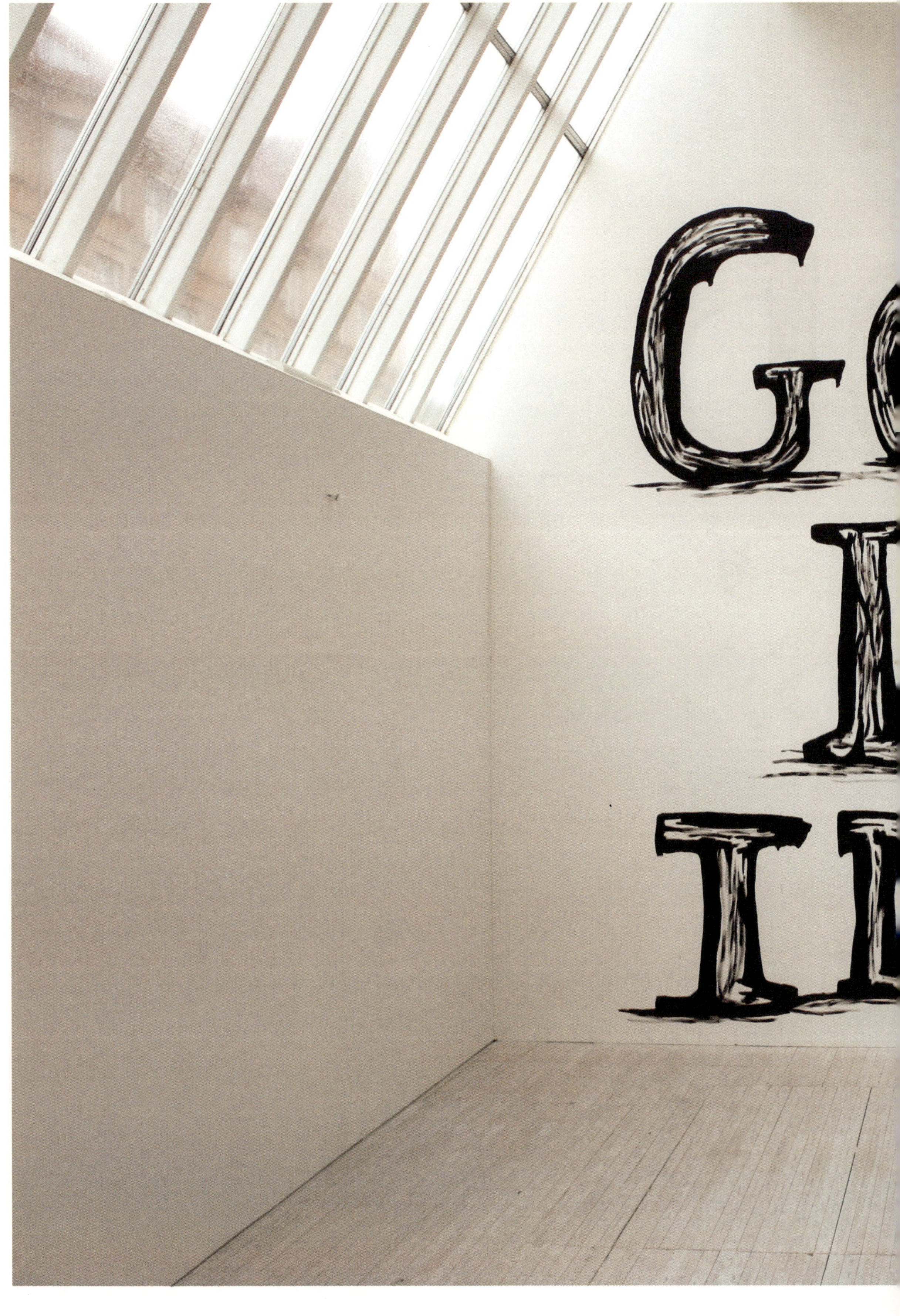

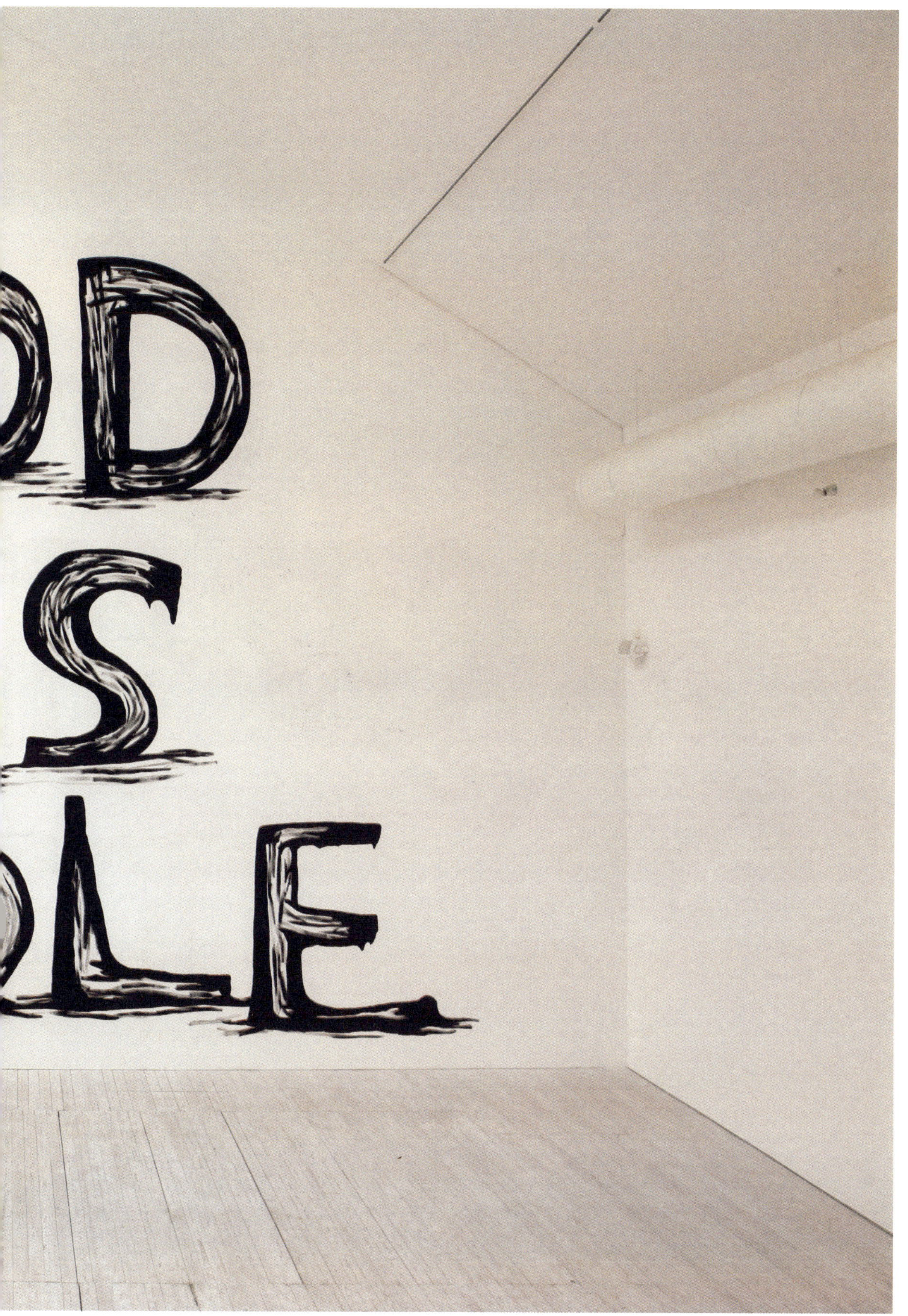

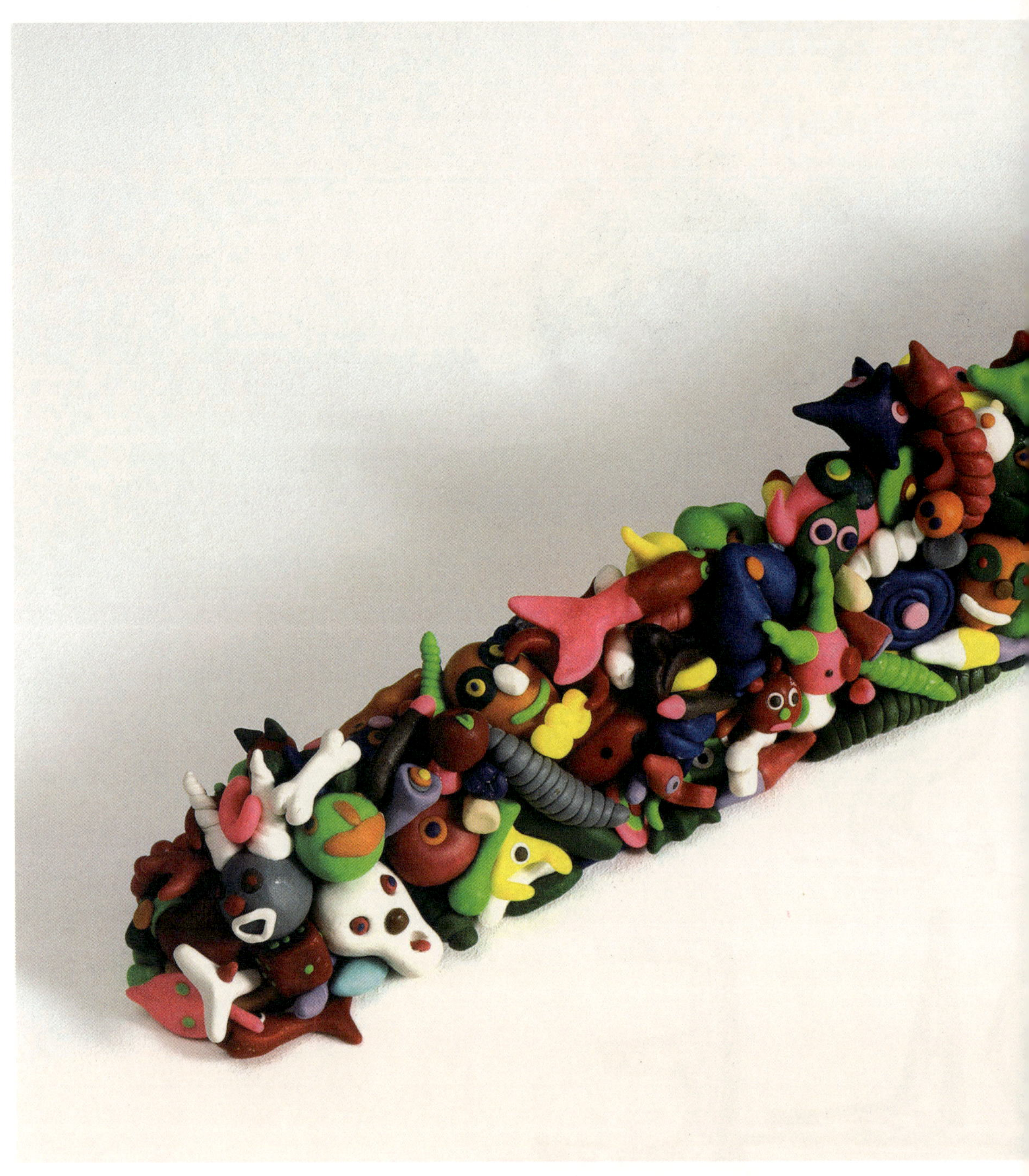

The Contents of the Gap between the Refrigerator and the Cooker, 1995

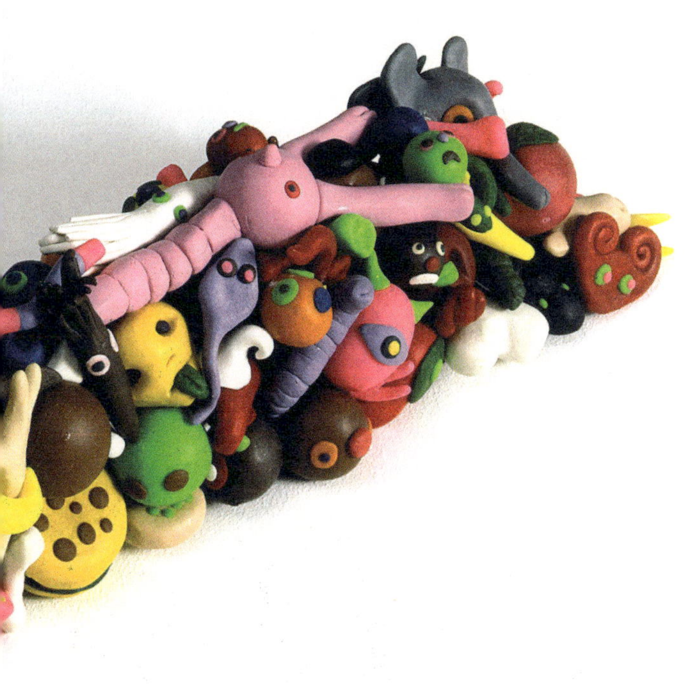

List of Works

Measurements are given in centimetres
height before width and depth

p.23
Leisure Centre, 1992
C-print
25.7 x 25.5
Courtesy the artist

pp.164–65
*The Contents of the Gap between
the Refrigerator and the Cooker,* 1995
Plastic and acrylic paint
57 x 9.5 x 11.5
Private Collection, London

p.56
Big Nut, 1996
Cast bronze and acrylic paint
27 x 25 x 23
Courtesy the artist and Stephen
Friedman Gallery, London

p.18
Ignore This Building, 1996
C-print
30.5 x 40.6
Courtesy the artist

p.20
Lost, 1996
C-print
30.5 x 40.6
Courtesy the artist

p.22
Imagine the Green is Red, 1998
C-print
30.5 x 30.5
Courtesy the artist

p.19
One Day a Big Wind will come and...,
1998
C-print
20.3 x 20.3
Courtesy the artist

p.17
Pumpkin, 1998
C-print
25.2 x 24
Courtesy the artist

p.21
River for Sale, 1999
C-print
30.5 x 40.5
Courtesy the artist

p.16
Untitled (Arson), 2000
C-print
40 x 30
Courtesy the artist

p.112
Black Forest Gateaux, 2001
Oil paint and acrylic composite
13 x 10.5 x 8
Private Collection

p.46
Nailed biscuit, 2001
Painted acrylic composite and nail
7 x 7 x 11
Courtesy the artist

p.47
What Decay Looks Like, 2001
Acrylic composite and mirror
Tooth: 17 x 9 x 7; Mirror: 130 x 100
Courtesy the artist and Stephen
Friedman Gallery, London

p.22
Anti-Depressants, 2002
C-print
28 x 41
Courtesy the artist

p.17
Balloon, 2002
C-print
30.5 x 38
Courtesy the artist

p.113
Five years of Toenail clippings, 2002
Glass and toenails
Sphere: 32 (dia)
Private Collection, Switzerland

p.18
Hate, 2002
C-print
30.5 x 41.3
Courtesy the artist

p.57
Nutless, 2002
Taxidermy squirrel and tree stump
48.5 x 35 x 31
Private Collection, Switzerland

p.159
Strange Toy for Strange Child, 2002
Fabric, polystyrene balls and felt pen
800 x 8 x 8
Courtesy the artist and Stephen
Friedman Gallery, London

p.21
Teeth, 2002
Black-and-white photograph
48.8 x 39
Courtesy the artist

p.64
Unfinished Letter, 2003
Painted steel
68 x 38 x 49
Courtesy the artist and
private collection, Switzerland

p.117
Wooden Tooth, 2003
Wood
22.9 x 38.1 x 29.2
Courtesy the artist and Anton Kern
Gallery, New York

pp.66–77
Untitled (Photographs with Text), 2005
20 black-and-white photographs
with text
Each: 40.5 x 30.5
Courtesy the artist

pp.62–63
New Friends, 2006
Animation, 1 minute
Museum Ritter. Marli Hoppe-Ritter
Collection, Waldenbuch/Germany

p.43
Cheers, 2007
Rubber waders and
polyurethane foam
145 x 45 x 58
Courtesy the artist and Stephen
Friedman Gallery, London

p.147
Door, 2007
Acrylic on canvas
230 x 130.5
Private Collection, Switzerland

pp.162–63
God is Idle, 2007
Wall painting
Dimensions variable
Courtesy the artist

p.39
Hanging Sign, 2007
Steel, wood and acrylic paint
51 x 79 x 10
Private Collection

pp.50–51
Keys, 2007
Steel
99 x 39 x 19
Courtesy the artist

pp.128–29
Light Switch, 2007
Single-screen black-and-white
projected animation, audio track
1 minute 29 seconds
Tate: Purchased 2008

p.155
OoO..., 2007
Acrylic on canvas
100.5 x 100
Private Collection, Switzerland

p.125
Stick figures having sex on car hood, 2007
Metal figures and car hood
50 x 158 x 112
Courtesy the artist and
Stephen Friedman Gallery, London

p.40
The Bell, 2007
Brass bell and aluminium sign
Bell: 31 x 17 x 17, Sign: 7 x 10 x 9
Arts Council Collection, Southbank
Centre, London

p.41
Tomorrow, 2007
Acrylic on canvas
100.5 x 100
Private Collection, Switzerland

p.59
Bone Clock, 2008
Polyester bone and clock mechanism
44 x 9.5 x 6
Courtesy the artist and
Stephen Friedman Gallery, London

pp.110–11
Conveyor Belt, 2008
Animation, 3 minutes 7 seconds
Museum Ludwig Köln

p.38
Crushed Ladder, 2008
Aluminium
Dimensions variable
Courtesy the artist and
Anton Kern Gallery, New York

p.131
Do Not Linger At The Gate, 2008
Powder-coated steel
229.5 x 131.2 x 10
The Frank and Cherryl Cohen
Collection

p.48
Gravestone, 2008
Granite and gold leaf
122 x 61 x 10
Private Collection, Switzerland

pp.160–61
Sleep, 2008
Animation, 8 minutes
Museum Ludwig Köln

pp.118–19
The Philosopher, 2008
Painted ceramic and cacti
23 x 25 x 38
Courtesy the artist and
Stephen Friedman Gallery, London

pp.126–27
Ones, 2009
Animation, 3 minutes 9 seconds
Courtesy the artist

p.35
Ostrich, 2009
Taxidermy ostrich
195 x 160 x 95
Courtesy the artist and
Stephen Friedman Gallery, London

pp.120–23
Untitled, 2009–
Painted steel and fibreplast
Dimensions variable
Courtesy the artist, Galleri Nicolai
Wallner, Copenhagen, and Stephen
Friedman Gallery, London

p.114
Bomb, 2010
Glazed ceramic
25 x 43 x 25
Courtesy the artist and
Stephen Friedman Gallery, London

pp.36–37
Boots, 2010
Glazed ceramic
Dimensions variable
Courtesy the artist and
Anton Kern Gallery, New York

p.115
Ceramic Ear, 2010
Glazed ceramic
50 x 30 x 8
Courtesy the artist

pp.44–45
Finger, 2010
Bronze
194 x 3 x 3
Private Collection, Germany and
courtesy Anton Kern Gallery, New York

p.55b
Fist, 2010
Bronze
6.4 x 11.4 x 10.8
Courtesy the artist and
Anton Kern Gallery, New York

p.61
I'm Dead, 2010
Taxidermy puppy, wooden sign
and acrylic paint
70 x 15 x 25
Hamilton Corporate Finance Ltd

pp.52–53
IT, 2010
Bronze
10.2 x 12.7 x 1.9
Courtesy the artist and
Anton Kern Gallery, New York

p.116
Rib Cage, 2010
Steel and plaster
52.7 x 78.1 x 36.2
Courtesy the artist and
Anton Kern Gallery, New York

p.54
Ring, 2010
Bronze
1 x 2.5 x 2.5
Courtesy the artist and
Anton Kern Gallery, New York

p.54
Ring, 2010
Bronze
1.3 x 3.2 x 3.2
Courtesy the artist and
Anton Kern Gallery, New York

p.54
Ring, 2010
Bronze
1.3 x 3.2 x 3.2
Courtesy the artist and
Anton Kern Gallery, New York

p.54
Ring, 2010
Bronze
1.6 x 1.3 x 1.3
Courtesy the artist and
Anton Kern Gallery, New York

p.55t
Screw, 2010
Bronze
6.4 x 17.8 x 6.4
Courtesy the artist and
Anton Kern Gallery, New York

p.158
Swords and Daggers, 2010
Patinated bronze in eight parts
Dimensions variable
Courtesy the artist and Stephen
Friedman Gallery, London

p.58
The dead and the dying, 2010
40 glazed ceramic figures
Dimensions variable
British Council Collection

pp.132–45
Untitled, 2010
Acrylic on paper
Dimensions variable
Courtesy the artist

pp.156–57
Eggs, 2011
Glazed ceramic
Dimensions variable
Courtesy the artist, Yvon Lambert

p.96
Untitled, 2011
Ink on paper
29.7 x 21
Private Collection

p.97
Untitled, 2011
Ink on paper
29.7 x 21
K is S Collection, Paris

p.96
Untitled, 2011
Ink on paper
29.7 x 21
Collection Nick van Woert, Brooklyn

List of Works Exhibited, but Not Illustrated

It's Freezing In Here, 2000
Neon
90 x 130
Courtesy the artist and Galerie
Francesca Pia, Zurich

The Letter, 2009
Animation, 2 minutes
Courtesy the artist

Untitled, 2011
Selected drawings
Ink on paper
29.7 x 21
Courtesy of the artist, Yvon Lambert.

Headless Drummer, 2012
Animation, 1 minute
Courtesy the artist

Untitled, 2012
Selected paintings
Acrylic on paper
75.5 x 56
Courtesy the artist and Stephen
Friedman Gallery, London

Very Large Cup of Tea, 2012
Glazed ceramic
Cup: 38 x 50 x 40, Saucer: 7 x 55 x 55
Courtesy the artist

(Auto)biography

1968
Born in Macclesfield, England.

1970
Family moves to Oadby, Leicestershire.

1972
Develops keen interest in dinosaurs.

1977
Fails Cycling Proficiency Test.

1981
Buys his first album: *Kings of the Wild Frontier* by Adam and the Ants.

1982
Visits Tate Gallery for the first time, to see a retrospective of works by sculptor Jean Tinguely.

1986
Obtains UK driving licence.

1987
Obtains A Level in Art (grade D).

1987–88
Enrols on Art and Design Foundation Course at Leicester Polytechnic. Meets Jonathan Monk, who becomes a close friend.

1988
Moves to Glasgow to study in the department of Environmental Art at Glasgow School of Art (with Jonathan Monk).

1991
Awarded Honours Degree (2:2).

1991–95
Works part-time in community art education for Glasgow City Council.

1992–96
Takes up post as a gallery guide at Centre for Contemporary Arts (CCA), Glasgow. Also works on exhibition installations for the gallery.

1992
First group exhibition: *In Here*, Transmission Gallery, Glasgow.

Self-publishes first book: *Slug Trails*.

1993
Provides title for *My Little Toilet*, an exhibition curated by Jonathan Monk. The exhibition is held at a flat shared by DS, JM and Jacqueline Donachie, and includes work by them and most of their friends.

Accidentally damages work by Cathy de Monchaux while installing it at CCA. The artist appears not to notice. Or maybe she does but is too kind to say anything.

1994
First group exhibition outside the UK: *Some of My Friends*, Galleri Campbells Occasionally, Copenhagen.

1995
Participates as an extra in the movie *Trainspotting* (along with half the population of Glasgow).

First solo exhibition, *Map of the Sewer*, held at Transmission Gallery, Glasgow.

A drawing by DS appears on the cover of *Frieze* magazine (Issue 25, November–December), to accompany Michael Bracewell's article on the artist, 'Jesus Doesn't Want Me for a Sunbeam'.

1996
Becomes a tenant at Glasgow Sculpture Studios.

First book on sale that is not self published: *Err* (Bookworks, London).

First drawings are sold, priced £50 each.

1997
First solo exhibition at Galerie Francesca Pia, Bern.

First solo exhibition at Galleri Nicolai Wallner, Copenhagen.

First solo exhibition at Stephen Friedman Gallery, London.

1998
First solo exhibition at Yvon Lambert, Paris.

Publishes first of many books with Redstone Press, London: *Why We Got the Sack from the Museum*.

1999–2000
Weekly cartoon runs in *The Independent* on Sunday.

2000
Designs *Cocaine & Heroin* salt and pepper shakers.

Participates in *British Art Show 5* (organised by Hayward Touring, London), touring to venues in Edinburgh, Southampton, Cardiff and Birmingham.

2001
Obtains California Driver's License.

Solo exhibition at Center for Curatorial Studies (CCS), Hessel Museum of Art, Bard College, Annandale-on-Hudson, New York.

2002
Solo exhibitions at Camden Arts Centre,
London; UCLA Hammer Museum,
Los Angeles; and Musée d'art moderne
et contemporain (MAMCO), Geneva.

First solo exhibition at Anton Kern
Gallery, New York.

2003
Collaborates with artist collective
Shynola on promotional video for 'Good
Song' by the band Blur.

Commissioned by Art on the Underground
to create billboards for Gloucester Road
Underground Station, London.

Solo exhibition in the project space at
Kunsthaus Zürich.

2005
Makes a short film (with Chris Shepherd)
for Channel 4 based on his 2003 book
Who I Am and What I Want. The work was
commissioned by animate! and funded by
Arts Council England and Channel 4.

Takes up yoga.

Worried Noodles (The Empty Sleeve)
is published by German record label
Tomlab. It is an empty record
sleeve with a book of faux lyrics.

Begins drawing weekly cartoon for
The Guardian newspaper.

2007
Worried Noodles CD is published, with
tracks by 39 musicians, using lyrics from
the original songbook.

Designs record cover for Deerhoof's
album *Friend Opportunity*.

Solo exhibition, *Everything Must Have a
Name*, at Malmö Konsthall, Sweden.

2008
Solo exhibition at BALTIC Centre for
Contemporary Art, Gateshead.

Included in group exhibitions *Life on
Mars: 55th Carnegie International*,
Carnegie Museum of Art, Pittsburgh,
Pennsylvania, and *Laughing in a
Foreign Language* at Hayward Gallery,
Southbank Centre, London.

Collaborates on a series of painted
diptychs for *Jonathan Monk & David
Shrigley Corroborative Paintings* at
Galeria Estrany – de la Mota, Barcelona.

2009
Solo exhibitions at Bergen Kunsthall and
Kunsthalle Mainz (*New Powers*).

Begins drawing fortnightly political
cartoon to run in *New Statesman*
magazine.

2010
Included in group exhibition *Rude Bri-
tannia: British Comic Art* at Tate Britain,
London.

Begins work on *Pass the Spoon* (a sort-
of opera) with composer David Fennessy
and director Nicholas Bone.

David Shrigley at Kelvingrove – a series
of interventions in the collections of the
Kelvingrove Art Gallery and Museum,
Glasgow – is conceived for Glasgow
International Festival of Visual Art.

Creates animation for the Save the Arts
Campaign in the UK.

2011
Pass the Spoon is performed at
Tramway, Glasgow.

2012
First major UK survey exhibition, *David
Shrigley: Brain Activity* at the Hayward
Gallery, Southbank Centre, London.

Pass the Spoon is performed at Traverse
Theatre, Edinburgh and Queen Elizabeth
Hall, Southbank Centre, London.

Bibliography and Further Reading

Artist's Books

Fragments of Torn Up Drawings,
BQ Berlin, 2011.

Red Book, Redstone Press, London, 2009.

Hand, BQ, Cologne, 2008.

Ants have Sex in your Beer, Redstone
Press, London, Chronicle Books,
San Francisco, 2007.

This is a Paper Trinket for You to Wear,
Bywater Brothers Editions, Toronto, 2006.

Photographs with Text, BQ, Cologne, 2005.

Worried Noodles (The Empty Sleeve),
Tomlab, Cologne, 2005.

Blocked Path, Galleri Nicolai Wallner,
Copenhagen, 2004.

It Is It, Nieves, Zurich, 2004.

Kill Your Pets, Revolver, Frankfurt, 2004.

Let's Wrestle, Redstone Press, London,
Chronicle Books, San Francisco, 2004.

Rules, Redstone Press, London, 2004.
22 postcards.

Joy, Redstone Press, London, 2003.
22 postcards.

Leotard, BQ, Cologne, 2003.

Who I Am and What I Want Redstone Press,
London, Chronicle Books, San Francisco,
2003.

Yellow Bird with Worm, Kunsthaus
Zurich, 2003.

Evil Thoughts, Redstone Press, London,
2002. 24 postcards.

Human Achievement, Redstone Press,
London, Chronicle Books, San Francisco,
2002.

Do Not Bend, Redstone Press, London, 2001.

Grip, Pocketbooks, Edinburgh, 2000.

Hard Work, Galleri Nicolai Wallner,
Copenhagen, 2000.

The Beast Is Near, Redstone Press,
London, 1999.

Blank Page and Other Pages, Modern
Institute, Glasgow, 1998.

Centre-Parting, Little Cockroach Press,
Toronto, 1998.

Order of Service, The Armpit Press,
Glasgow, 1998.

*To Make Meringue You Must Beat The
Egg Whites Until They Look Like This,*
Galleri Nicolai Wallner, Copenhagen,1998.

Why We Got the Sack from the Museum,
Redstone Press, London, 1998.

*Drawings Done Whilst On The Phone To
Idiot,* The Armpit Press, Glasgow, 1996.

Err, Bookworks, London, 1996.

Let Not These Shadows Fall Upon Thee,
Tramway, Glasgow, 1996.

Enquire Within, The Armpit Press,
Glasgow, 1995.

Blanket of Filth, The Armpit Press,
Glasgow, 1994.

Merry Eczema, Black Rose, Glasgow, 1992.

Slug Trails, Black Rose, Glasgow, 1992.

Monographs and Exhibition Catalogues

*What The Hell Are You Doing? The
Essential David Shrigley,* Canongate
Books, Edinburgh, 2010. Introduction
by Will Self.

David Shrigley: As Soon As Possible
Centro de Arte Caja de Burgos, Spain,
2007. Text by Katrina M. Brown.

*David Shrigley: Everything Must Have A
Name,* Malmö Konsthall, Sweden, 2007.
Interviews by Jacob Fabricius and David
Bellingham.

The Book of Shrigley, Redstone Press, London, Chronicle Books, San Francisco, 2005.

David Shrigley, Domaine de Kergué-
hennec, France, 2002. Text by Neil
Mulholland and Frederic Paul.

David Shrigley, Center for Curatorial
Studies, Bard College, Annandale-on-
Hudson, New York, 2001. Texts by
Amada Cruz and Russell Ferguson.

Audio / Visual

David Shrigley: Brain Activity, Hayward
Publishing, 2012, 7-inch vinyl picture disc.

Worried Noodles, Tomlab, Cologne, 2007.
2 Audio CDs of 39 songs by 39 artists.

Forced to Speak with Others, T/A Azuli
Records, London, 2006. Audio CD.

Who I Am and What I Want, Collaboration with Chris Shepherd and animate!,
London, 2005. DVD.

Acknowledgements

The artist would like to thank:

Stephen Friedman Gallery, Galleri Nicolai Wallner, Anton Kern Gallery, Galerie Yvon Lambert, Galerie Francesca Pia and BQ Berlin.

James Newport, James Rigler, Calum Stirling, Andy Knowles, Kim Shrigley, Nick Evans, Martin Young, Stuart Grant, Emilka Radlinska, Gavin Mitchell, MP Lancaster, Maria Manton, Chris Shepherd, Andrew Sunley-Smith, Sam Smith, Glasgow Sculpture Studios, Redstone Press, Powderhall Bronze, ESP Powder Coating Glasgow, Frieze Film, Robert Sinclair, Colin Morrison-Ignatieff, staff at Hayward Gallery and Inventory Studio, London.

Hayward Gallery, Southbank Centre would like to thank:

Jane Beese, Head of Contemporary Music; Ciaran Begley, Jeremy Clapham, James Coney and Mark King, and the Hayward Art Handling Technicians; Rebecca Connock, Participation Producer; Hannah Dewar, Hayward Intern; Helen Faulkner, Marketing Manager; Ignatz Johnson-Higman, Graphic Designer; Ben Larpent, Classical Music Programme Manager; Shân Maclennan, Creative Director, Learning and Participation; Rohini Malik Okon, Participation Producer; Alison Maun, Bookings and Transport Administrator; Mike McCart, Director, Partnership and Policy; Philip Miles, Graphics Production; Gillian Moore, Head of Classical Music; Lucie Paterson, New Media Officer; Deborah Power, Publication Sales Manager; Mary Richards, Art Publisher; Faye Robson, Publishing Coordinator; Xian Rodriguez, Assistant Registrar; Antonia Shaw, Hayward Intern; Ed Smith, Technical Director; Adam Thow, Head of Retail and Buying; Daniel Wallis, Learning and Participation Project Manager; Daniel Webb, Marketing Officer; Imogen Winter, Registrar; Helena Zedig, Press Manager.

Special thanks to all of the museums, galleries and collectors who supported this exhibition with loans (see list of works), and all those who wish to remain anonymous.

This exhibition has been made possible by the provision of insurance through the Government Indemnity Scheme. The Hayward Gallery, Southbank Centre would like to thank HM Government for providing Government Indemnity and the Department for Culture, Media and Sport and Arts Council England for arranging the indemnity.

Copyright Credits

The publisher has made every effort to contact all copyright holders. If proper acknowledgement has not been made, we ask copyright holders to contact the publisher. All works of art are © the artist unless otherwise stated.

© Richard Wentworth. All Rights Reserved, DACS 2011 p.26; © Succession Marcel Duchamp/ADAGP, Paris and DACS, London 2011 p.29; Ink, pencil, colored pencil, and watercolor on paper, 14 ½ x 23 in. Originally published in *The New Yorker*, February 21, 1983. The Saul Steinberg Foundation, New York © The Saul Steinberg Foundation/Artists Rights Society (ARS), NY/DACS, London p.82t

Photographic Credits

The provider of the image is listed first, followed by the name of the photographer in brackets. All images are courtesy the artist unless otherwise stated.

Courtesy akg-images (Rainer Hackenberg) p.30t; Courtesy Arts Council Collection, Southbank Centre, London p.40; Photo: Walter Bayer pp.44-45; Courtesy Ruth Clark Photography p.60; Courtesy Digital Image Museum Associates/LACMA/Art Resource NY/Scala, Florence p.30b; Courtesy Stephen Friedman Gallery pp.56, 59, 159, 164-65; Courtesy Stephen Friedman Gallery (Mark Blower) pp.118-19; Courtesy Anton Kern Gallery, New York pp.38, 54, 55t, 55b; Courtesy Yvon Lambert (Didier Barroso) pp.156, 157; Courtesy M – Museum (Kristien Daem) p.158; Courtesy Gary MacLennan Photography pp.1-8, 181-88 and endpapers; Courtesy Malmö Konsthall (Helene Toresdotter) pp.162-63; Courtesy The Museum of Modern Art, New York/Scala, Florence pp.31, 82b; Courtesy The Pace Gallery p.82t; Courtesy Dan Perjovschi p.28; Private Collection/The Bridgeman Art Library p.29; Photo: Helene Toresdotter pp.162-63; Courtesy Museum Ritter. Marli Hoppe-Ritter Collection, Waldenbuch/ Germany pp.62-63; Courtesy Galleri Nicolai Wallner (Anders Sune Berg) p.106; Courtesy David Shrigley, Yvon Lambert pp.89 ('vegetables'), 91 ('Footprint' and 'The Artist…'), 92 ('Social Unrest…'), 93 ('I Am A Cat-Walk Model…'), 94 (top-left, feet stepping into shoes), 96 ('This Is Nothing'), 98 (top-right, bird on canvas); Courtesy Richard Wentworth and Lisson Gallery p.26

Published on the occasion of the exhibition
David Shrigley: Brain Activity

Hayward Gallery, London
1 February – 13 May 2012

Curator: Cliff Lauson
Exhibitions Assistant: Jessica Cerasi

Published by Hayward Publishing
Southbank Centre
Belvedere Road
London, SE1 8XX, UK
www.southbankcentre.co.uk

Art Publisher: Nadine Monem
Publishing Coordinator: Faye Robson
Sales Manager: Deborah Power

Design: Inventory Studio, London
Printed in the UK

A catalogue record for this book
is available from the British Library

ISBN: 978 1 85332 297 6

This catalogue is not intended to be
used for authentication or related
purposes. The Southbank Board Limited
accepts no liability for any errors
or omissions that the catalogue may
inadvertently contain.

Distributed in North America,
Central America and South America by
D.A.P. / Distributed Art Publishers, Inc.
155 Sixth Avenue, 2nd Floor
New York, NY 10013
tel: +1 (0)212 627 1999
fax: +1 (0)212 627 9484
www.artbook.com

Distributed in the UK and Europe,
by Cornerhouse Publications
70 Oxford Street
Manchester, M1 5NH
tel: +44 (0)161 200 1503
fax: +44 (0)161 200 1504
www.cornerhouse.org/books

Front cover: *Untitled,* 2010.
Image courtesy the artist.

Tracks from the *Brain Activity 7"*
can be heard for a limited time here:
southbankcentre.co.uk/shrigley/seveninch

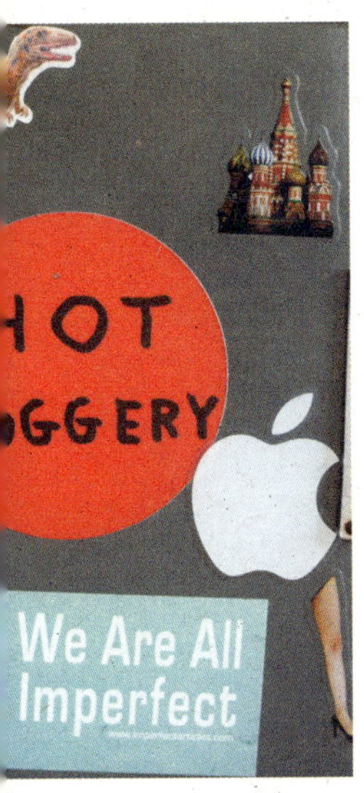
HOT
GGERY
We Are All
Imperfect

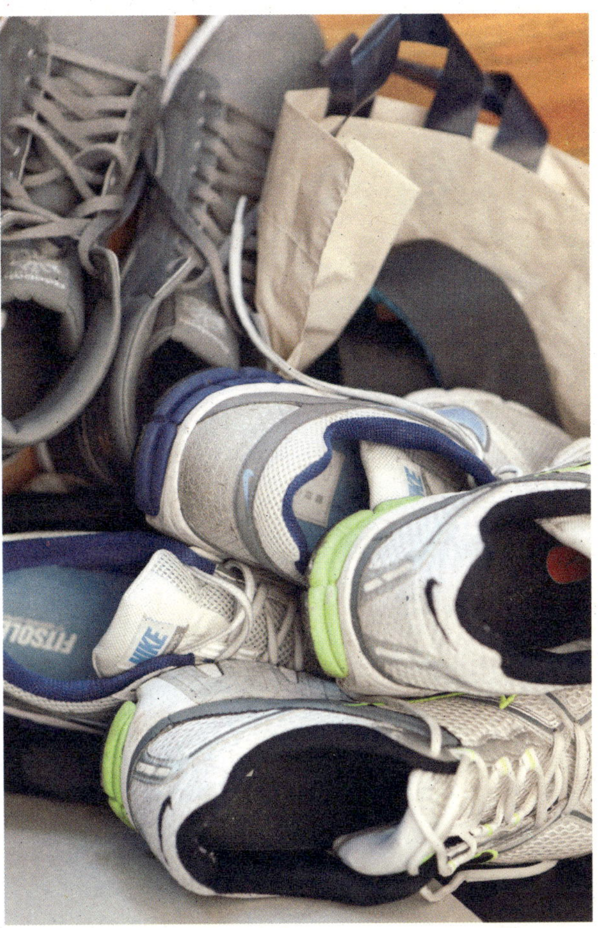

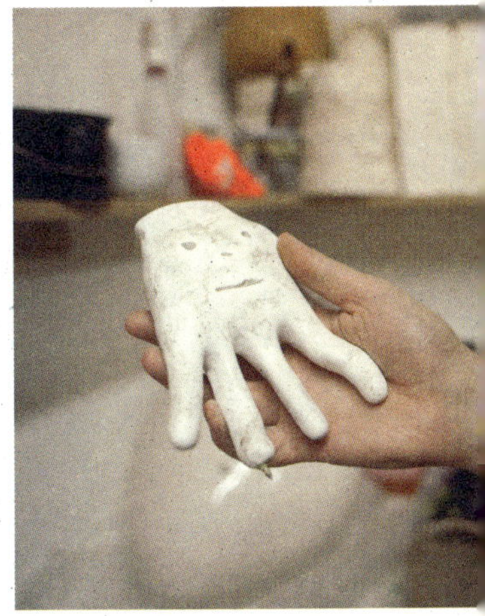

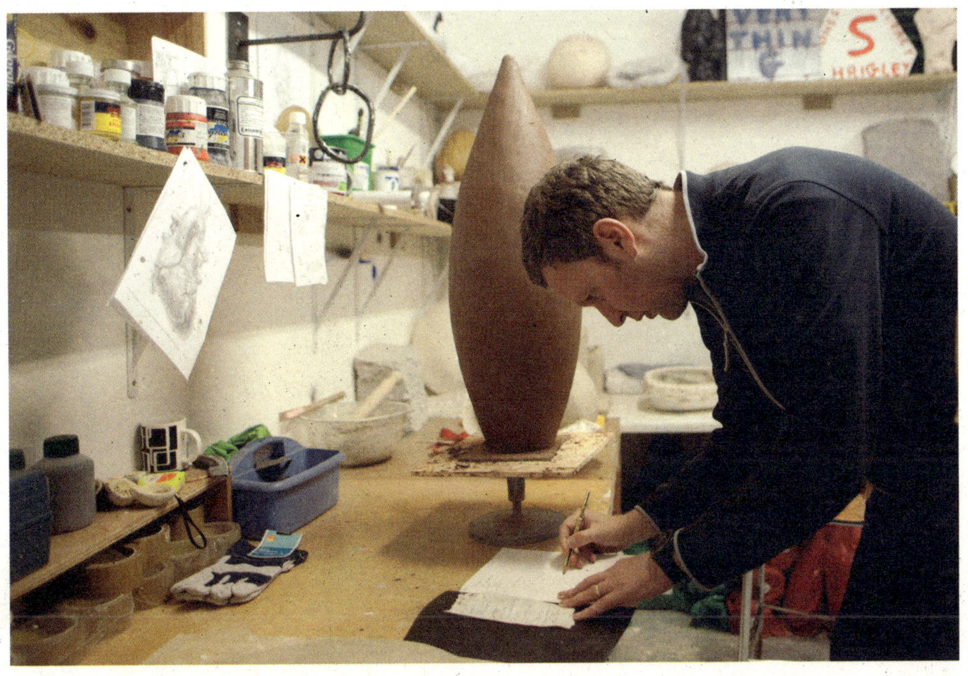

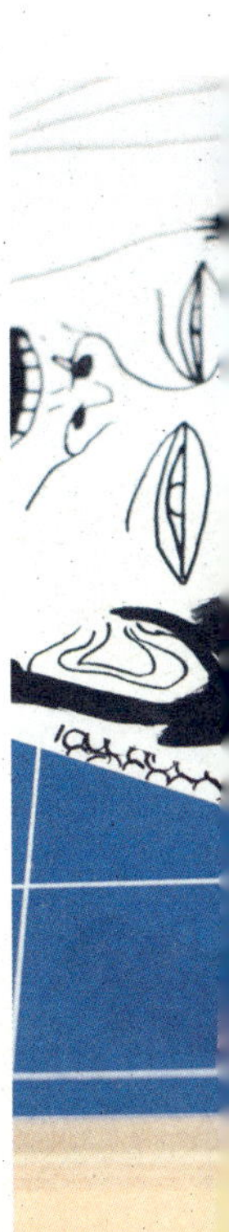

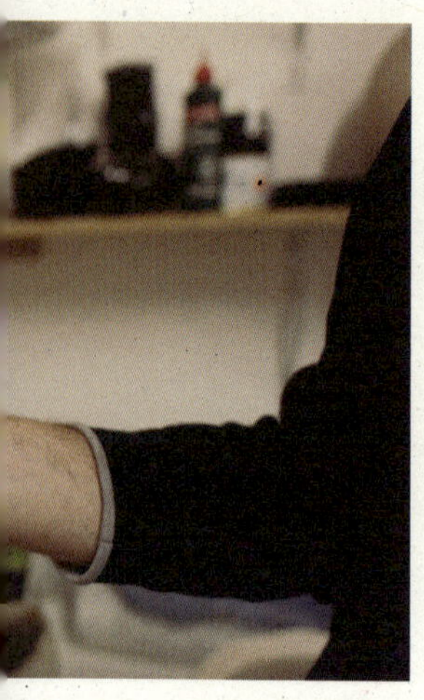

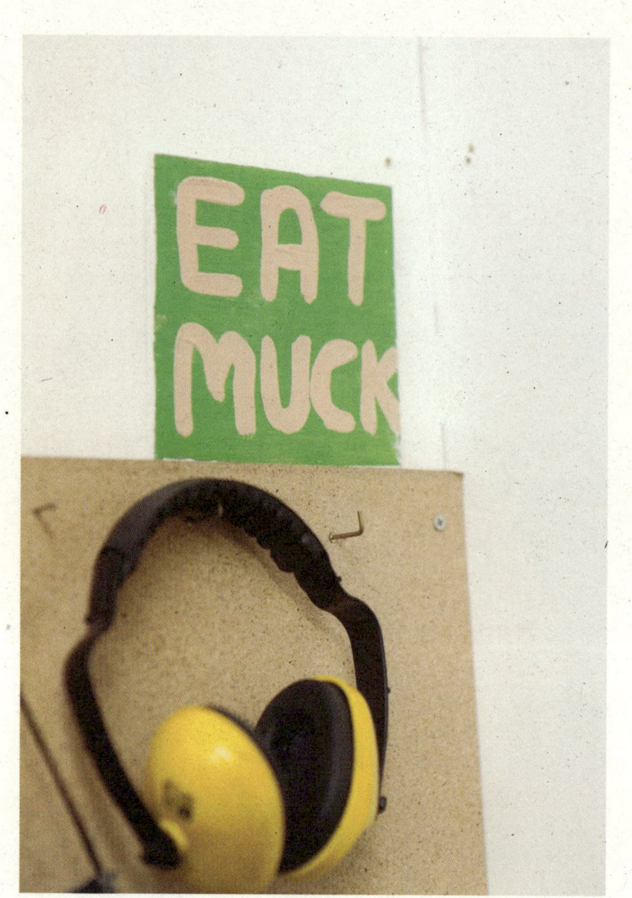
EAT
MUCK

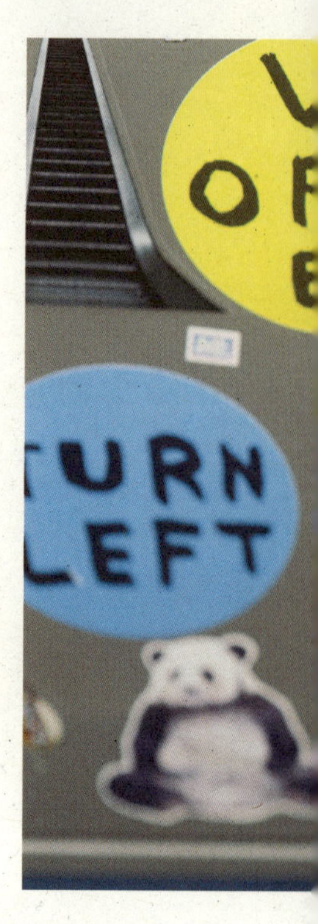
OF
TURN
LEFT

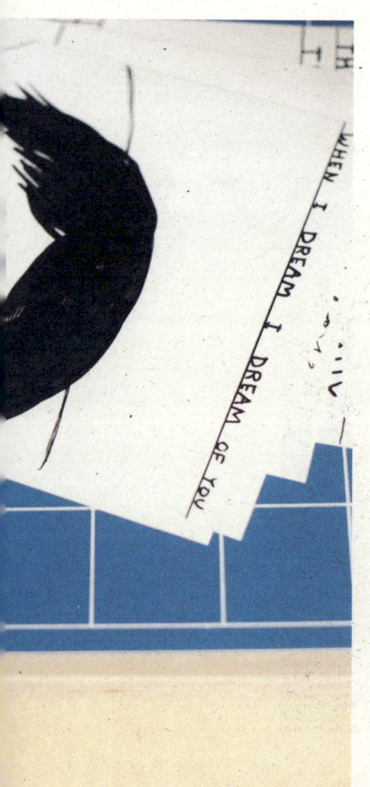
WHEN I DREAM I DREAM OF YOU

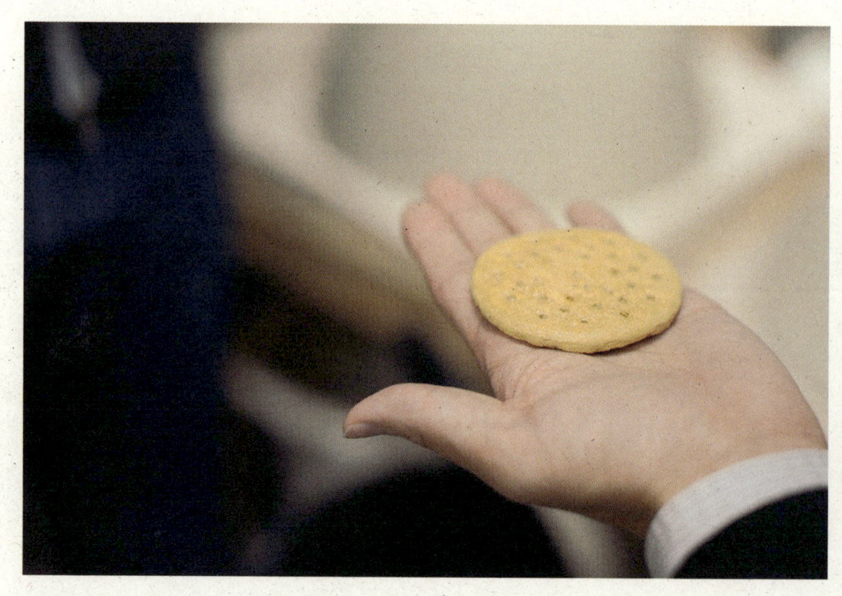

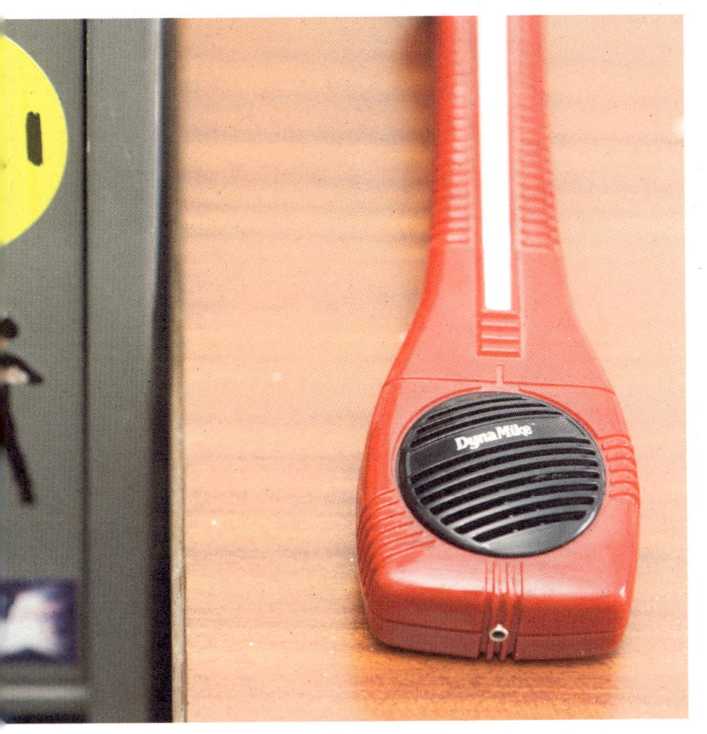

Dyna Mike

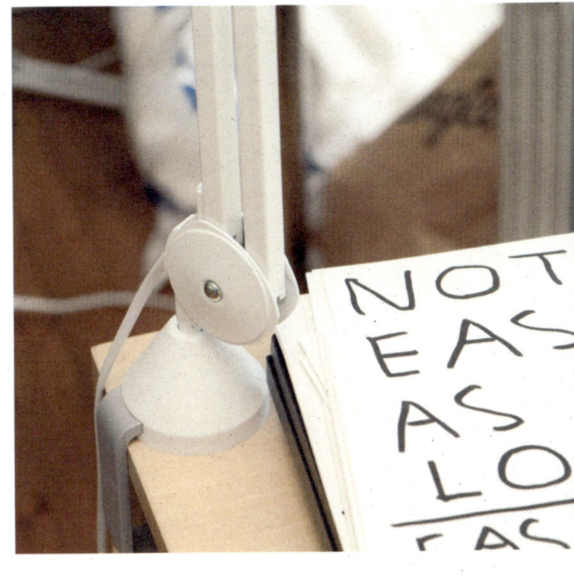

NOT
EAS
AS
LO
EAS

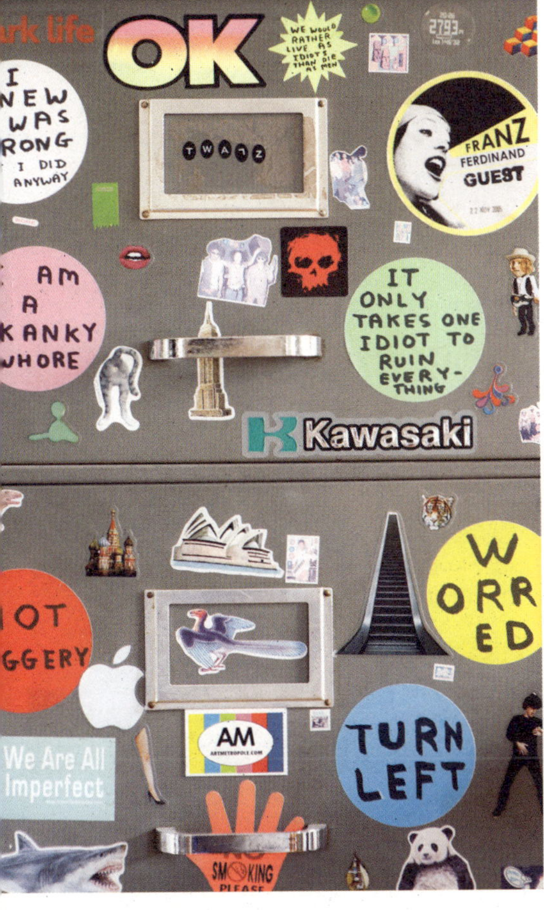

ark life
OK
WE WOULD RATHER LIVE AS IDIOTS THAN DIE AS MEN
2793
I NEW WAS RONG I DID ANYWAY
TWATZ
FRANZ FERDINAND GUEST
I AM A KANKY WHORE
IT ONLY TAKES ONE IDIOT TO RUIN EVERY-THING
Kawasaki
NOT GGERY
We Are All Imperfect
AM ARTMETROPLE.COM
WORRED
TURN LEFT
SMOKING PLEASE

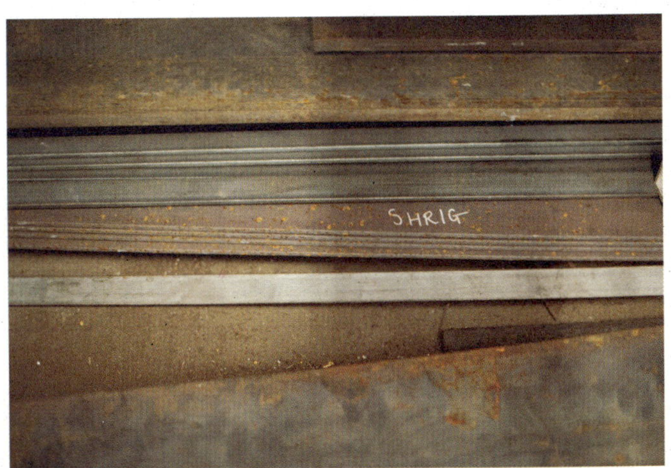

SHRIG

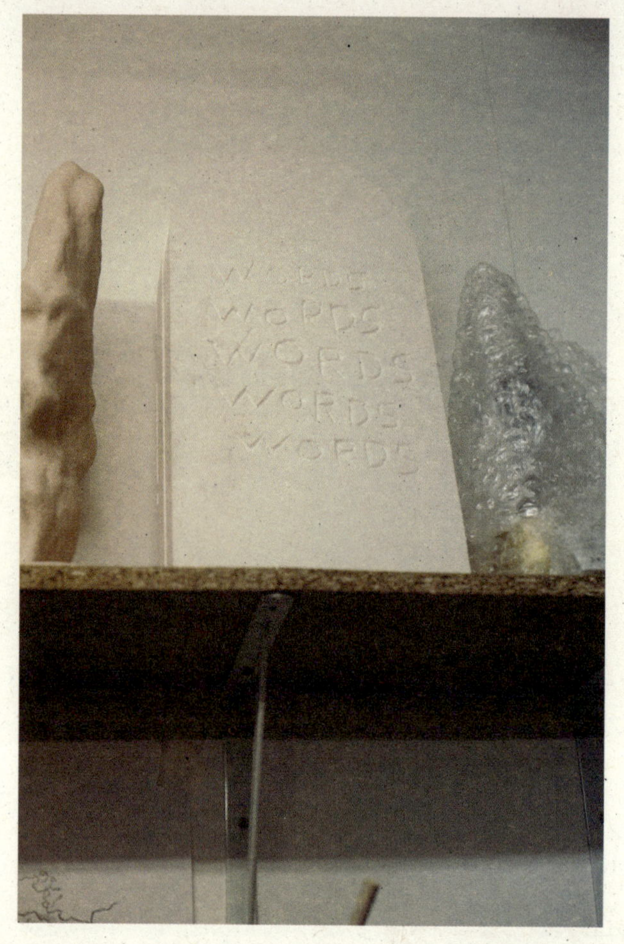

WORDS
WORDS
WORDS
WORDS
WORDS

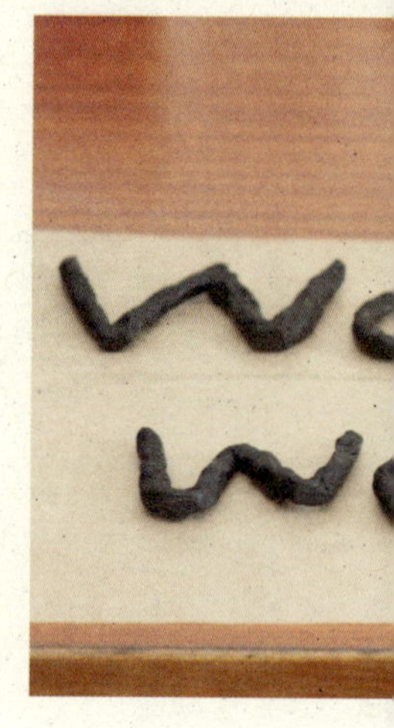

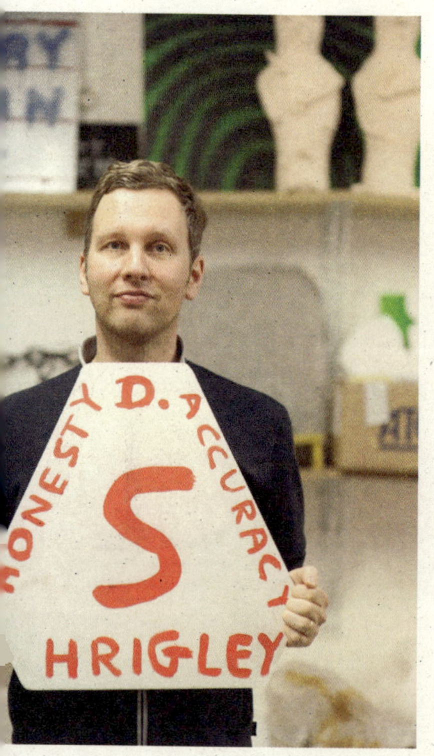

HONESTY D. ACCURACY
S
HRIGLEY

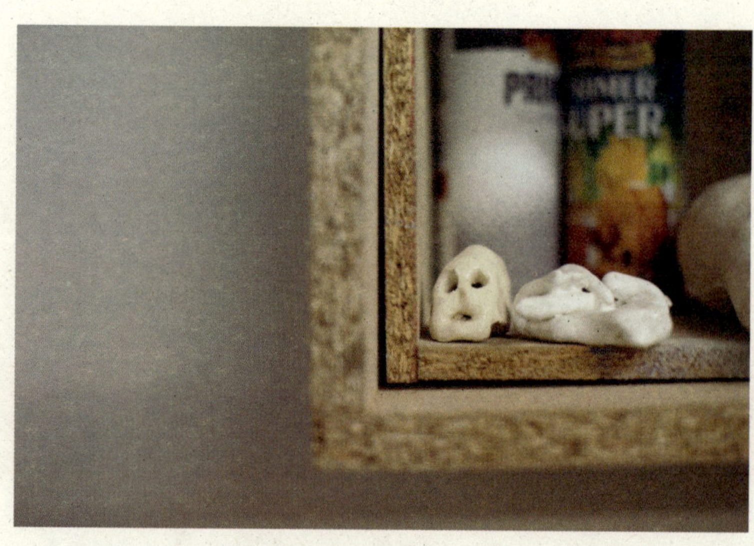

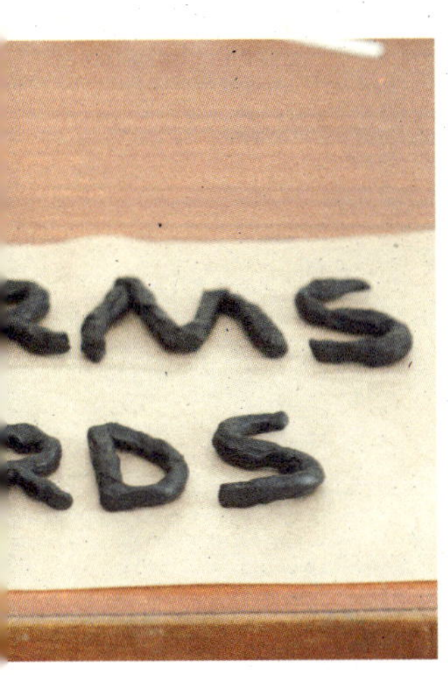

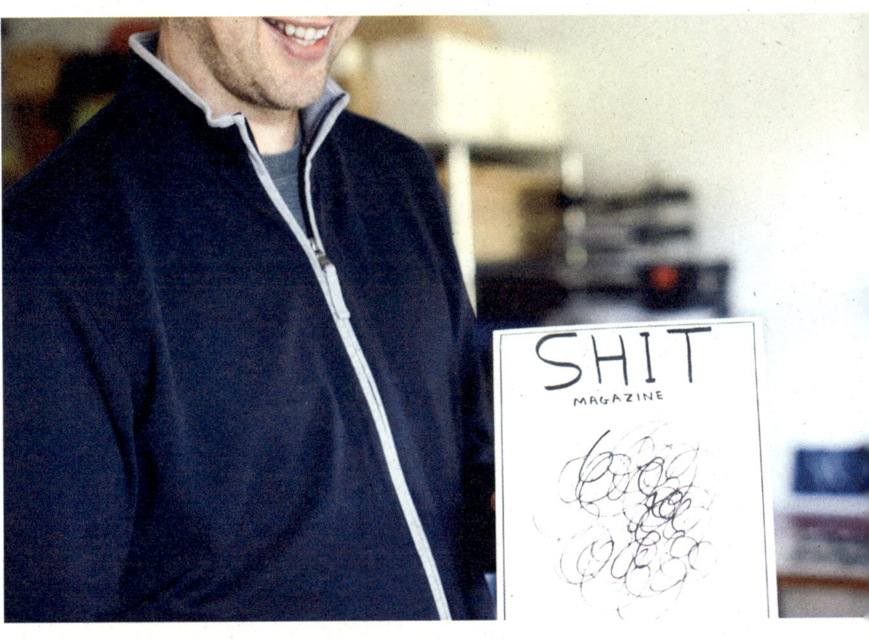

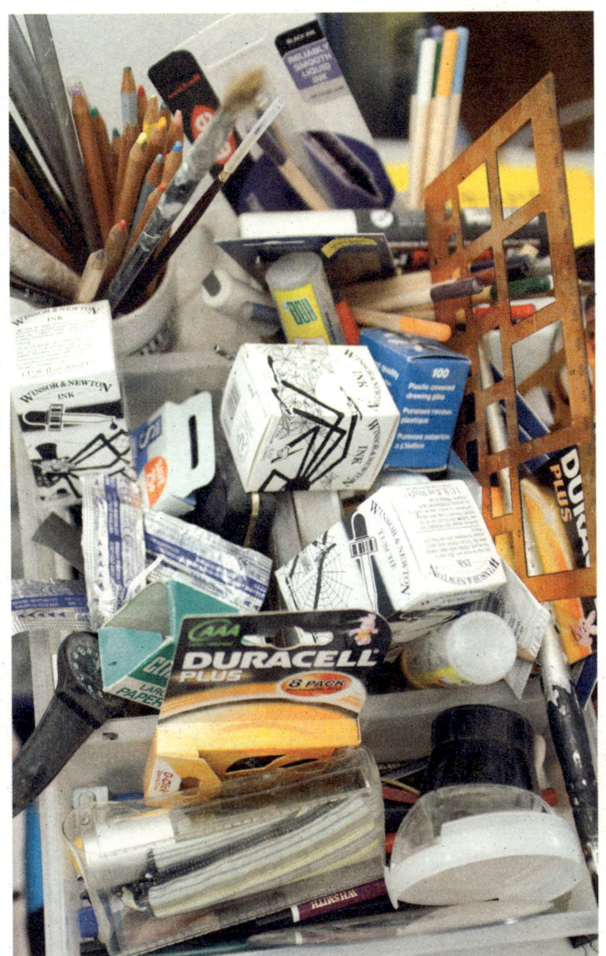

REMIND YOURSELF

THAT YOU ARE

ILL

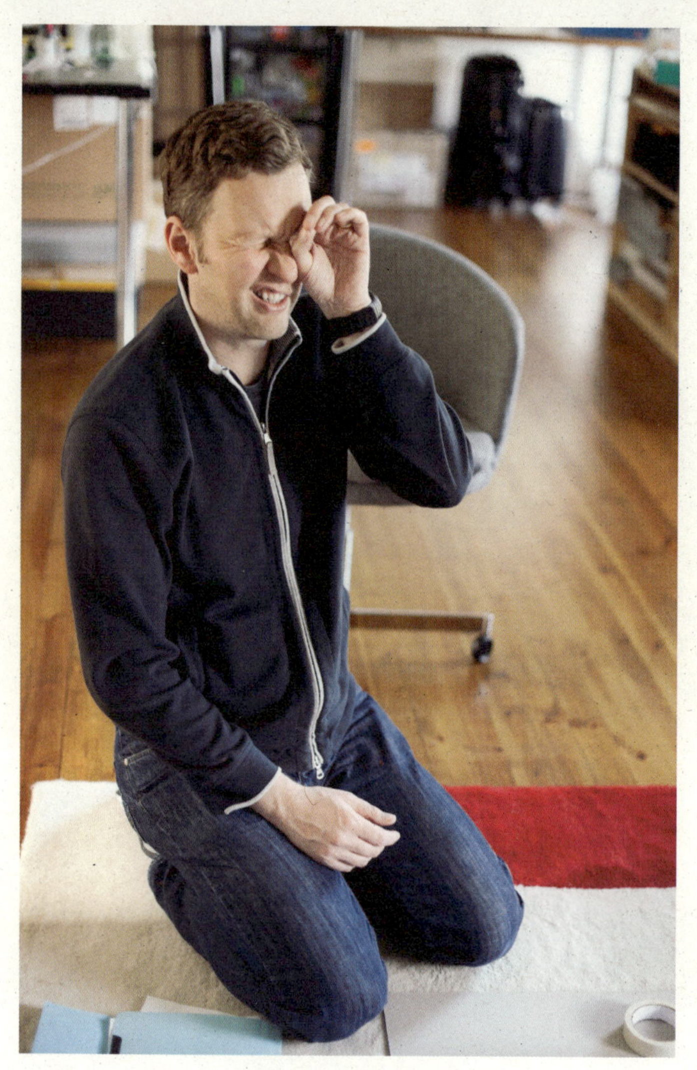

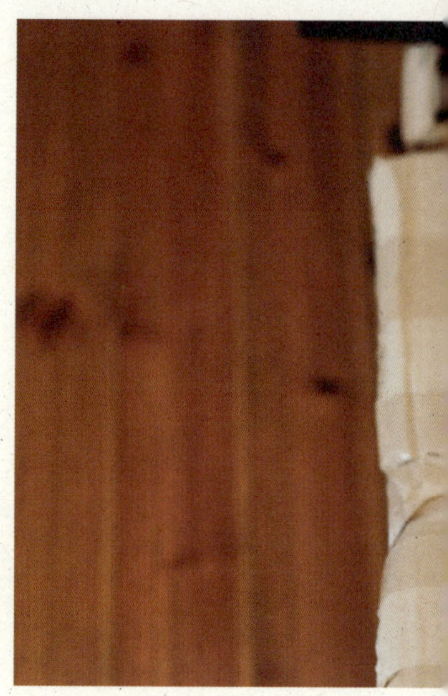

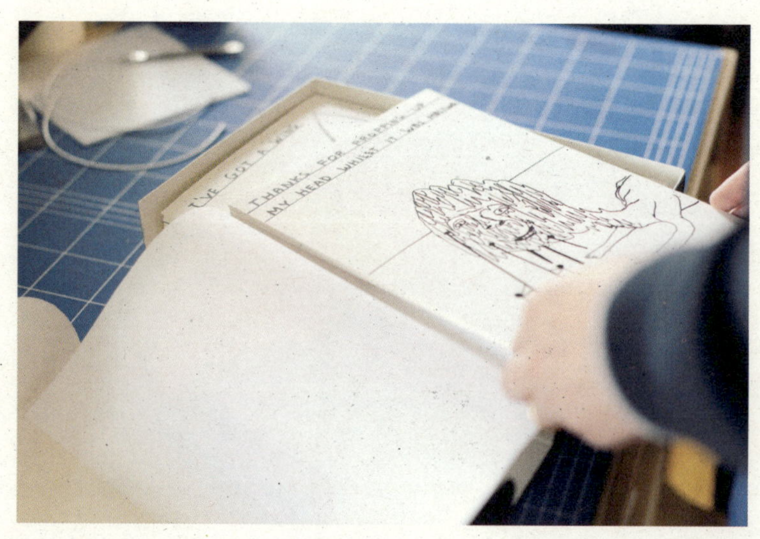

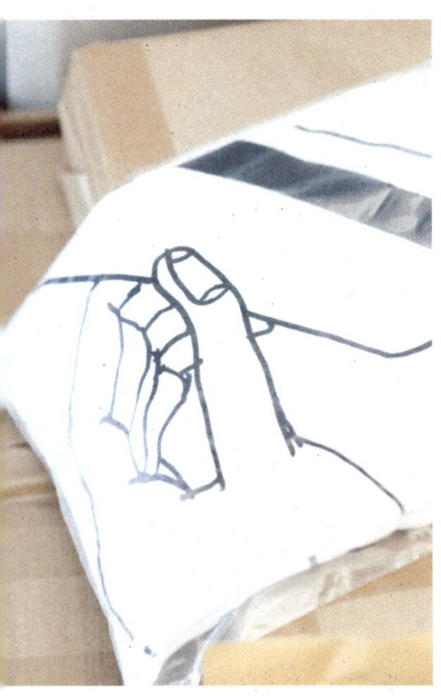
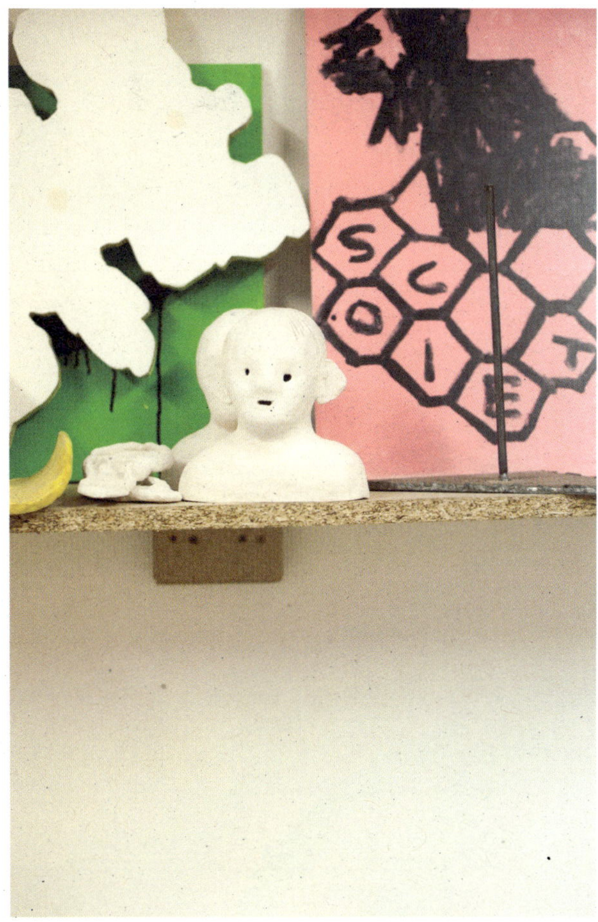
SC
OIE
T
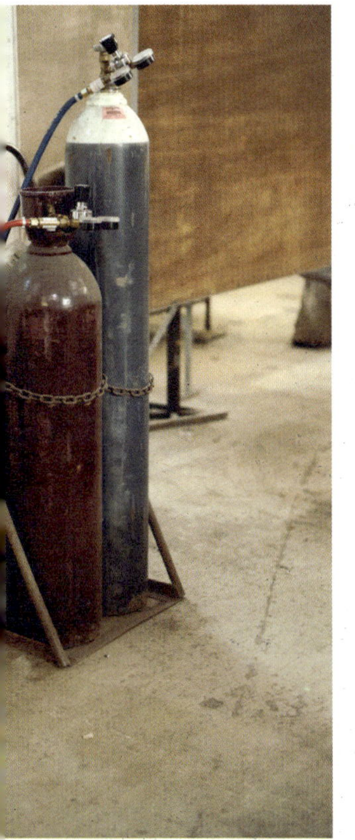
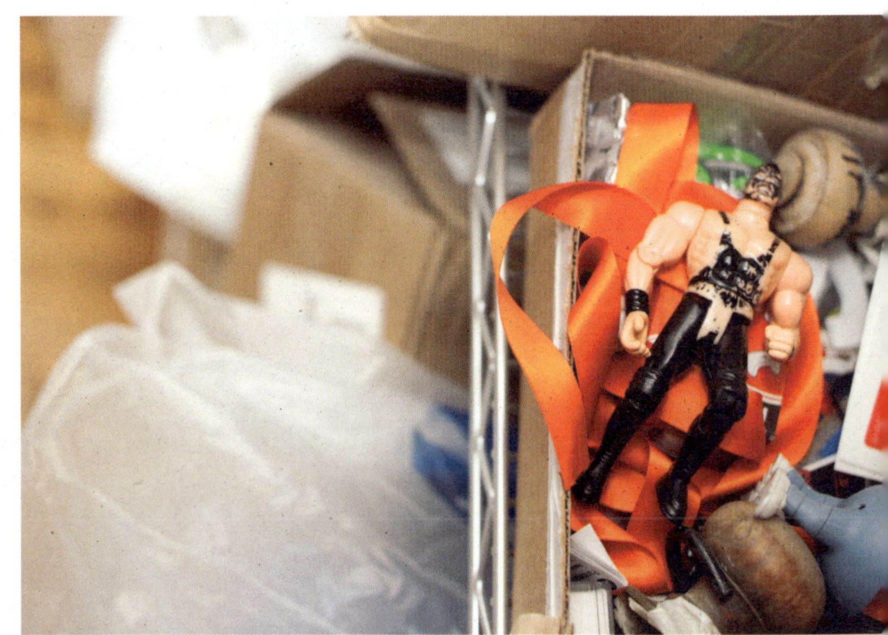

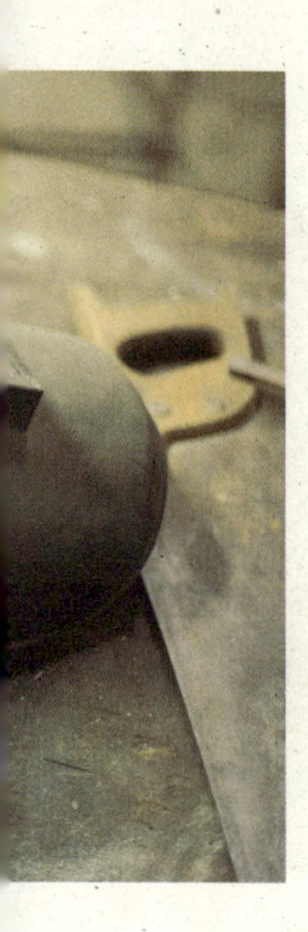
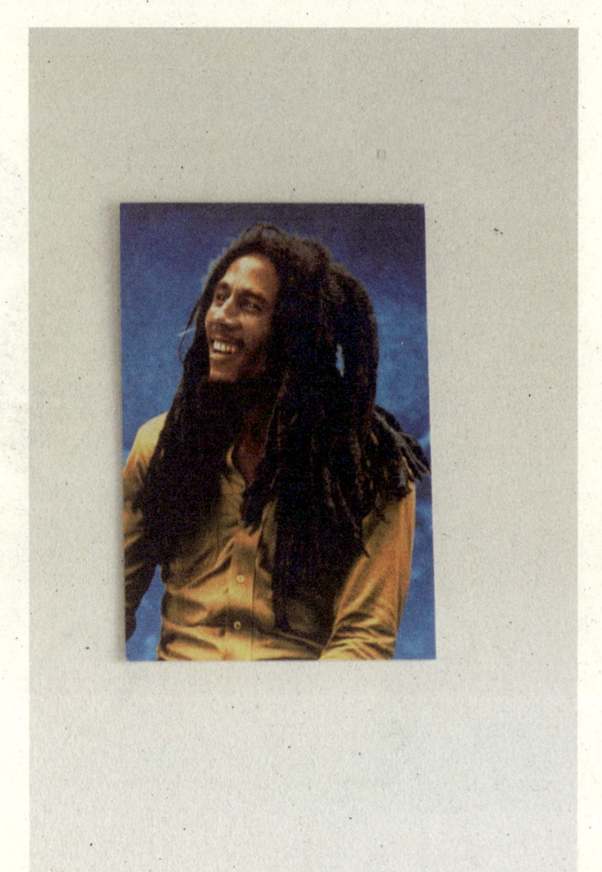
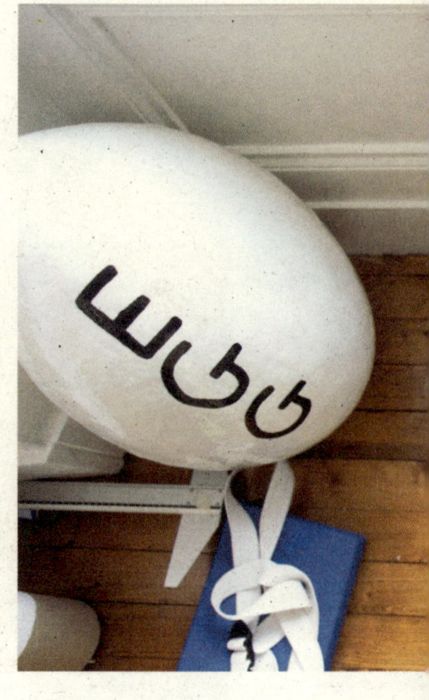

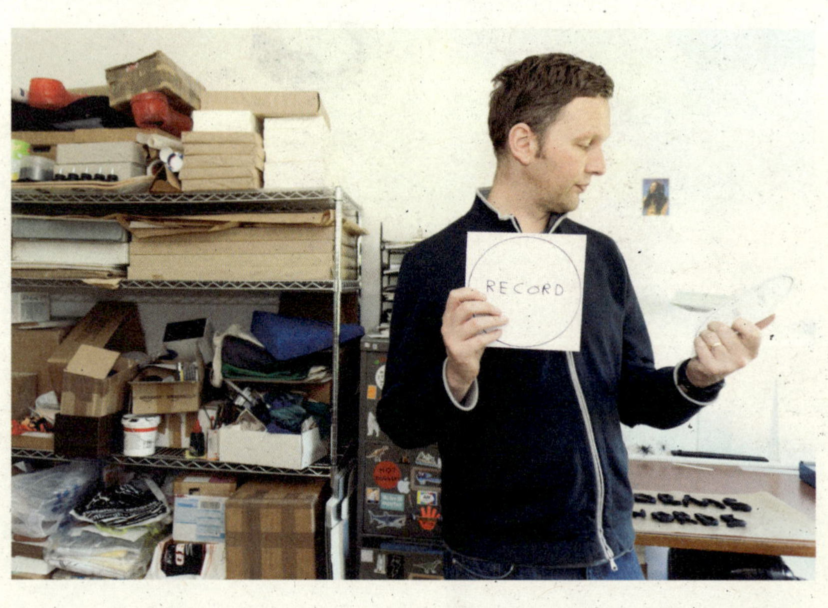
RECORD